Collectible Fountain Pens

Parker, Sheaffer, Wahl-Eversharp, Waterman

Glen B. Bowen

Library of Congress Catalog Card No. 82-90494
ISBN No. 0-910173-001

Revised 1986

Additional copies of this book may be ordered
at $17.95 postpaid from the publisher:

L-W Book Sales
Box 69
Gas City, IN 46933

Printed in the United States of America

To my wife Susan, for her patience and editing
assistance, to my wonderful children, Krissy and
David and to Bob Moline who gave me my first
fountain pen, a magnificent 1920's Lifetime Sheaffer.

ACKNOWLEDGEMENTS

At the outset, I had not fully understood the time, labor and knowledge it would take to compile, edit and publish this book. As it began to evolve, I soon realized the necessity of seeking out professional, knowledgeable people for advice and support. Without their help this book could not have been published.

I especially want to thank Don Lavin for reviewing the early manuscript, offering expert advice, and allowing some of his fountain pens and advertisements to be reproduced in this book.

I give my sincere thanks to Thomas Frantz, patent officer, Sheaffer-Eaton, div. Textron; to Lauren Schuller, public relations, and to archivists Anne Naeser and Jeanette Clark of the Parker Pen Company;

To Ivory Leininger for her excellent photography of my pen collection; and

To Cheryl Jenkins for her help and support.

And finally, for their technical production advice and encouragement, I wish to thank Norm Hirsch, Jim Forbing, Sam McMichael, Donald Behling, Les Davis, and Jim Gebek of Des Plaines Publishing, Don Lindstrom, Norm Harris, Bill Schoefield, Louis Sito, Bill Colbert and Bob Carley of the *Chicago Sun-Times* and David Roefer of Liberty Engravers.

CONTENTS

PREFACE

I have compiled and published this book in the hope that it will stimulate new interest in my favorite hobby, pen collecting.

Understandably, people still give me funny looks when they learn of my seemingly unique interest in old fountain pens. It has not occurred to them that fountain pens might qualify as a collectible.

An interesting test of vintage is to mention the words "fountain pen" to someone in his twenties and you are likely to get a blank stare. Try the same two words on a person over 35 and a look of delight will cross his face as he fondly remembers his school days and his favorite pen.

In a *Chicago Sun-Times* article by Jane Gregory in November 1980, she wrote:

Still a relatively new hobby, accumulating fountain pens used to be considered an eccentric pursuit of a few individuals who didn't need the acceptance granted to more popular forms of collecting. Then, about five years ago, the idea of pens as desirable objets d'art began to catch on. The demand started to push prices up and the race was on.

The ballpoint is partially responsible for the fountain pens' retreat to the prestige market and the failure of many a pen company. Prior to the introduction of the ballpoint, fountain pens were an everyday part of life. Now they have become a hot new collectible!

Collectible Fountain Pens

Introduction

The Value of Anything and Pens

Condition Influences Value

INTRODUCTION

Collectible Fountain Pens is designed to make identifying, dating and pricing early fountain pens easy. It is a ready reference for collectors, antique and collectible dealers and other pen enthusiasts.

The Big Four, as they have been labeled — Parker, Sheaffer, Wahl-Eversharp and Waterman — were selected for this guide because they represent the majority of quality fountain pens available today. Each of these manufacturers have uniquely interesting histories which have been blended with product development data, corporate goings-on and general conditions in the nation and world during their reign.

The book is divided into five sections. The first section deals with the somewhat difficult task of appraising the value of fountain pens. As the art of collecting and cataloging fountain pens becomes more sophisticated, so will the method of correctly assessing a pen's value. Meanwhile, one must depend on the somewhat reliable system of supply and demand to set prices.

The remaining sections introduce each of the four pen companies. A brief, comprehensive history is given for each company followed by an extract of its product development. The extract is very helpful in identifying early fountain pens and pencils.

National advertising and life-size photos of the author's collection, two visual aids for identifying and valuing pens and pencils, are included in each section. The national advertising illustrates each company's new product introductions and promotions of their major product lines. These beautiful informative ads help us follow the development and innovations in the design and mechanics of pens of their day. Each ad introduces a new mechanical device, a newly designed shape or color, a style of marketing strategy or simply a nice piece of advertising art.

Finally, photographs of pens and pencils from the author's personal collection are reproduced as a pictorial chronology. The pens and pencils are dated, fully described and priced at current market value to the best of the author's knowledge. For practical purposes the values quoted in this book are based on pens in excellent condition, although some of the pens illustrated are in less than excellent condition. The value of pens can be reduced by any condition that detracts from their appearance or mechanics. A mathematical formula for valuing pens in various conditions is included.

Additional knowledge can be gained by developing contacts with local collectors. The exchange of pen information will enhance your experience. Also, you will have a network of collectors with whom you can trade pens and related paraphernalia.

No one can guarantee it, but if you buy quality pens in excellent condition, you should be making a good investment that can be cashed in just about anytime. Until then, enjoy!

THE VALUE OF ANYTHING AND PENS

The value of anything is based on the principle of supply and demand and possibly the inherent value of the raw materials that embodies the merchandise. Fountain pens are no exception.

Early fountain pens are generally plentiful, including many fine quality ones. Since the supply is abundant and the demand reasonably strong, their prices are relatively affordable. However, some pen models are scarce or even rare and are in very strong demand, thereby creating high prices.

The value of pens can be better understood when we examine the motivation behind the cast of players. There must be a thousand different reasons people become pen collectors, but eventually they usually settle into one of three categories or a blending of several.

The majority of collectors tend to be somewhat passive about their hobby. An attitude develops that causes the passive collector to find a maximum price he will pay for a pen regardless of its value to others. Their collections are fairly generalized and spotty, with only a few scarce or rare pens. The passive collector will buy most of his pens at flea markets, garage sales, occasionally an antique store or wherever he can find them below his price ceiling.

The more advanced collectors usually start out similar to the passive collectors, but something sparks their interest to a higher level — almost to an extreme obsession. The advanced collector becomes acutely aware of pen values and finds means to support an increasingly expensive hobby. The art of buying, selling and trading becomes part of the challenge and exhiliration and also provides investment funds for future purchases.

The advanced collector reaches a level of selectivity at which he must invest larger sums of money to gain the desired pens. This collector will not forget his roots — the "fleas," etc. — but also will seek out and establish a network of other collectors and dealers with whom to transact deals.

The Value of Anything and Pens Continued...

The third category is the dealer level. Although it does often happen, the dealers do not necessarily grow through the ranks to become dealers. A dealer's motivation is almost purely financial, although there is probably a developed appreciation for fountain pens. The fact that a dealer is usually more interested in commerce than in ownership separates him from the collector. Many advanced collectors rely on dealers to keep a steady flow of high quality pens going through the network, particularly pens of scarce or rare vintage. The prices paid for these pens very widely depending on availability and demand.

Fountain pen dealers tend to lead the market upwards, but they can not stray too far from what the traffic will bear. This is particularly true as more and more dealers enter the fountain pen market.

The fountain pens of certain manufacturers command higher prices than the products of others. Principally, this is a result of the quality standards set by each company. Another factor affecting value includes abundance within various regions of the country. This is related to the proximity of the plant and distribution centers and the production runs of particular models.

As a guide to novice collectors, the following listings show relative values of collectible fountain pens by brand or manufacturer. This is only a partial listing but it does represent the majority of pens available to the average collector.

High Value
Parker, Sheaffer, Wahl-Eversharp and L. E. Waterman. Others include, Conklin, Dunhill, John Holland, Le Boeuf, Mont Blanc, Moore, Mabie Todd and Swan.

Average Value
Aiken-Lambert, Chilton, Diamond Metal, Diamond Point, Dunn, Eclipse, Franklin, Gold Bond, Grieshaber, Ingersol, Liberty, National, Parkette, Security, Swallow, Salz Bros., Wahl-Oxford, Wasp, A. A. Waterman, Wirt.

Low Value
Arnold, Autopoint, Avon, Cavalier, Criterion, Eagle Pen Co., (Epenco), Esterbrook, Everlast, E. Faber, Fineline, Gem, Kreko, Majestic, Marxton, Morrison, Park Pen, Penman, Pioneer, Resevoir, Southern, Stafford, Traveler, Wallace, Waltham, Wearever, Windsor.

There are collectors that specialize in certain brands and are unmoved by what other collectors consider valuable.

Important Notice: The values given in this book for pens and pencils are based on my general knowledge of the current U.S. market. However, because of the many diverse factors that influence prices asked and paid for fountain pens and pencils, which include regional variations, their physical condition, urgency of demand, oscillation in supply, etc., the author bears no responsibility for loss to anyone and does not claim to be the final authority in pen and pencil values.

CONDITION INFLUENCES VALUE

As with most collectibles, condition influences the value of fountain pens. An established method of appraising condition does not exist to my knowledge. Therefore, this guide will divide condition into three categories: excellent, good and poor.

Excellent conditon: All parts original and in near perfect or new condition.

Good condition: All parts original or replaced with parts of like quality. Minor wear and slight discoloration acceptable.

Poor condition: Missing or damaged parts. Serious wear such as scratches and dents in barrels and caps. Plating seriously worn or missing.

The three conditions are assigned the following numerical values:

> *Excellent condition* - *100%*
> *Good condition* -   *66%*
> *Poor condition* -   *33%*

A pen that is worth $100 in excellent condition is valued at $66 in good condition and $33 in poor condition.

A pen may have multiple conditions. For example, a pen's barrel may be in excellent condition, but the cap is slightly discolored and the nib is missing its iridium writing tip. The pen's value is reduced by the less than excellent condition parts.

A pen's value that has parts in different conditions can be determined by assigning values to the parts as follows:

> *Barrel equals ⅓ of total value*
> *Cap equals ⅓ of total value*
> *Nib, feed and section equals ⅓ of total value*

The pen in our example has a barrel in excellent condition, a cap in good condition and a nib in poor condition. The pen's value is determined as follows:

> *Value in excellent condition: $100*
>
> *Value of barrel is $33.*
> *$100 x ⅓ x 100% = $33*
>
> *Value of cap is $22.*
> *$100 x ⅓ x 66% = $22*
>
> *Value of nib, feed and section is $11.*
> *$100 x ⅓ x 33% = $11*
>
> *Therefore, the pen's total value is $66*

Any pen in less than poor condition can be considered of no value other than for parts.

Parker No. 38, 18K Solid Gold Snake Mountings, Green Stone Eyes. Pen Photo about 1½ actual size to show detail. Picture compliments of Don Lavin.

The Parker Pen Company

The Early History

Extract of Product Development

National Advertising

A Pictorial Chronology of Pens and Pencils

1863 - George Safford Parker - 1937·

A Tribute From An Old Friend

George Parker of Janesville was laid away in the Oak Hill Cemetery yesterday. Such a man as he is sure of an impressive funeral in our country — but his was very simple except for the number of people gathered about him and the great masses of gorgeous flowers that piled up where he was. George Parker was an Episcopalian. But, as the cars of the funeral procession passed by Mercy Hospital where they had cared for him while he was ill — lined up by the roadside there stood the black robed Mother Superior and her black robed assistants, flanked by long rows of white robed nurses, each side — the row of bowed heads seemed a block long as the mortal remains of the man they were honoring because they loved him — passed by. Because I loved him too, their affectionate gesture touched me as no funeral could. It was impossible to put a tag on him you see.

This friend of mine was so warm in spirit that people seemed to love him automatically. He was handsome and so much alive, that he is going to seem the more dear to most of us. Our country hasn't many of his type left. They are the best argument I know for our social system as it stands.

From the time he sat behind his favorite horse on the race track of the Janesville County Fair until he became an international figure in American Industry he was a "good sport" as we say. America considers that the first condition of the True American Gentleman — and it is. Just as it is the first condition of one in England. He became a great traveler, always curious. He got about a lot in far away places, not omitting the dangerous Yangste in China — and the ideal mate for him, his wife "Martha" was never very far away from "George." I imagine he was what we call a "selfmade man." But, as his friends knew, he was no selfish one.

By instinct he was a patron with strong likes and dislikes and salty tastes. He was a success in the best sense of that equivocal term in our country. What is America going to do without him and his kind? They are fast falling away from us — these grand fellows — developed in personality and correlation by their own resourcefulness — leaving their beloved sons and daughters, who have had no such luck, to "carry on."

A generation will carry on but the basis for "carrying on," and the scene, is changing with astonishing rapidity.

Will America bury that subsequent generation with similar feelings of admiration, respect, and love? I believe America will.

Frank Lloyd Wright, Taliesin, Wisconsin, July 23rd, 1937.

The Parker Pen Company: The Early History

George Parker was born November 1, 1863, at Shullsburg, Wis., 69 miles from Janesville, Wis., whose leading citizen he was destined to become. He was descended from William and Mary Parker, who migrated to Connecticut from Dover, England in 1636, and his father and mother were among the pioneers who treked from New England and settled the Mid-West.

When Mr. Parker was still a child, his parents migrated in a covered wagon from Shullsburg to a farm near Fayette, Iowa. Here Geo. S. Parker followed the life of so many of those early farm boys, working long hours in the fields during planting, growing and harvest seasons, and, in winter, attending a nearby country school and helping with the farm chores.

Here George Parker grew to sturdy manhood, obtained all the schooling the district had to offer, and then matriculated at Upper Iowa University. But the greatest lessons that he learned were from the school of experience taught by old Mother Necessity.

While attending Upper Iowa University, young George S. Parker began thinking of a career. He had had his fill of farm work as it was performed in those days, sans modern machinery and modern housing. His mother, too, according to his writings, concluded that he was not cut out to till the soil, and she tactfully told him so.

In the old YOUTH'S COMPANION, of which he was an avid reader, he saw an advertisement of the Valentine School of Telegraphy, Janesville, Wis. Until then he had been wavering between a medical and railroad career. The Valentine advertisement settled this. He saved up $55 for tuition, went to Janesville, and enrolled.

Mr. Parker must have been a very adept pupil, for within a year he was on the teaching staff himself. The salary was meager, and to augment his income he obtained the agency of the John Holland fountain pen manufactured in Cincinnati.

As time has disclosed, this chance induction into the pen business started Mr. Parker on a manufacturing career, which started a new pen company that has since become the largest and most famous in all the world.

Its products are sold in every nation on the globe except Japan and Russia, and are favored and advertised in 91 countries.

It came about thus:

Mr. Parker, the teacher of telegraphy, sold the John Holland pens to his students. When the pens gave trouble, the students brought them to their youthful teacher. He felt an obligation in the matter, felt obliged to diagnose the ailments. And although he was not then versed in the intricacies of pen assembly, he took them apart and put them together, until, like Walter Chrysler with his first motor car, he had acquired the "know how."

"This necessitated my purchasing some simple tools," Mr. Parker related, "including a small scroll saw, a lathe, cutter, etc., so that I could repair the pens."

Inasmuch as the students soon learned they could rely on him to correct their faulty pens, the more pens Geo. S. Parker sold, the greater became his labors in servicing them.

First discouragement, then disgust. "I can make a better pen myself," Geo. S. Parker confided to Geo. S. Parker. What happened he vividly told in a recital of his experiences written only a few months before his death.

"Anyway," he wrote, "with my scroll saw, file, and other tools, I made up a feeder, eventually fitted it into a holder — and lo and behold, it worked! What's more, it worked well. The next step was to take out a patent. I knew nothing about this, but it didn't take me long to learn. When I had scraped up $5, I sent it away to a patent attorney in Washington, and had the pleasure of sending to Mr. H.A. Seymour some $80 more, and eventually got my patent." (Dec. 10, 1889, scarcely a month following the election of Benjamin Harrison over Grover Cleveland, then ending his first term as President of the United States.)

"In the meantime, I was working with the H. A. Goodrich Company to manufacture some fountain pens for me in one or two gross lots, which they did, charging me a big price, but which I was willing to pay for getting them stamped, 'Geo. S. Parker.' As I previously told you, I was living at the Myers House, and being of a nature that always mixed with other fellows, it did not take me long to get acquainted with some of the travelers who inhabited that more or less famous hostelry, so that I made arrangements with some of these boys to take the pens out as a sideline. Of course, in those days, to sell a bill of a quarter of a dozen or half a dozen was going some, but they did occasionally send back a little order."

"At that time along came an insurance man, with long, flowing sideburns. His name was W.F. Palmer. He wanted to insure me, but I did not have money enough. However, he was anxious to get into the fountain pen business, too. That was the inception of Mr. Palmer's and my partnership, which lasted nearly throughout his entire life. A finer chap than the late W.F. Palmer never lived".

"Not a lot of capital was necessary in the early days of the company. I sold a half interest in my patents and the little business for $1,000 to Mr. Palmer, but he made out the check payable to The Parker Pen Company, and so this $1,000 was used in the development of the business instead of for me personally."

Meantime, Mr. Parker made an application for a patent, and ran into difficulties. He found there was a patent issued in the East to a man by the name of Mr. Pikard. So he wrote to Mr. Pikard to see if he would be willing to sell his patent. Lo and behold, the letter came back unclaimed. Mr. Parker wrote to the postmaster in the town of Mr. Pikard's address and he had never heard of him.

Mr. Parker recalled, "I went to New York, to the old Waldorf Astoria, and looked over their library of city directories. Pikard, being a peculiar name, was somewhat difficult to find. Finally I located a man by this name over in Jersey City. So the next day I dropped over to Jersey City,

and, would you believe it, this was the very man I had been searching for. Just like a needle in the haystack, finding him."

"Yes, he had been in the pen business but had not made a go of it. I took him over to New York and bought the patent from him for a few hundred dollars. This patent is the same we used all along for the Duofold, except we improved it considerably, so much that these improvements were patented."

Throughout this period of Parker Pen history patents were applied for in rapid succession. The company's early patent history runs something like this: First patent on December 10, 1889, followed by an over-under feed, March 18, 1890; and June 30, 1891, an improved type of over feed.

About the time of the World's Columbian Exposition in Chicago, George S. Parker patented a feed resembling the Lucky Curve. The date was December 12, 1893. This crude forerunner had two bent prongs on the rear, and this led up to the invention of the Lucky Curve feed, patented a year later, December 4, 1894.

With 1898 came the Spanish-American War, Roosevelt's Rough Riders, "Remember the Maine," and the capture of Manila Harbor by Admiral Dewey. In the meantime, George S. Parker was making more pens than ever for soldiers, sailors and the public.

His agile brain worked nights on new inventions. For example, on June 28 of that year, he was granted a patent which showed the first slip-fit type of outer cap. Prior to that, outer caps fitted on what is called the section. This new type cap slipped over the barrel and formed a snug fit. It was a major improvement in pens of that day. It continued as the reigning method for many years.

On April 4, 1899, Mr. Parker patented the jointless pen, and advertised it in national magazines heavily — or as heavy as advertising went in those days. His invention was a radical departure, eliminating the leakage so prevalent in joint type pens.

On July 17, 1900, Mr. Parker took out another important patent, incorporating a taper on the inside of the outer cap. This made the cap fit more securely to the barrel.

Roosevelt the Rough Rider was now Roosevelt the President. Only a year or two earlier Marconi's first wireless message was flashed across the Atlantic. The first mechanically filled Parker fountain pen made its appearance. The year was 1904 and it marked one of the most important advances in fountain pen history. The patent date was May 3.

Up to this time pens had been filled with eye-droppers. This new pen had a semicircular metal bar running the length of the barrel with a pressure bar attached on the inside to deflate the rubber ink sac. The sac was attached to the section, similar to present sac-type pens. In addition, a little lever was attached to the filling mechanism that was designed to slip up and release the apparatus for the filling process.

On January 3, 1905, Mr. Parker applied for a patent on a spear-head feed. He described it as "my improved instrument." He had discovered that a drop of ink would form in the point of any fountain pen suspended over paper. He answered the problem with the spear-head feed, which collected the excess ink and prevented blots.

Thus, by 1905 the Parker fountain pen embodied four great major improvements:

First, the Lucky Curve feed which drained the ink back into the reservoir by capillary attraction when the pen was upright in the pocket. This prevented ink from gushing into the outer cap and onto the nib section around the nozzle when the heat of the body expanded the air in the barrel;

Second, the slip-type outer cap which formed a seal with the barrel instead of a leading joint with the section of nozzle;

Third, a new filling mechanism; and

Fourth, the spear-head which prevented any excess ink from flowing on the nib.

On May 27, 1907, George S. Parker was granted a patent on what he termed the level lock clip. This clip would lie flat in the cap when the pen was in use. When the pen was capped, the barrel pushed the clip into position. Thus the clip gripped the cloth and held the pen firmly in the pocket. This clip was thereafter used on all of the slip-fit outer caps, until the caps were discontinued.

Parker further improved the Lucky Curve feed with a patent issued April 25, 1911. This provided for a cut in the end that contacted the barrel and allowed the ink to drain back freely into the sac.

On June 4, 1912, the first safety cap was patented. Parker called the pen that featured the safety cap the Parker Jack Knife Safety Pen. Its convenient size and clipless, ink-tight cap made it the handiest pen of its day. Carried in pocket or purse, it never leaked.

Four years later, on September 5, 1916, a washer clip was patented. Because this arrangement placed the clip at the extreme top of the pen, Parker pens from that date forward could be placed deeply and neatly in the pocket. The washer clip was conceived by one of the employees in the Parker plant, William E. Moore. He voluntarily assigned his invention to the company, and the company, in recognition of his devotion to Parker, paid him a royalty for the life of the patent — 17 years. One other very impor-

tant creation of those earlier days was the press button filler. This, in turn, was followed by the button filler extending through the end of the barrel, and concealed by the blind cap.

World War I brought a sudden demand for writing equipment from soldiers away from home. What they wanted was a pen which could be used during lulls in the static trench warfare that was typical of the great holocaust. Completely reversing the trend to self-fillers he had helped start himself, George Parker came up with a tough little pen that worked on ink made from a pill of black pigment and water.

"In order to give the soldiers all the information as to where the ink tablets could be found," wrote Mr. Parker, "we put the tablets in a little blind cap at the end of the holder, and so that the boys would not overlook the fact that this was an ink compartment we made it red, the rest of the pen being black.

"We sold vast quantities of these pens which were shipped through the War Department to the boys over in France, and it would not surprise me if there were many of the American Expeditionary Force who still have these fountain pens today. Their benefit was that the user simply had to drop a tablet in the barrel, fill the barrel with water, and he had a complete ink plant."

In 1918 The Parker Pen Company's sales passed $1 million for the first time—a figure now representing a fraction of the company's annual advertising budget

In 1919 the company built an all-brick five-story building to house its growing manufacturing and office facilities. Although the business was healthy, the building had been providently planned so that it could be converted quickly into apartments should pen sales fall off. As Parker said, "We were going ahead, but we spent a lot of time looking over our shoulders."

Like many of the major pen companies, Parker is essentially a family affair. The founder's elder son, Russell, came into the business in 1914. His other son, Kenneth, joined the company in 1919.

Russell Parker eventually became directly responsible for all phases of the company's operation except advertising and sales and rose to the position of vice president and general manager. His death in 1933 left a gap in the organization.

Kenneth Parker had served with the Naval Air Service during World War I and afterwards spent a year with the Lord and Thomas advertising agency. When he came with the pen company, he brought along some marketing ideas that were to bear fruit and change the entire complexion of the pen industry. At the time, practically all pens were black, with a uniform price of $2.75.

It was about that time that a Parker salesman, Lewis M. Tebbel, came up with an idea for a startling new pen. It would be bigger than anything on the market, have a larger ink capacity, a great gold point, and would boast a spectacular, vivid orange-red barrel. Tebbel, who was trying to crawl from under a disastrous personal sales slump, even had a name for the flashy "he-pen" — the Duofold. Most shocking suggestion of all was that it should cost about seven dollars, more than twice the accepted price.

Kenneth Parker quickly endorsed the idea. He thought it had far-reaching potential and spearheaded the new pen project. The 25-year old promoter called in his friend, Lucius Crowell, an advertising executive who was handling the Parker account, and they planned a market test in Chicago. Chicago retailers yelped loudly when they saw the new pen. Bluntly they questioned the sanity of trying to market something like the Duofold, which they held to be a mutation. They gave numerous reasons why it wouldn't sell. Price was the one Parker and Crowell heard most often.

They then decided to go out and survey people and find out from them whether or not the pen would sell. With ten salesmen who were carefully instructed to present a tray full of pens — including a Duofold — to householders and ask for an expression of choice, Parker and Crowell got the test under way.

When the two-week experiment ended, results showed that the new pen was the choice of 62% of the people interviewed. Also, enough people ordered the pen to pay for the survey and allowed Parker and Crowell to think about a national advertising and selling campaign.

Soon after the pen appeared, the company's sales graph fluttered, then moved skyward. In four years, by 1925, sales had quadrupled. In the short space of half a decade, the little Wisconsin pen company had vaulted into a place of international renown.

In 1923 the company expanded its export organization when it established a factory in rented quarters in Toronto, Canada. In 1932, the company purchased a building on University Avenue. In 1966, Canadian operations were moved to a new, modern site.

And early in 1923, Duofold pens in the conventional black were added to the line. The Duofold was capturing pen markets the world over.

A new sales policy, providing a sliding scale of discounts, and the Duofold's popularity, enabled the distribution of large numbers of floor display cases. Prior to this improvement Duofold orders had largely been confined to a few dozen at a time to be placed in pen cases of other makes. In the next few years, sales doubled, trebled, quadrupled, and more.

But its fast start had only given Parker a lead on other pen makers. There was no guarnatee that some company wouldn't come along and knock Parker from its perch. Late in 1924, about two and a half years after the start of the Duofold advertising, a competitor announced a jade green lifetime pen at $8.75, made of nonbreakable material, and guaranteed for life.

Few months passed before this new challenger gained a foothold. The non-breakable material, plus the lifetime guarantee, had a strong appeal to the public. the Duofold, at that time, was made of comparatively brittle rubber. The barrels and caps were relatively fragile. Soon Parker, too adopted a new nonbreakable plastic.

In the summer of 1926, the company announced the nonbreakable Duofold. What followed put new blood, new life, and new impetus into Parker sales. Many may remember those stirring announcements in color spreads and color pages in national magazines and newspapers:

"NONBREAKABLE BARRELS

Dropped From Airplanes — 3,000 Feet — Without Harm"

"HURLED 25 STORIES TO CEMENT

Picked up Unbroken"

"OVER THE RIM OF GRAND CANYON

It Struck the Jagged Rocks — Half a Mile Below — Unharmed"

Parker notified its dealers and the press when these stunts were to take place, and saw to it that each drew a full crowd of people. Parker sales for 1926 set a record.

The Duofold had made Parker the leader in the high-priced pen field. This represented about 75% of the company's unit sales and meant a more desirable net profit to dollar volume ratio.

Green jade was added to the Duofold line, and company officials began to think of ways to capture the low-priced market; first, by the introduction of a black school pen, called Parker D Q (Duofold Quality) at $3.50; next by the introduction of a line of slender pens in beautiful pastel shades. These were announced to the public in color advertisements in the summer of 1926.

Another notable development was the inauguration in 1926 of the Parker desk set line, with ball and socket receptacle. About this time the Wahl Company also appeared with a ball and socket receptacle and the W.A. Sheaffer Pen Company claimed rights to certain other features. The result was that Parker, Sheaffer and Wahl pooled their rights and patents, and organized the Pen Desk Set Company, which, in turn, licensed other manufacturers.

In 1927 two new Duofold colors — "mandarin yellow" and "lapis blue" — were added. Another effort was made in 1928 to gain a large portion of the low-priced market. The hero of this unsuccessful venture was a pen called "True Blue" at $3.50.

A solid marketing stroke, however, was the introduction of the Parker Duofold DeLuxe in black and pearl at $7.50, $8.50 and $10.00 in the Fall of 1928. In 1929, an important change was made in the whole Parker pen and pencil line. Both pens and pencils were redesigned and streamlined. The old gold crown cap was dispensed with, and in another "first," the pencil cap was made to match the outer cap of the pen.

From time to time refinements were introduced, including in 1930 the vest-pocket duette in Duofold colors. Then in July of that same year, green and pearl was added to the black and pearl in the Duofold DeLuxe. By that time the bottom had fallen out of the stock market. Fortunes were lost, and everyone could hear the screech of industry's brakes as company after company watched sales figures plummet. The Parker Pen Company was no exception. Its profits in 1930 were about half those of the previous year.

Fighting back, Parker Pen greeted 1931 with a new color in the $5 and $7 Duofold, — burgundy and black. This was extensively advertised. But sales continued to fall away. Early in the summer the company launched its new pen-cleaning ink — Parker Quink.

Meantime Kenneth Parker and the research and development department had been working on a plan for a chromium desk base which required no socket. In its place was a spring hook into which the clip of the pocket pen could be snapped so that the outer cap formed a socket and held the pen. This was named the Pen-Parker, and heavily advertised in the Spring of 1932. Whether due to the article itself or the financial panic which was sweeping America, the new desk pen product was not a success.

During this period, the Parker research and development department was engineering a new sacless filling mechanism operated by a plunger and diaphragm. This, in

time, became the filling mechanism of Parker's Vacumatic pen. The troublesome rotting of rubber sacs was soon to be eliminated.

Anticipating the introduction of the new Parker Vacumatic in the late Fall or early Spring of the following year, plans were made in 1932 to liquidate the company's world-wide stock of Duofolds. The method adopted was simple. Startling advertisements were published in the national magazines and leading newspapers, containing the following headlines:

"OLD PENS AND PENCILS ACCEPTED AS CASH

Toward the Famous Parker Duofold"

or

"WE'LL GIVE YOU UP TO $2.50 FOR AN OLD PEN —

ANY MAKE Toward A Brand New Parker Duofold"

The plan worked very well. Dealer's stocks were substantially reduced. Further reduction was obtained in December 1932 and in January and February of 1933, by offering a Duofold pencil, free, with the Duofold pen. Reorders from dealers, of course, were largely for Vacumatics and the new pen was first announced in THE SATURDAY EVENING POST on March 18, 1933.

The public was charmed by the style and beauty of the laminated pearl barrel and smart arrow-style clip. This original and exclusive creation was designed by Joseph Platt, a gifted New York artist. Moreover, the enlarged ink capacity—102% greater than the Duofold of comparable size — was very alluring to the public. The Vacumatic was a sales success from the start.

From 1933 to 1940 it was the Parker Vacumatic. But behind the scenes its successor was being engineered and readied for introduction. This new idea in pens was to have a numerical designation.

Practically all inks on the market in the 30's dried by evaporation. It was possible to speed up the evaporation, but the difficulty was that the fluid would dry not only on paper but on the pen point. Parker finally developed a suitable fast-drying fluid which dried by penetration into paper. It had a fault. The alkali in it ate up the pyralin of the pen barrel, tending to hasten the deterioration of ordinary rubber sacs. To combat the problem, the company began work on a pen with a resistant barrel. Lucite, the same material from which World War II bomber turrets and noses were made, provided a partial solution to what was being sought.

Starting with the Lucite barrel, Parker worked around it and began to experiment with some new pen ideas. Eventually the "51" was developed and somewhat of a legend was slated to begin. In 1940, the Parker "51" appeared in a few places in Brazil. In this overseas market test, the pen created no great stir, but Parker refined it still more and introduced it in the U.S. in 1941 at a price of $12.50.

Although the term "51" is identified as a pen in almost every part of the world, people have seldom seen the reason for it. Actually the company had three reasons when it chose the name "51." According to Kenneth Parker, "51" had been chosen because: (1) The pen came out of research in 1939 — the firm's 51st anniversary; (2) The company wanted to designate it with a non-alphabetic symbol which would not subtract from the prime trademark — the Parker name; (3) The figure translates into any language automatically, important for export conscious Parker.

More than a quarter of a million dollars was spent to develop the "51" pen, and at the time this made it the biggest project ever undertaken by the firm. Corporate nerves were understandably tense as the pen was sent out to the market place to prove itself. First reports about the pen's sales were slightly less than encouraging, but once it had taken hold, it captured the high-priced field and the company had itself another winner.

Then came World War II. During most of 1942 Parker and the rest of the companies in production of essential writing equipment were allowed to make all the pens they wanted, dependent only on the then increasing shortages of brass, copper, rubber and other war materials. In December of 1942 the War Production Board changed things when it put these items on its critical list and chopped pen production exactly in half. To stay in business, the company shifted to more expensive materials — silver, gold, etc., which were not high on the critical list.

By 1948 things were creeping back to normal, and the company got ready for a buyer's market. The original "51" was then nine years old, and had either to be replaced or dramtically modified to spark consumer interest.

One of the company's biggest problems was the development of a pen that would not leak at high altitudes. Reduced pressure caused ink to escape. A modified "51," which was "airplane-ized" and boasted a new method of filling and many other advances, was Parker's answer to the problem.

In 1948 the company scored again when it brought out a lower-priced line of pens — the "21." Trading on the world-wide preference for the "51" look, the company kept the basic design without putting in the high-priced refinements. People grabbed the "21" as soon as it appeared, and six months later Parker had 60% of the more-than-five-dollars pen market.

In August of 1950 Parker, for the first time in sixteen years, came out with a pen below $5 called the Parkette. The Parkette at $3 featured an interchangeable point. Designed for school and office utility use, the Parkette had a point of resilient octanium, styling similar to the "51." It was offered in red, black, grey and blue. The matching pencil sold for $2. The public did not snap up the Parkette as it had previous entries and the new pen was soon dropped from production.

In January of 1954, 9 years after the introduction of the Reynold's ballpoint, Daniel Parker, a grandson of George S., released the company's first ballpoint pen for marketing. It was called the Jotter and it was different. It had an oversize cartridge which wrote five times as long as ordinary ball pens. Moreover, the cartridge rotated each time the button was pressed, assuring even, longer wear. The pen was made entirely of stainless steel and nylon, tough and handsome. A 400-pound man could stand on the twin-walled barrel without denting it. A further difference of the Jotter was that, for the first time, a ball pen offered a variety of point sizes to suit the individual hand.

Kenneth Parker had kept his promise and the consumer was quick to recognize it. From March, when first production models reached the stores, to January of the following year, a total of 3,500,000 Parker Jotters were sold. This, in spite of the fact that the Jotter was priced well above existing ballpoints.

During 1954, the company introduced Jotter models ranging from $2.95 to $8.75. Some of these were designed as matching companions to the famed "51" and "21" fountain pens. Production boomed, taxing even the limits of a handsome new plant, Arrow Park, opened but a year earlier.

In January of 1955, one year after announcing the Jotter, Parker unveiled another new product. It was the Parker Liquid Lead pencil, first change in pencils in 200 years. Its point was unbreakable, and it never needed sharpening.

Consumers were a bit slow to take to the new Liquid Lead pencil when it reached the market place in May. This was because it was a totally new product and people were hesitant to try it. But as the year progressed, sales of the Liquid Lead pencil began to climb and by Christmas of

1955, 2,000,000 had crossed retail counters into consumers' hands. The early enthusiasm was not sustained, however, and the product was phased out in the early sixties.

In September of 1956, Parker Pen announced to the world that "the great natural force of capillary attraction had been harnessed to provide, for the first time, a fountain pen that fills itself, writes instantly, will not leak or blot, and even will write in an inverted position." The pen was known as the Parker 61. Developed after years of intensive research by a fifty-man laboratory team, the new pen was hailed as "unlike any pen in this world — or any other."

The Parker 61 fills simply by removing the barrel top and dipping the exposed inner cell into ink. Unlike conventional pens it has no filling lever, tube, ink sac or cartridge — in fact the functioning unit has no moving parts. The inner cell is covered with a "hydrophobic" (water-shedding) material that eliminates need for wiping the filling unit after withdrawal from the ink.

In September of 1957, some three and one-half years after Parker introduced its first ballpoint pen, it announced a revolutionary improvement which set the Parker Jotter apart from any pen on the market. Parker's metallurgy had created the first ball specifically designed for writing — a tiny textured tungsten carbide sphere with thousands of microscopic paper grippers on its surface. All previous ballpoints had used a common steel ball bearing as a writing tip.

In 1960, Parker introduced its first cartridge fountain pen, the Parker 45. It had a 14-karat gold point, unusual in pens retailing at $5; Its point was interchangeable at the pen counter; And it could be converted to a conventional fountain pen merely by inserting a cartridge-shaped refillable "converter."

In 1962 another product was introduced. A result of ten years of handwriting research, the VP (for very personal) offered a gently contoured grip that could be dialed to best fit the user's own writing style. (Each of us holds a pen in a slightly different position when writing.) The VP continued the very personal concept by offering a wide selection of point sizes.

In 1964, Parker challenged consumer buying habits by introducing a new, high-styled fountain pen costing $25. Named the Parker 75, it is made almost entirely of solid sterling silver and trimmed in gold. Its 14-karat gold point, available in over a score of distinctly different sizes, ranging from needle fine to extra broad, is adjustable to fit any writing angle.

Dramatically publicizing this top-of-the-line model, Parker released a specially engraved, limited-edition 75 made of Spanish "pieces of eight" recovered off the Florida coast. The treasure, lost in 1715 when galleons carrying the precious cargo sank in a hurricane, lay undisturbed until spectacular discovery almost two and a half centuries later. Parker offered some of this silver, in the form of a "treasure pen," to would-be beachcombers who are also discriminating penmen.

Spurred by the success of the sterling 75, Parker in 1965 added another precious-metal model to the line, this one plated with 14K gold. The use of precious Vermeil provided yet another luxury 75 model. Sales statistics and enthusiastic letters have since borne out Parker's feeling that these most giftable writing instruments would help restore interest in personalized, pleasurable handwriting and induce a pride of ownership impossible with "throwaway" pens that are, at best, functional.

In 1966, Parker introduced a "soft tip" product called Touche' and also made available "soft tip" refills for most of its higher end products. The Classic line of slim-contour ball pens was offered to the market in 1967, and the product has been made available in a variety of finishes and metals since that time to meet the demands of various world markets. The Classic line remains one of Parker's best sellers today at a popular price point.

A product with Titanium components was launched in 1970. Called the T-1, the space-age metal product had to be dropped within a few years because it proved to be technically unsuitable for writing. In 1972, the famed Parker Duofold, Big Red, was revived as a ball pen and soft-tip to mark the 50th anniversary of the successful "Roaring 20s" product and to ride the wave of "nostalgia" that had been sweeping the country. The product eventually became an item for the specialty advertising industry. The roller ball mode of writing was brought into the Parker family in 1975 with Systemark, a modular line of pens with interchangeable refills — a ball pen, soft tip, and a roller ball called "Floating Ball".

A number of models and lines, developed at various Parker operations, were marketed worldwide through 1981. Among them was the full line Parker 180 that featured a reversible fountain pen nib and futuristic styling. From Parker England came the Parker 25 line, and from Parker Germany came novelty pens such as Swinger, a neck pen; Multi, a puzzle pen, and Blimpy, a desk pen in the shape of an egg.

From Parker U.S.A. came a women's designer pen, Ms. Parker, with fashion influence by Emilio Pucci. A new line of gift writing instruments was introduced in 1981 as the company's world pen, the Parker Arrow. It featured a highly stylized, tri-faceted, diamond cut and engraveable arrow clip, a modern restyling of the original arrow clip that first appeared in 1932 on the Parker Vacumatic. Parker Arrow has become the leading highline product for the company during the early 1980s.

From its humble beginnings under the brilliant entrepreneurship of George S. Parker, The Parker Pen Company has today grown to become a leading international manufacturer of quality writing instruments. Parker products are sold in 150 countries — more than any other quality-pen competitor, with the features of the products advertised in more than 40 different languages. About 80 percent of the sales of the company's Writing Instrument Group are from outside of the United States.

The mission of the current management is to assertively compete in every viable segment of the quality writing instrument market — worldwide. And, the company will do so based on its fastidious quality requirements, efficient service worldwide and a lifetime guarantee on every writing instrument that bears the Parker brand name.

The Parker Pen Company:
Extract of Product Development

1888   George S. Parker established the company.

1889   The first patent for Parker's new pen and ink feed was registered on December 10.

1890   An over-under feed was patented March 18.

1891   W.F. Palmer and George Parker began partnership as sole owners.

1891   An improved over feed was patented June 30.

1892   The Parker Pen Company was incorporated in February.

1893   A feed resembling the Lucky Curve was patented December 12.

1894   The Lucky Curve feed was patented December 4.

1898   A slip-fit outer cap was patented June 28.

1899   The Jointless pen was patented April 4.

1900   • Gold filigree "Lucky Curve" pens introduced.
           • A taper on the inside of the outer cap was patented July 17 to make cap fit more securely.

1903   A vest pocket pen called the Bulldog Special was introduced.

1904   The first mechanically filled Parker was patented May 3.

Parker Product Development Continued...

1905   A patent for the spear-head feed was applied for on January 3.

1906   The Emblem pens for secret orders were introduced.

1907   • The level lock clip was patented May 27.
• The No. 37 Sterling Silver Snake pen introduced.
• The No. 38 18K solid gold Snake pen introduced.

1911   An improved Lucky Curve feed was patented April 25.

1912   The first safety cap was patented in June. Later used in the Jack Knife pen.

1914   The Black Giant and Red Giant pens were introduced.

1916   • The button filler was introduced.
• The Ivorine line of pens made from milk curd were introduced.
• The Jack-Knife Safety pen with a transparent barrel made of bakelite was introduced.
• The washer pocket clip was patented September 5.

1918   The Safety-Sealed feature was introduced.

1920   Parker introduced its first mechanical pencil.

1921   • The Duofold pen was introduced in the Chicago Tribune on November 22, 26, 30 and December 3, 8, 14, 17, 20, 22. The Duofold was a rich Pompeian Brown with jet black trim. It had a heavy gold nib and bold pocket clip. This pen did not have a cap girdle.
• New Ivorine pens were introduced in time for Christmas in shades of purple, green, mauve, taupe, transparent Bakelite and black.

1922   • The Duofold De Luxe and Duofold Junior De Luxe were introduced in April in Chinese Red with wide rolled gold or solid gold cap bands.
• The Duofold Junior and Lady Duofold were introduced in November.
• The Parker Duette gold filled pen and pencil sets were introduced.

1923   • The gold girdle reinforcement was added to the Duofold cap.
• Flashing Black was added as new color for Duofold.
• The College Pen was introduced in black. It had the look of a Duofold, but was not marked such.
• The first Canadian marks appeared on Duofolds assembled in Toronto.

1924 . • Flashing Black was added to Duofold Junior and Lady Duofold in April.
• Duofold pencil was introduced in April with a small pocket clip and could be purchased singly or as Duette set with Duofold or Lady Duofold.
• Duofold "Big Bro." pencil was introduced in December as a mate for the Over-size Duofold pen.

1925   • Duofold Junior Over-size pencil was introduced .
• Lady Duofold pencil was introduced.

1926   • Nonbreakable Duofolds of Permanite were introduced in summer.
• Mottled Green color was added to pens and pencils.

Parker Product Development Continued...

- The Petite pastel pens and pencils were introduced in May. Pastel shades were Magenta, Mauve, Naples Blue, Beige Gray, and Coral.
- Black vintage bands appeared on Mottled Green pencils.
- The non-clog pencil feed was introduced which could propel lead in or out.
- The Parker D.Q. school pen was introduced in black with a white-gold cap girdle.
- The first Parker desk sets introduced. The sets featured a rotating ball-and-socket receptacle.

1927
- Duofold imprint on pen barrel became smaller than in previous years.
- Parker Pastels introduced new pattern in February that was very similar to the Moire Pattern.
- Announcement of April 1, that Parker makes no charge to service Duofold pens.
- Parker Pastels introduced in May and new Moire Pattern of broken lines in five pastel shades: the green shade became Apple Green; pencils had the black vintage bands.
- New colors introduced in June included Lapis (Mottled Blue) and Chinese Yellow.
- In September, the new colors Lapis and Chinese Yellow were called Lapis Lazuli Blue and Mandarin Yellow respectively.
- Pressureless Touch writing was announced in September.
- New colors for desk pens were announced in December including Jade, Mandarin Yellow, Lacquer-red, Lapis Lazuli Blue and Black with colored Moire pattern tapers.

1928
- Split cap girdles were introduced on Duofold
- "Guarantee Forever against all defects" was introduced for all Duofolds.
- True Blue pens and pencils were introduced in Moderne Blue-and-White design aimed at the low price market.
- The Imperial Duofold introduced in October in Moderne Black and Pearl, was described as Silvery, Beautifully Tridescent. This pen was later called Duofold De Luxe.

1929
- The entire line of Parker pens were redesigned and introduced in Streamline Shapes. The pens were tapered at each end.
- The pencils' gold crowns were dispensed with and they were redesigned in the new Streamline Shape to match the pens.
- The Convertible pens were introduced. A pocket cap with clip was included with every Desk Set pen. This combination made two pens of one—for pocket—for desk.
- The Lucky Curve name was discontinued.
- True Blue line of pens and pencils were discontinued.
- Vest-Parker pens were introduced. These midget Duofolds were also convertible for desk sets.

1930   Moderne Green and Pearl Duofolds were introduced.

1931
- The Black and Burgundy Red Duofolds were introduced.
- Quink Ink, a pen-cleaning ink formula was introduced in early summer.

1932
- The Penparker was introduced in chromium and black finished metal. It was promoted as a desk base for Parker pens.
- Sea Green Pearl and Black Duofolds were introduced.
- A line of Parker Duettes were introduced at economy prices in mahogany & white, grey & red and blue & black colors.
- A "Thrift-time Pocket-Desk Pen Travel Set" was introduced in the Fall. The low priced set included a $3 Parker pen, desk base and attachable desk taper. The better set included a Duofold pocket pen. Some sets included matching pencils and Quink Ink.

1933
- The new Vacumatics were announced in March in the Saturday Evening Post. The

Parker Product Development Continued...

Vacumatics were completely restyled. Features included: 102% more ink capacity, new arrow pocket clip, cap and barrel made of laminated pearl and jet horizontal stripes, the nib was fashioned in platinum and gold and featured a reversible point, it was sacless and vacuum filled and their barrels were opaque.
- The Lifetime guarantee was discontinued with introduction of the new Vacumatics.
- Visible ink supply was introduced for Vacumatics in September and the opaque models were discontinued.

1937 Speedline Vacumatics were introduced in September for the Major, Maxima and Senior models. Cap band was imprinted Parker.

1939 The Vacumatic Repeater pencil was introduced.

1940 • The Blue Diamond was introduced in April and signified "Guaranteed for Life".
- The Imperial Vacumatic pen and Writefine pencil were introduced in solid colored barrels and gold-filled caps. The Blue Diamond appeared on the pens.

1941 • The famous Parker "51" was introduced and was named after Parker's 51st Anniversary commemorating the year the pen came out of research in 1939.
- The high Velocity "51" ink for "51" pens was introduced. It was designed to slow-down evaporation and step-up penetration to dry as you write.

1947 The "VS" pen was introduced. It was produced in black, blue, gray and rust barrel colors and had a "Lustraloy" cap with a straight pocket clip.

1948 • Superchrome permanent ink was introduced in five colors.
- The Demi-Size "51" was introduced.
- The "21" was introduced in a design similar to the "51" with a straight cap pocket clip. The "21"'s nib was made of Octanium.
- The Aeor-Metric "51" was introduced with these new features: foto-fill filler, visible ink supply, pli-glass reservoir, ink flow governor, five layer insulation, hi-flite leak prevention, greater writing mileage, plathenium-tipped point, "Live Metal" clip and five other significant advances.

1948 The new "51" Signet Set was introduced in chased lined 12K golf-filled cap and barrel and lined with silver. The pen and pencil were available in regular and demi-size.

1949 The Presidential "51" was introduced in solid gold in August. It had Sterling inner parts.

1950 • The "51" Flighter Set was introduced in "Lustraloy" with a gold-filled arrow clip and cap girdle. The Aero-Metric ink system was featured in this pen.
- The Parker "51" received the 1950 Fashion Academy Award for exceptional styling, precision and craftsmanship.
- The Parkette was introduced in August but was soon dropped from production because of lagging sales.
- The "51" Special was introduced in May with an Octanium nib. It was offered in four colors; red, black, grey and blue.
- The Flaminaire Butane Lighter was introduced in September, ran a short, unsuccessful course and was discontinued.

1954 The Jotter ball point pen was released in January and featured an oversize ink cartridge. The Jotter was made entirely of stainless steel and nylon and offered a variety of point sizes. Some Jotters were designed as matching companions for the "51" and "21" pens.

Parker Product Development Continued...

1955   The Liquid Lead pencil was introduced in January and reached the market place in May. The pencil sold well for awhile, but was phased out in the early sixties.

1956   The Parker 61 was announced in September and featured a natural capillary filling system with no moving parts. The original model had a two-tone gold cap.

1957   The T-Ball Jotter was introduced and featured a textured tungsten carbide ball that prevented skipping.

1959   ● The Parker 61 Jet Flighter was released in September and featured gold-filled cap, barrel and trim and was tested to 40,000 feet aloft.
● The Parker International Jotter pen was introduced in December with a gold-filled cap, barrel and clip and featured the T-Ball point.

1960   The Parker 45 was announced and featured an ink cartridge. It was named after the Western pistol.

1962   ● The VP (for very personal) was released in June and offered a contoured grip that could be dialed for best fit.
● A Special Edition pen was fashioned from the Atlas booster rocket which made John Glenn the first American Astronaut to orbit the earth on February 20, 1962. Only 250 of these pens were produced and were given to heads of state in foreign countries and a few VIPs here and abroad.

1964   The Parker 75 was announced in October and was made of solid Sterling silver and trimmed in gold. It featured an adjustable dial grip.

1965   ● The Parker 75 Spanish Treasure Fleet was announced in November. It was fashioned from silver recovered from the Spanish Treasure Ship that sank in 1715. The pen's barrel was engraved with the words "Sterling Silver, Spanish Treasure Fleet, 1715". Only 4821 pens were manufactured.
● The Parker 75 Insignia was introduced in 14k gold-filled cap, barrel and trim.
● The Parker 75 became available in Vermeil. It was made of 14K gold over Sterling.

1970   The Parker T-1 was announced in April and was made almost entirely of titanium. Manufacturing the T-1 was no easy task because titanium is so tough. It was discontinued in 1971.

1972   The famed Parker Duofold was revived under the label of Big Red, with the updated version utilizing interchangeable ball pen and soft tip writing modes. Millions are still being sold to those who nostalgically recalled the Roaring 20s — and those young enough to think Big Red was something new.

1975   Parker premiered a modular line of pens named Systemark. Highlighted by a Floating Ball pen, which uses a liquid ink like a fountain pen, the system also featured interchangeable soft tip and plastic tip stylus refills.

1976 thru 1979   Among the writing instruments offered in the late 1970s included the Parker 180, dual-line nib fountain pen; the Parker 25 line from England; the Parker 50 line; the "women's only" designer pen influenced by Italy's Emilio Pucci, called Ms. Parker; and a novelty "neck pen" called Swinger.

1981   Parker introduced a contemporary line of gift writing instruments, the Arrow, featuring a highly stylized and engraveable pocket clip which is a modernization of the Parker Arrow symbol that has been recognized world-wide since 1932 when it was first used. The line includes a ball pen, 0.7 mm mechanical pencil, roller ball and fountain pen. These different models are offered in several finishes: gold-filled, matte black with gold trim and stainless steel.

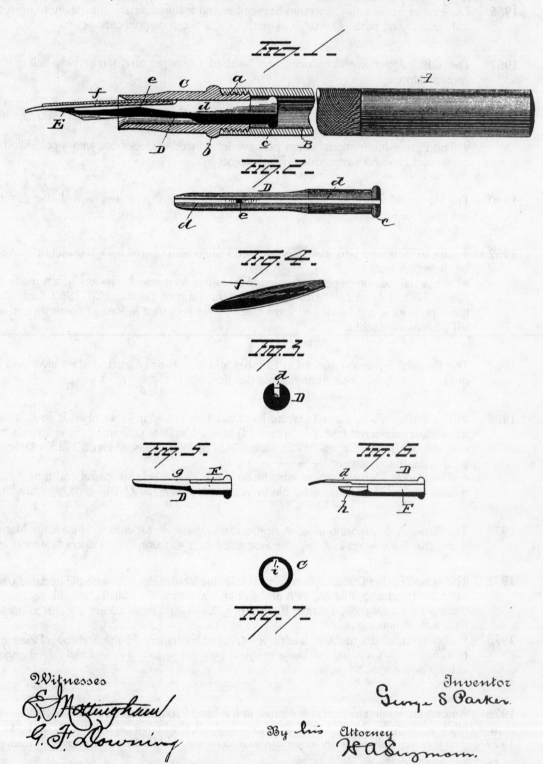

(No Model.)

G. S. PARKER.
FOUNTAIN PEN.

No. 416,944.   Patented Dec. 10, 1889.

Parker's original fountain pen patent issued December 10, 1889.

(No Model.)

G. S. PARKER.
FOUNTAIN PEN.

No. 512,319.   Patented Jan. 9, 1894.

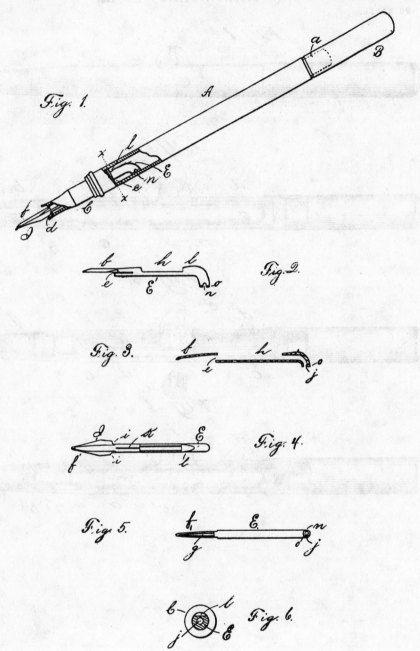

WITNESSES:

Otis D. Swett.

Samuel A. Groff

INVENTOR

George S. Parker

BY

Chas D. Swett,

ATTORNEY.

Parker's famous Lucky Curve feed patent issued January 9, 1894.

No. 758,930.   PATENTED MAY 3, 1904.

G. S. PARKER.
FOUNTAIN PEN.
APPLICATION FILED NOV. 30, 1903.

NO MODEL.

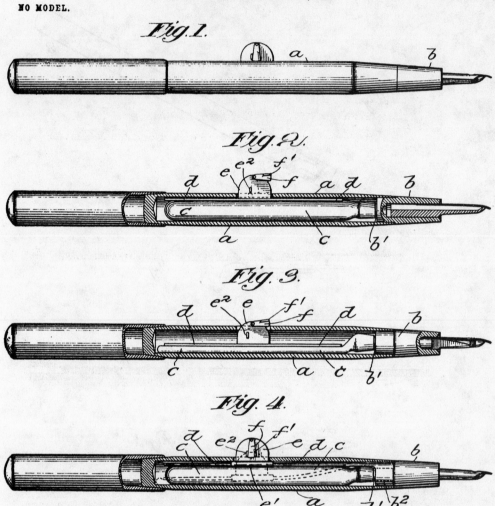

Fig. 1.

Fig. 2.

Fig. 3.

Fig. 4.

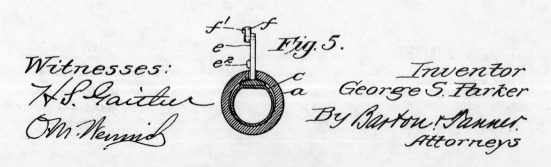

Fig. 5.

Witnesses:
H. S. Gaither
O. M. Wennich

Inventor
George S. Parker
By Barton & Tanner
Attorneys

THE NORRIS PETERS CO., PHOTO-LITHO., WASHINGTON, D. C.

Parker's first mechanically filled fountain pen patent issued May 3, 1904.

No. 778,997.   PATENTED JAN. 3, 1905.

G. S. PARKER.
FEEDER FOR FOUNTAIN PENS.
APPLICATION FILED MAY 9, 1904.

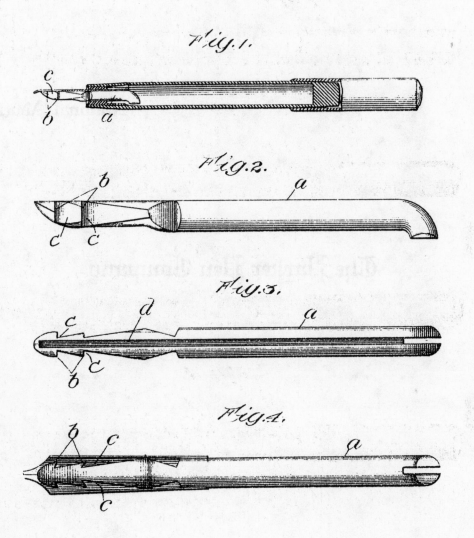

Witnesses.   Inventor,
Geo. C. Davison.   George S. Parker
W. W. Leach   By Barton & Banner
                                                       Attorneys.

Parker's spear-head feed patent issued January 3, 1905.

National Advertising

The Parker Pen Company

BUY THE

Parker

LUCKY CURVE

Fountain Pen

BECAUSE—IT IS A
GOOD PEN
· PARKER PEN ·

INKY FINGERS—only one of the nuisances that an uncertain pen makes. No trouble ever with the

GEO. S. PARKER FOUNTAIN PEN.

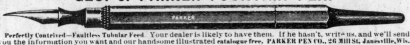

Perfectly Contrived—Faultless Tubular Feed. Your dealer is likely to have them. If he hasn't, write us, and we'll send you the information you want and our handsome illustrated catalogue free. PARKER PEN CO., 26 Mill St., Janesville, Wis.

Parker Advertisement — 1894

othing **more appropriate** or **more pleasing for a present than a**

GEO. S. PARKER FOUNTAIN PEN

Catalogue No. 6, Gold Trimmed. Price, $3.00. Sent Postpaid on Receipt of Price

nufactured in many different styles from the low in price to the more expensive for the elaborate and ly cases. If you do not own a Parker Fountain Pen you have no idea of the real comfort and convenience e derived from its use. Valuable patented improvements owned by us and used exclusively in these s. Every Pen sold on a guarantee to give satisfaction or money refunded

"My Parker Fountain Pen is simply perfect. After using several kinds I can say, this is the only one I have found satisfactory. It does not spill the ink and yet is always ready for use. I carry it constantly." GEO. H. ELLIOTT, M.D., 228 W. 11th St., New York.

r dealer is likely to have these goods, if he hasn't write us for our handsome catalogue and interesting ited matter which we mail free, and we will have your order filled direct

PARKER PEN CO., 10 Mill St., Janesville, Wis.

Parker Advertisement — 1897

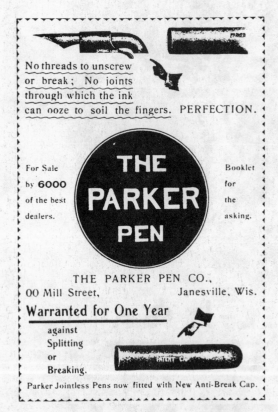

No threads to unscrew or break; No joints through which the ink can ooze to soil the fingers. PERFECTION.

For Sale by **6000** of the best dealers.

THE PARKER PEN

Booklet for the asking.

THE PARKER PEN CO.,
OO Mill Street,   Janesville, Wis.

Warranted for One Year

against Splitting or Breaking.

Parker Jointless Pens now fitted with New Anti-Break Cap.

Parker Advertisement — 1900

Lucky Curve

FEED

A Scientific Improvement

It is a Genuine **PARKER** Fountain Pen

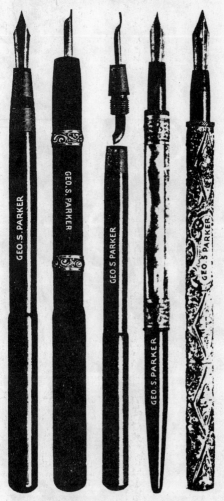

PEN COMFORT is the insurance afforded to those who use the

Parker Lucky Curve

Smooth, swift, sure. Parker Pens glide over the paper so easily pleasant thoughts are sure to flow.

Parker Advertisement — 1899

Parker Advertisement — 1902

A Christmas Suggestion

The GEO. S. PARKER Fountain Pen

LUCKY CURVE   LUCKY CURVE

A Christmas Suggestion

Are you perplexed and bothered to know what to select for a Christmas present for some dear friend, for some boy or girl, for a young lady or young gentleman, for mother, father, sister, or brother? There is no present, of moderate price, which you can buy that will give such pleasure and satisfaction as will a Parker Pen. It is a useful article, which will last a lifetime and be a constant pleasure to the owner. For your convenience, I will illustrate a few of the most popular numbers. My catalogue however shows many additional styles.

No. 1.   **Plain Barrel Parker Lucky Curve.**   **Price $1.50.**   Has the "Lucky Curve" Screw Joint. Does not have the Anti-Break Cap. Either over or under Feed. A very good pen and warranted.

No. 1.
Price $1.50

A neat little pen. It is the lowest in price of any Parker "Lucky Curve" made.

No. 20.
Screw Joint
or Jointless
$2.50

This is a splendid pen for the money, and it is just the thing for the school boy or school girl. It is so simple and strong that it can hardly be gotten out of order. If you want to send a thrill of pleasure through "that boy" or "that girl," you can do it with a Parker No. 20.

No. 24.
Screw Joint
or Jointless
$4.00

No. 23. This number can be supplied when so desired, with practically same size barrel as No. 20, but the pen is a full size larger than the preceding number. The larger pen affording, as it does, the different "feel," will richly repay anyone to purchase this pen if they are connoisseurs. Price $3.00.

No. 24.   **Price $4.00.**   This pen is much larger than the general run of pens, and they are purchased by those who know just what they want, and can afford to pay the higher price necessary for the larger and finer pen. If you feel like spending $4.00 for a fountain pen, and purchase this pen, we feel safe in saying one year hence $10.00 would not buy it if another could not be purchased. It has a "feel," too, all its own. We can recommend it as one of the finest pens ever made. (This pen fitted for manifolding, Shorthand or Bookkeeping when so ordered.)

No. 25.
Screw Joint
or Jointless
$5.00

LUCKY CURVE

The "Lucky Curve" is a scientific improvement which, by its peculiar construction, not only feeds the ink perfectly from the barrel to the pen, but prevents the ink from leaking and getting over the outside of the nozzle to soil the fingers when next used. My little booklet, "The Reason Why," tells all.

THE LUCKY CURVE

Absolutely the Best Pen in the World

If I could convey to you how much real pleasure, comfort and satisfaction there is in store for you, should you decide to become an owner and user of one of my Fountain Pens, I am sure you would not long be without. I have never been satisfied with making merely a good pen, but am making what is acknowledged to be

Honest pens that will wear, and capable of many years of satisfactory use. In fact, I issue an Accident Policy with each pen, which not only guarantees each pen to be entirely satisfactory, but it Insures Against Breakage of the Gold Pen, Cap, Barrel, Feeder, Nozzle, and, in fact, any part except the Gold Pen. Such vital and necessary patented improve[...]

A Charming Christmas Gift
PARKER *LUCKY CURVE* FOUNTAIN PEN

A SENSIBLE, PRACTICABLE AND USEFUL GIFT
FOR FATHER, MOTHER, BROTHER, SISTER, WIFE OR SWEETHEART

No. 1. PRICE $1.50. PLAIN BARREL PARKER LUCKY CURVE. A neat little pen. Has the "Lucky Curve" screw joint. Does not have the "Anti-Break" Cap. Either over or under feed. A very good pen and warranted. It is the lowest in price of any Parker "Lucky Curve" made.

No. 20. PRICE $2.50. PLAIN OR CHASED BARREL. Made with smooth or threaded end where fingers grasp the fountain. One of the most popular numbers we make. Can be supplied in either black or mottled rubber. Fine, medium, coarse or stub pen, as wanted.

No. 33. PRICE $5.50. GOLD. This pen is our leader for the new styles. It is certainly the biggest value ever put into a pen retailing for less than $6.00. Neat, tasty and a real beauty. Same design in Sterling Silver No. 34. Price, $4.50.

No. 35. PRICE $10.00. GOLD. GENTLEMAN'S SIZE. Barrel and cap entirely covered with heavy 18-k. plate, which will last for a lifetime. A magnificent creation. The delicate beauty of the handwork done on this cannot be appreciated until seen. Surely a finer present than this could hardly be devised.

No. 14. PRICE $5.00. STERLING SILVER FILIGREE No. 16. GOLD $6.00. The silver inlaid over the vulcanite, making a most striking looking pen. Space is reserved on name plate for engraving name of owner. No. 16 same pattern as above. Solid 18-k. gold plate, will wear for years. Price $6.00. If you want to spend as much as $5.00 or $6.00 for a fancy fountain you need have no fear of regretting selecting this style.

No. 15. PRICE $7.00. PEARL BARREL WITH GOLD BANDS. Just out. One of the prettiest in our line of fancy pens. Gold filigree on Cap. Name plate, so the name of owner can be engraved on same. This cut does not begin to show the beauty of this magnificent creation.

EMBLEM PENS. PRICE $12.00 AND $12.50. For the first time we show this pen, we are prepared to supply the Parker Pen with the emblem of almost any of the more prominent orders. The cut shows the general style. The emblem is on solid (not plated) gold band. Makes a fine present for some secret order man. K. of P., K. of C., I. O. O. F., Blue Lodge Chapter, $12.00. Shrine, Knight Templars and others, $12.50.

DID YOU ever see some friend take the cap off the pen point end of a fountain pen and then look dark, and finally take a piece of paper and wipe off the nozzle? If you have you may be sure it was not a Parker Lucky Curve Fountain Pen.

"What! Do you mean to say that this common and disagreeable feature is eliminated in the Parker?"

Most certainly we do, for to prevent that trouble the famous Lucky Curve was invented.

"Then why is it everyone who uses a fountain pen does not buy a Parker?"

Simply because some people do not take time the same as you do, to inform themselves as to what to buy and what not to buy and buy something merely because they do not inform themselves of something better.

"But will you please tell me how it is the Lucky Curve makes the Parker cleanly while others soil the fingers?"

Very gladly.

TO ILLUSTRATE

In the common kind of fountain pens you will find, if you unscrew the nozzle from the barrel, that the feeder is cut off almost coextensive with the thread end. Unscrew the Parker and you will find the feeder

THIS SHOWS THE LUCKY CURVE

extending for a short distance and in the form of a curve—hence the phrase "Lucky curve." This curved end is made so that when its face is in position it will just touch against the side of the barrel. This face also has a little slit or mouth which communicates with the main channel of the feeder. Just as soon as the fountain is inverted, as it is when carried in the pocket, the ink passes down through the ink channel, which is a capillary channel, to the mouth of the feeder, where it is in turn delivered to the side of the barrel and by it carried along to the reservoir, and the feed channel is quickly emptied. Consequently when the cap is next removed from the Parker Pen, the nozzle is found as clean and dry as when the pen was first put in the pocket. In the common and old style pens of other makes nothing has been made to provide for care of ink in the feed channel after the pen has been returned to the pocket and which has caused so many blackened fingers and dissatisfaction in using.

No intelligent person would, knowingly, run into trouble if they could avoid it; and a safe rule in purchasing a fountain pen and not be imposed upon, is to unscrew the nozzle and examine the thread end. **SEE THAT IT HAS THE LUCKY CURVE.**

Many thousands of dealers all over the world sell the Parker Pen. If yours does not, and he tries to sell you just as good a pen without the "Lucky Curve" tell him he cannot fool you, but in such cases we will gladly fill your order direct.

PARKER PEN COMPANY   MILL STREET, JANESVILLE, WIS.

See the above advertisement in the December Magazines

You'll Know It Won't Leak
When You See
The *Ink Scoot Down*

Make This Test Yourself

IN a "regular" fountain pen, standing point up in your vest pocket, is a straight feed tube. Below it is a space of air. Below the air is the ink.

The tube stays full of ink, even though the pen is standing point up.

Now, your body, 95° hot, warms the air in the air space. This makes it expand, and to get out, it pushes through the feed tube. It pushes out the feed tube ink, smearing up the writing end of the pen.

Down in a Parker Fountain Pen, is a *curved* feed tube. Below it is the air space, and below the air is ink, as per usual.

The instant you set your Parker in your pocket, that "Lucky Curve" feed tube sucks all the ink out, down into the reservoir, as you see. Thus the ink is out before the air gets warm and ascends.

What makes the "Lucky Curve" suck the ink? The end of the "Lucky Curve" feed tube, touching the wall of the barrel, creates Capillary Attraction. Capillary Attraction is a force of Nature that makes flower stems suck water and lamp wicks suck oil.

Unscrew any Parker Fountain Pen; fill the feed tube with ink; touch the "Lucky Curve" to the barrel wall as in above picture; watch the ink scoot down. Thus prove there is no ink in the Parker feed tube to leak out and smear your fingers.

When writing, Parker Pens behave and stay on the job; made in all styles, self-filling, safety and standard; plain, gold or silver mounted. All have 14-K gold pens with iridium points; prices $1.50 to $20.

New pocket clip cleverly withdraws into cap when you write, and comes out when you again put cap over the pen.

If dealer doesn't keep them, send us his name, and we'll sell you direct from our complete catalogue. Address

Parker Pen Co., 98 Mill Street, Janesville, Wisconsin
New York retail store, 11 Park Row, Opposite Post Office

Style 33
Price $4.50

Geo. S. Parker

Why hesitate to get a Parker today? We protect dealer from loss if you return pen.

PARKER LUCKY CURVE FOUNTAIN PEN

PARKER LUCKY CURVE FountainPens

Cleanly— Because of the LUCKY CURVE

I guarantee over my signature that you will find the Parker the most cleanly, most efficient and satisfactory of all fountain pens.

With the Lucky Curve it is a step ahead of any other in construction, readiness and dependability.

There is a bigger use for such a pen than mere pocket convenience—it will save energy and increase the accuracy of office workers, students, or anyone who uses ink. You can get a point perfectly suited to your writing habits—sold on ten days' test trial—insured against breakage for a year, and fully guaranteed.

Geo. S. Parker

No. 42½—Neat, simple, elegant. Space for owner's name.

No. 46—18-k. gold-filled filigree design. Corrugated, tinted pearl slab.

No. 52—Sterling hammered silver, Swastika design.

The PARKER Jack-Knife Safety

This little pen combines rare handiness, unusual convenience and highest efficiency.

No matter what position you carry it—even upside down—it doesn't leak.

It goes easily in a lady's purse or handbag. Safe from loss in a man's lower vest pocket, or even in his trousers pocket with his jack-knife, there is absolutely no danger of leaking, and it is always instantly available for use.

No springs, valves or disappearing mechanism to get out of order. It is durable for a lifetime.

Baby size, like illustration, with No. 2 pen, $2.50. With larger size gold pen, $3.00, $4.00 and $5.00, according to size.

Sold by Dealers on Ten Days' Test Trial

My idea is to have PARKER Pens sell themselves. It's a case of "Try Before You Buy," with the Parker. Any dealer will let you carry any Parker Pen ten days before he calls it a sale. That's so you can be sure to get the size barrel and pen point most satisfactory to you—and to let the PARKER prove its superiority and cleanliness. If the pen is not as good as I recommend it, take it back and your money will be refunded. A year's insurance policy against accidental breakage and a binding guarantee with every Parker Lucky Curve Fountain Pen. If you can't find a Parker dealer write to me. Prices range from $1.50 to $250.00.

Beautiful catalog showing all styles, designs and prices—free.

PARKER PEN COMPANY
GEO. S. PARKER, PRESIDENT
118 Mill St., Janesville, Wis.

BRANCHES
PARKER PEN CO. (Retail), 11 Park Row, New York City
Canadian Branch: BUNTIN, GILLIES & CO., Hamilton and Montreal, Canada
European Branch: PARKER PEN CO., Stuttgart, Germany

PARKER JACK-KNIFE SAFETY

X-Ray View of Parker Lucky Curve Fountain Pen

The Thing That Makes a Pen Write

Keeps the Parker from *Leaking*

WHY does a pen write? Because the *touch* of the pen point to the paper creates *Capillary Attraction*—that curious force in Nature that makes sponges absorb, lamp wicks draw, etc., etc. This Capillary Attraction draws the ink from the pen point onto the paper.

Why does a fountain pen leak? Because when you set an ordinary fountain pen in your vest pocket, point up, all the ink does not run down into the reservoir below. Some stays up in the straight feed tube leading to the pen point.

When your body heat—98 degrees—reaches the air in the pen barrel, the air expands—rushes up through the inky feed tube—pushes the ink up and out around the pen point—messes the writing end of the pen—and *blacks your fingers* when you remove the cap.

Now the Parker, unlike other fountain pens, has a *curved* feed tube—the famous Parker Lucky Curve. The end of it touches the barrel wall. This *touch* creates *Capillary Attraction*, which draws all the ink down out of the feed tube when you turn pen up, and before the air expands.

Thus the thing that makes a pen write is the same thing that keeps the Parker Pen from leaking and smearing the fingers—to wit: *Capillary Attraction*.

14k gold pens with hardest Iridium points make Parkers write without scratching. Parker Spear Head Ink Controller won't let ink flow too fast or too slow New Parker Disappearing Clip clutches like a drowning man, but *disappears* when you write. Price 25 cents additional.

Standard Style Parker Lucky Curve Fountain Pens $2, $2.50, $10 and upward, according to size and decoration.

NEW PARKER JACK KNIFE SAFETY PEN

can't leak in any position in any pocket. Comes also in pen knife size for lady's purse. Prices $2. $3, $4 $5, and up.

Get a Parker on trial. Dealer will nd any time within 10 days of purchase, if you're not overw elmingly pleased. If your dealer doesn't keep Parkers, write us for complete catalog.

Nothing like getting a Parker Fountain Pen *to-day*.

Parker Pen Co., 106 Mill Street, Janesville, Wis.
New York Retail Store, 11 Park Row, opposite Post Office

No. 14
Jack Knife Safety Pen, Sterling Silver. Price, $5. 18K. gold plate, $6.

No. 20½
Beautiful Chasing on Barrel and Cap. Price $2.50

No. 42½
Gold Bands. Space for Engraving Name Price $4.50

MAKE THIS TEST YOURSELF

PARKER
LUCKY CURVE
FOUNTAIN PEN

For Christmas?

You'll find the right answer in a

PARKER LUCKY CURVE

FOUNTAIN PEN

"What shall I give for Christmas?" Solve the question simply and at once. Jot down Parker Fountain Pens at the top of your Christmas shopping list. A Parker Pen will give pleasure to the recipient and reflect credit on the judgment of the giver. You cannot find a more acceptable gift than a Parker Fountain Pen. It's a pen of character and quality. A dainty Christmas gift box with every pen.

GEO. S. PARKER.

PARKER JACK KNIFE SAFETY

Wonderfully handy! The most convenient pen made and the cleanest, too, on account of the Lucky Curve and special lock feature that shuts in the ink and makes it absolutely leak-proof. It's always safe, carry it as you will—upside down or right side up—in any pocket, like a jack knife or small pencil. Just the thing for a lady's purse or hand-bag.

NEW PARKER SELF-FILLER

This is my latest pen and my latest success. It's as far ahead of other self-fillers in efficiency as the express train was over the prairie schooner. The Parker Self-Filler is unique—nothing else just like it. Looks like a regular Parker Standard Fountain Pen, but you press the button and in three seconds it fills itself. Has smooth barrel—no unsightly obstructions to interfere with easy handling. Any one will be delighted with this Self-Filling Pen. It's a gift that will pleasantly remind the user of the giver for a lifetime.

No. 14—Jack Knife Safety with ring. Sterling silver, $5. Gold plated, $6. The Ladies' Favorite.

No. 20
Standard or Self-Filler, $2.50; with level lock clip. $2.75.

No. 42½—Standard or Self-Filling, $4.50; with gold-filled level lock clip, $5.00. Space for name on gold band.

No. 20½—Jack Knife Safety with ring for suspending by chain. $2.75. Very popular.

No. 33
Gold-Filled, $5.50. Sterling Silver, $4.50. Space for name. Neat, tasty, a real beauty.

No. 57
Awanyu Aztec design, hammered silver, $10. Gold-filled, $12. More elaborate design, $20. Space for name. A splendid gift.

HOW TO GET THEM

You can get Parker Fountain Pens in a great variety of styles and sizes to suit every fancy—Jack Knife Safety, Self-Filler, and Standard Pens—at prices from $2.50, $3, $4, $5, and up. Level lock clip on Standards and Self-Fillers, 25c. extra. Complete assortments now at 15,000 dealers. If you cannot locate a dealer, write for our catalog, or send price named in this advertisement and we will supply you.

The Lucky Curve

The exclusive feature that has made the Parker the cleanly pen.

Parker Pen Company,

18 MILL STREET, JANESVILLE, WIS.

You are cordially invited to visit our New York **Retail Store** in the big Woolworth Building

Parker Advertisement — 1913

SANTA CLAUS SUGGESTS
PARKER SAFETY-SEALED FOUNTAIN PENS

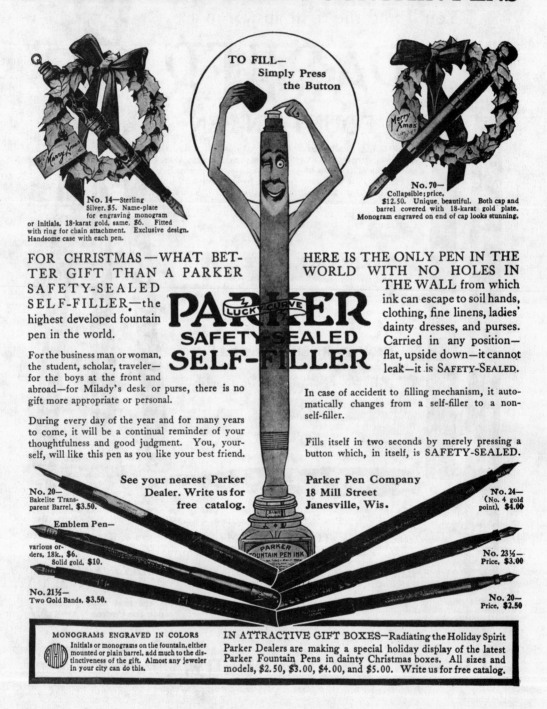

TO FILL—
Simply Press
the Button

No. 14—Sterling
Silver, $5. Name-plate
for engraving monogram
or initials, 18-karat gold, same, $6. Fitted
with ring for chain attachment. Exclusive design.
Handsome case with each pen.

No. 70—
Collapsible; price,
$12.50. Unique, beautiful. Both cap and
barrel covered with 18-karat gold plate.
Monogram engraved on end of cap looks stunning.

FOR CHRISTMAS—WHAT BETTER GIFT THAN A PARKER SAFETY-SEALED SELF-FILLER.—the highest developed fountain pen in the world.

For the business man or woman, the student, scholar, traveler—for the boys at the front and abroad—for Milady's desk or purse, there is no gift more appropriate or personal.

During every day of the year and for many years to come, it will be a continual reminder of your thoughtfulness and good judgment. You, yourself, will like this pen as you like your best friend.

PARKER
LUCKY CURVE
SAFETY-SEALED
SELF-FILLER

HERE IS THE ONLY PEN IN THE WORLD WITH NO HOLES IN THE WALL from which ink can escape to soil hands, clothing, fine linens, ladies' dainty dresses, and purses. Carried in any position—flat, upside down—it cannot leak—it is SAFETY-SEALED.

In case of accident to filling mechanism, it automatically changes from a self-filler to a non-self-filler.

Fills itself in two seconds by merely pressing a button which, in itself, is SAFETY-SEALED.

See your nearest Parker
Dealer. Write us for
free catalog.

Parker Pen Company
18 Mill Street
Janesville, Wis.

No. 20—
Bakelite Transparent Barrel, $3.50.

Emblem Pen—

various orders, 18k., $6.
Solid gold, $10.

No. 21½—
Two Gold Bands, $3.50.

No. 24—
(No. 4 gold
point), $4.00

No. 23½—
Price, $3.00

No. 20—
Price, $2.50

MONOGRAMS ENGRAVED IN COLORS
Initials or monograms on the fountain, either
mounted or plain barrel, add much to the distinctiveness of the gift. Almost any jeweler
in your city can do this.

IN ATTRACTIVE GIFT BOXES—Radiating the Holiday Spirit
Parker Dealers are making a special holiday display of the latest
Parker Fountain Pens in dainty Christmas boxes. All sizes and
models, $2.50, $3.00, $4.00, and $5.00. Write us for free catalog.

USED IN THE ARMIES AND NAVIES OF THE WORLD

For Christmas give

PARKER
LUCKY CURVE
SAFETY-SEALED
FOUNTAIN PENS

FOR the boys at the front, for relatives, friends and sweethearts. The enduring gift, always appreciated, always useful.

Parker Self-fillers are *safety-sealed*, the new type "no holes in the wall" fountain pens. Ink can't get out to soil clothes or uniform.

In event of injury to interior mechanism, the pen automatically changes from a Self-filler to non-Self-filler without interruption of service. Because of these exclusive features it's the pen for the army and navy, where only dependable pens are wanted.

Your search for suitable gifts is at an end—decide on PARKER FOUNTAIN PENS. The name is your guarantee of quality.

Obtainable at most stores where fountain pens are sold.

PARKER PEN CO., 11 Mill St., Janesville, Wis.

In Dainty Gift Boxes

Easy to Fill

THE GEORGE S. PARKER "LUCKY CURVE"

No. 20—$2.50
No. 21— 3.50
No. 51— 3.50
No. 24— 4.00
No. 14—
Sterling, 5.00
No. 14—Gold
Plate, 6.00

Parker Clips
75c extra

Ink tablets in place of fluid ink for soldiers' use, box of 36, for 10 cents.

At leading dealers.

New Parker PATENT Clip held in place like washer. Drops pen to level of pocket. Pen does not protrude or bunch under pocket lapel of uniform.

Parker Advertisement — 1917

Parker Advertisement — 1917

Parker Advertisement — 1918

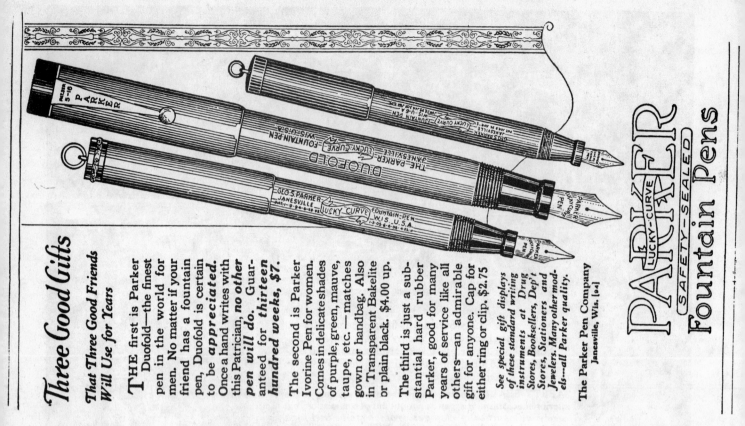

Three Good Gifts

That Three Good Friends Will Use for Years

THE first is Parker Duofold—the finest pen in the world for men. No matter if your friend has a fountain pen, Duofold is certain to be *appreciated.* Once a hand writes with this Patrician, *no other pen will do.* Guaranteed for *thirteen hundred weeks, $7.*

The second is Parker Ivorine Pen for women. Comes in delicate shades of purple, green, mauve, taupe, etc.— matches gown or handbag. Also in Transparent Bakelite or plain black. $4.00 up.

The third is just a substantial hard rubber Parker, good for many years of service like all others—an admirable gift for anyone. Cap for either ring or clip. $2.75

See special gift displays of these standard writing instruments at Drug Stores, Booksellers, Dep't Stores, Stationers and Jewelers. Many other models—all Parker quality.

The Parker Pen Company
Janesville, Wis. [04]

Parker Advertisement — November 1921

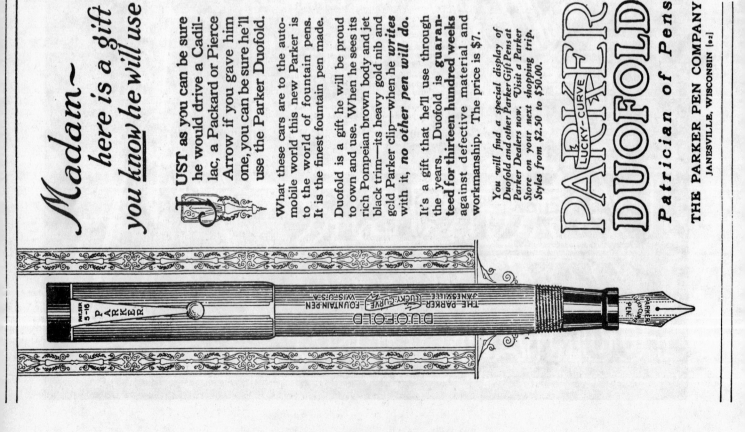

Madam~
here is a gift
you *know* he will use

JUST as you can be sure he would drive a Cadillac, a Packard or Pierce Arrow if you gave him one, you can be sure he'll use the Parker Duofold.

What these cars are to the automobile world this new Parker is to the world of fountain pens. It is the finest fountain pen made.

Duofold is a gift he will be proud to own and use. When he sees its rich Pompeian brown body and jet black trim—its heavy gold nib and gold Parker clip—when he *writes* with it, *no other pen will do.*

It's a gift that he'll use through the years. Duofold is guaranteed for thirteen hundred weeks against defective material and workmanship. The price is $7.

You will find a special display of Duofold and other Parker Gift Pens at Parker Dealers now. Visit a Parker Store on your next shopping trip. Styles from $2.50 to $50.00.

THE PARKER PEN COMPANY
JANESVILLE, WISCONSIN [02]

Parker Advertisement — December 1921

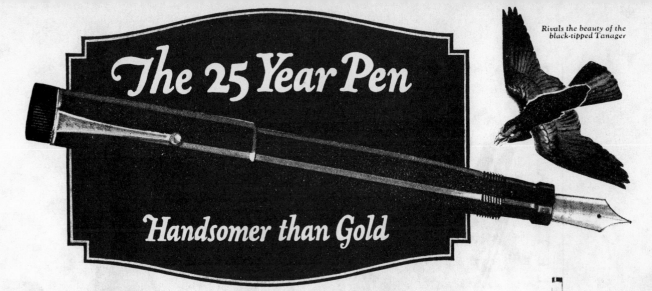

The 25 Year Pen

Handsomer than Gold

Rivals the beauty of the black-tipped Tanager

The new pen classic; with a point like a smooth jewel bearing, and an Over-size Barrel that resembles Chinese lacquer

Created by GEO. S. PARKER
inventor of the leakproof "Lucky Curve"

IT TOOK MR. PARKER 30 years to produce this super-pen, but it took America only six months to reward his infinite pains with a triumph unparalleled in the whole pen industry. In this short time the Parker Duofold has become the leading seller at prominent pen counters in New York, Chicago, San Francisco and dozens of cities. It seems that the higher a pen's perfection, the swifter and more sweeping its popularity.

Men and Women of America

We invite you to step up to the first good pen counter you come to and see its lacquer-like beauty. Note how soft this shade of Chinese-red; how smart the black-tipped ends and neat gold pocket-clip.

Grasp it! Get the business-like feel of its fit, weight and balance in your hand.

Compare its over-size barrel with the ordinary pen to note how much more ink the Duofold holds.

Then write with this Native Iridium point set in extra thick gold—so smooth it needs no "breaking in," so hard and life-enduring we can guarantee it for 25 years for wear and mechanical perfection.

Write also with pens of other makes. The Duofold successfully challenges any other pen on earth regardless of price. We, too, manufacture higher-priced pens with costly mountings and know all kinds. Try, yourself, to find another anywhere that writes so steadily and smoothly.

We are supplying dealers as rapidly as possible with this pen that wears like a smooth, hard jewel. But if you don't find it near by, have your dealer take your order subject to your approval after trial. Or write us giving your dealer's name.

Note the classic simplicity of its outlines

Do you know any other pen you can pass from man to man and have it suit all hands and hold its original point?

No pump or lever to catch on clothing and spill the ink

The PARKER LUCKY CURVE
Duofold
The 25 Year Pen

OVER-SIZE
$7

Lady Duofold $5
Chatelaine or Hand Bag Size

Duofold Jr. $5
Same except for size

THE PARKER PEN COMPANY · JANESVILLE, WISCONSIN
CHICAGO   NEW YORK   SAN FRANCISCO   SPOKANE

IT RIVALS THE BEAUTY OF THE SCARLET TANAGER

The HE pen

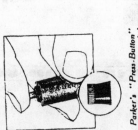

Now The Duofold De Luxe
And The Duofold Junior De Luxe

In response to the demand for "the 25-year Pen" in a more ornate and sumptuous style we have created the Duofold De Luxe and the Duofold Junior De Luxe. Both of these pens are equipped with a wide heavy rolled gold band on the cap. We thought there could be no more beautiful fountain pen than the standard Duofold with its rich laquer-like Chinese red barrel and cap with black tips. But the addition of a gold band enhances the richness of appearance of these pens and makes them unquestionably not only the finest writing instruments made but also the handsomest.

There could be no finer or more suitable gift than one of these pens. It is a gift that will serve continuously for many years and give happy satisfaction all the while. Offhand we think of no article which is used so frequently and continuously as a fountain pen. It is constantly in sight, in mind, and in the hands of the person thus favored. Therefore, it is a perfect gift.

The Duofold De Luxe with the rolled gold band retails for $10.00; with a solid gold band, $15.00. The Duofold Junior De Luxe with a rolled gold band retails for $7.00; with a solid gold band, $10.00.

Parker Duofold
The 25 Year Pen
OVER-SIZE $7
Duofold Jr $5   Lady Duofold $5

NOW GOLD GIRDLE, AS WELL AS POCKET-CLIP OR RING, INCLUDED FREE

Rivals the beauty of the Scarlet Tanager

The New
Gold Girdle
—The Last Loving Touch

We've Made Parker Duofold a Finer, Stronger Pen than Ever; Yet Kept the Price Where It Was—the Point Still Guaranteed 25 Years

PARKER DUOFOLD—the classic of pens—is one of the few things left that give you 100 cents value for your good old American dollar. Measured by fountain pen standards this Over-size beauty is a $10 pen for $7.

Our price is possible only because the Duofold's boundless popularity has afforded us large quantity production, thus scaled down the cost per pen. Now we've been able to add a strong Gold Girdle that reinforces the cap. And adds the crowning touch to its beauty. This was $1 extra before.

Thus now more than ever is Parker Duofold *the Gift superb!* A pen you can pull out in public and be proud of. A pen you can lend without fear because no style of writing can distort its 25-year point. A pen so super-smooth and rhythmically balanced *that your hand can't get away from its lure!*

We make Parker Duofold in plain black too, but recommend the black-tipped, lacquer-red Duofold for it's handsomer than gold and the color makes it hard to lose. But whichever your choice, to have Duofold's classic quality the pen must be stamped—"Geo. S. Parker—DUOFOLD—Lucky Curve." Look carefully.

Phone this newspaper for names of Parker dealers if you do not know where to get Duofold Pens.

Step up to the first good pen counter today and buy Parker Duofold on 30 days' approval

Parker
LUCKY CURVE
Duofold
OVER-SIZE $7
With The 25 Year Point

Duofold Jr. $5
Same except for size

Lady Duofold $5
With ring for chatelaine

THE PARKER PEN COMPANY, JANESVILLE, WISCONSIN
Manufacturers also of Parker "Lucky Lock" Pencils

5 Minutes at a Duofold counter

Rivals the beauty of the Scarlet Tanager

and *Your Christmas Shopping Is Done!*

To the Men and Boys Give
Parker Over-Size Duofold $7 or Duofold Jr. $5

To the Women and Girls Give
Slender Lady Duofold
with Wide Gold Girdle for Monogram, $5

THEY'LL never lay aside this black-tipped, lacquer-red classic with the polished Iridium-tipped point, guaranteed 25 years for mechanical perfection *and wear!*

"Handsomer than Gold!" is the popular verdict wherever the Duofold is seen. Its smart Chinese color makes it a treasure to carry and a hard pen to lose when you lay it down. It's a good gift for you to be judged by when friend shows friend what you gave for Christmas.

Neat gold pocket-clip or gold ring-end for ribbon, as well as rich ★gold girdle, now included free.

Leading pen counters in all cities—large and small—are supplying Christmas Duofolds to merry throngs.

Take your Christmas list with you today—get your shopping all done in five or ten minutes.

THE PARKER PEN COMPANY
Manufacturers also of Parker "Lucky Lock" Pencils
Factory and General Offices, Janesville, Wis.

Parker *LUCKY CURVE* Duofold
OVER-SIZE $7
With The 25 Year Point

Duofold Jr. $5
Same except for size

Lady Duofold $5
With ring for chatelaine

Red and Black Color Combination Reg. Trade Mark U.S. Pat. Office

Lady Duofold $5
Ribbon $1 extra

Over-Size $7

Written with a Parker by
Glenn W. Miller, guard on Iowa's famous team
and now captain

PARKER ANNOUNCES
a new one for students

Parker College Pen

—the Note-taker Pen, $3

Strong metal girdle reinforces cap
Large ring-end links to note-book
—A pocket-clip if you prefer—
No extra charge for either

WE asked about 1000 students at seventeen universities and colleges the kind of pen they wanted.

The majority preferred the Parker, but not all could afford to pay the Parker Duofold price.

So we set to work and produced this black beauty—the Parker College Pen— formed on Duofold's classic lines and made by the same crafts-guild.

We gave it a 14k gold point tipped with polished Iridium, and a good healthy ink capacity; then we added two things we could find on no other pen of this size below five dollars—a metal girdle to reinforce the cap; and an extra large ring link to fasten to the student's note-book. These features are included free, or a pocket-clip instead of ring-end.

The Parker College Pen is an ink-tight pen. Ask to see it—note its shapeliness and balance. Try other pens too, and see how super-smooth the Parker is in comparison.

THE PARKER PEN COMPANY, JANESVILLE, WIS.
Manufacturers also of Parker "Lucky Lock" Pencils

The **Parker** College Pen *LUCKY-CURVE* **$3**

Banded Cap—Large Ring or Clip—Duofold Standards

FOR SALE BY

THE TOOL BOX OF THE BRAIN

Graduation's New Gift

Parker Duofold Duette

Duofold Pen and Pencil to match

in satin-lined Gift Case De Luxe

Handsomer Than Gold—Mightier Than the Sword

DOING princely honor at Graduation to the sons and daughters of your friends wins not only the life-long affection of the Graduates, but of their parents, too. For to this Day they have all looked forward for years—it's the Day when Youth embarks on Life's Career.

No better gift to start the Graduate than these two fine Tools of Hand and Brain—the Parker Duofold Duette. For Duofold's balanced swing and infinite smoothness *inspire* writing.

This classic Duette is the newest of Gifts—this Graduation is its first. And it is beautifully prepared for giving—the black tipped lacquer-red Duofold or Lady Duofold Pen and the Duofold Pencil to match, nestling in a satin-lined Gift Case de luxe, for which no extra charge.

The pen has the super-smooth Point that is guaranteed 25 years for mechanical perfection and wear—the Pencil has Non-clog Propeller that turns the lead both OUT and IN. All are built and finished with jeweler's precision—there is nothing finer.

Duofold Pen or Pencil can be bought singly, or in Duette Sets. With the Sets we include the handsome Gift Case free.

Any good pen counter will supply you. Order now in time for engraving. If a dealer hasn't the Parker models desired, don't accept an inferior make, but write us giving dealer's name.

THE PARKER PEN COMPANY · JANESVILLE, WISCONSIN

Parker Duofold Pencils to match the Duofold Pen, $3.50

NEW YORK · CHICAGO · SAN FRANCISCO · SPOKANE

THE PARKER FOUNTAIN PEN COMPANY, LIMITED, TORONTO, CANADA

*Red and Black
Color Combination
Reg. Trade Mark
U.S Pat. Office*

Pen has 25 Year Point - Pencil turns lead OUT and IN

Rivals the beauty of the Scarlet Tanager

Satin-lined Gift Case included in Sets—$8, $8.50 and $11—according to size

The Chief Attraction at
Christmas Headquarters
Parker Duofold Duette
in Satin Lined Gift Case de luxe

ORDER early—for as Christmas nears, there'll be standing room only at the counters where Parker Duofold Pens and Pencils are sold.

Many late shoppers were turned away last year empty handed—the supply of these beautiful sets was wholly inadequate. If you were one of those you know how true this is—how timely our caution to choose your Parker Duofolds ahead of all other gifts.

No other pen and pencil set can take the place of the Parker Duofold Duette in the hearts and hopes of your loved ones.

The shapely Black-tipped Lacquer-red Pen with Hand-size Grip, Free Swinging Balance and 25-year Point. And to match it, the Hand-size Pencil that turns lead OUT and IN.

Pens and Pencils sold separately if desired: Parker Over-size Duofold Pen, $7; Pencil, $4; Duofold Jr. size Pen, $5; Pencil, $3.50; Lady Duofold Pen, $5; Pencil, $3.

Now ready at all good pen counters.

THE PARKER PEN COMPANY · JANESVILLE, WIS.
NEW YORK • CHICAGO • SAN FRANCISCO
THE PARKER FOUNTAIN PEN COMPANY, LIMITED, TORONTO, CANADA
THE PARKER PEN COMPANY, LIMITED, BUSH HOUSE, STRAND, LONDON, W.C.

Red and Black Color Combination Reg. Trade Mark U.S. Pat. Office.

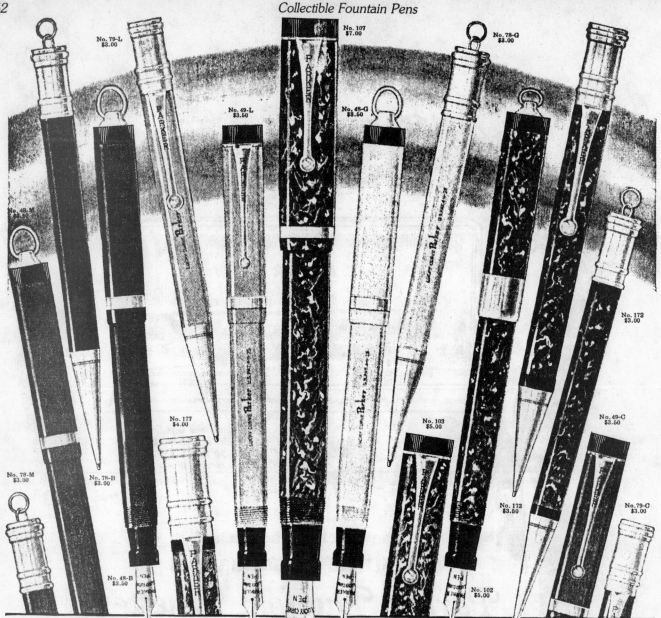

Fashion's Newest Arrival   *Petite Pens and Pencils*

Pastel Shades—Non-Breakable Barrels

Created by Parker—Acclaimed by Style Authorities Everywhere

Magenta, Naples Blue, Mauve, Beige Gray, Coral—and in larger sizes Mottled Green

FASHION has placed its stamp of approval on these alluring Parker creations that harmonize perfectly with the new color schemes and give women an opportunity to add a telling color-note to their costumes.

And women are buying these new Parker pens and pencils not only for their style and beauty but for the writing excellence that the Parker skill insures.

The Pens have the Parker 14k gold hand made point tipped with polished iridium, and the Ink-tight Duo-sleeve Cap, a safeguard to hands and clothes.

The Pencils have Parker's Non-clog Feed that turns the lead IN and OUT—easily filled by slipping a new lead into the tip. Both Pens and Pencils have Barrels of Permanite—Parker's new lustrous, non-breakable material.

Step to the nearest pen counter today and ask to see the "Parker Pastel Shades". But be sure to look for the name Parker on the barrel.

THE PARKER PEN COMPANY
JANESVILLE, WISCONSIN
OFFICES AND SUBSIDIARIES:
NEW YORK • CHICAGO • ATLANTA
SAN FRANCISCO
TORONTO, CANADA • LONDON, ENGLAND

Parker
Lucky Curve Pens and Pencils

Parker Advertisement — September 1926

Style's Newest Idea

To Accent Her Costume—Magenta,
Mauve, Coral, Beige Gray, Naples Blue

Parker Pastel Sets
Only $6.⁵⁰ Complete

The Pens $3.50 · The Pencils $3 · Non-Breakable Barrels · 14k Gold Points

NO lovelier, no more telling effect has made its appearance in women's accessories in years!

Petite Pens and Pencils in black-tipped Mauve, Magenta, Naples Blue, Coral, or Beige Gray—designed and selected by fashion authorities.

Quite as smart and practical for the college girl and business woman if you please, as for the social leader.

And any of these Parkers is sold separately, if desired, or in Parker Duettes at $6.50

the set, with Gift Box deluxe included.

All the smart shops and better stores are showing these Parker Pastels—just help yourself to colors of your choice.

To be sure of Non-Breakable Barrels, highest Writing Excellence and absolute Ink-tight Protection ask dealers for "Parker Pastel Shades" by name, and look with critical care for the stamp "Parker" on the barrels.

THE PARKER PEN COMPANY, JANESVILLE, WIS.
OFFICES AND SUBSIDIARIES:
NEW YORK · CHICAGO · ATLANTA
DALLAS · SAN FRANCISCO
TORONTO, CANADA
LONDON, ENGLAND

Parker
Lucky Curve Pens and Pencils

Parker Jade Pens and Pencils with Non-Breakable Barrels are like the famous Parker Duofold Pens in everything save color.

Black-tipped Jade
in larger sizes. Oversize Pen, $7; Pencil, $4; Junior size Pen, $5; Pencil, $3.50; Lady size Pen, $5; Pencil, $3.

Parker Advertisement — October 1926

Base of Opal Pearl on
Shell Permanite, Complete
with Parker Duofold Jr. Pen, $16.50

Black Glass Base,
with 2 Parker
Duofold Jr. Pens,
$27.50;
Over-size, $31.50

Parker's
Complete Ball-
and-Socket
Action
permits the
Pens to lie
level without
drying

Oval Black Glass Base, with
2 Parker Duofold Jr. Pens,
$31; Over-size, $35

First Christmas for Parker Desk Sets!

*—the Ones That Let the Pens
Lie Down Without Drying*

Non-Breakable Permanite Barrels—25-Year Duofold Points

Tapered Fountain Pens in attractive Desk Bases—pens that hold their own ink, so the desk can be freed of steel pens, pen holders and ink stands—

These are the newest, the most exciting Gifts that have appeared this Christmas.

But all the more reason to select the Set that lets the pens not only tilt and stand upright, but also lie level when not in use, still keeping the points ever moist with ink, ready to write *instantly!*

That's exactly why popular favor has turned to Parker Desk Sets with Ball-and-Socket action. No other is like it. It keeps the pens out of harm's way—it lets this set be slipped in a drawer and locked up.

Besides, you have here the celebrated Parker Duofold Pens with non-breakable Permanite Barrel and point guaranteed 25 years, not only for mechanical perfection but *for wear!*

Any good pen counter can supply you if you specify the original "Geo. S. Parker Duofold." Write for illustrated circular if no Parker dealer is near.

THE PARKER PEN COMPANY, JANESVILLE, WISCONSIN
OFFICES AND SUBSIDIARIES:
NEW YORK · CHICAGO · ATLANTA · DALLAS · SAN FRANCISCO
TORONTO, CANADA · LONDON, ENGLAND

Parker
Duofold Desk Sets

Gift Box   *Included*

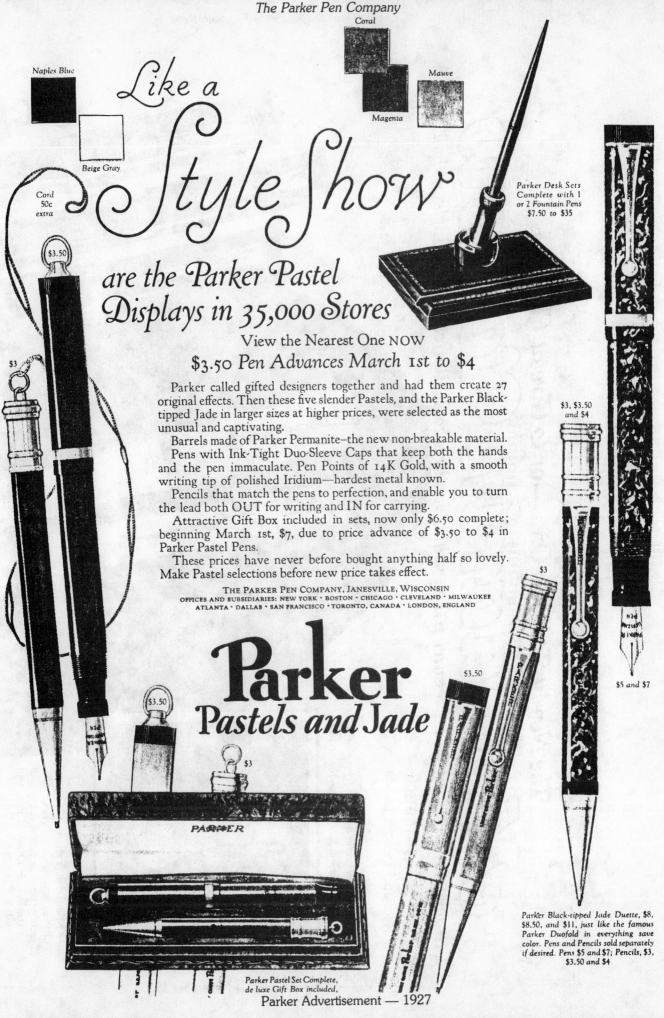

Naples Blue

Beige Gray

Cord
50c
extra

Coral

Mauve

Magenta

Like a Style Show

are the Parker Pastel Displays in 35,000 Stores

View the Nearest One NOW
$3.50 Pen Advances March 1st to $4

Parker Desk Sets
Complete with 1
or 2 Fountain Pens
$7.50 to $35

Parker called gifted designers together and had them create 27 original effects. Then these five slender Pastels, and the Parker Black-tipped Jade in larger sizes at higher prices, were selected as the most unusual and captivating.

Barrels made of Parker Permanite—the new non-breakable material.

Pens with Ink-Tight Duo-Sleeve Caps that keep both the hands and the pen immaculate. Pen Points of 14K Gold, with a smooth writing tip of polished Iridium—hardest metal known.

Pencils that match the pens to perfection, and enable you to turn the lead both OUT for writing and IN for carrying.

Attractive Gift Box included in sets, now only $6.50 complete; beginning March 1st, $7, due to price advance of $3.50 to $4 in Parker Pastel Pens.

These prices have never before bought anything half so lovely. Make Pastel selections before new price takes effect.

THE PARKER PEN COMPANY, JANESVILLE, WISCONSIN
OFFICES AND SUBSIDIARIES: NEW YORK · BOSTON · CHICAGO · CLEVELAND · MILWAUKEE
ATLANTA · DALLAS · SAN FRANCISCO · TORONTO, CANADA · LONDON, ENGLAND

$3, $3.50 and $4

Parker
Pastels and Jade

$5 and $7

Parker Black-tipped Jade Duette, $8, $8.50, and $11, just like the famous Parker Duofold in everything save color. Pens and Pencils sold separately if desired. Pens $5 and $7; Pencils, $3, $3.50 and $4.

Parker Pastel Set Complete, de luxe Gift Box included.

Parker Advertisement — 1927

The Newest Thing to Own—or to Give at Christmas

Mandarin Yellow

Extraordinary Beauty in a Pressureless Pen with Non-Breakable Barrel—28% Lighter than Rubber

3 Sizes—6 Points—
and Pencils to Match

*This handsome color adapted from this Vase,
found by Geo. S. Parker in the Orient*

Mandarin Yellow—long se-
cluded among Oriental Art Ob-
jects—now is given the world
in the Parker Duofold Pen, and
Duofold Pencil to match.

This rare and exotic color was
found by Geo. S. Parker in a

The New Parker Pen at $3.50

in the *Ultra Modern* Style
Blue-and-White,
Non-Breakable Barrels
The Greatest Value
Ever Offered At This Price!

You have never held a sweeter pen—so light, so well balanced, so responsive, so easy and so sure in use.

We showed scores of different pens to hundreds of pen users and asked, "Which do you like best?" They picked this one.

You'll do the same among pens at this price at any counter.

A *Modern* Blue-and-White

Of the latest modern design —trim, neat, beautiful in color —you'll want it for its *looks alone.*

And after you have written with it, it will be yours for life. And only $3.50, too!

Try it at your nearest pen counter today—choice of long or short model.

THE PARKER PEN CO., JANESVILLE, WIS.
OFFICES AND SUBSIDIARIES
NEW YORK • BOSTON • CHICAGO
ATLANTA • DALLAS • SAN FRANCISCO
TORONTO, CANADA • LONDON, ENGLAND

Parker
"Three-Fifty"

*Parker
"Blue-and-White" Pencil,
to match Pen, $3*

Long or Short Pen

Just the thing for school

NEW

Parker's Newest is the de luxe Duofold in

MODERNE BLACK & PEARL

Silvery Beautifully Iridescent

—*Guaranteed Forever against all defects

Silvery, luminous crystals of pearl are combined with Parker's jet Permanite to produce these beautifully iridescent effects in this new Black and Pearl Duofold.

Parker's Black and Pearl designs are unduplicated, and as *moderne* as the moment and the mode.

The pens are $10, $8.50 and $7.50, according to size; pencils, $3.50, $4 and $5; pairs (smartly matched), $11, $12.50 and $15. A handsome individual or double box goes with them at no extra charge.

Non-breakable, 28% lighter than a rubber pen. Perfect balance in your hand.

Pressureless Touch, as in all Duofolds, permits instant, steady, fastest writing with no pressure from your fingers—no effort—no fatigue—because the feather-light weight of the *pen itself* is sufficient to bring it into perfect operation.

36 years' experience, 47 improvements, 29 pen patents—all have contributed to the development of this master pen.

And it is *guaranteed forever against all defects* which assures you satisfaction that is *permanent.*

There couldn't be a finer present to one you want to please.

The imprint, "Geo. S. Parker—DUOFOLD," is stamped on every barrel so you may know you have the genuine. Be sure to look for it.

THE PARKER PEN COMPANY, JANESVILLE, WIS.
OFFICES AND SUBSIDIARIES:
NEW YORK · BOSTON · CHICAGO
ATLANTA · DALLAS · SAN FRANCISCO
TORONTO, CANADA · LONDON, ENGLAND

*Senior Pen, $10; Junior, $8.50
Juniorette or Lady, $7.50
Gift box included*

*To prove Parker Duofold is a pen of lifelong perfection, we offer to make good any defect provided complete pen is sent by the owner direct to the factory with 10¢ for return postage and insurance.

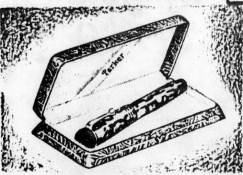

Parker
Imperial Duofold

See the New *Streamline* Shapes *for* Christmas *in* Parker Duofold *Matched* Pens and Pencils

*The Parker Duofold Fountain Pen is made to give lifelong satisfaction. Any defective parts will be replaced without charge provided complete pen is sent to the factory with 12c for return postage and registration.

Pocket Cap & Clip included with Every Desk Pen. Giving Two Pens in one. Convertible Duofold is Parker's Greeting & Surprise this Christmas

Obtainable only in Parker Pens and Pencils is this beautiful, symmetrical *Streamline* shape; also a Pocket Cap and Clip now included with *every* Desk Set Pen. This combination makes 2 pens of one — for pocket — for desk.

Parker originated this double-duty feature — no other pen is convertible. Screwing on a tapered end transforms it to a Desk Pen. Removing the taper restores it to a Pocket Pen.

Thus those who give Parker Desk Sets will give a Pocket Duofold, too; and those who give Parker Pocket Pens alone will be giving also half of a Desk Set. To have a desk set later their loved one need get only a base and taper.

No other pens and pencils set so low or look so neat in the pocket. The clip starts — not halfway down the cap — but at the *tip!*

Pressureless Point, Non-breakable Permanite Barrel, 24% greater ink capacity than average, size for size, and *guaranteed against all defects.

Good dealers everywhere are ready with Parker's Streamline shapes for Christmas.

THE PARKER FOUNTAIN PEN COMPANY, Ltd.
Toronto 3, Ontario

Parker Duofold Convertible $5-$7-$10

SIR ARTHUR CONAN DOYLE, *Author of*
"SHERLOCK HOLMES"
Used Parker's Pressureless Writing Pen

Now...
Black and
Burgundy
Red

A new—a breath-taking Beauty by Parker

at three dollars less than the usual ten dollar price scale

PEN GUARANTEED FOR LIFE

The Same Pen Two Ways
As a Pocket Pen,
—converted for Desk
Only the Parker serves as two Pens in one without extra cost. Take from pocket, attach slender taper, and you have a Desk Pen, at will.

Now comes Parker's famous Pressureless Writing in a jewel-like Pen of iridescent Black and Burgundy Red.

A Pen as elusively colorful and radiant as wine-colored crystal, yet non-breakable — and *Guaranteed for Life!*

A streamlined Beauty, balanced in the hand—low and non-bulging in the pocket, or handbag.

A Pen that writes with Pressureless Touch

—Parker's 47th Improvement. Its golden glide is as subconscious as breathing—aids clear-thinking—gives birth to your best ideas.

Go to the nearest pen counter and look for the name—"Geo. S. Parker—DUOFOLD"—on the barrel. That name means 17.4% greater ink capacity than average, and *Guarantees* the Genuine *for Life.*

The Parker Pen Company, Janesville, Wisconsin. *Offices and Subsidiaries:* New York, Chicago, Atlanta, Buffalo, Dallas, San Francisco; Toronto, Canada; London, England; Berlin, Germany.

Black and Burgundy Red
$5 and **$7**

Parker *Duofold*

PEN GUARANTEED FOR LIFE

Other Parker Pens, $2.75 to $10
Pencils to match all Pens, $2.50 to $5

Parker Advertisement — 1930

Have You Seen the *New*

Penparker?

Comes without charge

. . . but only for a limited time with the Parker Duofold Pen

Marvelous invention — parks the *pocket* pen on your desk—upright —ready to use all day

1 Take from pocket

Pen may be used with or without taper

2 Snap pocket clip to Penparker grip. Done in a second or two.

gives you a Complete Desk Set

This utterly new KIND of pen stand has just been created by Parker—world's leading pen manufacturer. It gives you a place to park the Parker *pocket* pen on your desk and use it 8 hours a day extra. It all but hands you the pen when you are ready to write—because it holds the point down and the barrel erect—ready for your hand.

We are giving a million of these Penparkers, at no charge, with Guaranteed for Life Parker Duofold Pens purchased promptly, at $10, $7, or only $5. We want hosts of people to discover personally how Parker Desk Sets double the use of the Parker Convertible Pocket Pen.

We will give not only the Penparker with the Pen, but also a tapered end to attach to your pen, a 30,000-word bottle of Parker *Quink*—the quick-drying, pen-cleaning ink—this complete Ensemble, handsomely cased in a velour-lined gift box—*a $2 value—for which you pay nothing.* Just the thing for birthday gifts, bridge prizes, etc.

Penparker Ensembles including Duofold Pencils to match— with Envelopener tapered end (a handy paper cutter on the end of the pencil), only $2.75 or $3.25 extra. See the nearest Parker dealer before these gift Penparkers are gone. We may have to end this offer any day.

THE PARKER PEN CO., Janesville, Wis.   *154A*

Handsome chromium and black finished metal, modern design—the Penparker is a credit to the finest desk. The Parker Duofold Pens and Pencils, such as the radiant Burgundy and Black and Sea Green Pearl and Black, are all style leaders. Our finest and latest streamlined models.

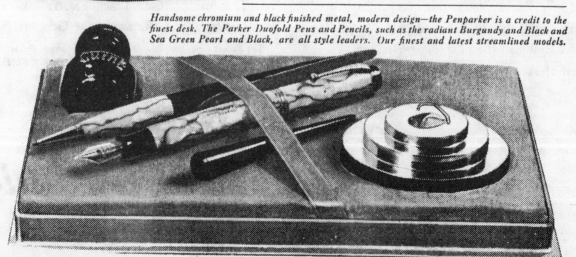

Parker Advertisement — Spring 1932

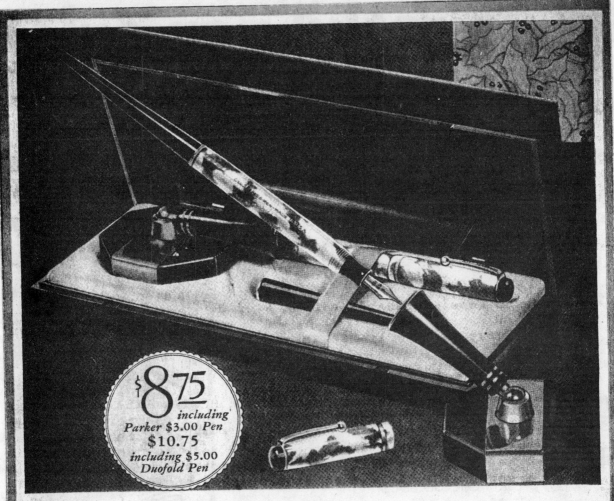

$8 75 including
Parker $3.00 Pen

$10.75
including $5.00
Duofold Pen

A *Thrift-time* Christmas Creation

BY PARKER

Pocket-Desk Pen Travel Set *in Permanent Bakelite Case*

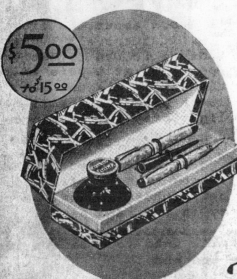

$5 00 to $15 00

No one ever received this gift before—a beautiful new Parker Fountain Pen Desk Set in a permanent Bakelite Travel Case. A gifted jewelry designer created this ensemble including a small octagonal ebony pen stand with golden bands.

The Pen is one of Parker's newest streamlined styles, for Pocket and Desk use both. Attach the tapered end, and it's a Desk Pen. Attach the cap and clip, and it's a pocket model. Five seconds makes the change. And these fittings come in the set without extra charge.

You are asked as much for pens of some makes as Parker asks for this entire set. It seems that Parker alone has caught the spirit of thrift-time. Furthermore, even the Parker Duofolds at $5 have 22% to 69% more ink capacity than some pens priced 50% higher.

The number of these exclusive Travel Sets is limited, so see them at your dealer's before they are gone.

THE PARKER PEN COMPANY, *Janesville, Wisconsin*

Entire Ensemble Only $8.75. Includes Duofold Pocket Pen with attachable Desk Pen Taper, pencil to match, leads, and bottle of Quink—the new, quick-drying ink. Other ensembles, including Parker Pen and Pencil, $5 to $15.

Parker Duofold

PEN GUARANTEED FOR LIFE $5 ▾ $7 ▾ $10
Other Parker Pens $2.75 to $3.50 — Pencils to match them all $2 to $5

Parker Advertisement — December 1932

Up go retail pen sales

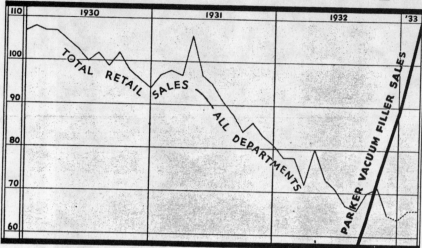

Due to Parker's revolutionary new Vacuum Filler Pen

"Sold 28 in one day"

SAYS TEXAS DEALER

"Sold $1,253.⁵⁰ the first month"

SAYS CHICAGO DEALER

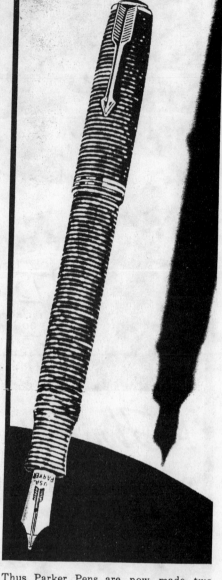

An utterly new idea in fountain pens has turned pen sales skyward.

Vacuum Filling in fountain pens, introduced in the new Parker Vacuum Filler, is the idea that is reviving sales in the higher price range. It has kept the Parker factory running Sundays and holidays as well as full time daily. A positive antidote for the depression.

A dealer in San Antonio sells 28 Vacuum Filler Pens the very day they arrive. A dealer in Chicago sells 134 Vacuum Filler Pens the first month, and 71 pencils to match.

To be advertised starting with March 18th Saturday Evening Post ad on page one

Records like these, remember, were made *before* any Vacuum Filler advertising appeared. To further stimulate sales the Saturday Evening Post of March 18 (out March 14) will carry the first sensational announcement of this revolutionary new pen: "sacless — vacuum filled" — "holds 102% more ink" — "reversible point of platinum and gold writes two ways" — "barrel styled in striped laminations, as shimmering as velvet — a patented style."

"What a pen!" says the public. And thousands of people are discarding guaranteed-for-life pens to get the new, the world's finest — the Parker Vacuum Filler. They're paying $7.50 for this revolutionary new pen *without a guarantee for life* — thus proving the wisdom of the new policy of "*no lifetime guarantee*" urged by 20,000 retailers and adopted by Parker on this new Vacuum Filler Pen.

Dealers feel that the purchaser of a guaranteed-for-life pen is taken out of the pen market. This puts the dealer in the business of servicing pens free, instead of selling pens for profit. That's why dealers welcome Parker's no lifetime guarantee policy on the Vacuum Filler.

This marvelous pen is the goal sought by pen makers for two generations. It is Geo. S. Parker's masterpiece — the crowning achievement of his long career as the world's leading pen maker.

Thus Parker Pens are now made two ways: the famous Parker Duofold (with rubber sac) at $5 and $7; and the new Parker Vacuum Filler (sacless) at $7.50.

The fountain pen sales curve is going up — bringing back the quick-turnover days. Send now for actual records of other dealers' sales and Parker's Vacuum Filler proposition to put your own pen department sales up and keep them up.

Parker VACUUM FILLER

PEN $7.50 — PENCIL TO MATCH $3.50

Parker Advertisement — March 1933

Start Out the *Young Moderns* with this *Modern Pen*-

AMERICA'S NO.1 GRADUATION GIFT

Visible ink supply

Holds 102% more ink

(Less than actual size)

Laminated Pearl Set comes in smart *Plaskon Gift Case* at no extra charge. A permanent container for cigarettes or jewels

Scratch-proof..Two-way point

It will turn their Ideas into Money!

It's the *First Choice whenever Student Bodies are asked, "Which Pen Would You Prefer?"

Because it Holds 102% More Ink —shows when to refill—is GUARANTEED Mechanically Perfect!

Help your favorite graduate turn learning into earning by giving him —or her—this marvelous Parker Vacumatic—the revolutionary invention that does what no other pen can do. He'll carry it over his heart for life!

Due to its double ink capacity

*Based on independent surveys, including university survey of the magazine SALES MANAGEMENT, AMERICAN BOY Magazine survey, national pen census of Recording & Statistical Corp., Robert L. ("Believe It or Not") Ripley survey of college students, and others.

and visible ink supply, it never halts and balks one's efforts by running dry in the midst of one's work. But what *most* distinguishes this miracle pen is this—it gives the world these long-desired features in a sacless pen that's MECHANICALLY PERFECT! This is worth ALL features *of all other pens combined!*

Unlike ordinary sacless pens, the Vacumatic contains NO SLIDING PISTON—No "ONE SHOT" PUMP. Its unique filler is sealed in the top *where ink can never touch the working parts*—never corrode or decompose them.

Go today to any good pen counter and see this laminated Pearl

Beauty that shows the ink level when held to the light. Try its Scratch-proof Point of precious Platinum combined with solid Gold. But be sure the pen you select has this smart ARROW clip. That identifies this patented Parker. The Parker Pen Co., Janesville, Wis.

Parker
VACUMATIC
GUARANTEED MECHANICALLY PERFECT
Junior, $5; $7.50   Pencils, $2.50;
Over-Size, $10 $3.50 and $5

*Today
the Curtain Rises*
ON THE PEN OF
HIGHEST PEDIGREE...

Full →
TELEVISION
Ink Supply

Illustration less
than actual size

Scratch-Proof Point of Platinum & Solid Gold

A New and SUPERLATIVE Model
of the Revolutionary Vacumatic

PARKER'S *SPEEDLINE* MAJOR and MAXIMA, $8.75 and $10

Attend Original Showing September 1 to October 1—
Start Fall Earning or Learning on a New High Plane

*New Speedline Shape
with enlarged
Ink Capacity,
Self-governed Flow,
33⅓% More Gold,
and of course
Parker's smartly
laminated Pearl
And Jet Style*

TODAY there takes place at all good pen counters the curtain-raising on the king of all pens—the new Parker Speedline Vacumatic, in three sizes.

A conquering Pen is this, because it never starts anything that it cannot finish.

For example, it gives continuous year-round mileage if you merely fill it 3 or 4 times from one birthday to the next. Eight or ten fleet seconds does the trick.

When held to the light its transparent laminations show the ink level at all times. Hence you can refill at any odd moment, so it won't run dry.

A wholly original and exclusive Style—shimmering Pearl and Jet—now with new, restful Speedline shape, smartly laminated.

Not merely a 1938 style, but also a 1938 mechanism! And every Parker Vacumatic is GUARANTEED mechanically perfect, with no coddling asked or expected.

By all means see this pedigreed Beauty at once at any good store selling pens. The Parker Pen Company, Janesville, Wisconsin.

Makers of Parker Qu*ink*, the amazing new ink that cleans a pen as it writes. 15¢, 25¢, and up at any store selling ink.

(Less than actual size)

HOLDS 102% MORE INK
THAN OUR FAMOUS DUOFOLD

Parker

$7⁵⁰
8⁷⁵
10

Speedline VACUMATIC REG. T. M.
GUARANTEED MECHANICALLY PERFECT
Junior or Juniorette, $5 · Standard or Slender Standard, $7.50
Speedline Major, $8.75 · Speedline Maxima or Senior Maxima, $10
Pencils to match, $2.50, $3.50, $3.75 and $5

Birthday Gifts
GUARANTEED for LIFE
by Parker

Parker's
BLUE DIAMOND
means
Guaranteed
for Life

FULL
TELEVISION
Ink
Supply

New Imperial Vacumatic Pen and Writefine Pencil with gold-filled monogrammed caps Sets. $17.75 and $19.75

Maxima Vacumatic
(oversize), $10;
Major (illustrated)
or small Debutante, $8.75;
Junior or Sub-Deb, $5

Dearest—The lovely Parker Vacumatic Pen you sent has made me well enough to sit up and write you how wonderful you are to think of it.

Matched Parker Vacumatic Pen and Writefine Pencil Sets in lovely jewel cases,
$8.50 to $19.75

HAPPY BIRTHDAY, DADDY, FROM ALL OF US.

SAY, WHAT A BEAUTY! THERE'S PARKER'S BLUE DIAMOND MARK, AND I KNOW WHAT THAT MEANS.

Yes, Gorgeous Gifts for Weddings, Prizes, and Convalescents, Too

When you give the lovely laminated Pearl Parker Vacumatic—*Guaranteed for Life* by Parker's Blue Diamond—*you make yourself warmly remembered for life* by a Gift that the owner *will use continually and cherish for life!* In all the world there is not another like it.

For one thing it contains NO rubber ink sac or piston pump like ordinary pens. It has, instead, a revolutionary Diaphragm Filler sealed in the top—thus *provides nearly twice as much room for ink* as old sac styles.

Due to its patented Television barrel, when you hold this shimmering, streamlined Beauty to the light, you SEE the level of ink *at all times.*

The Point is special, fine-grained, resilient 14 K Gold, tipped with high-polished Osmiridium—*as smooth as oil!*

See and TRY the genuine Life-guaranteed Parker Vacumatic—not some "near-vacumatic," or any second best. All good pen counters are now demonstrating. To show your true affection, give the *real thing.*

The Parker Pen Co., New York, Chicago, San Francisco.
Factories at Janesville, Wisconsin and Toronto, Canada.

"ONE-HAND" FILLER
The EASIEST, most convenient to fill, as proved by independent experts testing 24 models of various makes.

Writefine Pencils to match
$3.50 to $6

Exclusive Laminated Pearl Pens
$5 to $13.75

Parker
GUARANTEED FOR LIFE
REG. T.M. VACUMATIC

Pens marked with the Blue Diamond are guaranteed for the life of the owner against everything except loss or intentional damage, subject only to a charge of 35¢ for postage, insurance, and handling, provided complete pen is returned for service.

This Christmas

KEEP PARKER'S NAME

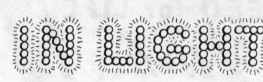

PEOPLE WILL BE LOOKING FOR IT!

"51"
- ten years ahead

IN more than a dozen separate, independent surveys, from coast to coast, the people have selected Parker as their unquestioned preference in fountain pens. Sales records prove that, this Christmas, more people will buy Parker than any other pen or pen and pencil set!

Make it easy for your customers to find the pen that they've already said they want! Display and demonstrate your Parker merchandise. Run tie-in ads in your local papers, announcements over your local radio station. Harness up, for your store, the full pulling power of Parker's national advertising, the broadest, hardest-hitting, most consistent campaign in pen-selling experience.

Get Parker's name up IN LIGHTS . . . and keep it there. People will be looking for it!

♦

PENS and SETS

The phenomenal
new Parker "51"

Imperial Vacumatic

Laminated Pearl Vacumatic

Sac and Sacless Duofold

Parker Writefine Pencils

Parker Desk-Pen Sets

Parker Qu*ink* and "51" Ink

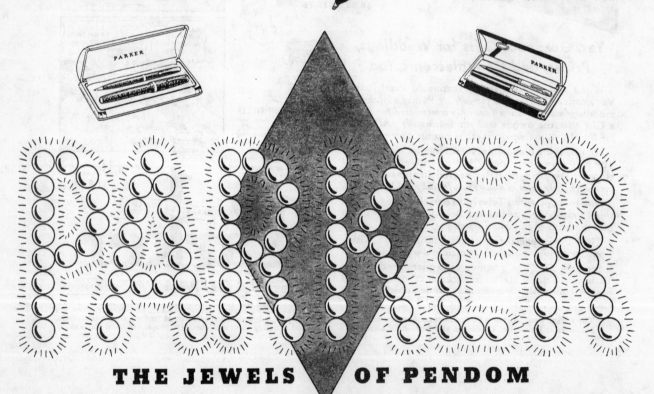

THE JEWELS　OF PENDOM

WITH THE FAMOUS BLUE DIAMOND GUARANTEED CONTRACT

Parker Advertisement — November 1941

COPR. 1941, THE PARKER P

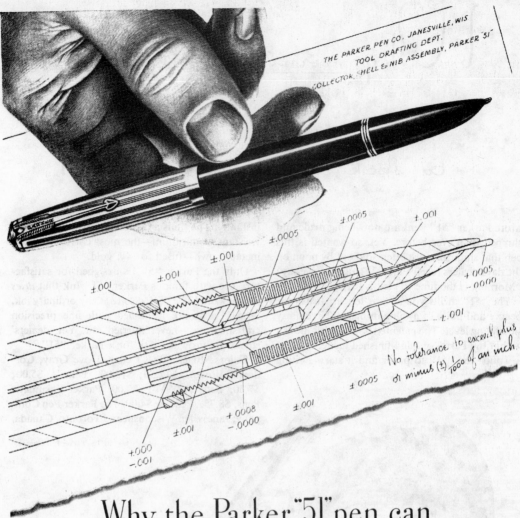

THE PARKER PEN CO. JANESVILLE, WIS.
TOOL DRAFTING DEPT.
COLLECTOR, SHELL & NIB ASSEMBLY, PARKER "51"

No tolerance to exceed plus or minus (±) $\frac{1}{1000}$ of an inch.

Why the Parker "51" pen can never be "mass produced"

PRECISION CRAFTSMANSHIP, MEASURED IN THOUSANDTHS OF AN INCH, MAKES THIS THE WORLD'S "MOST WANTED" PEN.

Parker 51's are limited by their very precision. The craftsmen who make them work to standards of accuracy never before attained in fountain pens. Their pride in producing 51's equals the pride of those who own them.

One day you'll have your own "51". You'll discover its whisper-smooth writing. You'll find that only the "51" is designed for satisfactory use of Parker "51" Ink that dries as it writes. And you'll be glad you waited. More 51's *are* coming. Place a reservation order at your Parker dealer's now.

Colors: Black, Blue Cedar, Dove Gray, Cordovan Brown. $12.50; $15.00. Pencils, $5.00; $7.50. Sets, $17.50 to $80.00. Parker Vacumatic Pens, $8.75. Pencils, $4.00. The Parker Pen Company, Janesville, Wisconsin and Toronto, Canada.

"Writes dry with wet ink!"

PARKER "51"

Copr. 1946 by
The Parker Pen Company

Why morning is the time to seek a Parker "51"

More Parker "51" pens are now being made and shipped than ever before. Yet, so wanted is this pen that shipments are often sold out by noon on the days dealers receive them. That's why we say: "Morning is the time to seek a Parker '51'."

The "51" thrills you at first touch. It has the beauty and poise of a thing in flight. No clumsy side-filling lever. The patented "51" filler is hidden within the barrel of hand-finished lucite.

Touch the "51" to paper and it starts writing instantly. The tip is a ball of micro-smooth, wear-resistant Osmiridium—the most corrosion-proof metal known—fused to 14K gold.

Only the Parker "51" is designed for satisfactory use with famous Parker "51" Ink that *dries as you write!* The "51" also uses any ordinary ink.

"51" pens are fashioned with fine precision craftsmanship—never hurried out. Yet, dealers' stocks are growing. Ask for a Parker "51".

Colors: Black, Blue Cedar, Dove Gray, Cordovan Brown. $12.50; $15.00. Pencils, $5.00; $7.50. Sets, $17.50 to $80.00. Parker Vacumatic Pens, $8.75. Pencils, $4.00. The Parker Pen Company, Janesville, Wisconsin and Toronto, Canada.

Copr. 1946 by The Parker Pen Company

"Writes dry with wet ink!"

*It's new...
it's a beauty...
it's a Parker!*

New
**PARKER
"V-S" PEN**

NEVER BEFORE
...SO FINE A PEN FOR
ONLY **$8⁷⁵**

Any way you look at it—this new Parker "V-S" bears the hallmark of distinction. In style, in performance . . . it's years ahead of anything in its price class.

Yes, never before has so fine a pen been offered for so little money. In every detail—from micro-smooth point to trim slip-on cap—you'll find this a fine precision writing instrument.

Best of all, this pen is a Parker. And that means you can expect years and years of writing pleasure from it. We invite you to come in . . . see and inspect this exciting new Parker "V-S" today!

- 4 points to choose from: fine, medium, broad, stub.
- Writes at any angle.
- Fills in just two strokes.
- 14K gold point.
- Special micro-smooth tip for easy writing.
- Cap slips on, locks without twisting.
- Take your choice of 4 brilliant colors: Black, Blue, Gray, Rust.
- Only $8.75 with tarnish-resistant Lustraloy cap. Handsome matching pencil. $4.00.

IN THE HAND OF

Vilhjalmur Stefansson, world-famous scientist and explorer, who has contributed much to our knowledge of the northern polar regions. He is editor of the popular book, "Great Adventures and Explorations."

World's most wanted pen...

Parker "51"

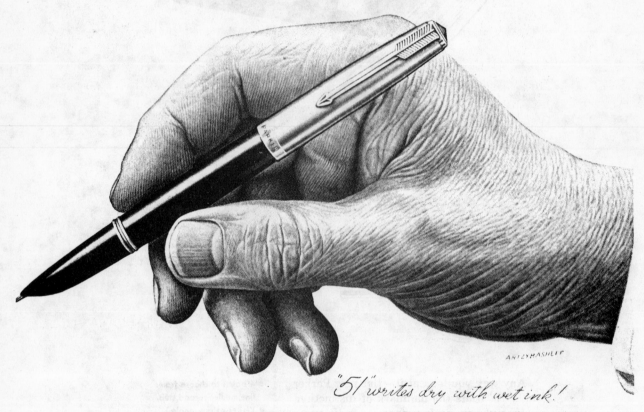

"51" writes dry with wet ink!

NORTH—south—east—west—Parker "51" is the preferred writing instrument.

77 surveys in 29 countries proclaim its popularity. Even in far-off Sydney, Australia, for example, the preference for Parker exceeded that of the *next three leading makes combined!*

Here is a pen of simple, unspoiled beauty. Precision-made from cap to point. You choose from a wide range of individualized custom points. Each starts on the instant—glides across the paper with light and eager touch.

Only the "51" is designed for satisfactory use with new Parker *Superchrome*—the super-brilliant, super-permanent ink that *dries as it writes!*

See the "51" today. An ideal gift for birthdays and anniversaries. Choice of distinctive colors. Individual "51" Pens (including the new *demi-size*), $12.50; $15.00. Pencils, $5.00; $7.50. Sets, $17.50 to $80.00. The Parker Pen Company, Janesville, Wis., U.S.A., and Toronto, Can.

Copr. 1948 by The Parker Pen Company

Parker Advertisement — April 1948

For those who
prefer a
smaller pen...

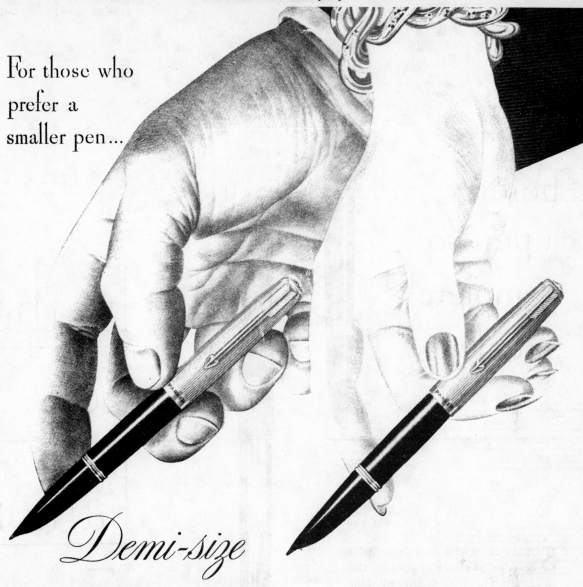

Demi-size

a new Parker "51"...world's most wanted pen

New...jewel-like...the *demi-size* is a true "51" in everything but dimensions. Created especially for the man or woman who prefers a smaller pen.

Less than 5 inches long, the *demi-size* Parker "51" clips neatly to a woman's handbag in an upright position. Fits even a man's shallow shirt pocket. To many hands, the compact, balanced design brings new comfort . . . greater flexibility.

Precision-made throughout, the *demi-size* offers a wide range of custom points. You choose the one that best brings out the full individuality of your handwriting. For added color and character, you'll want to use new Parker *Superchrome* Ink. Created for use only in "51" Pens—this super-brilliant, super-permanent ink actually *dries as it writes!*

See the new *demi-size* today. Choice of colors. $12.50, $15.00. Pencils, $5.00, $7.50. Matched Sets, $17.50 to $80.00. The Parker Pen Company, Janesville, Wis., U. S. A., and Toronto, Canada.

Copr. 1948 by The Parker Pen Company

Parker "51"...writes dry with wet ink!

PARKER
Superchrome **INK**
FOR THE "51" PEN ONLY

NEW! Wholly different—created by leading scientists. World's most brilliant permanent ink—and it *dries as it writes!* Choice of 5 colors. Priced at only 50 cents.

Parker Advertisement — June 1948

Never before a pen so completely satisfying

It's the new Parker "51"

SUCH writing ease, such dependability never before existed in any pen. Only now have new materials made them possible.

14 precision advances mark the new "51". With it, writing is *gliding*. Even filling becomes a pleasure—quick and sure. You *see* the ink level. There's a new guard against leaking—even at the highest flight levels.

But these are only a few of new 51's advantages. To learn the full story, *try* the new pen now at your Parker dealer's. Choose yours—for keeping or giving—from 7 rich colors and black. Custom points.

Pens, $13.50 up. Pencils, $6.75 up. Sets, from $19.75. The Parker Pen Company, Janesville, Wis., U. S. A.; Toronto, Can.

NEW FOTO-FILL FILLER • VISIBLE INK SUPPLY • PLI-GLASS RESERVOIR • EXCLUSIVE INK FLOW GOVERNOR • 5-LAYER INSULATION • HI-FLITE LEAK PREVENTION • GREATER WRITING MILEAGE • PLATHENIUM-TIPPED POINT • "LIVE METAL" CLIP —5 OTHER SIGNIFICANT ADVANCES.

World's most wanted pen...

writes dry with wet ink!

Parker Advertisement — March 1949

Luxurious giving

for that special gift occasion

<u>new</u> Parker "51" *Signet Set*

It's the New "51" pen and pencil in a beautiful new all gold-filled design

A style-setting masterpiece by Parker! And the Signet Set features the remarkable New Parker "51" Pen—with 14 precision advances!

Both pen and pencil in this new "51" set are exquisitely appointed. Chased lines across 12 K gold-filled cap and barrel, form a dramatic design . . . highlighted by a signet area for owner's name or initials. Pen barrel is lined with silver . . . to prevent corrosion.

Signet Set in new jewel gift case, is available in either regular or *demi-size*. Limited quantities only—so make your selection now. It's the gift unsurpassed. $49.75 (tax included).

Parker "51" *Flighter* Set
and Matching
RONSON LIGHTER

No Money Down!

pay only $1.00 weekly

Complete Set
$35.75

A Gift Combination to please every man! The famed Parker "51" ...winner of the 1950 Fashion Academy Award for distinctive design. Crafted of sleek Lustraloy in a truly modern mode...the *Flighter* has the new exclusive Aero-metric ink system which assures a smooth, steady no-skip line...even at hi-flight atmospheric conditions. Choice of custom points. Matching Lustraloy pencil has continuous feed mechanism. Ronson lighter is precision made for continuous satisfactory service. Chromium finish matches pen and pencil.

All three pieces engraved free.

"A *new* Parker... how perfect!"

Give your grad the winner

1950 Fashion Academy Award

. . . for exceptional styling, precision and craftsmanship

 **new Parker "51"**

with the exclusive

Aero-metric Ink System!

● First choice for superb writing ease. Only New "51" has remarkable Aero-metric Ink System . . . faster filling, greater ink capacity . . . meters the ink in a faultless skip-free line. Give your grad the writing perfection of the world's most-wanted pen. Choose beautiful New "51" at your dealer's now. 8 colors.

Finest at any price. New Parker "51" Pen and Pencil gift set, Lustraloy caps **$19⁷⁵** *NO F. E. TAX*

Single "51" pens $13.50 up.
Gold sets $29.75 up. (F. E. tax incl.)

Both pens *write dry* with super-brilliant Superchrome Ink.

new Parker "21"

Sure to please your grad—and it costs so little to give!

● Never before so fine a precision writing instrument at such a low price. Parker 21's point is made of Octanium, a new 8-metal alloy that gives magic writing ease. Concealed, fast-action filler . . . visible ink supply . . . many other luxury features make New "21" a perfect graduation gift. Choose a smart new "21" gift pen or set today. Blue, green, red or black.

Parker Advertisement — 1950

Finest at a medium price New Parker "21" **$5⁰⁰** *NO F. E. TAX*

Matching "21" pencil $3.75 "21" Pen and Pencil set $8.75

. . . and remember PARKER for Father's Day, Birthdays, Weddings, Anniversaries and all Gift Occasions

Copr. 1950 by The Parker Pen Company

JUST IN TIME TO HELP YOU
CELEBRATE YOUR 50th YEAR!

Parker's
newest baby
...the ball point
Jotter

You've been around for the christening of most of our youngsters. You've had a big part in their bringing up, too, helped them make their way to the top, watched them succeed throughout the world. Duofold, Vacumatic—they're retired now, of course—but you remember them well. Ever-youthful "51" and brother "21" are in their prime today.

And now comes infant Jotter, as lively a young'un as we've ever seen and sturdy Parker stock to the core. It's everything a ball point pen *should* be, but *never has been* till now. Parker's new Jotter ball point has all the makings of a favorite nephew to his stationer uncles.

THE PARKER PEN COMPANY
Janesville, Wisconsin, and throughout the world

Parker Advertisement — April 1954

At last! A pencil that sharpens itself as you write—and cannot break!

New **PARKER LIQUID LEAD** Pencil

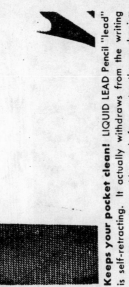

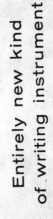

Keeps your pocket clean! LIQUID LEAD Pencil "lead" is self-retracting. It actually withdraws from the writing point when not in use. No need of any retracting mechanism because the LIQUID LEAD Pencil cannot leak or seep.

Entirely new kind of writing instrument

It seemed that all possible tools for putting thoughts on paper had been developed. Then, up with something excitingly new and thoroughly practical came Parker. It's called a LIQUID LEAD Pencil. Try this fascinating new Parker invention at your pen counter. Deluxe model—$3.95. Choice of 5 colors. Replaceable cartridge and extra eraser—39¢. Models also available to match Parker "51" and "21" Pens, and Jotter Ball Pens.

And you can erase that LIQUID LEAD line! It's just the same kind of line you make—and erase—with ordinary lead pencils. A blessing for those who make mistakes. A convenience that no ball point pen can possibly give.

Sharpens itself as fast as you write! Never a broken point. The new LIQUID LEAD Pencil is all set to write—instantly—for thousands of words without reloading. When it does run out you simply slip in a new cartridge.

Rolls words on paper smooth as silk! Parker's tiny ball-bearing pencil point writes the cleanest line you've ever known. And the LIQUID LEAD Pencil line comes through clearly on as many as 12 carbons.

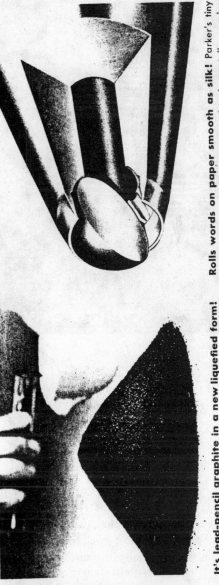

It's lead-pencil graphite in a new liquefied form! Parker has developed a way of blending genuine pencil graphite into a brand new form so that the LIQUID LEAD Pencil gives you the best of pencil and ball point pen writing.

PARKER

◆ **LIQUID LEAD**®

PENCIL

PARKER ◆ LL, Liquid Lead, arrow are trade-marks of The Parker Pen Company

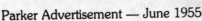

Parker Advertisement — June 1955

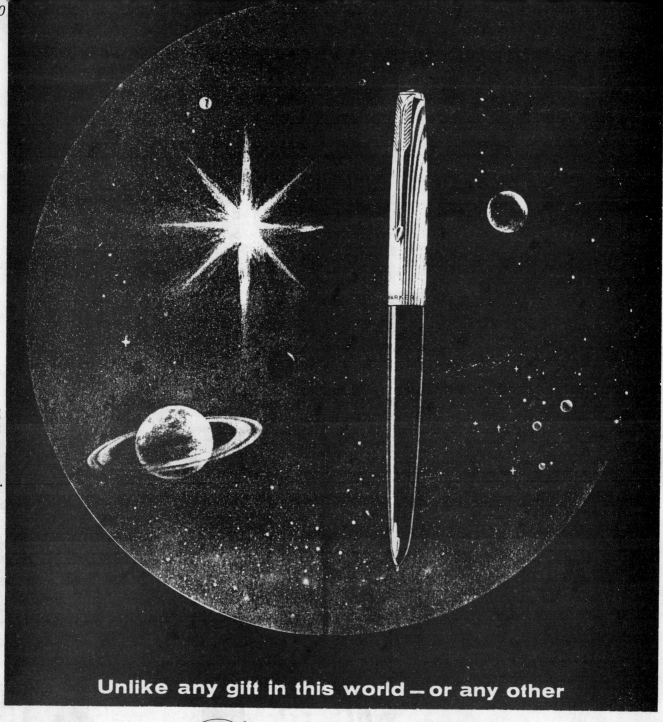

Unlike any gift in this world—or any other

Parker 61

The only fountain pen that fills itself by itself—it has no moving parts

In its first Christmas Season, the Parker 61 is the distinguished gift for those friends who appreciate the new, the unusual—quite flattering to them and to you.

The Parker 61, with its frankly revolutionary capillary ink system, fills itself, writes effortlessly, dependably—even on a high-flying plane.

You have a choice of rich colors and gleaming caps—all strikingly beautiful. The Parker 61 is $20 or more.

The Parker 61, alone among fountain pens, fills itself by itself. It fills itself cleanly—through the end opposite the point. It's done by capillary action in just 10 seconds—the shining point need never be dipped in ink.

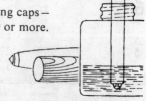

For a demonstration of the fabulous new Parker 61 come to our Stationery Department.

Parker Advertisement — September 1956

Two reasons why the Parker 75 is the only gift for some people you know

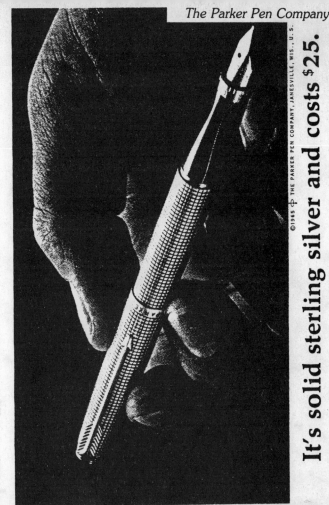

©1965 ✦ THE PARKER PEN COMPANY, JANESVILLE, WIS., U.S.

It's solid sterling silver and costs $25.

The Parker 75 is not a gift to be given lightly.

You choose the person who receives the 75 as carefully as you've chosen the pen . . . someone who has a liking for the finer things in this life . . . like clean, classic design, and sterling silver.

You choose someone who would appreciate writing with the world's first personal-fit pen. With the new Parker 75 he can adjust the 14K gold point to the exact writing angle he desires — a

relaxed, comfortable angle he'll never lose, because of the sculptured grip. His fingers nest in its curvatures in exactly the same way every time the pen is picked up.

Assuredly the Parker 75 is not for everyone on your gift list. But it is the only gift for some of the people you know. You decide which ones.

Also see the new matching Parker 75 International ball pen.

Solid sterling silver, $12.50. ✦**PARKER**

Maker of the world's most wanted pens

Parker Advertisement — November 1965

Unlike any gift in this world —or any other!

Parker

61

The only fountain pen that fills by itself— it has no moving parts

Newest—most unusual Christmas gift! New Parker 61 fills itself in 10 seconds by capillary action . . . no pumping, twisting, squeezing. No moving parts. Parker 61 with its revolutionary capillary ink system writes effortlessly, clearly . . . even on a high-flying plane. Choice of new rich colors and gleaming caps. Priced from

$20⁰⁰

Parker Advertisement — September 1956

THE PARKER 61 JET FLIGHTER

...Tested and proved as the finest and *safest* Pen in Flight

Eight miles up! Flashing along at 600 miles an hour, this United Air Lines DC-8 Mainliner carried the Parker 61 Jet Flighter Pen through the same kind of rigorous testing United Air Lines insists on for all its operational equipment. The Parker 61 Jet Flighter performed superbly. From sea level to 40,000 feet aloft, it started instantly wrote smoothly with the ink metered precisely, evenly. Behind this trouble-free performance is Parker's exclusive "escape chamber" design that safely houses excess ink as air pressure changes . . . ink that would otherwise leak or blot. No wonder the Parker 61 Jet Flighter Pen to log its new DC-8 Mainliner jet flights.

PEN $17⁵⁰

With matching mechanical pencil $27.50

It's the perfect gift for the air traveler, for everyone who demands trouble-free pen performance. See the exciting new Parker 61 Jet Flighter at your Parker Franchised Dealer now.

Parker

Makers of the world's most wanted pens!

Parker Advertisement — September 1959

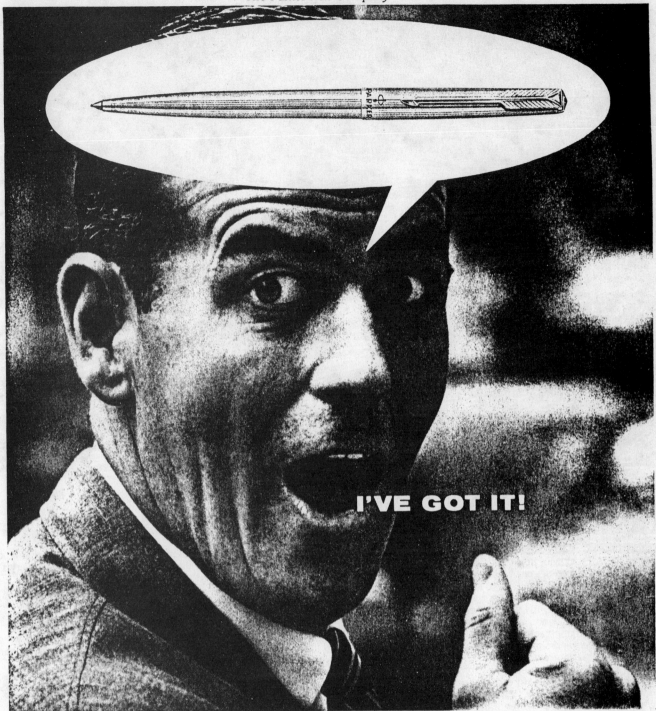

I'LL GIVE DAD A PARKER INTERNATIONAL PEN

Brilliant idea! He's going to give pater a Parker International for Christmas. Dad hasn't had a gift like this since his gold watch days. But he's a pretty good judge of value, so he'll recognize Parker quality the minute he hefts the slim precisely-balanced International Pen.

And he'll like the precise way it writes. Parker's textured, porous T-BALL point is guaranteed not to skip . . . its giant cartridge is guaranteed not to run dry for a full year.*

Examine the Parker International Jotter Pen. See for yourself why it is such a respected pen . . . why it makes such a magnificent gift for someone who appreciates quality.

See Parker's Written Guarantee

THE PARKER INTERNATIONAL PEN

$12.50

Insignia Model

Parker

MAKERS OF THE WORLD'S MOST WANTED PENS

Parker Advertisement — December 1959

©1966 ⊕ THE PARKER PEN COMPANY, JANESVILLE, WIS. U.S.A.

From sunken Spanish treasure, a collector's edition of the Parker 75. It costs $75.

On the morning of July 30, 1715, the Spanish Treasure Fleet was homeward bound from Veracruz, carrying gold and silver for the royal mint of King Philip V.

As the eleven proud galleons proceeded up the coast of Florida, the sky blackened. All that day rising winds and a stinging spray signaled an approaching storm.

That night the wind shifted to east-northeast and the great hurricane struck. Shrieking like a thousand banshees, the titanic winds mauled the rolling ships, shattering them against the treacherous Florida reefs. By dawn over 1,000 crewmen and more than $14 million in gold and silver had vanished into the sea.

Now—2½ centuries later—this fabulous treasure is being salvaged from the ocean's floor. Enough of the prized silver has been purchased by The Parker Pen Company to craft a limited collector's edition of the Parker 75 fountain pen.

This unusual pen is distinguished by the mint mark of Mexico City which appears on the cap. The "eagle of purity," a quality hallmark established by Philip V of Spain in 1715, is coin-stamped in the base. The barrel itself is engraved with the words "Sterling Silver, Spanish Treasure Fleet, 1715."

Even without its rare silver, this 75 would be a once-in-a-lifetime sort of pen. Write with it: you'll sense immediately that *here* is the world's first personal-fit pen. You can adjust the 14K gold point to the exact writing angle you desire . . . a relaxed, comfortable angle that you will never lose, thanks to the 75's sculptured grip. Your fingers nest in its curvature in exactly the same way every time the pen is picked up.

This collector's edition of the Parker 75 comes to you in an attractive hand-rubbed walnut gift box.

When the supply of these limited edition pens is exhausted, there won't be any more. Ever. So this could well be the rarest pen of all time. It costs $75.

Intrigued? For the name of your nearest dealer, write to The Parker Pen Company, Janesville, Wisconsin 53545. We'll tell you where to see the pen with a heritage that began two and one-half centuries ago.

✦ **PARKER**

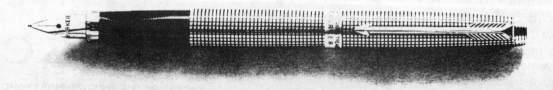

A limited edition of the Parker 75 crafted of silver from the sunken Spanish Treasure Fleet. $75.
Parker Advertisement — January 1966

The finest fountain pen ever made...

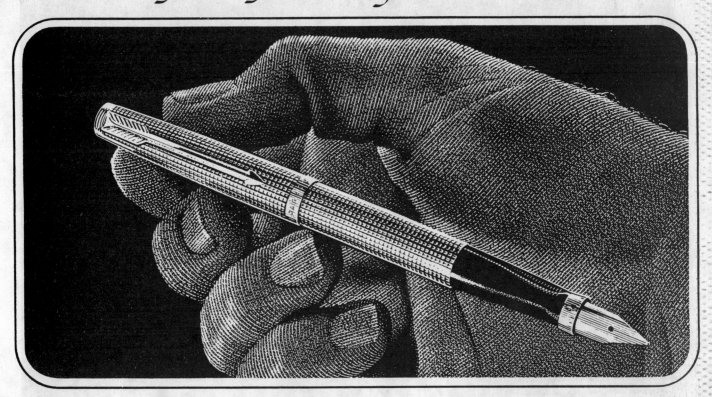

the magnificent Parker 75, now sheathed in radiant Vermeil, a work of art in precious metals

Magnificent in both concept and design, the Parker 75 takes on added excellence, thanks to its Vermeil exterior. Warmer than silver alone, richer-looking than any ordinary gold finish, the Vermeil on the Parker 75 is finest fourteen karat gold applied to sterling silver. A centuries-old process, reaching its greatest eminence during the reigns of Louis XIV and Louis XV, Vermeil is today enjoying a re-birth and is found on more and more objets d'art.

As a possession of lasting beauty, the Parker 75 has no peer. It is also a pen that adjusts itself to the hand. It can be tailored exactly to the way its owner writes! The sculptured grip nests his fingers comfortably in its curvatures. The point can be adjusted to the exact angle at which he writes.

Because the hand stays relaxed, there is more opportunity to form each letter gracefully, expressively.

The ease of writing is enhanced by the cushion flexing of the fourteen karat point. Point sizes are available for all writing styles from a very fine Accountant to the bold Broad. There is also a choice of filling methods! The Parker 75 fills easily and cleanly from an ink bottle or it may be loaded with the convenient reserve ink cartridges.

See the Parker 75 at your dealer's soon...in the new Vermeil of 14K gold-fill on sterling silver, the 14K gold-filled Insignia, and in sterling silver. Matching ball pens for each model are available.

PARKER

Maker of the world's most wanted pens

Parker Advertisement — March 1966

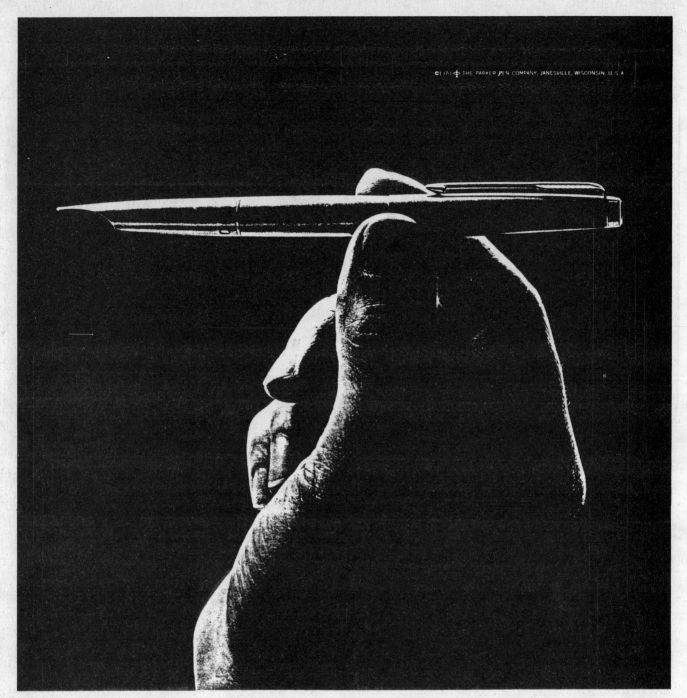

© 1970 ✶ THE PARKER PEN COMPANY, JANESVILLE, WISCONSIN, U.S.A.

Hold the metal that's going to Mars in your hand. And write.

It's titanium.

The metal so strong it's exploring the universe in space ships.

The metal so light it can fly at speeds three times the speed of sound.

Shock-proof, crack-proof, nearly everything-proof titanium.

Now Parker makes it a pen.

The Parker T-1.

One strikingly beautiful streak of titanium from its cap all the way to its point. With a finish that glows with an other-worldly luster.

And a way of writing that's as close to flying as any pen's ever come. The T-1 jets across paper. Pouring out words as quickly as you think them. Because its ink flows freely and easily to its point.

And it carries ink longer without evaporation.

This pen even lets you change your stroke. From fine to medium. Or from medium to bold. With a tiny dial hidden under its point that you can turn to suit your mood.

This is the Parker T-1. In titanium.

Now the wonder metal is a wonder pen.

Other Parker pens to own or give, from the $1.98 Jotter Ball Pen to the $150 Presidential Fountain Pen.

T-1 COMING AT YOU.

PARKER T-1 $ 20

Parker Advertisement — April 1970

Parker Launches the T-1

T-1. The Space Age pen. It's made of titanium. The metal proved in the lunar landing module. And now the metal for the spacecraft that will take man to Mars.

Titanium. More indestructible than stainless steel, yet twice as light. Virtually shock-crack-corrosion-everything-proof. And now titanium is a pen. A pen that glows with an other-worldly luster.

And get the point: the pen is the point. One sleek sweep of titanium all the way to the tip. Titanium makes it possible.

And under the point is a dial. Turn it and the line width adjusts. From fine to medium. Or from medium to broad. Two point widths that adjust for any writing requirement. Makes gift selection easy, and only two point sizes for you to inventory.

T-1. Superb resistance to leakage and dry-out. The world's largest ink cartridge. Space Age packaging. And a down-to-earth retail price of $20. Matching Ball Pen or Cartridge Pencil, $12.50.

Your Parker man will be in soon with details. He'll tell you, modestly, the T-1 is backed by our biggest promotional campaign since the Jotter ball pen.

T-1. The Space Age pen for personal communication is here. It's the pen that's taking off. Better get ready for the launch.

✦ PARKER
Maker of the world's most wanted pens.

Chronology Of Pens And Pencils

The Parker Pen Company

1. 2. 3. 4. 5. 6. 7. 8. 9. 10. 11.

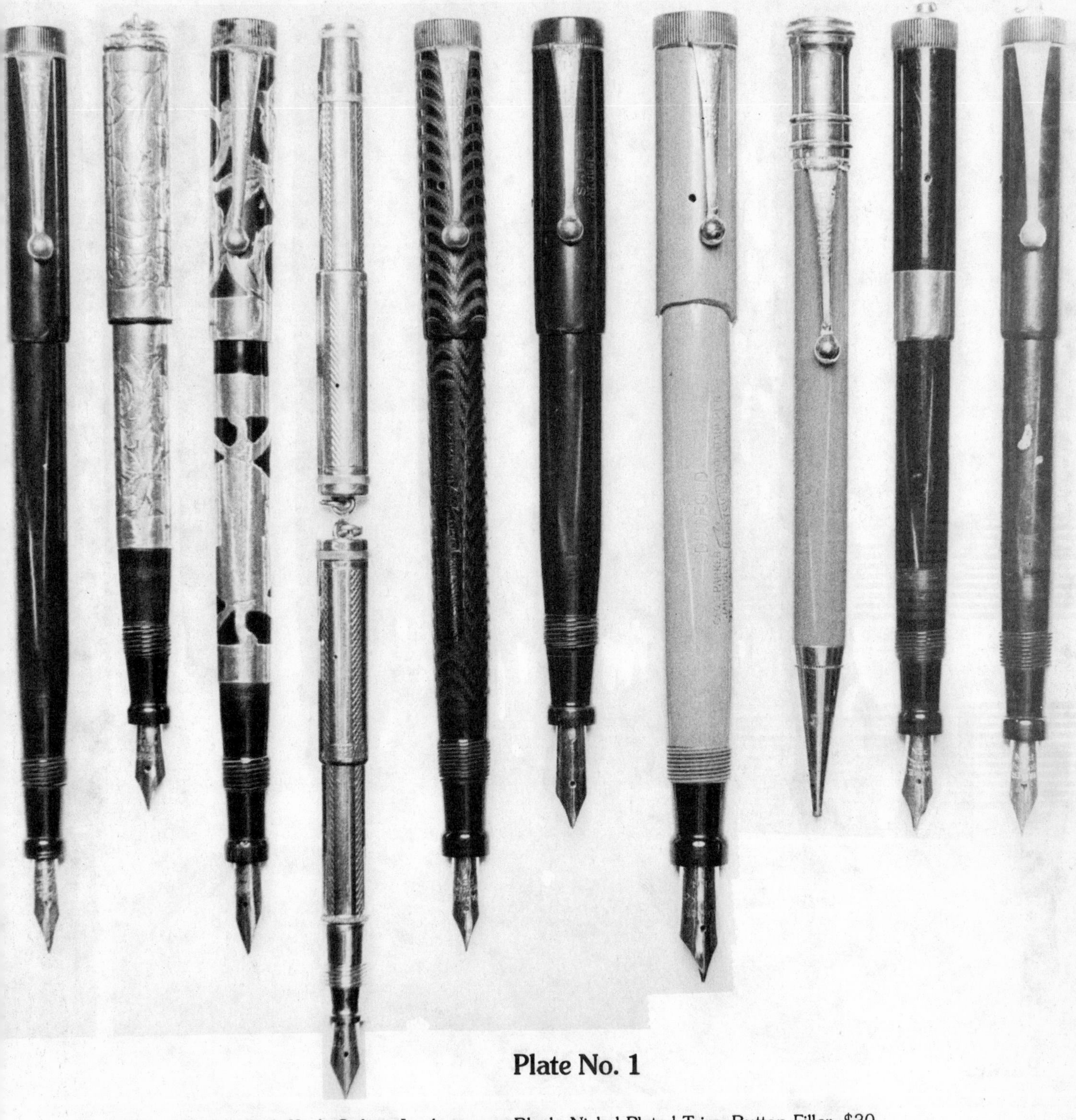

Plate No. 1

1. 1917 Parker Jack-Knife Safety, Lucky curve, Black, Nickel Plated Trim, Button Filler, $30.
2. 1918 Parker #32, Sterling Cap and Barrel, Button Filler, Ribbon Ring, $75
3. 1918 Parker #14, Black, Sterling Overlay, Button Filler, $75
4. 1922 Parker Lucky Curve Midget, Gold Filled, Button Filler, Ribbon Ring (Closed), $35
5. 1922 Parker Lucky Curve Midget, Gold Filled, Button Filler, Ribbon Ring, $35
6. 1920 Parker Lucky Curve, Black Chased, Nickel Plated Trim, Button Filler, $25
7. 1920 Parker Jack-Knife Safety, Lucky Curve, Black, Gold Filled Trim, Button Filler, $35
8. 1921 Parker Duofold, Lucky Curve, Pompian Brown, Gold Trim, Button Filler, Large Imprint, $150
9. 1924 Parker Duofold Sr. Pencil, Red, Gold Filled Trim, $75
10. 1924 Parker Lady Duofold, Lucky Curve, Black, Gold Filled Trim, Button Filler, Ribbon Ring, $25
11. 1921 Parker Lucky Curve, Black, Gold Filled and Nickel Plated Trim, Button Filler, Combination Clip and Ribbon Ring, $25

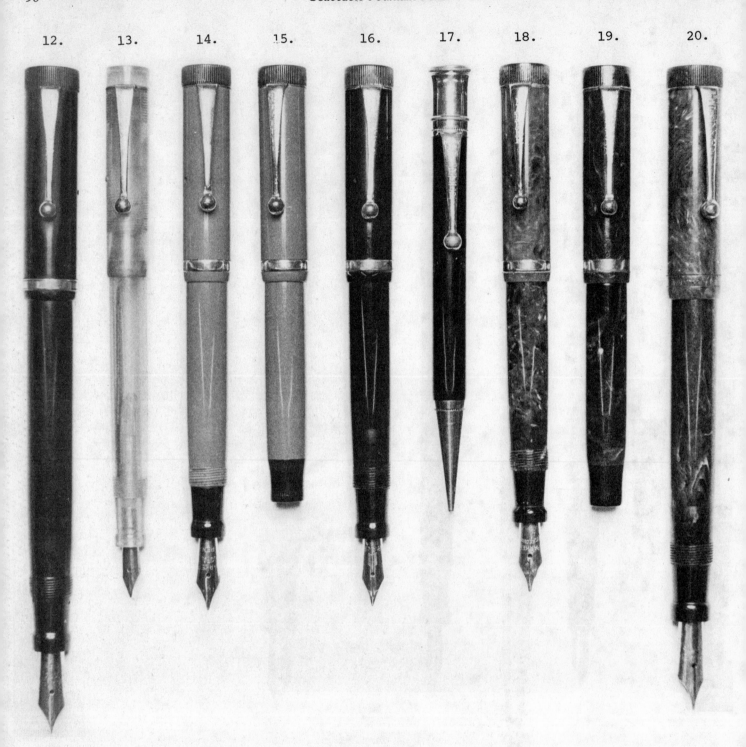

Parker

Plate No. 2

12. 1923   Parker Duofold, Lucky Curve, Black, Gold Filled Trim, Button Filler, $75
13. 1923   Parker Lucky Curve, Clear Bakelite, Gold Filled Trim, Button Filler, $50
14. 1923   Parker Duofold Jr., Lucky Curve, Red, Gold Filled Trim, Button Filler, $30
15. 1923   Parker Duofold Jr., Lucky Curve, Red, Gold Filled Trim, Button Filler (Closed), $30
16. 1924   Parker Duofold Jr., Lucky Curve, Black, Gold Filled Trim, Button Filler, $35 (Replacement nib, note arrow)
17. 1925   Parker Duofold Pencil, Black, Gold Filled Trim, $35
18. 1926   Parker Duofold, Lucky Curve, Mottled Green, Gold Filled Trim, Button Filler, $30
19. 1926   Parker Duofold Jr., Lucky Curve, Mottled Green, Gold Filled Trim, Button Filler (Closed), $30
20. 1926   Parker Lucky Curve, Mottled Green, Gold Filled Trim, Button Filler, $75

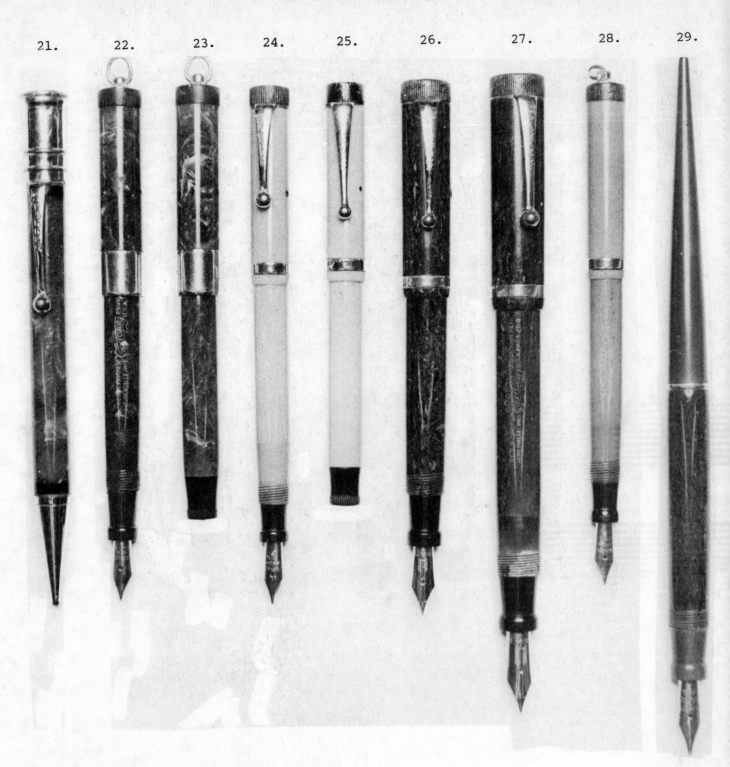

21. 22. 23. 24. 25. 26. 27. 28. 29.

Parker   Plate No. 3

21. 1926 Parker Pencil, Mottled Green, Gold Filled Trim, $40
22. 1926 Parker Lucky Curve, Mottled Green, Gold Trim, Button Filler, Ribbon Ring, $25
23. 1926 Parker Lucky Curve, Mottled Green, Gold Filled Trim, Button Filler, Ribbon Ring (Closed), $25
24. 1926 Parker Lucky Curve, Petite Pastel, Beige Gray, Gold Filled Trim, Button Filler, $30
25. 1926 Parker Lucky Curve, Petite Pastel, Beige Gray, Gold Filled Trim, Button Filler (Closed), $30
26. 1927 Parker Duofold Jr., Lucky Curve, Lapis Blue, Gold Filled Trim, Button Filler, $40 (Replacement Nib)
27. 1927 Parker Duofold, Lucky Curve, Lapis Blue, Gold Filled Trim, Button Filler, $90 (Replacement Nib)
28. 1927 Parker Lucky Curve, Petite Pastel, Mauve, Gold Filled Trim, Button Filler, Ribbon Ring, $30
29. 1927 Parker Duofold Jr., Lucky Curve, Desk Taper, Lapis Blue, Gold Filled Trim, Button Filler, $30

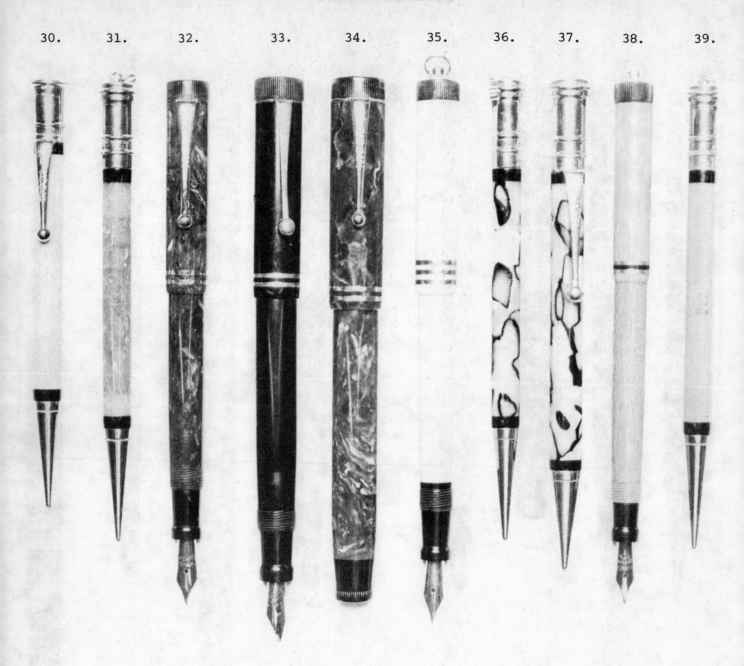

Plate No. 4

Parker

30. 1927   Parker Duofold Pencil, Chinese Yellow, Gold Filled Trim, $40
31. 1927   Parker Pencil, Jade, Gold Filled Trim, Ribbon Ring, $30
32. 1928   Parker Lucky Curve, Jade, Gold Filled Trim, Button Filler, $25
33. 1928   Parker Duofold, Black, Gold Filled Trim, Button Filler, $35
34. 1928   Parker Lucky Curve, Jade, Gold Filled Trim, Button Filler (Closed), $75
35. 1929   Parker Lady Duofold, Lucky Curve, Mandarin Yellow, Gold Filled Trim, Button Filler, Ribbon Ring, $60
36. 1929   Parker DeLuxe Duofold Pencil, Black and Pearl, Gold Filled Trim, Ribbon Ring, $40
37. 1929   Parker DeLuxe Duofold Pencil, Black and Pearl, Gold Filled Trim, $50
38. 1929   Parker Pastel Lucky Curve, Magenta Moire Pattern, Gold Filled Trim, Button Filler, Ribbon Ring, $40
39. 1929   Parker Pastel Pencil, Magenta, Gold Filled Trim, Ribbon Ring, $30

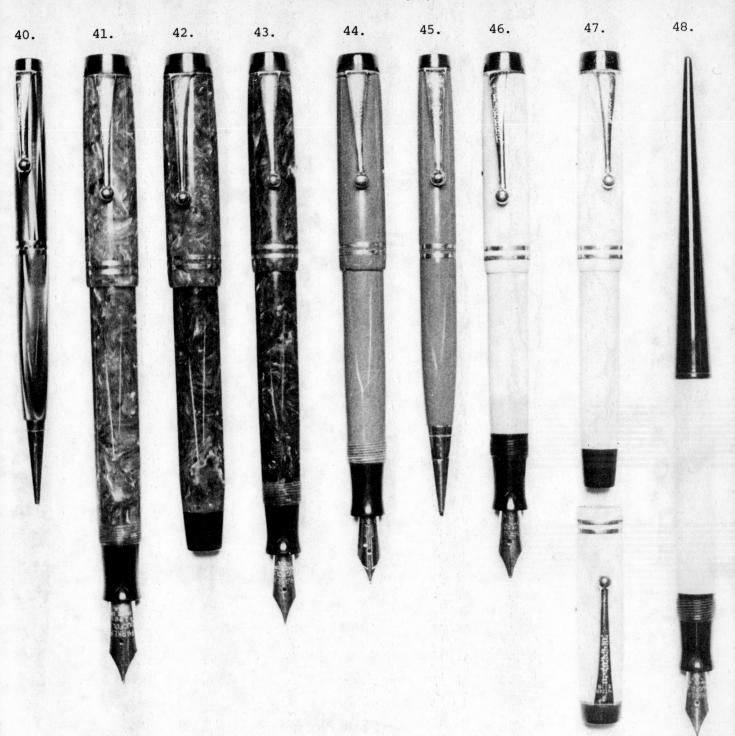

Parker

Plate No. 5

40. 1928 Parker Pencil, True Blue, Blue and White Barrel, Gold Filled Trim, $20
41. 1929 Parker Duofold, Jade, Gold Filled Trim, Button Filler, $40
42. 1929 Parker Duofold, Jade, Gold Filled Trim, Button Filler, Canadian Marks, (Closed), $50
43. 1929 Parker Duofold, Jade, Gold Filled Trim, Button Filler, $35
44. 1929 Parker Duofold, Red, Gold Filled Trim, Button Filler, $25 (Replacement Nib)
45. 1929 Parker Duofold Pencil, Red, Gold Filled Trim, $25
46. 1929 Parker Duofold, Mandarin Yellow, Gold Filled Trim, Button Filler, $50
47. 1929 Parker Duofold, Mandarin Yellow, Gold Filled Trim, Button Filler (Closed), $50
48. 1929 Parker Convertible Duofold, Mandarin Yellow, Gold Filled Trim, Desk Taper and Cap, Button Filler, $75

49.   50.   51.   52.   53.   54.   55.   56.   57.

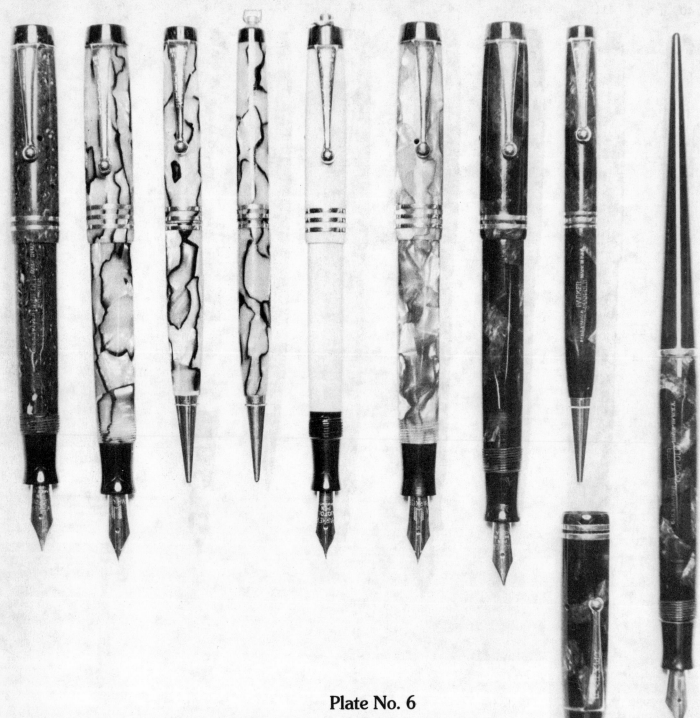

Plate No. 6

Parker

49. 1930 Parker Duofold, Lapis Blue, Gold Filled Trim, Button Filler, $35
50. 1930 Parker DeLuxe Duofold, Pearl and Black, Gold Filled Trim, Button Filler, $50
51. 1930 Parker DeLuxe Duofold Pencil, Pearl and Black, Gold Filled Trim, $35
52. 1930 Parker DeLuxe Duofold Pencil, Pearl and Black, Gold Filled Trim, Ribbon Ring, $35
53. 1930 Parker Duofold, Mandarin Yellow, Gold Filled Trim, Button filler, Combination Clip and Ribbon Ring, $65
54. 1930 Parker Duofold, DeLuxe Modern Green, Gold Filled Trim, Button Filler, $50
55. 1931 Parker Duofold, Burgundy Red and Black, Gold Filled Trim, Button Filler, $35
56. 1931 Parker Duofold Pencil, Burgundy Red and Black, Gold Filled Trim, $20
57. 1931 Parker Convertible Duofold, Burgundy Red and Black, Desk Taper and Cap, Gold Filled Trim, Button Filler, $50

58.   59.   60.   61.   62.   63.   64.   65.   66.

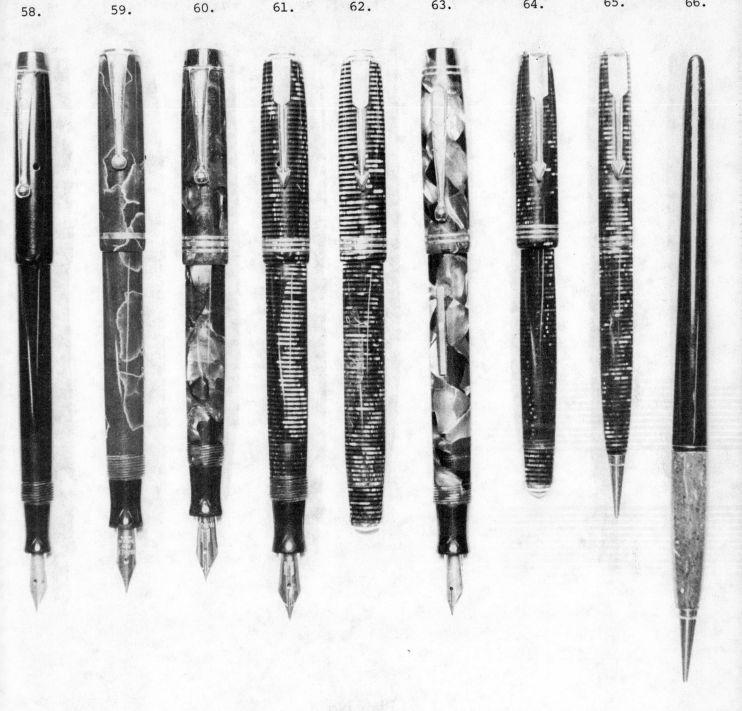

Parker

Plate No. 7

58.   1932   Parker, Black, Gold Filled Trim, Button Filler, $15
59.   1932   Parker Duette, Mahogany and White, Gold Filled Trim, Button Filler, $25
60.   1932   Parker Duofold, Sea Green Pearl, Gold Filled Trim, Button Filler, $20
61.   1933   Parker Vacumatic Maxima, Silver Pearl and Black Laminated, Chromium Trim, Vacumatic Filler, $40
62.   1933   Parker Vacumatic Maxima, Silver Pearl and Black Laminated, Chromium Trim, Vacumatic Filler (Closed), $40
63.   1933   Parker Parco, Burgundy Red and Black Marble, Gold Filled Trim, Button Filler, $25
64.   1933   Parker Demi-Vacumatic, Burgundy Red and Black Laminated, Gold Filled Trim, Vacumatic Filler (Closed), $20
65.   1933   Parker Demi-Vacumatic Pencil, Burgundy Red and Black Laminated, Gold Filled Trim, $20
66.   1933   Parker Duofold Pencil, Lapis Blue Barrel, Black Taper, Gold Filled Trim, $25

67.   68.   69.   70.   71.   72.   73.   74.   75.

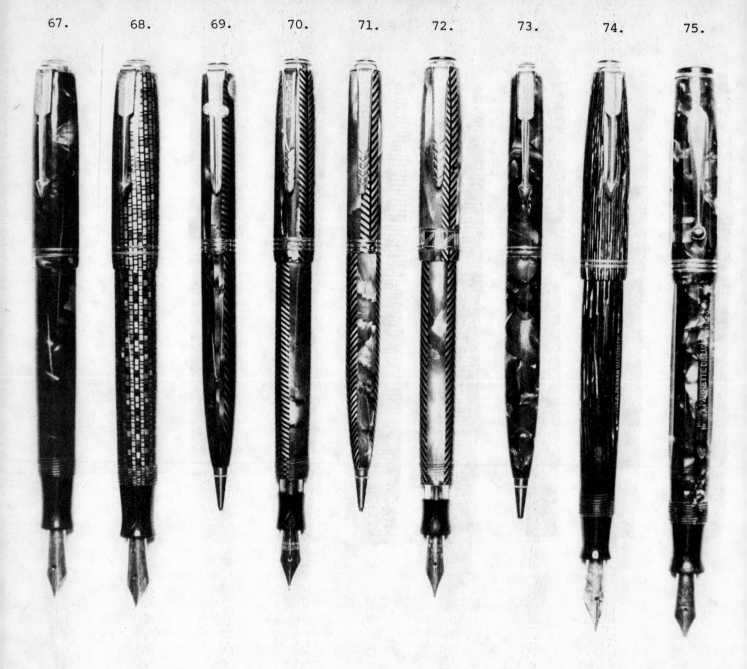

Plate No. 8

Parker

67.   1934   Parker Vacumatic, Burgundy Red and Black, Gold Filled Trim, Vacumatic Filler, $20
68.   1934   Parker Vacumatic, Gold and Black Web, Gold Filled Trim, Vacumatic Filler, $35
69.   1934   Parker Royal Challenger Pencil, Red and Black, Sword Clip, Gold Filled Trim, $30
70.   1934   Parker Royal Challenger, Copper Pearl and Black, Gold Filled Trim, Button Filler, $25
71.   1934   Parker Royal Challenger Pencil, Silver Pearl and Black, Chromium Trim, $25
72.   1934   Parker Royal Challenger, Silver Pearl and Black, Chromium Trim, Button Filler, $30
73.   1935   Parker Pencil, Sea Green and Black, Gold Filled Trim, $20
74.   1935   Parker Vacumatic, Silver Pearl and Black, Chromium Trim, Vacumatic Filler, $20
75.   1935   Parker Parkette DeLuxe, Red Pearl, Gold Filled Trim, Lever Filler, $20

76. 77. 78. 79. 80. 81. 82. 83. 84.

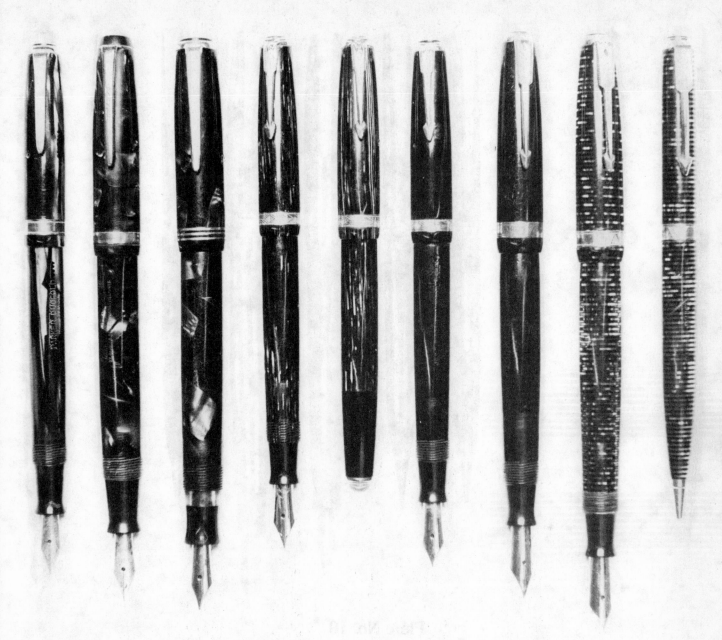

Plate No. 9

Parker

76. 1936 Parker Duofold, Copper Pearl and Black Geo, Gold Filled Trim, Button Filler, $25
77. 1936 Parker Challenger, Blue Pearl and Black, Gold Filled Trim, Button Filler, $15
78. 1936 Parker Deluxe Challenger, Red Pearl and Black, Gold Filled Trim, Button Filler, $20
79. 1937 Parker Demi-Vacumatic, Brown Pearl and Black, Gold Filled Trim, Vacumatic Filler, $20
80. 1937 Parker Demi-Vacumatic, Brown Pearl and Black, Gold Filled Trim, Vacumatic Filler (Closed), $20
81. 1940 Parker Demi-Vacumatic, Dark Brown, Gold Filled Trim, Vacumatic Filler, $20
82. 1940 Parker Blue Diamond Vacumatic, Black, Gold Filled Trim, Vacumatic Filler, $30
83. 1940 Parker Blue Diamond Vacumatic Major, Blue Pearl and Black Laminated Transparent Stripes, Gold Filled Trim, Vacumatic Filler, $40
84. 1940 Parker Pencil, Sea Green Pearl and Black Laminated, Gold Filled Trim, $20

85.   86.   87.   88.   89.   90.   91.   92.   93.   94.

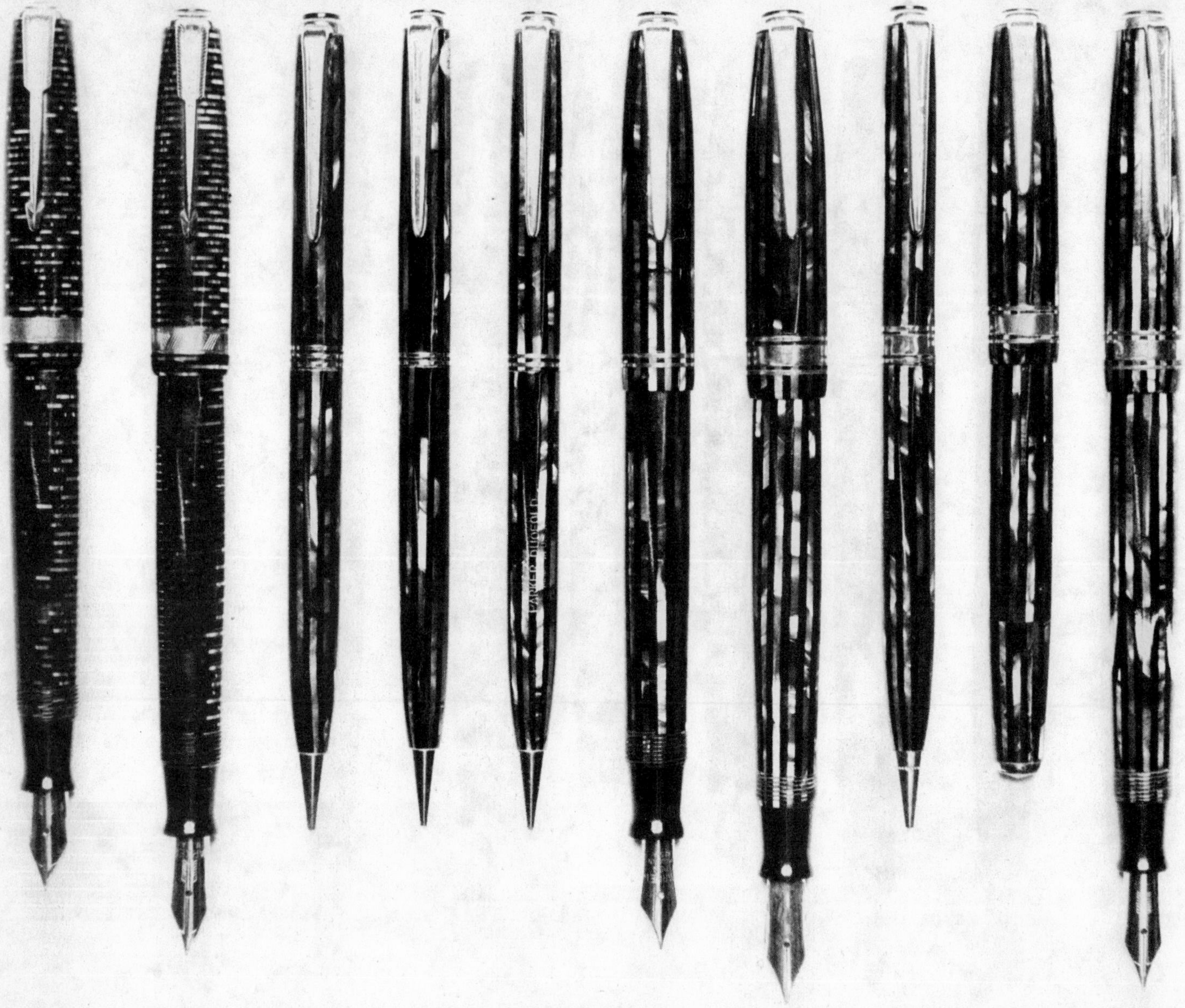

Plate No. 10

Parker

85. 1940 Parker Blue Diamond Vacumatic, Silver Pearl and Black Laminated, Nickel Filled Trim, Vacumatic Filler, $30

86. 1940 Parker Blue Diamond Vacumatic Major, Brown Pearl and Black Laminated, Gold Filled Trim, Vacumatic Filler, $40

87. 1940 Parker Pencil, Blue Pearl and Black Stripes, Gold Filled Trim, $20

88. 1940 Parker Duofold Pencil, Blue Pearl and Black Stripes, Gold Filled Trim, $20

89. 1940 Parker Duofold Pencil, Blue Pearl and Black Stripes, Gold Filled Trim, $20

90. 1940 Parker Duofold, Blue Pearl and Black Striped, Gold Filled Trim, Vacumatic Filler, $30

91. 1942 Parker Blue Diamond Duofold, Red and Silver Pearl and Black Stripes, Gold Filled Trim, Vacumatic Filler, $50

92. 1942 Parker Duofold Pencil, Red and Silver Pearl and Black Stripes, Gold Filled Trim, Button Filler, $35

93. 1943 Parker Blue Diamond Duofold, Blue Pearl and Black Stripes, Gold Filled Trim, Vacumatic Filler (Closed), $35

94. 1943 Parker Blue Diamond Duofold, Blue Pearl and Black Stripes, Gold Filled Trim, Vacumatic Filler, $45

95.   96.   97.   98.   99.   100.   101.   102.   103.

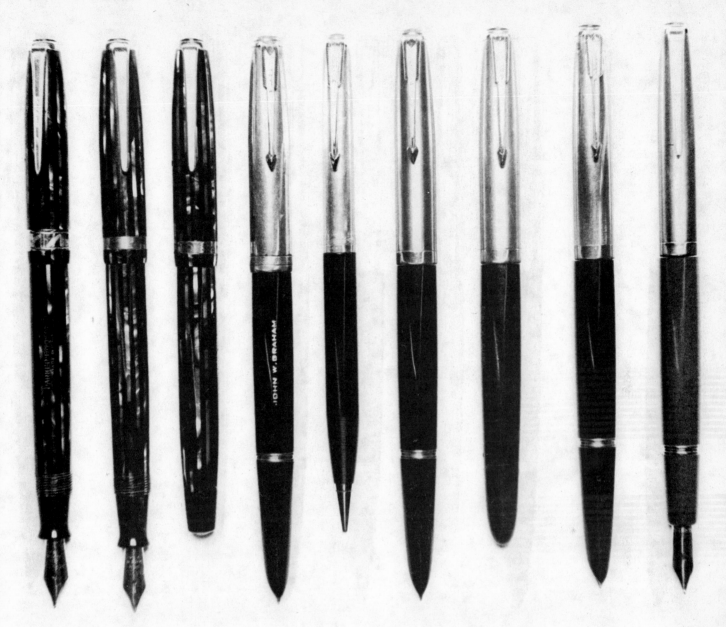

Plate No. 11

Parker

95.	1943	Parker Duofold, Green and Brown Pearl and Black Stripes, Gold Filled Trim, Button Filler, $35
96.	1940	Parker, Blue Silver Pearl and Black Stripes, Gold Filled Trim, Button Filler, $20
97.	1944	Parker, Blue Silver Pearl and Black Stripes, Gold Filled Trim, Button Filler (Closed), $20
98.	1941	Parker "51" Blue Diamond, Sterling Cap, Black Barrel, Gold Filled Trim, Vacumatic Filler, $65
99.	1941	Parker Pencil, Sterling Cap, Black Barrel, Gold Filled Trim, $40
100.	1945	Parker "51" Blue Diamond, Lustraloy Cap, Black Barrel, Gold Filled Trim, $30
101.	1945	Parker "51" Blue Diamond, Lustraloy Cap, Maroon Barrel, Gold Filled Trim (Closed), $30
102.	1946	Parker "51" Blue Diamond, Gold Filled Cap, Black Barrel, Gold Filled Trim, Vacumatic Filler, $45
103.	1947	Parker VS, Lustraloy Cap, Gray Barrel, $35

104.   105.   106.   107.   108.   109.   110.   111.   112.

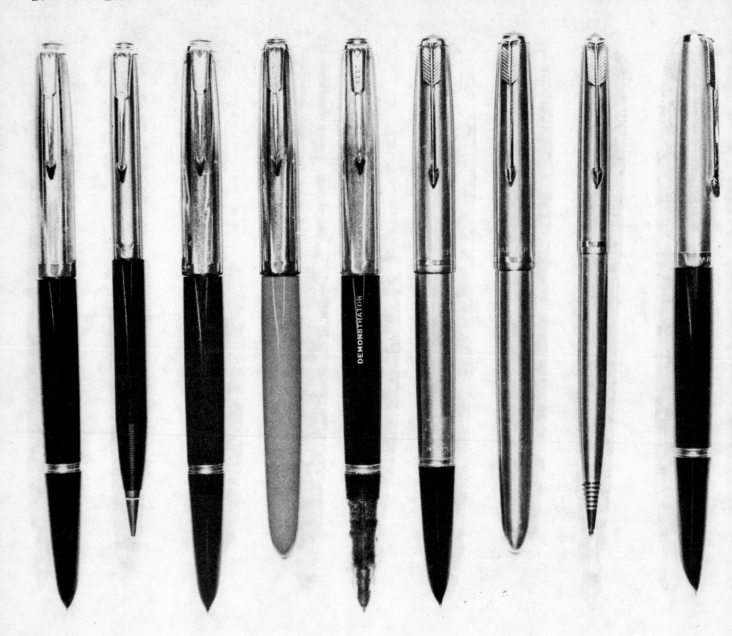

Plate No. 12

Parker

104. 1947 Parker "51" Blue Diamond, Sterling Cap, Black Barrel, Gold Filled Trim, Vacumatic Filler, $50
105. 1947 Parker Pencil, Lustraloy Cap, Black Barrel, Gold Filled Trim, $25
106. 1948 Parker "51" Blue Diamond, Gold Filled Cap, Aqua Barrel, Vacumatic Filler, $40
107. 1948 Parker "51" Blue Diamond, Gold Filled Cap, Gray Barrel, Vacumatic Filler (Closed), $40
108. 1948 Parker "51" Blue Diamond Demonstrator, Gold Filled Cap, Black Barrel, Vacumatic Filler, $50
109. 1950 Parker "51" Flighter, Lustraloy Cap and Barrel, Gold Filled Trim, Aero-Metric, $50
110. 1950 Parker "51" Flighter, Lustraloy Cap and Barrel, Gold Filled Trim, Aero-Metric (Closed), $50
111. 1950 Parker "51" Flighter Pencil, Lustraloy Cap and Barrel, Gold Filled Trim, $40
112. 1950 Parker "51", Lustraloy Cap, Black Barrel, Vacumatic Filler, $15

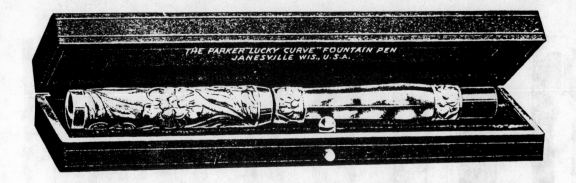

Above: Parker No. 47, Pearl Barrel, 18K Gold Filled Floral Design Mountings, with Box, $550

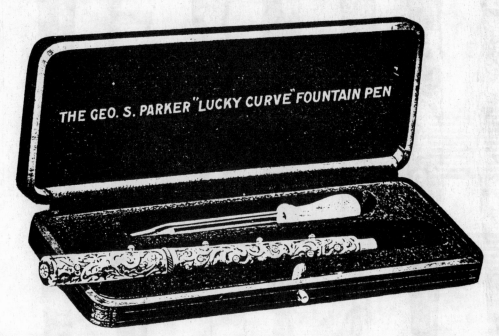

Middle: Parker, The Pen of Pens, Solid 18K Gold, Studded with Precious Gems. A large diamond is set in the cap crown. The smaller stones are diamonds, rubies, etc., set in an ornate mounting. $5,000 to $10,000

Below: Same as model in middle, except in a plain mounting. $5,000 to $10,000

Plate No. 13

Fancy Mounted Parker Eye Dropper Filled Pens
Circa 1905 - 1915

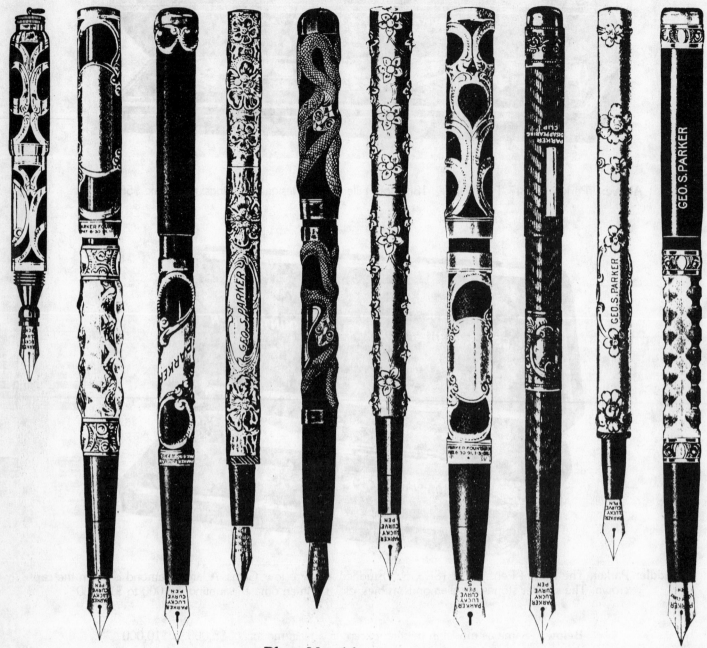

Plate No. 14

1. Parker No. 14, Baby Jack Knife Safety, Sterling Silver Mountings, $100
   Parker No. 16, Jack Knife Safety, Gold Filled Mountings, $100
2. Parker No. 15, Tinted Pearl Slab Barrel, Gold Filled Mountings, $250
3. Parker No. 33, Gold Filled Mountings, $175
   Parker No. 34, Sterling Silver Mountings, $175
4. Parker No. 36, Sterling Silver Mountings, $350
5. Parker No. 37, Sterling Silver Snake Mountings, Green Stones, $750-$1000
   Parker No. 38, Solid 18K Gold Snake Mountings, Green Stones, $1000-$1500
6. Parker No. 39, 18K Gold Filled For-Get-Me-Nots Mountings, Stone or Pearl Settings, $500
   Parker No. 54, 18K Gold Filled For-Get-Me-Nots Mountings, Sans Settings, $300
7. Paker No. 41, Gold Filled Filigree Design, $500
   Parker No. 31, Sterling Silver Filigree Design, $500
8. Parker No. 42½, Black Chased With Gold Filled Mountings, Level Lock Clip, $150
9. Parker No. 43, 18K Gold Filled Simple Floral Pattern, Dull Finish, $300
   Parker No. 44, Sterling Silver Simple Floral Pattern, Dull Finish, $300
10. Parker No. 45, Corrugated Pearl Slabs, 18K Gold Filled Mountings, $250

Plate No. 15

11. Parker No. 45, Jack Knife Safety, Pearl Barrel, Gold Filled Mountings, $300 (Not duplicate from Plate No. 14, Item 10)
12. Parker No. 46, Corrugated Pearl Barrel, Gold Plated Mountings, $300
13. Parker No. 47, Pearl Slab Barrel, Gold Filled Mountings, $500
14. Parker No. 49, Baby Jack Knife Safety, 18K Rolled Gold Mountings, $200
15. Parker No. 52, Hammered Sterling Silver Swastika Design Mountings, $1000-$1500
16. Parker No. 53, Solid 18K Gold Swastika Design Mountings, $2000-$3000
17. Parker No. 58, Gold Filled "Awanyu" Aztec Indian Design Mountings, $750-$1000
18. Parker No. 59, Elaborate Sterling Silver "Awanyu" Aztec Indian Design Mountings, $1500-$2500
     Parker No. 60, Elaborate 18K Gold Filled "Awanyu" Aztec Indian Design Mountings, $1500-$2500
19. Parker No. 61, Solid 18K Gold Plain Design Mountings, $500
20. Parker No. 62, Solid 18K Gold Floral Design Mountings, $500-$1000

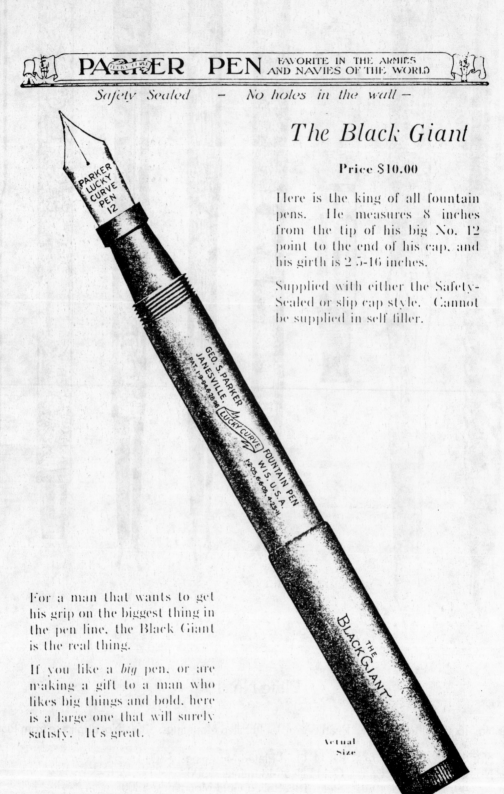

PARKER PEN FAVORITE IN THE ARMIES AND NAVIES OF THE WORLD

Safety Sealed   —   No holes in the wall —

The Black Giant

Price $10.00

Here is the king of all fountain pens. He measures 8 inches from the tip of his big No. 12 point to the end of his cap, and his girth is 2 5-16 inches.

Supplied with either the Safety-Sealed or slip cap style. Cannot be supplied in self filler.

For a man that wants to get his grip on the biggest thing in the pen line, the Black Giant is the real thing.

If you like a *big* pen, or are making a gift to a man who likes big things and bold, here is a large one that will surely satisfy. It's great.

Actual Size

The Sheaffer Pen Company

The Early History

Extract of Product Development

National Advertising

A Pictorial Chronology of Pens and Pencils

(Sheaffer-Eaton, Div. Textron)

1867 - Walter A. Sheaffer - 1946

THE founder and first president of The Sheaffer Pen Company, Walter A. Sheaffer, had a great understanding of the techniques of merchandising quality products. With it, he possessed a contagious enthusiasm for selling quality. This combination provided the spark of success that enabled his fledgling pen company to survive in a highly competitive situation where, normally, the odds were all on the side of failure. Mr. Sheaffer had not gained his merchandising skill easily. He had not been able to finish high school because financial need forced him to begin working early in life. He held a variety of jobs before becoming a partner in his father's jewelry business. There, and later in his own jewelry store, which he launched in Fort Madison in 1906, he perfected his merchandising skills. When he decided to risk his hard-won life's savings to go into the pen business at the age of 45, he was able to transfer these skills from the challenges of a small retail store to those of a manufacturer for national markets. He was president for 25 years and remained active in company affairs until his death in 1946.

The Sheaffer Pen Company: The Early History

(Sheaffer-Eaton, Div. Textron)

Walter A. Sheaffer was born in Bloomfield, Iowa, on July 27, 1867. He was one of five children of Jacob Royer Sheaffer and Anna Eliza (Wilton) Sheaffer. Walter dropped his formal education before completing high school and looked for employment in the jewelry business. He did not work in his father's jewelry store initially because Jacob had already employed a young orphaned nephew.

After learning the fundamentals of the jewelry business in Centerville and Unionville, Walter returned to Bloomfield in 1888 as a partner in his father's jewelry store. The partnership between Jacob and Walter Sheaffer continued until Jacob's death in 1916.

Walter married Nellie Davis of Pulaski, Iowa, on February 8, 1888. Two children were born to Walter and Nellie.

To help the jewelry store support the expense of this second family, Walter branched out into the piano and organ business and later into sewing machines.

After selling his first small house and putting the proceeds in the jewelry business, Walter purchased a larger house from his wife's grandmother. After paying off this home, Walter bought an eight acre property which he improved and later traded for a rundown 188 acre farm.

Upon getting this 188 acre farm into shape, Walter was ready to trade for a jewelry store in a larger town. Through an ad in a jewelry magazine, he learned of a store in Ft. Madison, Iowa, owned by M. L. Bowen. In April of 1906, Walter traded his 188 acre farm for the Bowen store. At the time, the store stock invoiced at $12,552.

One Autumn evening in 1907, while reading the local weekly newspaper, Walter noticed an ad for a Conklin pen having a filling device requiring a coin looking hump on one side of the barrel. Most pens of that day were filled with an eyedropper.

Walter felt that there should be some way of making a pen which could be filled without the mess and bother of an eyedropper or the protrusion of a coin-shaped hump on the barrel.

A few days later, he had the answer. He eliminated need for an eyedropper by putting a deflatable rubber sac in the pen barrel. And he eliminated the coin-shaped hump by using a lever and pressure bar to deflate the sac. The lever fitted smoothly into a shallow recess in the pen barrel.

Because of his experience in using and selling fountain pens of that era, Walter was convinced of the soundness of his invention. A patent was issued to him on August 25, 1908 covering the new idea.

The big industrial news of 1908 was the introduction by Henry Ford of a new-fangled contraption called the Model T automobile. Most people thought it would be lunacy to risk riding in it and that the trusty horse would never be replaced.

In the nation's capital, Congress passed a bill regulating child labor in the District of Columbia. The action created only minor interest across the land, and few realized it was the beginning of sweeping social reform that was to mark the years ahead.

It was not known at all that, in the small Iowa community of Fort Madison, a jeweler named W. A. Sheaffer was devising a new product that would revolutionize America's writing habits and pave the way for the birth of a manufacturing enterprise.

For Mr. Sheaffer, 1908 and the years immediately following were not only ones of invention and of improvement in the initial model of his revolutionary lever, self-filling pen; they were also years of debate and uncertainty.

He had an inborn instinct for merchandising and selling, which he had used to good advantage in building up a successful jewelry business. Now, it clearly told him that he had developed a product with great potential. To be doubly sure, he assembled a few of his lever-fill fountain pens and sent them to friends to try out. Their comments assured him the product was highly salable. The new pen, that needed no coin or eye dropper for filling, was a truly great advance.

But there was much more involved in deciding to go into the pen business. In 1912, there were 58 other companies in the industry, including several large, well-established firms. With this competition, the risk of failure would be high, despite a sound product.

Mr. Sheaffer talked over the idea with friends and other businessmen. Many advised against it. "You're secure now, with a business that will enable you to live comfortably," they said. "Why take a chance on losing everything?"

The argument was a good one. At 45, Mr. Sheaffer had years of hard work behind him. To get a pen business started would require all of his life savings and much more. Should he lose what he had, it might be impossible to regain similar financial security.

However, he decided to take the momentous step. In the spring of 1912, the workshop of the Sheaffer jewelry store became a pen factory and a Sheaffer sales office was opened in Kansas City, Mo., by George Kraker and Ben Coulson, former salesmen for the Conklin Pen Co.

Seven employees crowded into the small workroom to hand-make the first Sheaffer pens, including Mr. Sheaffer's young son, Craig. They were kept busy, working long hours a day, as Kraker and Coulson followed up their first sale — to the Missouri Store Co. of Columbia, Mo. — with ever-increasing orders. According to records, the prevailing wage in Fort Madison in 1912 was $3 to $5 a week.

From the outset, quality was the byword for Sheaffer pens. Mr. Sheaffer believed in it wholeheartedly, and his employees, sharing his enthusiasm, approached their jobs like craftsmen fashioning the fine watches that were out front on the shelves of the jewelry store.

With the success of this early operation, and with the interest of Kraker and Coulson in joining him as partners, Mr. Sheaffer was able to put together enough money to go into business officially. On January 1, 1913, the W. A. Sheaffer Pen Co. was incorporated for $35,000, with Kraker and Coulson owning 40 per cent of the stock. That year Mr. Sheaffer sold his jewelry business, and in a few months manufacturing operations were transferred to larger quarters on the upper floor of the Hesse building in downtown Fort Madison.

During the first year, the new company captured three per cent of the writing instrument market, chalking up sales of $100,000. Profits were $17,500, or 50 per cent of the initial investment.

Things looked bright for American and for the fledgling company in 1913. War clouds were gathering in Europe, but the trouble was far away. Congress had adopted the 16th amendment to the Constitution, granting the power to levy and collect taxes on income, and while this was a highly controversial issue, it did not affect greatly the optimism that everyone felt. The spirit of the time was more aptly symbolized by the fact that, in New York City, the world's tallest building rose. At 60 stories, the Woolworth Building towered 10 stories above any other skyscraper.

In the years immediately after 1913, despite rapidly increasing sales, the fate of the Sheaffer Pen Co. hung in the balance. It was a period of life-and-death legal battles and maneuvers to protect the company's patents against the challenges of other firms.

It pitted a small company, with limited financial resources, against some of the giants of the industry. Mr. Sheaffer led the fight. If he had lost any one of the cases the company would have been finished.

Accounts of the legal battles, told by Mr. Sheaffer himself, read in some instances like cloak-and-dagger mysteries. On one venture, traveling to New York to have important testimony checked, Mr. Sheaffer was followed by a private detective. He eluded him by stepping onto a subway train and then suddenly leaping off just as the doors were closing.

In 1916, the company moved to a former creamery building in Fort Madison on the site of the present Research and Development offices. A year later the old Morrison Plow Works was purchased, providing the company with its first full-scale plant facilities. The number of employees had risen to 100; in 1917 they produced about 100,000 pens. The models of that year had 11 parts, and 62 hand operations were performed in making and assembling them.

A Sheaffer factory was also opened in Kansas City. It was a plant that had been started by George Kraker when he left the company and attempted to set up a competitive operation, using Sheaffer patents. This was one of the threats Mr. Sheaffer succeeded in turning aside.

One of the main advances made possible by the purchase of the Morrison Plow Works was the installation of a Gold Nib Department. Previously, all Sheaffer pen points had been shipped in from the east. Whenever the train was late, or a shipment did not arrive on time, production was seriously affected or halted entirely.

At that time, there were only three men in the entire country who could do the quality nib work Mr. Sheaffer required. He personally induced one of them — Winfield Kay of Jersey City, N.J. — to move his operations to Fort Madison.

In 1919, the offices and manufacturing departments occupied a part of the Morrison Plow Works building. They made a striking contrast with the facilities of today. The office force consisted of W. A. Sheaffer, Craig Sheaffer and three others. The advertising manager opened the daily mail, when Mr. Sheaffer didn't do it himself.

Things really happened in America in the Twenties. Industry boomed in the aftermath of World War I. The League of Nations was formed to help insure a lasting peace. The first transcontinental airmail route was established between New York and San Francisco. Later, Lt. Comdr. Richard Byrd made the first flight over the South Pole. George Gershwin wrote the immortal "Rhapsody in Blue" in 1924. Football became one of the great American sports, spearheaded by the Notre Dame teams of the legendary Knute Rockne.

These were good things. Others were not so good. Prohibition brought on a wave of gangsterism unlike anything seen before. And in 1929, the free, easy, carefree living of the decade came to an abrupt, tragic end. On October 29, the day of the stock market crash, 16 million shares were sold in panic. The great depression lay ahead.

The fortunes of the Sheaffer Pen Co. followed right along with the period's industrial boom. Improvements in writing instruments brought Sheaffer to a position of industry leadership by the middle of the decade. In 1925, sales had risen from three per cent of industry volume to 25 per cent. The Morrison Plow Works buildings were modernized and enlarged to accommodate increased production. In 1928, Sheaffer stock was listed on the New York Stock Exchange. Manufacturing operations were under way in both New York and Kansas City, and sales and repair offices had been established in Chicago and San Francisco.

One of the foremost Sheaffer innovations of the Twenties was the development of a way to make pen caps and barrels of plastic, rather than the previously used hard rubber, which was highly breakable and precluded the use of color. It was not an easy task, and it cost the young company dearly in both time and money. The first attempt in 1920 ended in failure because the plastic material expanded too much when the temperature rose.

It was a disheartening experience, but Mr. Sheaffer was not accustomed to defeat. He pressed the project harder, using a new type of plastic. As a result, the company got a jump on the rest of the industry and was the first to introduce colored pens that were virtually unbreakable.

In 1921 Sheaffer startled the writing instrument world by introducing a pen priced at $8.75 — three times as much as the price of competitive products. The 14-karat gold point of the pen was guaranteed for the lifetime of the owner, another unheard-of move among pen companies.

This reflected Mr. Sheaffer's marketing philosophy. He felt that the pen was worth the money, and that when consumers became aware of the quality that was built into it they would be willing to pay the higher price. He was right; the first Sheaffer "Lifetime" fountain pen became the nation's No. 1 seller.

Early in the game, Mr. Sheaffer decided that the company must develop its own writing fluid, rather than depend on the products of others. In 1922, again after many months of costly research and some setbacks, the formula for Skrip writing fluid was perfected in the basement room that served as a laboratory. The new product proved better than any competitive ink and was an instant success.

Other developments in the Twenties included the propel-repel-expel pencil, the desk set, and streamlined, balanced design for writing instruments.

A 1926 employee manual, one of the first issued by the company, pointed out that the work day started at 7:30 and ended at 5:30, with an hour for lunch. The work week included Saturday mornings. For perfect attendance during a year (no absences or lateness except for jury duty) employees could earn a $25 bonus.

There was no parking problem at the plant in the Twenties, since only two or three employees drove cars. Many rode to work on the street car that ran near the plant. Summer heat, on the other hand, was a problem. Where practical, employees were allowed to bring their own small electric fans with them.

According to an early report, telephones were a scarce item in those days. There was one for the office and one for the plant.

Bookkeeping was several giant strides away from the data processing procedures of today. The accountants used what has been described as "a huge journal that covered an eight-foot slant top desk."

An employee recreation program was initiated in February, 1927, with the completion of the Clubhouse. A schedule of activities was posted for men and women. For those who like to paint mental pictures, gymnasium attire for the ladies included "shoes, black hose, black bloomers and white blouse."

By 1931, the depression had deepened and spread to include millions of Americans. There was hunger, and bread lines, and soup kitchens. The self-assurance that America had felt since the turn of the century was gone. Sweeping government programs were installed to fill the gap left when people felt they could no longer solve the problems for themselves.

Events that would lead to World War II had occurred in Japan and in Germany, but most Americans were too preoccupied with their own problems to notice. In Russia, the Communist Party had grown all-powerful during the Twenties. Here, in what appeared to be a helplessly backward land that could never be a threat to anyone, groundwork for the future was being laid.

America did not grind to a complete halt, of course, despite the rigors of the depression. In 1934 a DuPont company scientist invented a new synthetic fibre that was given the name Nylon. There were outstanding writers, like Thornton Wilder, whose play, "Our Town," won the Pulitzer Prize for drama. In 1938, Orson Wells scared millions with a chillingly well done radio program called "Invasion From Mars." Listeners thought it was real.

In Fort Madison, Iowa, the depression left its mark, just like everywhere else. Sheaffer sales held up well until 1931, then dropped off sharply. Yet the company was one of the last employers to cut its production schedules. Employees worked three days a week as the situation continued to worsen. Finally, when President Roosevelt declared a holiday that closed all banks across the nation, it was necessary to shut down entirely, except for a few office employees.

Fortunately, this complete standstill was short lived. Within a week the two main banks in Fort Madison were re-opened, and Sheaffer immediately resumed a three-day-a-week schedule.

Economic conditions were not all that plagued Fort Madison and the Sheaffer Pen Co. during the Thirties. Unbearably hot, dry weather during at least two of the summers resulted in almost complete crop failures in the area. At one point, work schedules at the company were set from 6 a.m. to 1 p.m. to avoid the hottest part of the day.

In the early Thirties, Sheaffer annual sales were about $7 million, but this was a healthy percentage of industry sales, which totaled about $30 million. The company was one of 50 writing instrument firms — actually fewer than had been in business 20 years before, in 1913.

During the dark days of the Thirties, Sheaffer people continued working together, and building. From Sheaffer laboratories came the Feathertouch two-way point, the plunger, visible barrel pen and the Fineline pencil. A line of office adhesives was also developed and put on the market.

One Monday morning, in the late fall of 1937, employees came to work to find plant guards securely bound, the vault broken into and stock valued at $50,000 missing. Coming just before Christmas, the loss was especially harmful. A bulletin was sent to all dealers asking them to advise the company if Lifetime fountain pens were offered for sale by anyone other than an authorized Sheaffer representative. "We hope in the near future to fill all orders completely," the bulletin added. The promise was fulfilled.

Strong relationships with dealers helped the company weather the depression. During the Twenties forthright policies had been developed, and the company followed them closely, treating all dealers with equal fairness.

During the heart of the depression, when most citizens across the nation had to accept reduced compensation and benefits, Mr. Sheaffer launched a profit-sharing plan for all company people. He felt the time had come to strengthen the company by giving employees a way to share in its growth. It was a program in which he believed deeply, and the depression did not stand in his way.

Except for a brief over-the-weekend dispute in 1918, employee relationships had remained excellent over the years. The formation of the WASPCO council in 1937 helped insure that they would remain so. The council, made up of employee representatives who met regularly with management, was to become a fixture in company affairs and an outstanding example of forthright communication in industry.

In the latter half of the decade the company further geared itself for the growth years Mr. Sheaffer felt certain lay ahead. A new office building was completed in 1937, and all accounting functions for the company were centralized in Fort Madison. Previously, part of this work had been done in the New York office. In 1939, 1,100 square feet of space was added to manufacturing facilities.

The scope of the company's manufacturing skills was expanded during this period. The first molding machine was purchased in 1937, enabling employees to produce some molded parts themselves and paving the way for large-scale precision operations of the future.

In 1938, having passed the 70-year mark, Mr. Sheaffer gave way as president to his son, Craig.

As the decade began, there was hope that America could stay out of the war that was engulfing other areas of the world. Yet, on all sides preparation for war and other emergency measures began to take place. No one who lived through it will ever forget the numbing shock of Pearl Harbor on December 7, 1941, or the events that followed: the British surrender of Singapore, the fall of Bataan and the Philippines, the mushroom atomic clouds over Hiroshima and Nagasaki, the birth of the jet age, the death of President Franklin D. Roosevelt in 1945.

The war had a widespread effect on Sheaffer operations, where planning for war work began as early as mid-1941. Major emphasis turned from the production of writing instruments to the manufacture of airborne communication plugs, bomb and artillery fuses, and an automatic radio tuning device for the armed forces. From the time the company received its first prime contract — for communication plugs — from the Army Signal Corps in September, 1941, until the cessation of hostilities, more than seven million of these units were produced.

The autotune device made by Sheaffer was a delicate apparatus with 1,000 separate parts in a set. To insure that it would function on high-flying bombers, each set had to meet severe tests — including a stay in 50-degree-below-zero temperatures. At the start of the war, these were custom made devices, but Shaeffer employees devised a way for mass producing them, while still maintaining the pin-point quality. In the course of the war, 80 per cent of all autotunes came from skilled Sheaffer hands. For this, and other achievements, an Army-Navy "E" award was presented to the company in 1944.

Three other war projects were launched in 1942, and production of Sheaffer writing instruments was at a comparative standstill. Most of those that were manufactured went to the armed forces.

Before all-out emphasis on war work began, Craig Sheaffer announced the changes to Sheaffer employees in a lengthy bulletin that gave two principal reasons for the course the company was following. First was duty. "Unless we lick the Axis, nothing else will be worthwhile," Mr. Sheaffer said. Second, the war effort "would help maintain full employment in Fort Madison." Mr. Sheaffer pointed out that there were critical shortages in materials needed to maintain full production of writing instruments. As many substitutions as possible had been made and cutbacks were inevitable unless something took up the slack.

Early in 1942 the company began remodeling a former paper mill at 18th St. and Avenue O in Fort Madison (now Plant No. 2). This plant went into operation in May of that year and was devoted completely to war production.

Both the quantity and quality of war products was a tribute to the skill of Sheaffer people. Women employees did more than their share as men went into the armed forces in increasing numbers. By 1944, 490 employees had been called, and there were four gold stars on the roster of names.

During the war employees were reminded of the nature of their work by a high wire fence that encircled the plant to keep out intruders. There were other changes. Bicycle parking stalls completed in 1942 reflected the effects of gas rationing. The serving of soup and hot coffee at the War Division was so well accepted that the program was installed at Plant No. 1. The cafeteria idea had come to stay.

Of major importance to employees was the announcement of an extension of the profit-sharing program to include a trust fund (or retirement) program. It was started in 1942, although it took several years to get approval of all details from the U.S. Treasury Department.

When the war ended, Craig Sheaffer led an all-out expansion program aimed at making up lost ground in the writing instrument field. It included new products that had been in development stages during the war years, new plant facilities and equipment, and new merchandising and sales plans.

A 30-minute film on war work had been prepared for showing to dealers to explain what Sheaffer people had been doing during the war and why the company's regular products were in such short supply.

New operations were opened in Quincy, Ill., and Mt. Pleasant, Ia. In Fort Madison, Plants No. 1 and No. 2 were changed back to normal production with all speed. An old button factory building at 12th St. and Avenue O was purchased and became Plant No. 5. (This is the site of the present Tool and Die Division.)

Engineering plans for the construction of a completely modern multi-million-dollar plant in Fort Madison were completed, but it was decided to delay this program until building costs and conditions were more favorable.

In the 1947 annual report to shareowners, Craig Sheaffer pointed out that pre-war prices were being maintained on most products in the line, despite rising costs for just about everything. With good customer reaction the future is favorable, Mr. Sheaffer said, "and the company will continue this policy as long as we are able to do so."

Methods improvements made this possible, and Mr. Sheaffer was right about the future being favorable. The main problem was that of keeping up with customer demand, and the company was able to regain its position of industry leadership in a comparatively short time.

A particularly significant advance was the installation of equipment to do all molding of pen caps and barrels in Fort Madison, which made possible sharp decreases in product cost.

Everybody benefited from the rush of success. Profit-sharing soared to new heights. So did wages, which accounted for 36 cents of each sales dollar in 1948.

One thing that happened during the war was destined to have a marked and lasting effect on the writing instrument market. This was the development of the ballpoint pen, which originally met the wartime need for a writing instrument with built-in ink supply. The ballpoint reached the consumer market amid great fanfare and was eagerly accepted, despite formidably high prices. Original models did not write well, nor did they live up to the claims made for them; but this proved only a temporary setback. The ballpoint was off and running.

The first Sheaffer ballpoints were manufactured at the Mt. Pleasant plant in 1947. They joined other important product developments of the Forties: the inner-spring clip, the Triumph sheath-type nib and the Touchdown filling mechanism.

In 1949, the plant in Quincy, Ill., was closed and the operations were moved to Fort Madison. That same year, the softball field at Employees' Park was dedicated. The war behind them, people were thinking about such things as baseball again. Major cloud on the horizon was the rising threat of Communism, evidenced by the halting by Russia of free traffic between Berlin and the Western occupational zones in 1948, and subsequent institution of the Berlin airlift.

The fabulous Fifties some called them. In many ways, they were. More Americans had more things than ever before. The stock market moved to new highs, reflecting the economic growth that was taking place.

It was also the decade of the "cold war." This was something new, a kind of war that was hard to put your finger on. There were border incidents, small brush fire battles, and brush fire battles that weren't so small — like Korea.

The most terrifying part of it all was the nuclear arms race. Russia had the bomb, too. The weapons became bigger and better until their destructive power could be imagined only in a nightmare.

One of the favorite topics of political conversation was the government debt. There was no such thing when the Sheaffer Pen Co. was started. Now the debt was edging toward $300 billion. This got people to thinking about taxes and inflation. People received more money than ever before, but it would buy less.

The first triumph of the space age went to Russia as news of Sputnik I hit the front pages. The first U.S. earth satellite, Explorer I, was launched in 1958. The race for the moon, and for the vast reaches of space beyond, had begun. Flash Gordon and Buck Rogers, comic strip heroes of the past, did not seem quite so comic any more.

On the sports front, Rocky Marciano became heavyweight champion of the world. The Brooklyn Dodgers won their first world championship in 1955, defeating the New York Yankees (who else?) in the World Series. Closer to home, the University of Iowa became a major college football power under the guidance of Forrest Evashevski.

Alaska became the 49th state in 1958. Hawaii would soon be No. 50.

In addition to growth at home, the Sheaffer Pen Co. grew overseas during the Fifties, as outlined elsewhere in this special supplement. Fort Madison became the hub of global operations.

In the spring of 1950 it appeared that disaster had struck in the form of fire that followed an explosion in the basement of the company's office building. An Associated Press wire story of that day said: "A raging fire is threatening to destroy the W. A. Sheaffer Pen Company's office building in Fort Madison, Iowa. Fire departments from Burlington, Keokuk and the Iowa Ordnance Plant have been called out to aid the Fort Madison Fire Department."

Fortunately, the blaze was brought under control quickly and most damage confined to the basement area. It was also fortunate that the explosion occurred in the new office building, which held up even though it appeared that the explosion had lifted the structure from its foundation. It was felt that the old factory area would certainly have been destroyed.

Contracts for construction of a new main plant in Fort Madison were signed in 1950. Construction was completed in 1952, and the Morrison Plow Works, which had served the company for over three eventful decades, was razed to become an employee parking lot. Sheaffer employees wrote a message to their counterparts of the year 2001. The documents were placed in a tube and sealed in the walls of the lobby of the new building.

In November, 1951, the 50 millionth Sheaffer pen came off the assembly line.

New emphasis was placed on research and development during the Fifties. Early in the decade the building that would house R & D facilities was enlarged and a complete second story added.

The Snorkel fountain pen, introduced in 1952, sparked a sales surge for Sheaffer in the mid Fifties. It was developed in great secrecy and launched with the greatest promotional campaign in the company's history.

Craig Sheaffer resigned as president in 1953 to become an Assistant Secretary of Commerce in Washington, D. C. Walter A. Sheaffer II succeeded him as president to direct the company through the closing years of its first half century.

In the mid Fifties Sheaffer employees pioneered in the development of the cartridge pen, which was to become the sales leader in fountain pens within a few years.

Hundreds of companies entered the writing instrument industry during the Fifties. By mid-decade, there were well over 200, as opposed to the 50 companies that had been in business a few years before. Many of these were extremely small operations selling unbranded, low-cost ballpoint pens. Singly, they were minor factors. As a group, they made a sizeable impression on the market and posed a new challenge for well-established brand manufacturers like Sheaffer.

In 1953 the company established a Tool and Die Division and built a new plant in Fort Madison on the site of the old button factory purchased after the war. In 1957 Sheaffer entered a field unrelated to writing instruments for the first time, purchasing Maico Electronics of Minneapolis, a manufacturer of hearing aids, acoustical equipment and miniature electronic devices.

For maximum efficiency, all domestic writing instrument manufacturing was consolidated in Fort Madison with the closing of the Mt. Pleasant plant.

Furnished and reprinted with permission by Sheaffer-Eaton, div. Textron. Also based in part on *The Palimpsest*, September 1952 by the State Historical Society of Iowa.

Sheaffer's Jewelry Store in Bloomfield about 1895.

W.A. and J.R. Sheaffer standing in doorway.

W.A. Sheaffer Pen Company:

Extract of Product Development

1907   W.A. Sheaffer invented lever filler mechanism

1908   Lever filler mechanism was patented.

1912   Second patent was issued for an improved pressure bar and lever construction.
1912   First production of Sheaffer pens.

1913   W.A. Sheaffer Pen Co. was incorporated in Iowa.

1914-1921   Introduction of long straight clip with large ball; imprinted Sheaffer-Clip.

1918   Propel-repel pencil was introduced and named Sharp Point.

1920   Lifetime pen was introduced

1921   Introduction of propel-repel-expel pencil.
1921-1929   Long straight clip with large ball; imprinted Sheaffer's.

1922   Formulation of Skrip Ink.

1924   Introduction of Pyroxylin (Radite) non-breakable barrels and caps.
1924   White Dot trademark was introduced.
1924   Oriental Mosaic was introduced in hand enameled and laquered yellow and green gold filled pens and pencils.
1924-1932   Jade Green color for pens and pencils was introduced.
1924-1945   Jet Black color for pens and pencils was introduced.
1924-1928   Introduction of Loaner pen, also called "Service Pen".
1924   First Sheaffer desk pen was introduced with fixed socket and metal base.

1925-1932   Long clip with hump and small ball; imprinted Sheaffer's.
1927   Desk Set with swivel socket was introduced.
1925   Introduction of the Titan extra large pencil.
1925   The Lifetime Student pen was introduced.

Sheaffer Product Development Continued...

1928	Split cap bands appeared on Sheaffer pens for the first time.
1928-1934	Black and Pearl design for pens and pencils was introduced.
1929	Introduction of Safety Skrip Bottle made of plastic.
1930	Introduction of Balanced Pen, streamlined with tapered ends.
1930	Marine Green and Black design was introduced.
1930-1931	Desk & pocket pen combination was introduced.
1930-1931	Pen and pencil combination introduced; never gained popularity.
1931	Introduction of Feather Touch with two-way point and Pladium plating.
1931	Autograph pens and pencils with 14K solid gold wide engraving bands were announced.
1931-1935	Grey Pearl with red veining design for pens and pencils.
1933-1934	Short clip with hump and small ball.
1933	Skrip bottle gets top well feature.
1934-1940	A low priced line named Wasp introduced.
1934	Plunger type sacless filling mechanism featuring visible ink supply introduced in Wasp Clipper.
1934-1936	Black and Grey Pearl design for pens and pencils.
1934-1938	Black with inlaid Mother-of-Pearl introduced for pens and pencils.
1935-1936	Short clip with hump and flattened ball; one year only.
1935-1949	Vac-Fil (Sacless) filling system added to Sheaffer pens.
1936-1943	Long clip (no hump) with rigid radius and flattened ball.
1936	Transparent gripping section to view ink supply.
1936-1939	Striated rose colored caps and barrels for pens and pencils.
1936-1945	Striated brown and gold colored caps and barrels for pens and pencils.
1936-1945	Striated black and grey pearl colored caps and barrels for pens and pencils.
1938	Introduction of the Fineline pencil utilizing lead 39% smaller.
1938-1945	Marine Green and black striated color for pens and pencils.
1939-1945	Red Pearl and black striated color for pens and pencils.
1939	Crest model with metal cap introduced.
1940-1941	Introduction of Clicker type pencil.
1940-1943	Over the top clip (military clip) for pens and pencils.
1941	Absorbent Magic Circle in ink bottle cap to keep threads clean on bottle.
1942	First Triump Lifetime conical nib introduced.
1945-1952	Clasp tuckaway clip on some models.
1945-1948	Solid Radite colors for pens and pencils.
1943-1977	Long clip with inner spring in cap.
1946	Introduction of first ballpoint pen called RAI Stratowriter made of gold filled metal.
1946	Slip on cap introduced for Stratowriter to protect clothing from ink.
1947	Safeguard Desk Set introduced.
1948	Introduction of injection molded plastic caps and barrels.

Sheaffer Product Development Continued...

1949   Touch Down pen filling system introduced.

1950   TM Thin Model pen line introduced.

1952   TM Thin Model pencil line introduced.
1952   Introduction of the Snorkel pen filling mechanism.
1952   First clicker type ball point introduced.

1953-1957   Tip Dip feed introduced for some models.

1955   Introduction of first low priced cartridge fountain pen.
1956   RC35 Skrip Ink with luminescent feature introduced.

1957-1958   Sterling silver tip to hold ball in ball point pen.

1958   Lady Sheaffer line in 19 designs introduced.

1959   PFM, Pen For Men line introduced with large diameter, inlaid nib.

1960   Lady Sheaffer line reduced to five designs.

1961   Safe guard clip with retractable mechanism.

1963-69   Lifetime cartridge pens introduced.

1965   Smoothie Marker pen with porous plastic marking tip.
1965   Twinwell FINE tip marker introduced.

1966   Stylus line introduced in slim pen, pencil and marker.

1967   Introduced Deskette desk pen and socket with adhesive for attaching to phone, etc.

1969   Soft Stroke ink marker introduced.
1969   No-Nonsense line of pens — copies of 1915-1918 pens.

1970   Nostalgia line; recreation of gold and silver filagree pens, limited quantities.

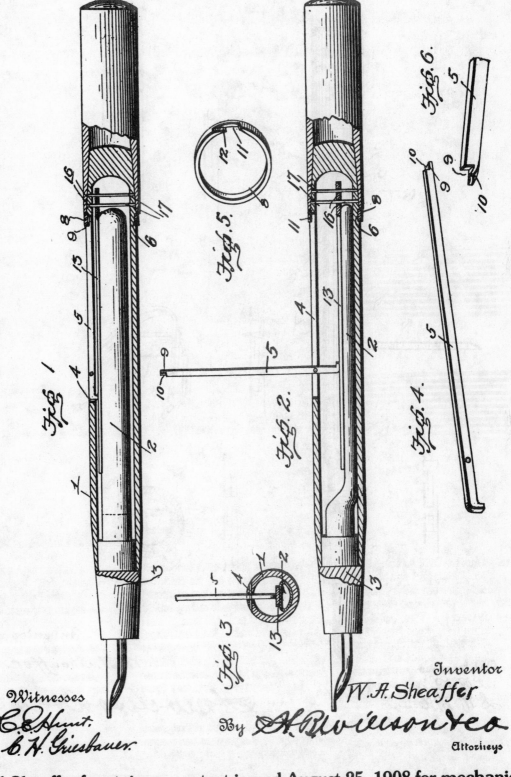

No. 896,861.

PATENTED AUG. 25, 1908.

W. A. SHEAFFER.
FOUNTAIN PEN.
APPLICATION FILED MAR. 2, 1908.

Fig. 1

Fig. 5.

Fig. 6.

Fig. 2.

Fig. 4.

Fig. 3

Witnesses
C. E. Hunt.
C. H. Griesbauer.

Inventor
W. A. Sheaffer
By H. R. Williamson & Co
Attorneys

The original Sheaffer fountain pen patent issued August 25, 1908 for mechanical lever filler.

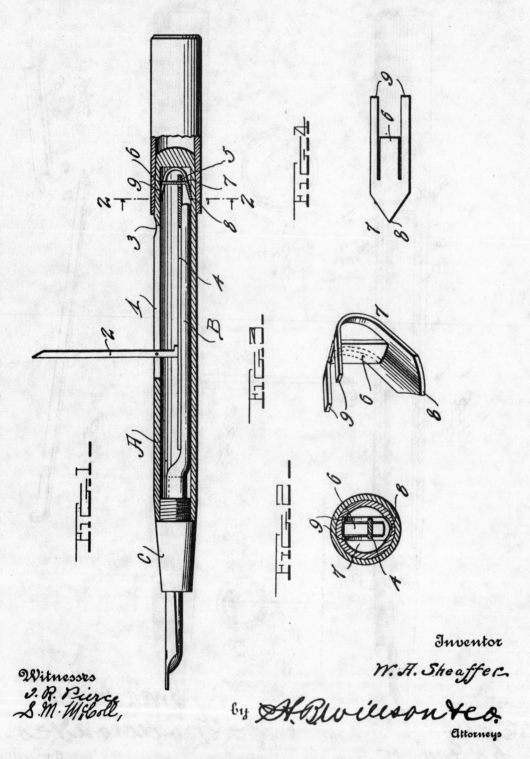

W. A. SHEAFFER.
FOUNTAIN PEN ATTACHMENT.
APPLICATION FILED MAR. 21, 1912.

1,046,660.   Patented Dec. 10, 1912.

Witnesses
J. R. Pierce
S. M. McColl,

Inventor
W. A. Sheaffer
by H. B. Willson & Co.
Attorneys

Sheaffer's improved filler mechanism. Patent issued December 10, 1912.

Price List of Parts and Repairs
For Sheaffer Self-Filling Pens.

When a new Gold Pen or any repairs are needed, send complete PEN, so new and old parts will fit perfectly.

Always mark your name and address and street number plainly on package. We will return package the same way it is received, unless otherwise instructed. If you desire package RETURNED BY REGISTERED MAIL, enclose additional STAMPS for same. WE WILL NOT BE RESPONSIBLE FOR PACKAGE SENT IN OPEN MAIL.

Empty out ink before mailing. Always send cash for repairs, which must include return postage.

Catalogue No.	FEED BAR	PEN SECT'N	CAP	BARREL	LEVER	METAL BAR	END PIECE	Ink Reser.	Allowance Old Pens on New No.	Each	GOLD PENS No.	Each
2 and 3	.30	.40	.30	.75	.30	.20	.10	.15	2	.20	2	1.00
4, 5 and 6	.35	.50	.40	1.40	.30	.20	.10	.15	3	.30	3	1.25
8	.40	.60	.50	1.85	.30	.20	.10	.15	4	.40	4	1.50
21 and 31	.30	.40	1.30	.75	.30	.20	.10	.15	5	.50	5	2.00
41, 51 and 61	.35	.50	1.40	1.40	.30	.20	.10	.15	6	.60	6	2.65
81	.40	.60	1.50	1.85	.30	.20	.10	.15	8	.80	8	4.00
34	.30	.50	.40	1.40	.30	.20	.10	.15				
341	.30	.50	1.40	1.40	.30	.20	.10	.15				

W. A. Sheaffer Pen Company, Fort Madison, Iowa, U. S. A.

GOLD PENS Repointed or straightened for 50 cents each. Repointed pens are not warranted to wear well nor to have same quality of point, as new pens. Pens smaller than No. 4 are seldom worth repointing.

1916

BULL'S EYE of PERFECTION

SHEAFFER'S FOUNTAIN PEN

THE NEW FAVORITE

Sold on 30 Days' Trial

Manufactured by
W. A. SHEAFFER PEN CO.
FT. MADISON IOWA

Fountain Pen Perfection
HAS BEEN EMBODIED BY SHEAFFER IN HIS

Self-Filling
Self-Cleaning
Non-Leakable
GUARANTEED PEN

Sheaffer's First Fountain Pen Catalog — 1916

SHEAFFER'S SELF-FILLING FOUNTAIN PEN

"THE NEW FAVORITE"

SHEAFFER'S Self-Filling Fountain Pen, the final result of many years experimenting, is the only pen on the market to-day that overcomes every objection of fountain pen users. The "Lever Filler" is the most simple of any filling device yet designed—A small lever sunk in the barrel—so simple it can be easily operated by a one arm writer or with one hand by anyone. Hold the pen between thumb and second finger, catch upper end of lever under nail of first finger, pull down lever, dip in ink, release lever and the pen is filled.

Only two seconds time required and the pen writes instantly. No shaking or coaxing to make it write. The operation of filling, which draws the ink up through the feed channels cleans the pen thoroughly each time.

NON-LEAKABLE

Owing to the peculiar construction, of the screw cap, the SHEAFFER Self-Filling Pen may be carried in any position with absolutely no danger of ink leaking.

Right side up or upside down, it's all the same. The "Lever Filler" cannot be operated by accident. But when you want to fill your pen there are no screws to turn—nothing to unlock—just pull down the lever. The pen fills completely every time the lever is operated, and does not depend on the ingenuity of the user.

This filling device is so cleverly constructed that it is practically invisible. No humps, rings, screws or buttons to bother with, or to mar the beauty of the pen. There is no forgetting to close the lever. It must be closed to get ink. No chance for accidents, inky fingers, or spoiled temper.

SHEAFFER'S SELF-FILLING FOUNTAIN PEN

THE fountain pen is now recognized as one of the necessities of modern life. Therefore it needs no words of praise from us to increase its favor. It has come to be as natural and important for the student, business and professional man to carry his fountain pen, as it is important and natural for the mechanic to carry his tools.

The Self-Filling pen has replaced the old style (fill with a dropper) in the same manner that the dropper filler replaced the steel pen, and the steel pen the goose quill.

In this world of rapid progress it was inevitable that some one would invent an improved and more perfect Self-Filling Fountain Pen, than the pen which replaced the dropper filler. Following the inevitable law of the survival of the fittest, when the new and better article comes along the old is pushed aside and becomes a thing of the past.

SHEAFFER'S Self-Filling Pen is the result of many years of study and experimenting on the part of the inventor, Mr. W. A. SHEAFFER. The men associated with him in the manufacture of this pen have had abundant experience in the fountain pen business. The SHEAFFER pen has been perfected to such an extent that to-day it has no rival worthy of the name as it stands head and shoulders above its nearest competitor.

Sheaffer's 1916 Catalog Continued...

SHEAFFER'S FOUNTAIN PEN

WRITING QUALITIES

The best thing about the SHEAFFER Self-Filling Pen from the user's standpoint is the ease with which it writes. You never have to jerk or coax the SHEAFFER Pen to write; it is always ready. Writes the instant you touch it to the paper. You can write fast or slow, forward or back hand and always there will be the steady, even flow of ink, which has won for the SHEAFFER its exalted position among fountain pens. The Air Chamber between the ink reservoir and the inside of the barrel keeps the SHEAFFER from sweating or dropping ink.

The Screw Cap with its air tight chamber keeps the pen point always moist and free from corrosion.

Nothing has been overlooked to make the SHEAFFER the most perfect and convenient pen possible to produce.

The best materials money can buy and an army of the most skilled workmen of the craft insure the SHEAFFER Self-Filling Pen to be perfect in every detail and the acme of fountain pen manufacturing.

SECTIONAL VIEWS OF SHEAFFER'S SELF-FILLING FOUNTAIN PEN.

View No. 1 shows elastic ink reservoir filled and "Lever Filler" closed. Also shows pen point in air tight chamber in cap. Notice how the end of the feed section fits tightly against the shoulder of cap forming the air tight chamber. This makes it impossible for the SHEAFFER Pen to leak, no matter in what position you may carry it. View No. 2 Shows "Lever Filler" open and elastic ink reservoir compressed ready for filling.

The cleaning and filling principles of the SHEAFFER Self-Filling Pen are most simple. Inside the barrel is the elastic ink reservoir made of soft rubber (View No. 1). To fill the SHEAFFER Pen, it is only necessary to pull down the "Lever Filler" as shown in View No. 2 compressing the elastic ink reservoir, then dip pen in ink, release lever, and it is filled instantly. The simple filling operation also cleans the pen automatically each time it is filled and you have no trouble with your pen becoming clogged up. If it is sometime necessary to give the pen a thorough cleaning on account of having poor ink or changing color of ink,

SHEAFFER'S FOUNTAIN PEN

cold water may be drawn in and discharged in the same manner as the ink. However if good writing fluid is used, the SHEAFFER Pen seldom needs cleaning.

You will notice in sectional view No. 2 that when the "Lever Filler" is opened, the ink reservoir is completely compressed, insuring the pen being filled to full capacity each time. In other Self-Filling pens the ink reservoir is not always compressed, as on account of their construction, whether the pen is filled completely or not depends entirely upon the ingenuity of the user.

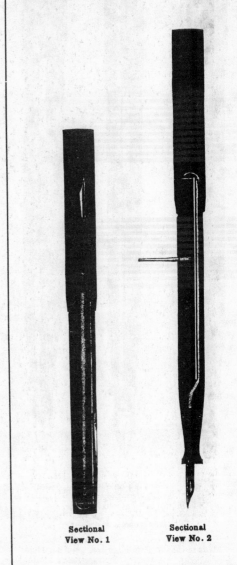

Sectional View No. 1   Sectional View No. 2

Sheaffer's 1916 Catalog Continued...

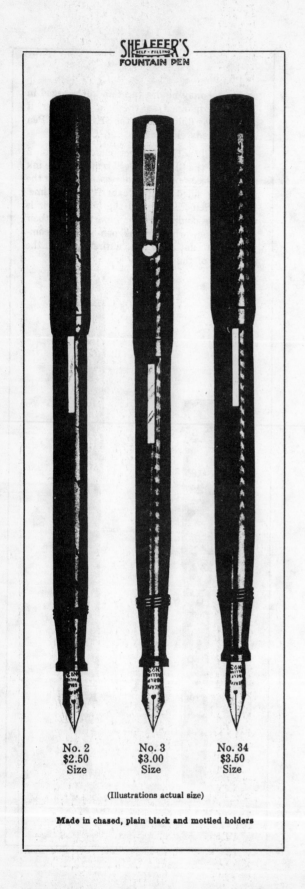

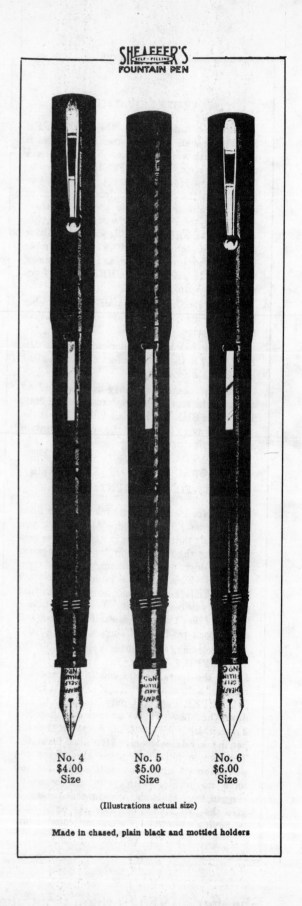

Sheaffer's 1916 Catalog Continued...

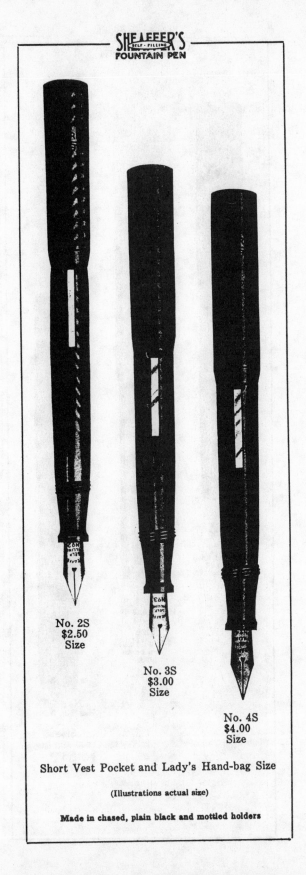

No. 2S
$2.50
Size

No. 3S
$3.00
Size

No. 4S
$4.00
Size

Short Vest Pocket and Lady's Hand-bag Size

(Illustrations actual size)

Made in chased, plain black and mottled holders

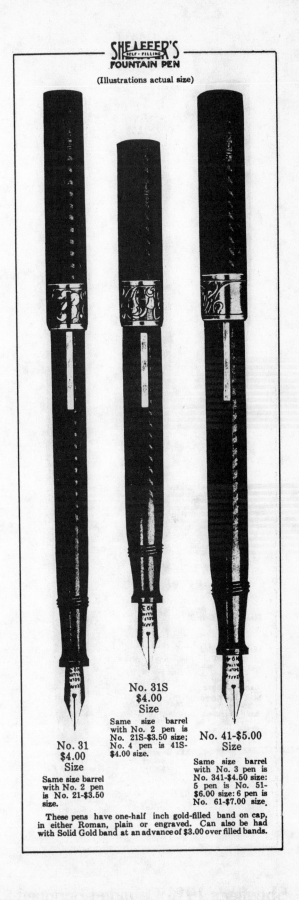

(Illustrations actual size)

No. 31S
$4.00
Size

Same size barrel
with No. 2 pen is
No. 21S-$3.50 size;
No. 4 pen is 41S-
$4.00 size.

No. 31
$4.00
Size

Same size barrel
with No. 2 pen
is No. 21-$3.50
size.

No. 41-$5.00
Size

Same size barrel
with No. 3 pen is
No. 341-$4.50 size:
5 pen is No. 51-
$6.00 size: 6 pen is
No. 61-$7.00 size.

These pens have one-half inch gold-filled band on cap,
in either Roman, plain or engraved. Can also be had
with Solid Gold band at an advance of $3.00 over filled bands.

Sheaffer's 1916 Catalog Continued...

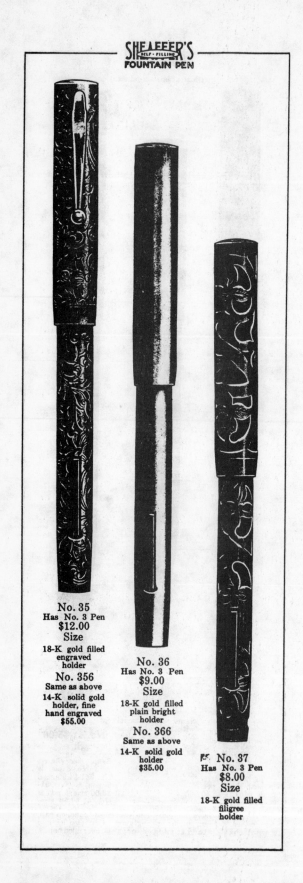

No. 35
Has No. 3 Pen
$12.00
Size
18-K gold filled
engraved
holder

No. 356
Same as above
14-K solid gold
holder, fine
hand engraved
$55.00

No. 36
Has No. 3 Pen
$9.00
Size
18-K gold filled
plain bright
holder

No. 366
Same as above
14-K solid gold
holder
$35.00

No. 37
Has No. 3 Pen
$8.00
Size
18-K gold filled
filigree
holder

No. 35S
Has No. 3 Pen
$12.00
Size
18-K gold filled
engraved
holder

No. 36S
Has No. 3 Pen
$9.00
Size
18-K gold filled
plain bright
holder

No. 37S
Has No. 3 Pen
$8.00
Size
18-K gold filled
filigree
holder

Sheaffer's 1916 Catalog Continued...

SHEAFFER'S
SELF-FILLING
FOUNTAIN PEN

SHEAFFER'S POCKET CLIP.

Attached to Any Sheaffer Pen, Metal 25c;
Gold Filled, $1.00; Solid Gold, $2.00.

The SHEAFFER Pocket Clip completes the SHEAFFER pen in every detail It is fastened at the top of cap with two arms extending through to the inside of cap and there being securely fastened, the end of the clip rests on a strong coil spring which fits in a pocket running straight across inside of the cap. This gives the SHEAFFER Clip the elastic and holding power necessary, and still makes it possible to attach to the pocket with one hand. It is fastened to the cap in such a manner as to not interfere with the air tight chamber or non-leakable feature of the pen.

This makes it the only attached clip to a Self-Filling, Non-Leakable Pen on the market.

OUR GOLD PENS.

The gold pens used in the SHEAFFER Self-Filling Pen are as good as can possibly be produced. We use 14K gold which is hand tempered and finished by the most skilled workmen to be found. Every variety of points can be had; in fact if you have a pen point that you are fond of, send it to us and we will make you an exact duplicate. Our gold nibs are pointed with the best grade of hard iridium. This metal comes from the Ural Mountains, of Russia and should not be compared with soft iridium used by most pen manufacturers.

SHEAFFER'S
SELF-FILLING
FOUNTAIN PEN

DIRECTIONS TO USERS OF SHEAFFER'S SELF-FILLING PEN.

When Filling—The first time, fill and expel the ink several times, so ink will adhere to pen point.

To Fill—Raise Lever until it is at right angles with barrel. Submerge gold pen and end of holder in ink. Close lever allowing pen to remain in ink for a few seconds until elastic ink reservoir has fully expanded.

To Clean—Place gold pen and end of holder in cold water, working lever back and forth several times.

Cap—Cap must be screwed on firmly to insure against leaking; always keep cap on pen when not in use.

Ink—Avoid muddy and Gummy Ink, special fountain-pen ink is best.

CAUTION—This pen is put together and adjusted by fountain-pen experts, and will not give satisfaction if taken apart or altered in any way.

A pen should be used several days, giving it a chance to get thoroughly wet. If it fails to write properly, after a fair trial, take it to the nearest SHEAFFER DEALER or mail it to us. We want every user of a SHEAFFER SELF-FILLING PEN, to be thoroughly satisfied.

W. A. SHEAFFER PEN COMPANY
FORT MADISON, IOWA, U. S. A.

Sheaffer's 1916 Catalog Continued...

FRONT VIEW OF 12-DOZEN FLOOR CASE.
Made also in 18, 24 and 36-Dozen Sizes.

SHEAFFER DISPLAY CASES.

The above is a photographic reproduction (front view) of the SHEAFFER 12-doz. floor case.

This case is built to show our pens to the best possible advantage, also with a view of enabling you to handle your fountain pen department in a convenient and profitable manner.

The case shown is in Golden Oak finish. However, we will furnish these cases in any finish desired, to match store fixtures.

The fronts of these cases are finished in plain panel with an ebony inlaid border. The back has a jeweler's mirror sliding drop door which allows dealer to handle his stock with perfect ease.

The lower part of the case is designed to hold surplus stock, advertising matter and supplies. THE GLASS USED IN THESE CASES IS HEAVY PLATE GLASS WITH POLISHED EDGE. IT IS PUT TO-GETHER WITH CLAMPS AND FELT WHICH MAKES IT AN ABSOLUTELY DUST PROOF CASE. The case stands on heavy solid bronze legs, six inches from the floor, making it a thoroughly sanitary case.

Taken altogether the SHEAFFER Floor Case is the finest looking and most sub-stantial of any show case ever built for displaying fountain pens.

Back View of 12-Dozen Floor Case.

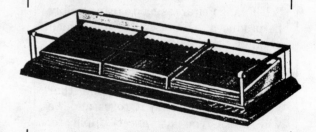

Three-Dozen Counter Display Case.

Also made in Two, Four and Six-Dozen Sizes.
Any Finish Desired.

Sheaffer's 1916 Catalog Continued...

The assembly and final inspection assures a perfect product.

All nibs are ground to perfect points of satin smoothness in the Sheaffer factory.

W. A. SHEAFFER
PRESIDENT
W. A. SHEAFFER PEN COMPANY

The 14K gold nib is tipped by hand with the hardest native iridium.

Pure minted gold from the government is melted and alloyed to make the Sheaffer pen.

Ball points, of iridium are fused to the nib of each pen.

All barrels, caps, and parts are shaped and polished in the Sheaffer plant.

Reprinted From Sheaffer's 1925 Catalog

Sheaffer Pen Points

Every operation in the construction of the Sheaffer pen is thoroughly inspected and tested to assure the dealer of securing perfect merchandise. Points of superiority in the Sheaffer pen give special selling arguments to dealers and their clerks in the sale of this product.

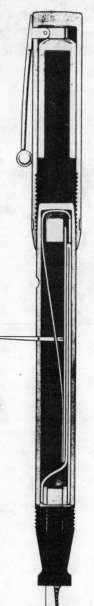

1. Clip inserted in cap and over inside cap so it cannot pull out.

2. Clip shank of optical spring metal that will retain its spring and holds firmly.

3. Ball clip tip holds firmly to any cloth, easy to slip over edge of pocket, and holds tightly without wearing or tearing the cloth.

4. Inside cap securely anchors the clip and forms an air-tight chamber for the point so it cannot leak or sweat in your pocket.

5. Section firmly seated against inner cap by perfectly cut threads. Screw cap prevents pen coming open in the pocket.

6. Banded cap avoids breakage and improves appearance.

7. Large sack of finest rubber latex permits plentiful supply of ink.

8. Filling mechanism lies flat, requires little room and is firmly fastened in place.

9. Filling lever fastened into place and locks in slot in the bar holding it in place. Remains flush and does not extend beyond barrel of pen.

10. Thumb-nail recess permits easy lifting of lever for filling.

11. Pressure bar entirely deflates sack and springs back when released. Return of filling mechanism to normal position does not depend on strength or elasticity of sack, which, therefore, expends energy to draw in the ink.

12. Lever is sufficiently long to entirely deflate the sack and assure a full ink supply.

13. Rubber section conveniently shaped to fit the fingers when writing.

14. Special comb feed assures instant flow of ink without skipping or flooding.

15. Points of solid 14K gold, alloyed and shaped in our own factory.

16. Points tipped with special iridium — hardest known metal. Iridium is fused on the gold tip and ground to a smooth writing ball point by our own jewel grinders.

17. Distinctive shape of the ring in all Sheaffer ring pens is designed for the purpose of permitting the ring to be fastened in the split ring of any loose-leaf binder.

All Sheaffer Pens are guaranteed against any defects or flaws of materials and construction.

Reprinted From Sheaffer's 1925 Catalog

SHEAFFER'S
PENCIL

The guarantee on the Sheaffer pencil is not a guarantee of implied perfection but is positive and definite, covering all the separate parts of the pencil, guaranteeing them unconditionally against imperfections or defects of material or construction. If, at any time, the pencil proves defective, it is to be returned to the factory and will be replaced without charge, providing the pencil does not show the results of misuse or abuse.

The points of superiority of this product are as follows:

1. Patented bell-shaped cap, light weight, neat design; not easily dented or mashed like a heavy, bulging cap.

2. Clip is firmly clinched through the barrel of pencil; no solder used in mechanism or barrel.

3. Spring clip shank of spring optical metal that retains its "spring" and holds firmly.

4. Ball clip tip holds firmly to any cloth. Easy to slip over edge of pocket and holds tightly without tearing or wearing the cloth.

5. Easily accessible lead magazine that holds a generous supply of leads.

6. Renewable eraser conveniently placed under the cap in the end of lead magazine.

7. Barrel of seamless drawn tubing—strong and not easily dented.

8. Drive shaft of pencil is light weight but durable tube—no threads to strip or wear out.

9. Fibre friction washer holds entire mechanism always firm so lead does not slip back.

10. Propel spiral screw, cut from solid brass rod, assures smooth operation of pencil and great strength.

11. Friction block, inserted under thirty pounds pressure, and seated without the use of solder. No solder used in the entire barrel.

12. Carrier of non-corrosive spring metal, will take indelible lead or crayon without rusting, springs into shape after using oversize leads and easily holds smaller leads.

13. Waspalumin push rod propelled by propel screw, drives through carrier and expels the last particle of unused lead. Clears tip so it cannot jam or clog.

14. Tip of same metal as barrel of pencil except the Jet, red and Jade pencils, the barrels are made of Radite. Improved appearance and will take oversize leads without jamming or clogging.

Reprinted From Sheaffer's 1925 Catalog

Lifetime Desk Set

When a fountain pen is open and left lying on the desk, the nib quickly dries out, and when required for use again, it will not write promptly. This objection to a fountain pen for desk use has been overcome with the Sheaffer Lifetime Desk Set. The pens in these sets are regular Sheaffer Lifetime pens with holders eight and one-half inches long that fit into statuary bronze finished desk receptacles. The nib fits into an almost air-tight compartment that protects it against damage and prevents it from drying out so it will always be ready for immediate use.

Sets are sold Single or Double, but pens are not sold separately from sets.

A rapid selling and perfect product, an item for aggressive retailers who maintain outside salesmen, opening up new avenues in sales. When once used, the convenience is so clearly appreciated that they are easily sold.

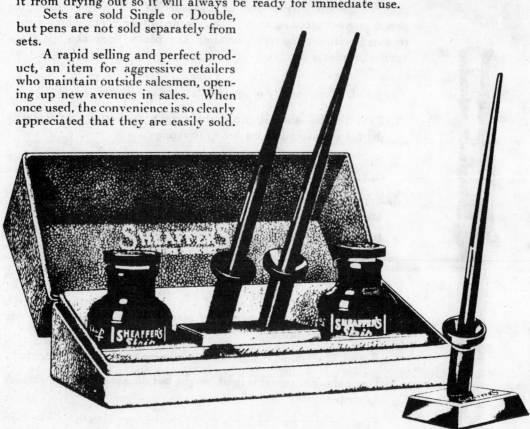

D. Set—Double	S. Set—Single
(Deset)	(Dones)
$20.00	$10.00
1 2 oz. bottle Skrip—red	1 2 oz. bottle Skrip—blue
1 2 oz. bottle Skrip—blue	1 Single Receptacle
1 Double Receptacle	1 No. 84 Lifetime Desk pen—black
1 No. 84 Lifetime Desk Pen—red	
1 No. 84 Lifetime Desk Pen—black	

Each set packed in attractive box.

Reprinted From Sheaffer's 1925 Catalog

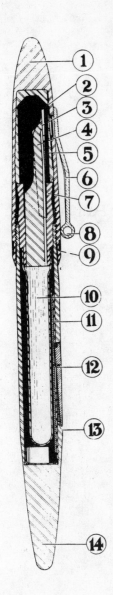

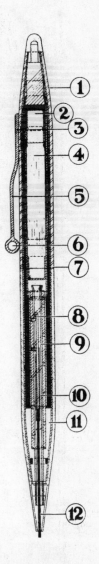

SHEAFFER'S

BALANCED LIFETIME
PEN AND PENCIL

The Balanced Pen:

1. Balanced cap.
2. Precious Iridium point, the world's hardest and one of the most costly metals. Fused on gold tip and ground to smooth writing surface.
3. Nib of 14 karat heavy gold, alloyed and shaped in Sheaffer's factory.
4. Special comb feed assures instant writing fluid flow without skipping or flooding.
5. Inside cap forms airtight chamber. Keeps point moist.
6. Clip shank of optical grade spring metal. Will retain its strength and hold firmly.
7. Section conveniently shaped to fit the fingers and firmly seated against inner cap by perfectly cut threads.
8. Ball clip tip holds firmly without wearing or tearing the cloth.
9. Gold filled band reinforces open end of cap.
10. Large sac of finest rubber latex permits plentiful supply of writing fluid.
11. Filling mechanism lies flat in barrel.
12. Filling lever is firmly fastened in place.
13. Thumb nail recess permits conveniently lifting of bar for filling.
14. Balanced end.

The Balanced Pencil:

1. Balanced end.
2. Renewable eraser conveniently placed in end of lead magazine.
3. Clip firmly clenched on brass bung through the balanced end of pencil, no solder used.
4. Easily accessible lead magazine holding generous supply of leads.
5. Clip shank of optical grade spring metal retains its resiliency and holds firmly.
6. Ball clip tip holds firmly to any cloth without tearing.
7. Barrel of unbreakable Radite.
8. Waspaluminum push rod propelled by propel screw, drives through carrier and expels the last particle of unused lead, clearing tip so it cannot clog or jam.
9. Propel spiral screw cut from heavy brass tube, assures a smooth operation and great strength.
10. Carrier made of non-corrosive spring metal. Will take indelible lead or crayon without rusting.
11. Friction block, inserted under heavy pressure, and seated without the use of solder.
12. Gold filled handsome tip.

Sheaffer's 1929 Lifetime Fountain Pen and Pencil. Cross Section Views

The Sheaffer Pen Company

(Sheaffer-Eaton, Div. Textron)

SHEAFFER'S

Big Business Demands
SHEAFFER'S PEN

Self Filling   Self Cleaning   Non Leakable

—because it embodies *all* the essential features of a
perfect Fountain Pen. Instant service. Steady, reliable
ink flow. Speed and ease from start to finish. Absolute
freedom from ink-spilling—carried in any position.

SHEAFFER'S Pen puts *brains* in your hand.
It is built for the man or woman who has no time to
waste. It is the pen of Big Business. And the pen
of Big Business is the pen for Everybody.

SHEAFFER'S Fountain Pen fills instantly from any
ink-well, with one touch of the finger. Cleans automatically
when filling. Has a smooth, clear surface without humps
or buttons. *SHEAFFER'S Pen is your pen—without a doubt.*

W. A. Sheaffer Pen Co., Fort Madison, Iowa.

Sold
by all
Leading
Dealers
$2.50 Up.

SHEAFFER'S
GUARANTEE

Have your dealer *fit your
hand* with SHEAFFER'S
Fountain Pen. If it fails to
suit you, he will refund your
money without question.

**Self Filling
Self Cleaning
Non Leakable**

New York   Chicago   Kansas City   Fort Madison

Sheaffer Advertisement — September 1914

Sheaffer Advertisement — 1916

WIN $350 WITH A SHEAFFER PEN

The SHEAFFER PEN is far the most practical and *always reliable* fountain pen. It does not leak. It always gives an even, steady flow of ink. It does not blot. It is ink-tight (carry it anywhere, anyhow)! It fills itself instantly by means of the lever self-filling device. There is nothing to lock nor forget to lock. Your favorite steel pen duplicated in a SHEAFFER. *Try the Pen and Test Your Skill in This Contest.* We want to give the public striking proof of

THE MERITS OF SHEAFFER'S SELF FILLING PEN

For this purpose, we offer $350.00 to the man, woman or child (expert engravers and draughtsmen excepted) who writes this sentence, "The Sheaffer Fountain Pen Has the Merits of All and the Faults of None," the greatest number of times upon a contest card supplied by one of our dealers.

There are but two conditions to be observed by competitors for this $350.00 prize: First, the sentence must be written with a Sheaffer Pen or a pen manufactured by the Sheaffer Pen Company; Second, the writing must be legible and done on a contest card furnished by a Sheaffer dealer. In case of a tie between contestants the full prize will be paid to each and the winning card or cards will be published. Get a contest card and the rules governing this interesting prize offer now. Contest closes December 21st, 1916.

SOLD BY GOOD DEALERS EVERYWHERE

Our No 2 $2.50 With Clip $2.75

W. A. SHEAFFER PEN CO. FORT MADISON, IOWA, U.S.A.

Sheaffer Advertisement — 1916

This Is The Pen

which has caused a greater stir among makers of fountain pens and dealers who sell them than any other fountain pen ever manufactured.

Its wonderful *lever self-filling device* has inaugurated a new principle in fountain pens. It is so much simpler and more effective that makers are abandoning every other type of self-filling in an effort to imitate the *Sheaffer*— and imitations only emphasize the quality of the *Sheaffer*.

Not only is the pen far in advance of other makes in its self-filling device; it always gives a steady, even flow of ink; doesn't blot; doesn't dry out. And it is ink tight no matter how you carry it. Your favorite steel pen can be duplicated in a SHEAFFER.

Ask to see the *Sheaffer* at your dealer's. If you don't know who has it, write

W. A. SHEAFFER PEN COMPANY

Fort Madison, Iowa

This is our No. 2—$2.50. Others up to $50. Write for catalog.

SHEAFFER'S
STEADY-FLOW SELF-FILLING
FOUNTAIN PEN

Sheaffer Advertisement — 1916

SHEAFFER'S
Self Filling Fountain Pen and Sharp Point Pencil
THE WORLD'S BEST WRITING INSTRUMENTS

There's a style to suit the taste and purse of every giver

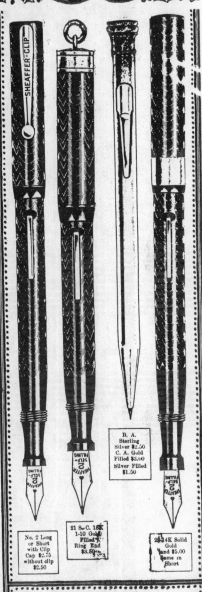

B. A. Sterling Silver $2.50 C. A. Gold Filled $3.00 Silver Filled $1.50

No. 2 Long or Short with Clip Cap $2.75 without clip $2.50

21 S. C. 18K 1-10 Gold Filled Ring End $3.50

24-14K Solid Gold and $5.00 Same in Short

IN selecting a Sheaffer Pen or Sharp Point Pencil for a Christmas gift, you can feel sure that it will not only meet with instant appreciation but will become doubly prized as time proves its daily usefulness and reliability. For the Sheaffer Pen does not blot nor leak and the Sharp Point Pencil is always sharp and always ready for use. The Gift of gifts for Army and Navy Boys.

Sold by Good Dealers Everywhere
UNDER MONEY BACK GUARANTEE

W. A. SHEAFFER PEN CO. Fort Madison, Iowa

SERVICE STATIONS
203 Broadway, New York City
1004 Consumers Bldg., Chicago
Monadnock Bldg., San Francisco

Sheaffer Advertisement — 1918

Sheaffer Advertisement — 1917

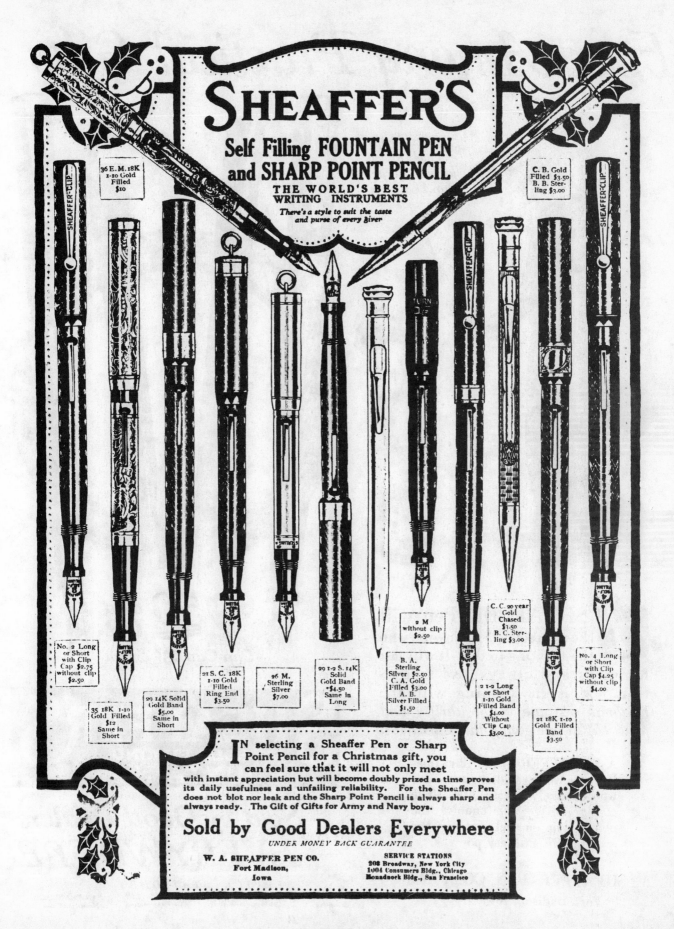

Sheaffer Advertisement — 1917

First Among Practical Gifts

"Jack, this Sheaffer will make it easy for you to write often. Don't forget"

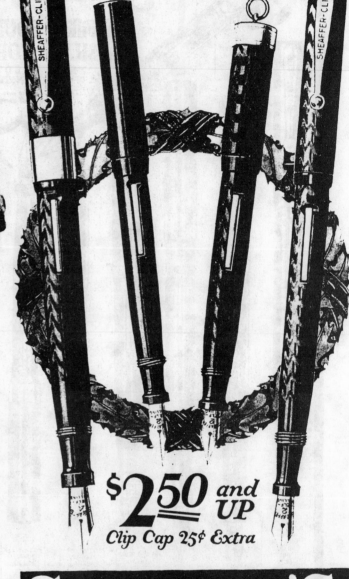

$2 50 and UP

Clip Cap 25¢ Extra

A SHEAFFER Pen will be appreciated by anyone who has writing to do. It will last for years and always give satisfaction. It is in keeping with the *national purpose to be thrifty and practical in our giving this Christmas.*

A SHEAFFER in the Christmas box to your soldier or sailor would surely please him. The *clip at top of cap* enables the pen to fit entirely under the lapel, in military pockets.

SHEAFFER'S
SELF FILLING
FOUNTAIN PEN

Sold by Good Dealers
EVERYWHERE

W. A. SHEAFFER PEN COMPANY
Fort Madison, Iowa

SERVICE STATIONS

NEW YORK CITY	CHICAGO	KANSAS CITY	SAN FRANCISCO
203 Broadway	504 Consumers Bldg.	Gateway Station	Monadnock Bldg.

Sheaffer Advertisement — 1918

Writes the Instant It Touches Paper

YOU use a fountain pen for convenience and to save time. If you have to bother with one, shake it and scratch around for awhile before you get it into working order, you waste more time than you save and are likely to lose your temper as well.

The SHEAFFER pen is always ready for action, and the last drop of ink flows as evenly and as smoothly as the first —*no skipping*, blotting or flooding. It automatically fills and cleans itself with the famous SHEAFFER lever-filler.

Every SHEAFFER pen is Ink Tight, too. You can carry it in any position—drop it in a bag or drawer without fear of leakage. The ink tube opens only to pressure on the point of the pen. It is the practical military pen because it fits down into the soldier's pocket and is *always ready*.

The Sheaffer is the Pen
for Universal Use

$2 50 Up

Clip Cap 25c

Sold by Good Dealers Everywhere

UNDER MONEY BACK GUARANTEE

W. A. SHEAFFER PEN CO.
Fort Madison,
Iowa

SERVICE STATIONS
203 Broadway, New York City
504 Consumers Bldg., Chicago
Monadnock Bldg., San Francisco

Always Ready for Action

The Sheaffer hikes Alaskan trails

Always Writes All Ways

UP in the North World where primitive men once took what came—and weighed the price in gold—they're getting "fussy-like" now.

And why not? Civilization has long since come. Civilization and the Sheaffer Pen. It's kind o' fitting, too; Alaska's the land of *do things*. The Sheaffer's the pen that does things.

The *Sheaffer Pen always writes all ways* so long as there's a drop of ink inside. It does not leak or blot, flood, sweat or skip.

In Greenland—in Patagonia—wherever men make marks-- some one has introduced the Sheaffer—the world's best pen. It's use is a happy habit. Sold by good dealers everywhere.

W. A. SHEAFFER PEN COMPANY
14-B Sheaffer Building, Fort Madison, Iowa
Service Stations:

New York, 440-4 Canal Street   Kansas City, Gateway Station
Chicago, 504 Consumers' Building   San Francisco, Monadnock Building

THE pen illustrated is No. 5, price, with clip, $5.25, a style that men are strong for. Dainty styles for dainty women, too. Other styles $2.75 and up with clip-cap.

SHEAFFER SHARP-POINT Pencil—a new idea in simplicity. Beautiful designs in silver-filled, sterling, gold-filled, solid gold. Pay as little as $1.00 for the Sheaffer Pencil with pocket-clip—as much as $50.00 for solid gold.
The Sheaffer SHARP-POINT Pencil illustrated is the Puritan style, in Sterling silver, No. BD—Price $3.00. In gold filled, No. CD—Price $3.50. In solid gold, No. DD—Price $22.50. ©1919 W.A.S.P.Co.

SHEAFFERS
SELF FILLING FOUNTAIN PEN

Sheaffer Advertisement — June 1919

On Land or Sea

In every place, position, or condition—when there is writing to do—the Sheaffer pen does it—to its last ink drop.

The Sheaffer *always writes all ways*—writes at the first touch. It can't blot, flood, skip, or ink the fingers. That's because of the special patented Sheaffer features. It is a perfect writing instrument.

And that, after all, is the character test of a pen.

Many beautiful models and mountings—for men, women—little folks, too. Sold by good dealers everywhere.

W. A. SHEAFFER PEN COMPANY

14C Sheaffer Bldg., Fort Madison, Iowa

Service Stations

New York, 203 Broadway
Chicago, 504 Consumer's Building
Kansas City, Gateway Station
San Francisco, Monadnock Building

Sheaffer "Giftie" Combination Sets consisting of Sheaffer Pen mounted in Sterling silver and Sheaffer SHARP-POINT Pencil, Sterling—Price $9.50. Combination set, gold filled—Price $13.50. Solid gold—Price $61.50.

Always Writes All Ways

Sheaffer Pens come in a variety of styles and prices, from $2.75 with clip cap and up.

The one above illustrated is No. 366 CRM mounted in 14K. gold—Price $30.00. In rolled gold, No. 36 CRM—Price $8.00. In Sterling silver No. 26 CRM—Price $7.00.

Sheaffer SHARP-POINT Pencils—good as the pen—entirely new idea—are simplified—efficient. From $1.00 to $50.00 with pocket clip.

The Sheaffer SHARP-POINT Pencil here illustrated is the Puritan style. In Sterling silver, No. BD—Price $3.00. In Gold filled, No. CD—Price $3.50. In Solid Gold, No. DD—Price $22.50.

SHEAFFERS
SELF FILLING FOUNTAIN PEN

Sheaffer Advertisement — August 1919

Sheaffer Advertisement — October 1919

A Never-Forgotten Gift

At any hour—in any place—day after day —the SHEAFFER pen proves itself the perfect writing instrument.

The SHEAFFER is a favorite gift for Yuletide, because like a story without end, this gift goes on—It *always writes all ways*. At the lightest touch, with ease and precision it goes—smoothly—fluently—flexibly.

Fluency of thought is never interrupted by blot—blur—sputter or skip. So perfect is the SHEAFFER'S response to the guiding hand, the thought seems transferred of itself to paper.

Special SHEAFFER Features distinguish it from all others. Many beautiful models and mountings—for men, women—little folks, too. Give this never-forgotten Christmas gift—discover its two-fold joy— a joy to give, a joy to receive. Sold by good dealers everywhere

W. A. SHEAFFER PEN COMPANY
149 Sheaffer Building,   Fort Madison, Iowa

New York City, 440-4 Canal St. ⎱ SERVICE ⎰ Kansas City, Gateway Station
Chicago, 604 Consumers Bldg. ⎰ STATIONS ⎱ San Francisco, Monadnock Bldg.

$2.50 and up. with clip cap $2.75 and up.

SHEAFFER Pen illustrated is No. 41-C, with band and clip of rolled gold, price $6.00

SHEAFFER Pen and Sharp-Point PENCIL, in "Giftie" Combination Sets, as shown in the illustration.— in sterling silver, $9.50; gold filled, $13.50; solid gold, $61.50

SHEAFFER'S
FOUNTAIN · SHARP-POINT
PEN · PENCIL

$1 and up

© 1919 W.A.S. Co.

THE SHEAFFER Sharp-Point PENCIL is "as good as the pen." The pencil illustrated is known as the "Engine Turned" Design, No. BB, sterling silver, $3.00; CB, 20-year gold filled, $3.50. Other designs, from $1.00 in nickel to $40.00 in solid gold.

Always Writes All Ways

Sheaffer Advertisement — February 1920

His Diary

Sept. 12—Arrived right side up. School again tomorrow and my SHEAFFER Fountain Pen is filled with words of wisdom. Someone very distracting on the other side of the desk. She is surely *some* peach. It takes a mighty good pen to write under such difficulties.

Her Diary

Sept. 12—Arrived safe. School opens tomorrow and my lovely new SHEAFFER quite prepares me to take down copious notes. Somebody very interesting came and sat opposite me today, and I noticed he uses a SHEAFFER too. So far our tastes agree.

Fashionable Ebony Finished Pen, illustrated below, with plain solid gold band and clip—No. 29C—$8.00

W. A. SHEAFFER PEN COMPANY, 237 SHEAFFER BUILDING, FORT MADISON, IOWA

CHICAGO   NEW YORK   KANSAS CITY   SAN FRANCISCO

Sheaffer Advertisement — August 1920

SHEAFFER'S PEN
AND PENCIL

Use Those 5-Minute Waits for Your Correspondence

CARRY a smooth-flowing SHEAFFER Fountain Pen and acquire this sensible habit of using spare time for writing—it not only makes the wait seem short but keeps you from falling victim to "neglected correspondence." Empty ink wells and scratchy pen points are responsible for most of the procrastination that causes so many letters to begin with—"Pardon my delay." The SHEAFFER Fountain Pen inspires writing not only because it is always ready and handy but it writes so beautifully and faithfully that your thoughts flow as smoothly as the ink.

Select the SHEAFFER best suited to your hand and taste from the varied assortment all Sheaffer dealers show, $2.50 to $50.00

W. A. SHEAFFER PEN COMPANY, 238 SHEAFFER BUILDING, FORT MADISON, IOWA

NEW YORK CHICAGO KANSAS CITY DENVER SAN FRANCISCO

Stylish Chatelaine Model illustrated below — No. 2 M. C. rolled gold crown, $3.50; No. 29 M. C. 14k gold crown, $6.50

Sheaffer Advertisement — October 1920

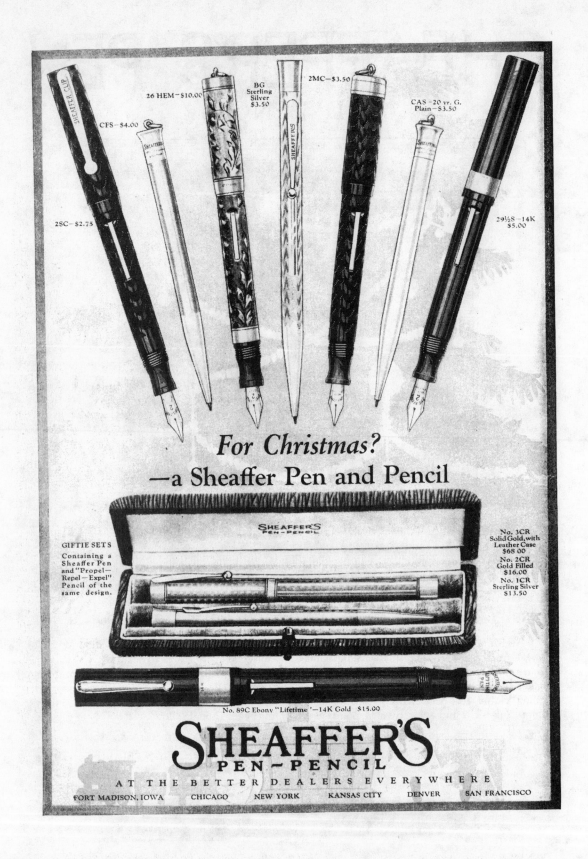

For Christmas?
—a Sheaffer Pen and Pencil

SHEAFFER'S
PEN–PENCIL
AT THE BETTER DEALERS EVERYWHERE
FORT MADISON, IOWA   CHICAGO   NEW YORK   KANSAS CITY   DENVER   SAN FRANCISCO

Sheaffer Advertisement — December 1920

SHEAFFER'S
LIFE TIME PEN

Painted by Coles Phillips expressly for W. A. Sheaffer Pen Co

Life Time Pen
illustrated, with
clip, $8.75

Adopted by Men Who Write in Big Figures

THE "Life Time" SHEAFFER is the most important advancement in Fountain Pen manufacture since the original lever-filler, which was invented by W. A. SHEAFFER. It is larger than the ordinary fountain pen and holds a much greater supply of ink.

Its extra heavy gold nib with indestructible iridium point writes with perfect smoothness and will stand the extra pressure necessary to make clear carbon copies —five, if necessary, just as easily as the hardest lead pencil.

W. A. SHEAFFER PEN COMPANY
301 Sheaffer Bldg., Fort Madison, Iowa

New York   Chicago   Kansas City
          Denver   San Francisco

AT THE BETTER DEALERS EVERYWHERE

SHEAFFER'S
MANIFOLD PEN

"All Right, Let Me Have Your Pen."

HE has landed the order. It remains only to be signed. Now—the crucial moment. Does the pen he carries write without hesitation? Bad thing for him if it doesn't write *perfectly*.

Avoid the risk of such embarrassing moments. Go to any good Stationer, Jeweler or Druggist and ask them to demonstrate to you the SHEAFFER No. 5 Manifold—$5.75 with clip.

That's the pen for you and everyone else who needs a pen that can be depended upon in every emergency, and under all conditions.

W. A. SHEAFFER PEN COMPANY, Fort Madison, Iowa

Chicago   New York   Kansas City   Denver   San Francisco

AT THE BETTER DEALERS EVERYWHERE

No. 5C Manifold Pen illustrated, $5.75   *Other popular models, $2.50 and up*

Sheaffer Advertisement — April 1921

SHEAFFER'S

PEN   PENCIL

The "Giftie Set"

COLES PHILLIPS

Painted by Coles Phillips expressly for the W. A. Sheaffer Pen Co.

A Gift of Irresistible and Enduring Charm

NOWHERE will you find a more pleasing or acceptable gift for Weddings, Birthdays or Graduations than the SHEAFFER Giftie Set—the De Luxe expression of sentiment and admiration.

The beauty, symmetry and mechanical excellence of this rare combination of efficient writing instruments make the SHEAFFER Giftie Set "a thing of beauty and a joy forever."

W. A. SHEAFFER PEN COMPANY, Fort Madison, Iowa

New York   Chicago   Kansas City   Denver   San Francisco

Set No. 1R, Sterling Silver, $13.50—illustrated.   Individual Pens, $2.50 to $50.   Individual Pencils, $1 to $50

AT THE BETTER DEALERS EVERYWHERE

Sheaffer Advertisement — July 1921

A typical mining scene in Tasmania whence comes the precious iridium for Sheaffer Pens
Photo © by W.D.Boyce Co.

11,000 miles away
they unearth the strange metal for this pen point

The South Seas yield more than romance and glamour. In Tasmania they have uncovered a strange, elusive mineral known as iridium. It is the hardest substance known to science, and next to radium the most expensive.

It is out of this odd metal, iridium, that the tip of SHEAFFER's famous "Lifetime" Pen is fashioned. It is the use of this metal, so trying and difficult to apply, that enables us to guarantee the point of "Lifetime" to last forever. It explains why a "Lifetime" point can make five carbon copies of a letter as easily as the hardest lead pencil without the slightest damage to the point, a thing hitherto unheard of in fountain pens.

As a writing companion for business men, travelers and novelists "Lifetime" is unsurpassed. Only $8.75. Other SHEAFFER Pens, $2.50 to $50.

Every SHEAFFER Pen has the original leverfiller—the invention of W.A.Sheaffer

Other "Lifetime" Superiorities
—larger ink capacity
—can't-lose clip
—leak-proof vacuum cap
—quick and simple filling
—the lever principle, invented by W.A.Sheaffer

W. A. SHEAFFER PEN COMPANY
Fort Madison, Iowa

Chicago   New York   Kansas City   Denver   San Francisco

SHEAFFER'S
PEN ~ PENCIL
AT THE BETTER DEALERS EVERYWHERE

Sheaffer Advertisement — October 1921

76,000

Names and Addresses written with a SHEAFFER PEN without repairs or perceptible wear. This unusual feat was accomplished with a Sheaffer Pen owned by Mr. Vuillmot.—See letter.

INTERESTING NEWS FOR EVERY STUDENT OF 1923

(Read carefully about the Lifetime family)

LIFETIME, the Senior Member, with very large ink capacity and unconditionally guaranteed nib.—$8.75

46 SPECIAL, the Youthful member next in size and quality to Lifetime —$5.00

22 STUDENT'S SPECIAL the Youngest Member, greatest value at the price.—$3.75

W. A. SHEAFFER PEN CO. FORT MADISON IOWA

"This is the engine of a fountain pen." Insist that yours bears the name "LIFETIME."

Evidence

700 K Street, N.E.,
Washington, D.C.

W. A. Sheaffer Pen Company,
Fort Madison, Iowa.

Dear Sirs:

It may be of interest to you to know that on September 12, 1922, I left Washington D.C. at 10 o'clock a.m. on a hike to San Francisco, California, chained and handcuffed to a wheelbarrow.

Before starting on this trip I procured from the stock of the Consolidated Supply Co. Stationers and Printers, 1342 G Street, N.W. Washington, D.C. one of the Fountain pens, and a Pencil.

The fountain pen I used in getting signatures and addresses of 76,000 people and in all the trip the pen never failed to write, never changed the point and never had any repairs whatsoever.

I am sending you this pen today so you can see the splendid condition that it is still in after having made this wonderful journey.

As this pen was just one of your regular pens and not made specially for this purpose, I think this has been a wonderful performance.

Yours very truly,

A. L. Vuillmot,
700 K Street, N.E.,
Washington, D.C.

The nibs of the whole Lifetime family are made under the personal supervision of Mr. Winfield H. Kay, the world's master nib maker, which guarantees smoothness of writing and durability.

Make the most economical purchase of your school year by selecting a member of the Lifetime family.

SHEAFFER'S
PENS—PENCILS
AT THE BETTER DEALERS EVERYWHERE

NEW YORK	CHICAGO	SAN FRANCISCO	DENVER
370 Seventh Avenue	506 Republic Bldg.	681 Market St.	502 Jacobsen Bldg.

There is only one Lifetime-- SHEAFFER'S

Identify the Lifetime
pen by this
white dot

Long-life is a matter
of substantial building

It is easy to build for a day. It is difficult to build a
thing that will withstand hard usage for unnumbered
years. But it is not only because of its *durability*
that the pen with the little white dot has had its out-
ranking success. It is a real achievement in art. It is a
faithful performer, instantly responding to the lightest
touch, yet capable of making several carbon copies.
With its brilliant radite barrel and its Sheafferized
nib, it is built for a lifetime of hard service and the
enduring enjoyment that comes from real beauty.

*Onyx or Italian
Marble "Lifetime"
Desk Fountain-
pen Set, $11*

"Lifetime°" pen in green or black, $8.75, Ladies', $7.50—pencil, $4.25
Others lower

At better dealers everywhere

SHEAFFER'S
PENS · PENCILS · SKRIP

W. A. SHEAFFER PEN COMPANY · FORT MADISON, IOWA, U.S.A.
New York   ·   Chicago   ·   San Francisco
W. A. Sheaffer Pen Co. of Canada, Ltd. · Toronto, Ont.—60-62 Front St., W.
Wellington, N. Z. · Sydney, Australia · London—199 Regent St.
° Reg. U. S. Pat. Off.

Sheaffer Advertisement — February 1928

Lifetime° desk fountain pen set complete with green Brazilian onyx base, $15.00 (Obtainable only through Sheaffer dealers.)

Pen springs to ready writing angle.

No retarding grips nor clutches.

Patent internal shoulder forms air-sealed chamber. Keeps pen clean, keeps tip moist.

Patented universal receptacle permits pen to lie flat in desk drawer.

Unseen niceties—
assurance of matchless performance

Sheaffers pay quick dividends. Pens and ink are saved, work goes easier, faster, better. For they excel not alone in styling but in mechanical merit. From their patented receptacles pens come lightly, without grip or hindrance—at the correct writing angle, not at random angles—and with tips moist and ready. Gracious pens in settings of splendor! Qualities prized for a lifetime! Compare thoughtfully. You'll choose Sheaffers!

Identify the Lifetime° Pen by this white dot

Lifetime° desk fountain pen sets, Brazilian onyx base, $12 up. Others $10 up.

At better stores everywhere

SHEAFFER'S
PENS·PENCILS·DESK SETS·SKRIP

W. A. Sheaffer Pen Company, Fort Madison, Iowa, U. S. A.
New York · · · · Chicago · · · San Francisco
W. A. Sheaffer Pen Co. of Can., Ltd. 169-173 Fleet St., Toronto, Ont.
Wellington, N. Z.   Sydney, Australia . 199 Regent St., London
°Reg. U. S. Pat. Off.

Skrip, successor to ink, 25-cent and larger sizes.

© W. A. S. P. Co., 1929

Lifetime Feathertouch WORLD'S LOWEST COST PEN

ONLY SHEAFFER HAS ALL SEVEN

Visulated . . . Lifetime°
Guarantee...2-way Feather-
touch° Point...Streamlined
Balance° . . . ONE-STROKE
Vacuum and Lever Filling,

takes in over 400 per cent
more SKRIP per stroke
than multiple stroke pens
. . . Visible SKRIP supply
. . . Dry-proof, Air-sealed

The White Dot
identifies the
Lifetime° pen

SHEAFFERS

$8.50 to $15   *Visulated*
VISIBLE TO THE LAST DROP · INSULATED FOR PERFECT FLOW

Full length
SKRIP
Visibility

$8.75
and
$10

$3.50

DRY-
PROOF
Desk Set,
with Lifetime
Pen, $10

A LIFETIME OF
SWEET PERFORMANCE—*at a few cents a year*

In a high school, college and business career you can wear out and throw away ten cheap pens. But if you live to a hundred your Sheaffer Lifetime° will not wear out; it is the only Lifetime° pen. With the ten pens you can never have the finest. But your Sheaffer will give endless satisfaction, for "Only Sheaffer Has All Seven of Today's Most Desired Pen Features." Sheaffer's Lifetime°, identified by the white dot, is the economical pen to own, the appropriate gift for graduations, weddings, birthdays, anniversaries, when this lasting token marks a lasting sentiment. Choose Sheaffer's, either Visulated or Vacuum type, each supreme in its field. ***All Sheaffer pen points are made of 14K solid gold for longer life and better writing qualities. Some companies are substituting cheap gold-plated brass and steel to increase profits. Have your dealer guarantee the pen you buy has a 14K solid gold point. If you buy a Sheaffer this guarantee is not necessary.***

SKRIP-WELL

Uses
the
Last
Drop   **15c**

Pen-SKRIP,
Successor
to Ink, 2-oz.
15c. Perma-
nent SKRIP
makes
better
business
records.

SHEAFFER'S
Skrip
THE SUCCESSOR TO INK

SHEAFFER'S

W. A. SHEAFFER PEN CO., FORT MADISON, IOWA • TORONTO, ONTARIO, CANADA
SHEAFFER PENS, ALL COLORS, $2.75 to $20

BOYS!   GIRLS!   GROWN-UPS!

WIN 2 FULLY EQUIPPED FORDS
OVER 1,000 BICYCLES!
°Reg. U.S. Pat. Off.

**FREE Scrap-Book Supplied: at Dealer's, with
Para-Lastik (15c up) or Make or Supply Your Own.**

Two National Contests! Skrip Scrap-Book Contest: use SKRIP
and PARA-LASTIK in your scrap-book—it may win! *ENTER NOW!*
Get Contest Rules at Your Dealer.   (Applies in U.S.A. Only)

Copyright, 1937, W.A. Sheaffer Pen Co.

Sheaffer Advertisement — May 1937

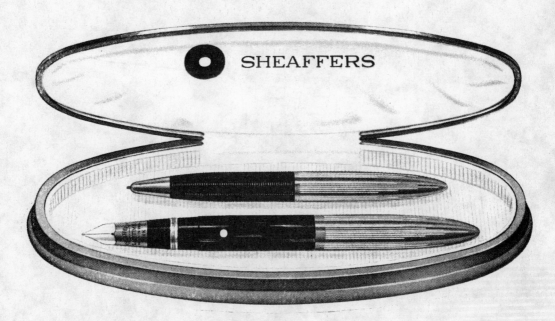

SHEAFFERS

This is the time to *Write!*

Now is the time for all good men and women to come to the aid of their country — with frequent letters to those we know in the U. S. Services at home and afar. You'll be well repaid, too, for you'll get letters back. W. A. Sheaffer Pen Co., Fort Madison, Iowa; Toronto, Ontario, Canada.

★ ★ ★

Above: Sheaffer's newest *Lifetime* *, CREST "TRIUMPH" TUCKAWAY, for men or women, carries safely in all positions in pocket or purse, $18.75 for the set. Other Sheaffer pens, all colors, $2.75 and up.

*All *Lifetime* pens are unconditionally guaranteed for the life of the first user except against loss and willful damage — when serviced, if complete pen is returned, subject only to insurance, postage, handling charge — 35c

Listen to SHEAFFER'S WORLD NEWS PARADE
with UPTON CLOSE
NBC Complete Network — Sundays, 3:15 P.M. E.W.T.;
2:15 P.M. C.W.T.; 1:15 P.M. M.W.T.; 12:15 P.M. P.W.T.

SHEAFFER'S

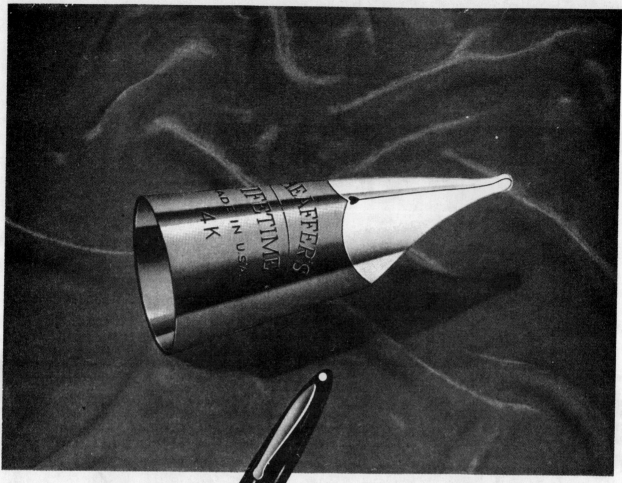

*Lifetime**

RIG. U.S. PAT. OFF.

"TRIUMPH" MODEL

SUPREME VALUE AMONG PENS

Greater worth—not alone in the use of *more* than twice as much gold as other pens selling at the same price—but in *how* and *why* more gold is used! This 14 karat gold Sheath Point, stronger because it is a cylinder, permits a *larger diameter* fluid feeding mechanism giving *safe* fluid control under all atmospheric conditions! W. A. Sheaffer Pen Company, Fort Madison, Iowa; Toronto, Ontario, Canada.

"TRIUMPH" *Lifetime** pen, with clip, $12.50; pencil, $5. "TRIUMPH TUCKAWAY" model, without clip, for men or women, carries safely *in all positions* in purse or pocket—pen, $12.50; pencil, $4. Other sets with 14K gold trim, $35 to $125.

*All *Lifetime* pens, identified by the White Dot, are unconditionally guaranteed for the life of the first user except against loss and willful damage—when serviced, if complete pen is returned, subject only to insurance, postage, handling charge—35c if you send it to the factory yourself; slightly more if you request the dealer to do it for you.

Listen to SHEAFFER'S WORLD PARADE with UPTON CLOSE
NBC Complete Network—Sundays, 3 to 3:30 P.M. E.W.T.;
2 to 2:30 P.M. C.W.T.; 1 to 1:30 P.M. M.W.T.;
12 to 12:30 P.M. P.W.T.

Copyright, 1944, W. A. Sheaffer Pen Co.
* Trademark Reg. U. S. Pat. Off.

SHEAFFER'S

THE BOTTLE WITH THE TOP WELL!

Top Well keeps fingers clean. Only SKRIP has the Top Well. SKRIP successor to ink. Regular size, 25c—School size, 15c.

Ask for Sheaffer's when you ask for Leads. Look for complete Sheaffer lead department containing all sizes, colors and grades—strong, smooth-writing, grit-free—Fineline leads were developed for Sheaffer by Jos. Dixon Crucible Co. Economy package, 25c; regular package, 15c.

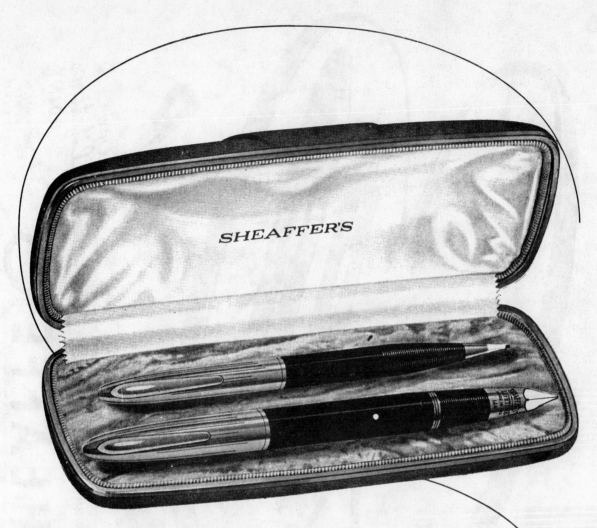

Born of war to serve in peace

These are the pens and pencils that are going to the men and women in the Services overseas. Quantities available for civilians are very limited, but Sheaffer dealers will take your reservations now.

Precision pen-making makes the new Sheaffer pens...precision gained by Sheaffer's skilled craftsmen in engineering fine instruments to help win the war. The new Sheaffer pens and pencils will change all your old thinking about writing ease—will give you new, fuller measures of smooth, utterly relaxed, perfectly-balanced writing satisfaction. Even if you know the pride of possession that goes with owning a post-war Sheaffer's, you'll be amazed anew that anything as good could be so greatly improved by re-designing and new engineering skill. W. A. Sheaffer Pen Co., Fort Madison, Iowa; Toronto, Ontario, Canada.

CREST "TRIUMPH" *Lifetime* pen, $15; pencil, $6; complete set, $21. Other sets with 14K gold trim, $35 to $150. Other pens $2.75 and up. Federal Excise Taxes Additional.

New Lifetime "TRIUMPH" *Pen* *New Fineline Pencil*

SHEAFFER'S

Sheaffer Advertisement — May 1945

THE NEW *Lifetime* POINT

THE WHITE DOT ON THE PEN IDENTIFIES IT!

New "TRIUMPH" Pens . . . New Fineline Pencils

SHEAFFER'S

Copyright 1945, W. A. Sheaffer Pen Co. *Trademark Reg. U. S. Pat. Off.

SHEAFFER'S

Friendship's finest token!

The satisfaction of giving (and getting) Sheaffer writing instruments is the satisfaction of giving (and getting) the best! . . . Put yourself on the receiving end—wouldn't you like to get the finest gift of its kind ever made—particularly when that gift becomes an intimate personal possession?

The answer, of course, is obvious. And just as obvious is the extra value built into Sheaffer pens and pencils. You'll see that extra value, if you'll eye and try before you buy!

W. A. Sheaffer Pen Co., Fort Madison, Iowa, U.S.A., and Toronto, Ontario, Canada.

Sheaffer's are still scarce, but supplies are increasing daily.

VALIANT TUCKAWAY pen, $12.50; pencil, $5; complete set, $17.50. Other sets, $3.95 to $150. Other pens, $2.75 to $100. Colors: Golden Brown, Marine Green, Carmine, Grey Pearl and Black. Federal excise taxes additional.

LISTEN EVERY SUNDAY to SHEAFFER'S WORLD PARADE—*NBC* Complete Network, 3 P. M. E.W.T.; 2 P.M. C.W.T.; 1 P.M. M.W.T.; 12 P.M. P.W.T.

Sheaffer Advertisement — November 1945

Color photograph by Léon DeVos

LOOK FOR *Value* WHEN YOU BUY A PEN ...
CHECK THE *"TRIUMPH"*

The selection of a fine writing instrument—to treasure as your own or to represent you as a gift—deserves thought and care ... The makers of Sheaffer's "TRIUMPH" urge you to examine it critically—to compare it with any other make at any price. You'll be sure to discover what science has proved—that "TRIUMPH" is the best-built, best-writing, best-value pen money can buy!

VALIANT "TRIUMPH" pen, $12.50; pencil, $5; complete set, $17.50.
Federal excise tax additional.   Other sets, $3.95 up.   Complete range of colors.

The **Lifetime** POINT

Unconditionally Guaranteed For First User's Lifetime Without Repair Charges!

New **Fineline** SLEEVE TIP

Reduces Lead Breakage!

SHEAFFER'S

Copyright 1946, W. A. Sheaffer Pen Co.   *Trademark Reg. U. S. Pat. Off
Licensed U. S. Patent No. 2170734

"TRIUMPH" Pens and Fineline Pencils

LISTEN EVERY SUNDAY to SHEAFFER'S PARADE with Carmen Cavallaro—*NBC Network,* 3 P. M. E. T.; 2 P. M. C.T.; 1 P. M. M.T.; 12 Noon P. T.

Sheaffer Advertisement — March 1946

*Color photograph by
John Paul Pennebaker*

Sheaffer's – tops in its field !

In writing instruments it's always Sheaffer's that set the quality standard . . .
STRATOWRITER proves it again! . . . STRATOWRITER is Sheaffer's newest writing sensation—the
dependable, trustworthy, quality-clear-through ball-pointed instrument. Neither pen
nor pencil, yet possessed of many of the best qualities of each, STRATOWRITER
is a gold-filled, precision-built, jewelry-like instrument—with a long-life
writing unit which will be replaced in its entirety (including factory-sealed
supply of Strato-Ink) at any time by your dealer for only $1.00.
Complete STRATOWRITER $15.00 Federal Tax included.

SHEAFFER'S
Stratowriter

Copyright 1947. W. A. Sheaffer Pen Co.

Rolls your writing on dry

POINT RETRACTED

LISTEN SUNDAYS to SHEAFFER'S PARADE, with Carmen Cavallaro—NBC Network, 3 p.m. E.T.; 2 p.m. C.T.; 1 p.m. M.T.; 12 noon P.T.
LISTEN SATURDAYS to SHEAFFER'S ADVENTURERS' CLUB—CBS Network, 11:30 a.m. E.T.; 10:30 a.m. C.T.; 9:30 a.m. M.T.; 8:30 a.m. P.T.

Sheaffer Advertisement — March 1947

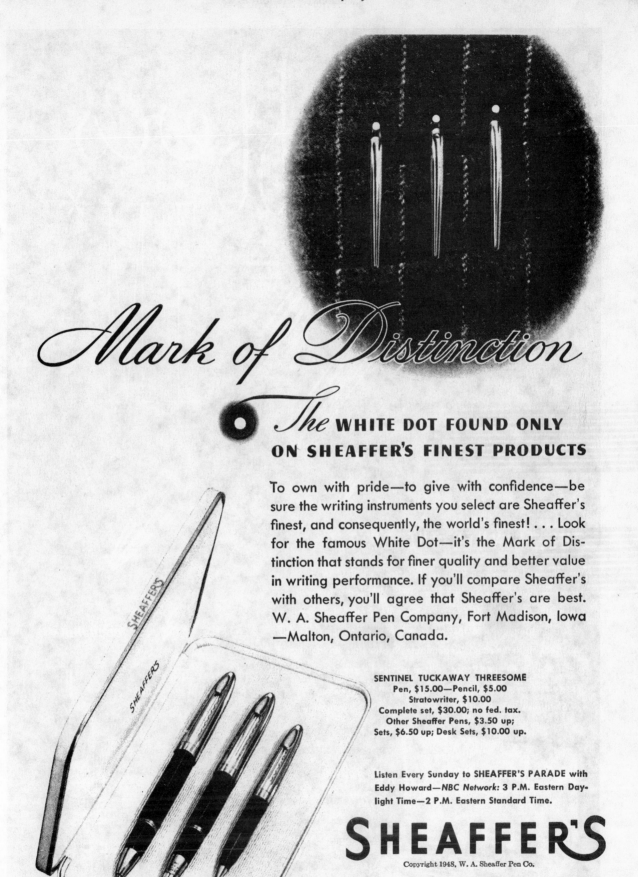

Mark of Distinction

The **WHITE DOT FOUND ONLY ON SHEAFFER'S FINEST PRODUCTS**

To own with pride—to give with confidence—be sure the writing instruments you select are Sheaffer's finest, and consequently, the world's finest! . . . Look for the famous White Dot—it's the Mark of Distinction that stands for finer quality and better value in writing performance. If you'll compare Sheaffer's with others, you'll agree that Sheaffer's are best. W. A. Sheaffer Pen Company, Fort Madison, Iowa —Malton, Ontario, Canada.

SENTINEL TUCKAWAY THREESOME
Pen, $15.00—Pencil, $5.00
Stratowriter, $10.00
Complete set, $30.00; no fed. tax.
Other Sheaffer Pens, $3.50 up;
Sets, $6.50 up; Desk Sets, $10.00 up.

Listen Every Sunday to SHEAFFER'S PARADE with Eddy Howard—*NBC Network:* 3 P.M. Eastern Daylight Time—2 P.M. Eastern Standard Time.

SHEAFFER'S

Copyright 1948, W. A. Sheaffer Pen Co.

Sheaffer Advertisement — May 1948

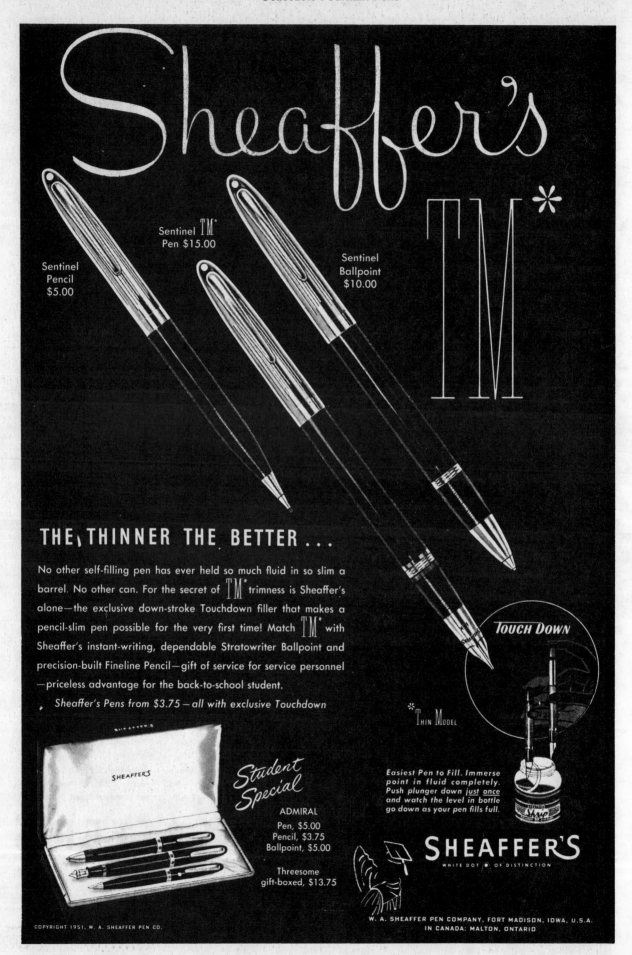

Sheaffer Advertisement — September 1951

THIS IS NEW!

Sheaffer's TM*

"SNORKEL"

Only once in a long while do you have a chance like this—to give a gift so completely new you can be sure no one has it. Sheaffer's TM with the "SNORKEL" is an entirely new invention that separates the two vital functions of a fountain pen... filling and writing. Filling is so much easier, quicker, cleaner—point never needs wiping. And this outstanding and completely new pen writes so much better you'll want to test it yourself at your Sheaffer dealer's. One trial and you'll know ...THIS is the gift!

SHEAFFER'S
WHITE DOT OF DISTINCTION

*Thin Model

Point never "dunked"— never needs wiping

CREST TM*
Completely New
Pen $25.00   Pencil $9.00
Ballpoint $9.00

Just in time for Christmas

W. A. SHEAFFER PEN COMPANY, FORT MADISON, IOWA, U.S.A.
IN CANADA: MALTON, ONTARIO
COPYRIGHT 1952, W. A. S. P. CO.

Sheaffer Advertisement — November 1952

BOLD NEW PEN DESIGNED FOR MEN

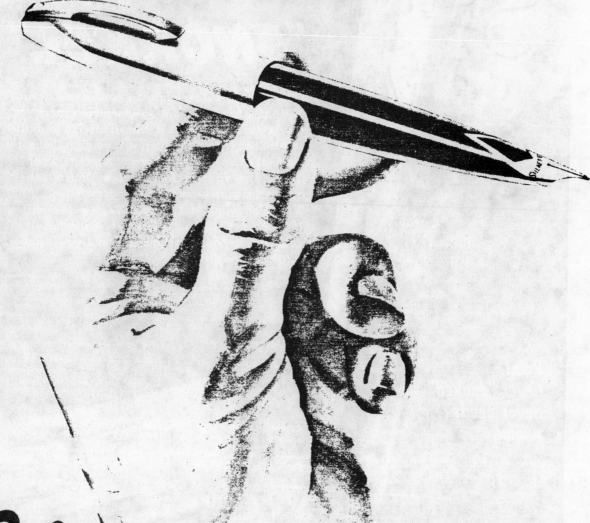

Sheaffer's **PFM** ™

Pen For Men

NO OTHER PEN HAS SO MANY
NEW, EXCITING, PRESTIGE FEATURES!

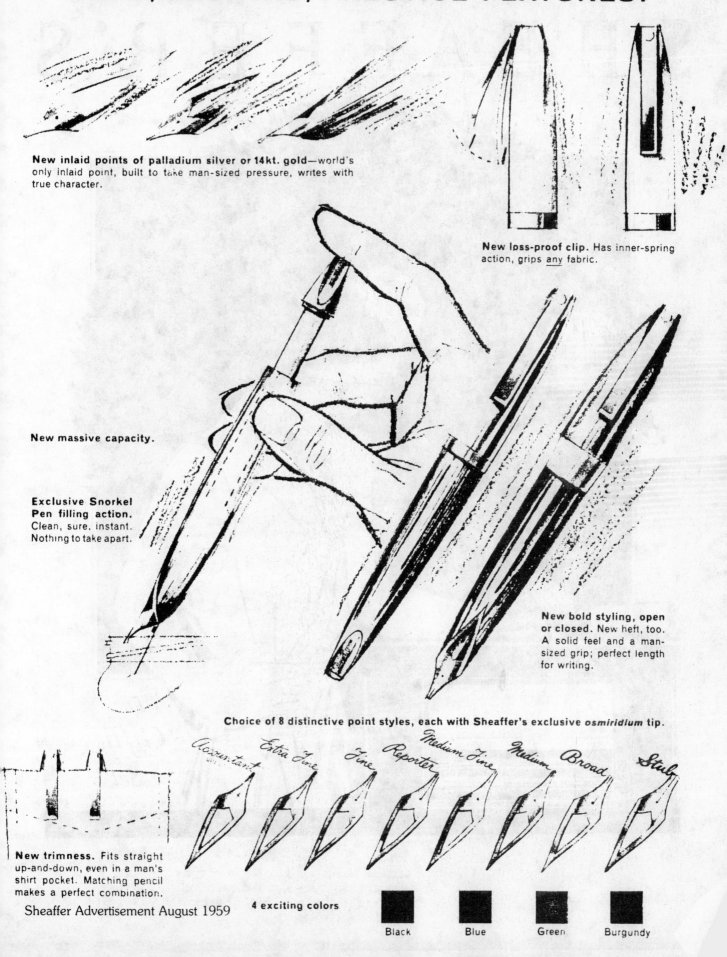

New inlaid points of palladium silver or 14kt. gold—world's only inlaid point, built to take man-sized pressure, writes with true character.

New loss-proof clip. Has inner-spring action, grips any fabric.

New massive capacity.

Exclusive Snorkel Pen filling action. Clean, sure, instant. Nothing to take apart.

New bold styling, open or closed. New heft, too. A solid feel and a man-sized grip; perfect length for writing.

Choice of 8 distinctive point styles, each with Sheaffer's exclusive *osmiridium* tip.

Accountant   *Extra Fine*   *Fine*   *Reporter*   *Medium Fine*   *Medium*   *Broad*   *Stub*

New trimness. Fits straight up-and-down, even in a man's shirt pocket. Matching pencil makes a perfect combination.

Sheaffer Advertisement August 1959   **4 exciting colors**

Black   Blue   Green   Burgundy

SHEAFFER'S

The "Giftie Set"

COLES PHILLIPS

Chronology Of Pens And Pencils

The Sheaffer Pen Company

(Sheaffer-Eaton, Div. Textron)

1.   2.   3.   4.   5.   6.   7.   8.   9.

Plate No. 1

Sheaffer

1. 1914   Sheaffer #34C, Black Chased, Nickel Plated Trim, Lever Filler, Long Straight Clip, Sheaffer-Clip Imprint $50
2. 1921   Sheaffer Lifetime T8C, Black Chased, Gold Filled Trim, Lever Filled, Long Straight Clip, $100
3. 1922   Sheaffer, 46 Special, Red, Gold Filled Trim, Lever Filler, Manifold Nib, Long Straight Clip, $50
4. 1924   Sheaffer #46 Special, Black Chased, Gold Filled Trim, Lever Filler, Ribbon Ring, $40
5. 1924   Sheaffer, 20½ SR, Black Chased, Gold Filled Trim, Lever Filler, Ribbon Ring, $40
6. 1924   Sheaffer, 20SR, Black Chased, Gold Filled Trim, Lever Filler, Ribbon Ring (Closed), $40
7. 1924   Sheaffer Pencil, EEM, Silver Filled Chased Metal, Ribbon Ring, $15
8. 1925   Sheaffer Oversize Pencil, SRC, Red, Gold Filled Trim, Long Straight Clip, $50
9. 1925   Sheaffer Oversize Pencil, Jade Green, Gold Filled Trim, Long Straight Clip, $50

10.   11.   12.   13.   14.   15.   16.   17.   18.

Plate No. 2

Sheaffer

10. 1925   Sheaffer 74SC, Lifetime White Dot, Black, Gold Filled Trim, Lever Filler, Long Straight Clip, $40
11. 1925   Sheaffer #3-25S, Black, Gold Filled Trim, Lever Filler, Ribbon Ring, $25
12. 1927   Sheaffer Lifetime White Dot, Jade Green, Gold Filled Trim, Lever Filler, Long Straight Clip, $75
13. 1927   Sheaffer #74C, Lifetime, Jade Green, Gold Filled Trim, Lever Filler, Ribbon Ring, $40
14. 1927   Sheaffer #5-30C, Jade Green, Black Cap and Barrel Ends, Lever Filler, Long Straight Clip, $30
15. 1927   Sheaffer #5-30C, Jade Green, Black Cap and Barrel Ends, Lever Filler, Long Straight Clip (Closed), $30
16. 1927   Sheaffer #5-30SC, Jade Green, Black Cap and Barrel Ends, Lever Filler, Long Straight Clip, $30
17. 1928   Sheaffer SJC, Pencil, Jade Green, Gold Filled Trim, Long Humped Clip, $50
18. 1928   Sheaffer #3-25SC, Black, Gold Filled Trim, Lever Filler, Long Humped Clip, $20

Collectible Fountain Pens

19.　　20.　　21.　　22.　　23.　　24.　　25.　　26.　　27.

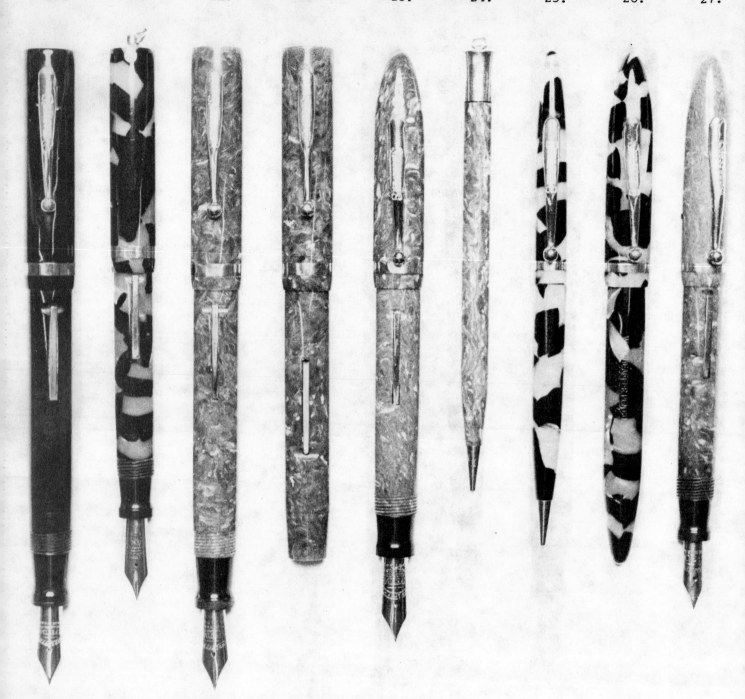

Plate No. 3

Sheaffer

19. 1928 Sheaffer 84C, Lifetime White Dot, Black, Lever Filler, Long Humped Clip, $60
20. 1928 Sheaffer K74SR De Luxe, Lifetime White Dot, Pearl and Black, Gold Filled Trim, Lever Filler, Ribbon Ring, $60
21. 1929 Sheaffer J8C, Lifetime White Dot, Jade Green, Gold Filled Trim, Lever Filler, Long Humped Clip, $75
22. 1929 Sheaffer J8C, Lifetime White Dot, Jade Green, Gold Filled Trim, Lever Filler, Long Humped Clip (Closed), $75
23. 1929 Sheaffer Lifetime White Dot, Jade Green, Gold Filled Trim, Lever Filler, Long Humped Clip, Stream-lined Style, $75
24. 1929 Sheaffer Pencil, Jade Green, Gold Filled Trim, Ribbon Ring, $25
25. 1930 Sheaffer SKT, Pencil, Pearl and Black, Gold Filled Trim, Long Humped Clip, $40
26. 1930 Sheaffer #5-30, Pearl and Black, Gold Filled Trim, Long Humped Clip (Closed) $40
27. 1931 Sheaffer #5-30, Jade Green, Gold Filled Trim, Lever Filler, Long Humped Clip, $40

28.   29.   30.   31.   32.   33.   34.   35.   36.

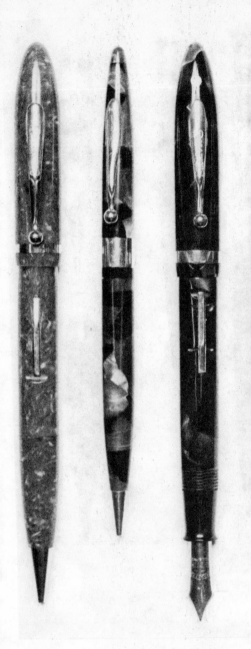

Plate No. 4

Sheaffer

28. 1932   Sheaffer Pen and Pencil Combination, Jade Green, Gold Filled Trim, Lever Filler, Long Humped Clip, $100
29. 1933   Sheaffer Pencil, Marine Green, Solid 14K Gold Trim, Short Humped Clip, $65
30. 1933   Sheaffer #5-10, Lifetime White Dot, Marine Green Pearl and Black, Gold Filled Trim, Lever Filler, Short Humped Clip, $45
31. 1933   Sheaffer Pencil, Marine Green, Gold Filled Trim, Ribbon Ring, $25
32. 1933   Sheaffer Lifetime White Dot, Grey Pearl and Red Veining, Gold Filled Trim, Lever Filler, Short Humped Clip, $45
33. 1933   Sheaffer Pencil, Grey Pearl and Red Veining, Gold Filled Trim, Short Humped Clip, $30
34. 1934   Sheaffer Lifetime White Dot, Ebonized Pearl, Gold Filled Trim, Lever Filler, Short Humped Clip, $75
35. 1934   Sheaffer Feather Touch, Marine Green, Gold Filled Trim, Lever Filler, Short Humped Clip with Flat Ball, $20
36. 1934   Sheaffer Feather Touch, Ebonized Pearl, Gold Filled Trim, Lever Filler, Short Humped Clip with Flat Ball, $30

37.   38.   39.   40.   41.   42.   43.   44.   45.   46.

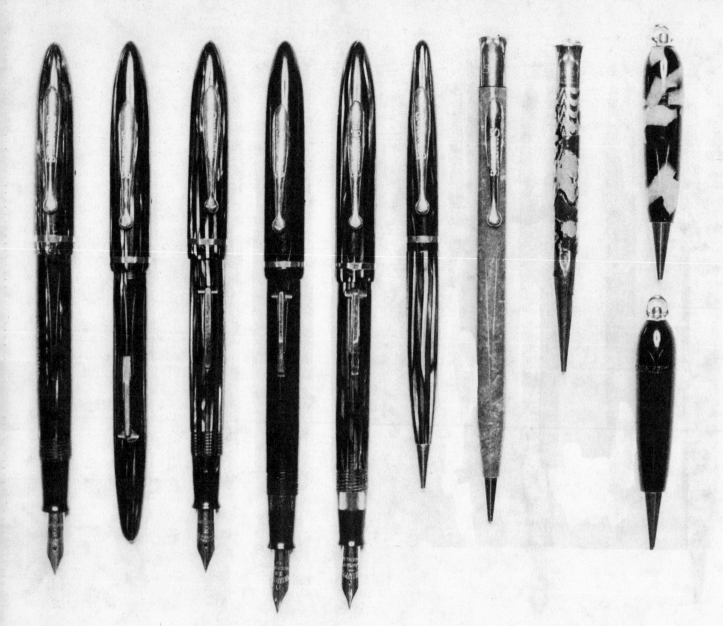

Plate No. 5

Sheaffer

37.	1934	Sheaffer, Rose Glow, Gold Filled Trim, Vacuum Filler, Short Humped Clip with Flat Ball, $15
38.	1934	Sheaffer #350 Golden Brown, Gold Filled Trim, Lever Filler, Short Humped Clip with Flat Ball (Closed), $15
39.	1934	Sheaffer, Golden Brown, Gold Filled Trim, Lever Filler, Short Humped Clip with Flat Ball, $15
40.	1934	Sheaffer #33, Black, Gold Filled Trim, Lever Filler, Short Humped Clip with Flat Ball, $30
41.	1935	Sheaffer Jr., #275, Marine Green, Chromium Trim, Lever Filler, Visulated, Short Humped Clip with Flat Ball, $30
42.	1935	Sheaffer, #250 Marine Green, Gold Filled Trim, Short Humped Clip with Flat Ball, $20
43.	1935	Sheaffer Pencil, Kelly Green, Gold Filled Trim, Short Humped Clip with Flat Ball, $30
44.	1935	Sheaffer Pencil, Oriental Mosaic, Gold Filled Chased, Ribbon Ring, $20
45.	1935	Sheaffer Golf Pencil, Black and Pearl Gold Filled Trim, Ribbon Ring, $15
46.	1935	Sheaffer Golf Pencil, Black, Gold Filled Trim, Ribbon Ring, $15

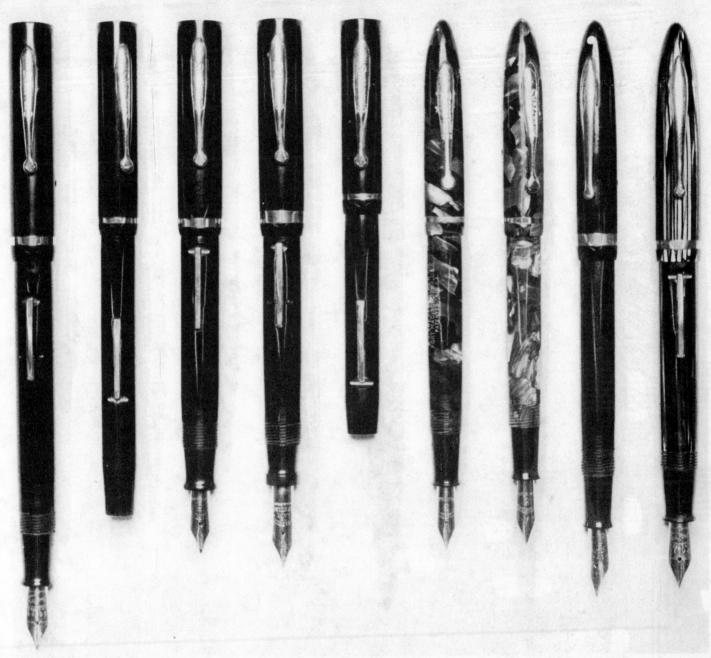

Plate No. 6

Sheaffer

47.	1935	Sheaffer Feather Touch, Black, Gold Filled Trim, Lever Filler, Short Humped Clip with Flat Ball, $20
48.	1935	Sheaffer Feather Touch, Black, Gold Filled Trim, Lever Filler, Short Humped Clip with Flat Ball, $20
49.	1935	Sheaffer #3-25, Black, Gold Filled Trim, Lever Filler, Short Humped Clip with Flat Ball, $20
50.	1935	Sheaffer Lifetime White Dot, Black, Gold Filled Trim, Lever Filler, Short Humped Clip with Flat Ball, $30
51.	1935	Sheaffer, Black, Gold Filled Trim, Lever Filler, Short Humped Clip with Flat Ball (Closed), $20
52.	1935	Sheaffer, Grey Pearl, Chromium Trim, Lever Filler, Short Humped Clip with Flat Ball, $20
53.	1935	Sheaffer, Grey Pearl, Transparent Barrel, Chromium Trim, Vacuum Filler, Short Humped Clip with Flat Ball, $20
54.	1936	Sheaffer Lifetime White Dot, Black, Gold Filled Trim, Vacuum Filler, Long Rigid Radius Clip, $30
55.	1936	Sheaffer Feather Touch, Gold and Black Striated, Gold Filled Trim, Lever Filler, Long Rigid Radius Clip, $25

56.   57.   58.   59.   60.   61.   62.   63.   64.

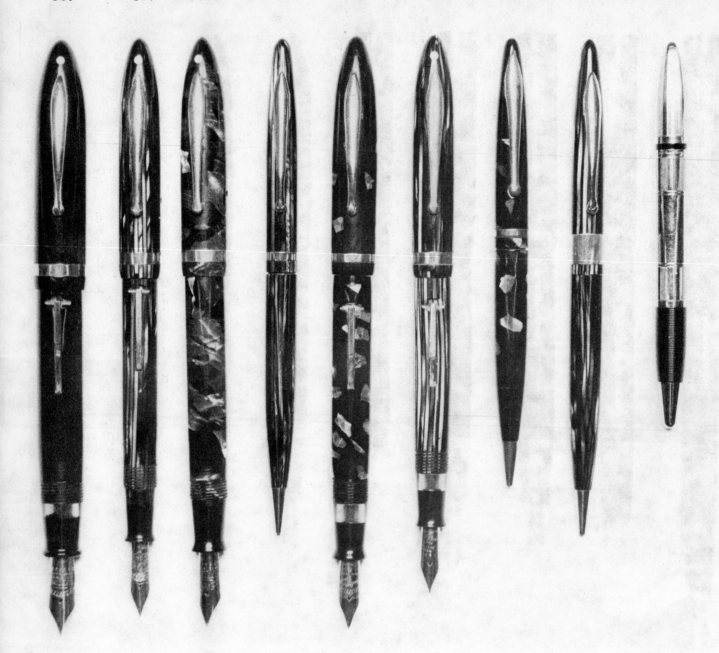

Plate No. 7

Sheaffer

56. 1937   Sheaffer Lifetime White Dot, Black, Gold Filled Trim, Lever Filled, Visulated, Long Rigid Radius Clip,
             $65
57. 1937   Sheaffer Sovereign Lifetime White Dot, Golden Brown, Gold Filled Trim, Lever Filler, Long Rigid
             Radius Clip, $35
58. 1937   Sheaffer Lifetime White Dot, Grey Pearl, Chromium Trim, Lever Filler, Long Rigid Radius Clip, $35
59. 1937   Sheaffer Pencil #400, Marine Green, Gold Filled Trim, Long Rigid Radius Clip, $25
60. 1938   Sheaffer D5W Feather Touch, Ebonized Pearl, Gold Filled Trim, Lever Filler, Visulated, Long Rigid
             Radius Clip, $35
61. 1938   Sheaffer Sovereign Lifetime White Dot, Grey Pearl, Chromium Trim, Lever Filler, Long Rigid Radius
             Clip, $35
62. 1938   Sheaffer Pencil, Ebonized Pearl, Gold Filled Trim, Long Rigid Radius Clip, $20
63. 1939   Sheaffer Pencil, Golden Brown, Gold Filled Trim, Long Rigid Radius Clip, $25
64. 1940   Sheaffer Tuckaway Pencil, Gold Filled Barrel, $20

65. 66. 67. 68. 69. 70. 71. 72. 73. 74.

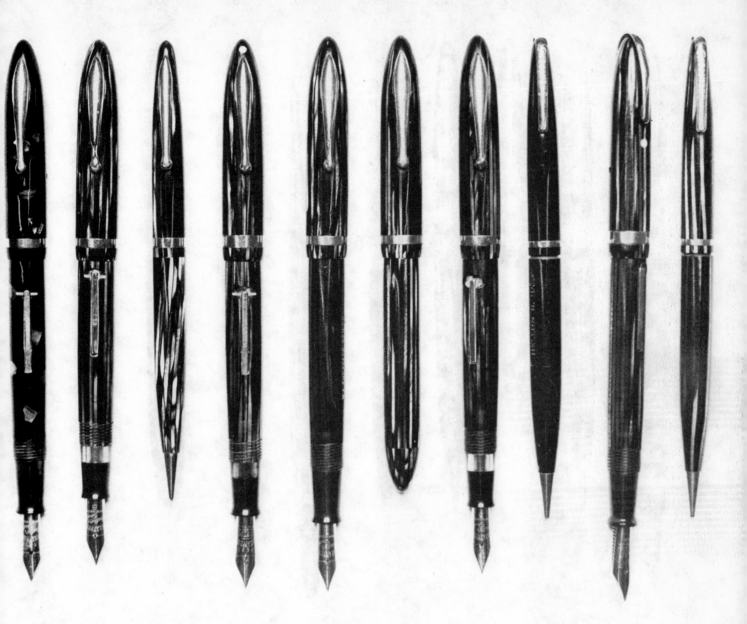

Sheaffer

Plate No. 8

65. 1938 Lady Sheaffer Feather Touch, Ebonized Pearl, Gold Filled Trim, Lever Filler, Short Rigid Radius Clip, $25

66. 1940 Lady Sheaffer Feather Touch, Marine Green, Gold Filled Trim, Lever Filler, Visulated, Short Rigid Radius Clip, $20

67. 1940 Lady Sheaffer Pencil #350, Marine Green, Gold Filled Trim, Short Rigid Radius Clip, $20

68. 1940 Lady Sheaffer Lifetime White Dot #875, Marine Green, Gold Filled Trim, Lever Filler, Short Rigid Radius Clip, $30

69. 1940 Lady Sheaffer Feather Touch, Golden Brown, Gold Filled Trim, Vacuum Filler, Short Rigid Radius Clip, $20

70. 1940 Lady Sheaffer #500 Feather Touch, Grey Pearl, Chromium Trim, Vacuum Filler, Short Rigid Radius Clip (Closed), $20

71. 1940 Lady Sheaffer #500 Feather Touch, Caramine (Reddish), Gold Filled Trim, Lever Filler, Visulated, Short Rigid Radius Clip, $20

72. 1941 Sheaffer Pencil, #300 Black, Gold Filled Trim, Over-the-Top Military Clip, $20

73. 1941 Sheaffer #875 Lifetime White Dot, Golden Brown, Gold Filled Trim, Lever Filler, Over-the-top Military Clip, $35

74. 1941 Sheaffer Pencil, #300 Golden Brown, Gold Filled Trim, Over-the-Top Military Clip, $20

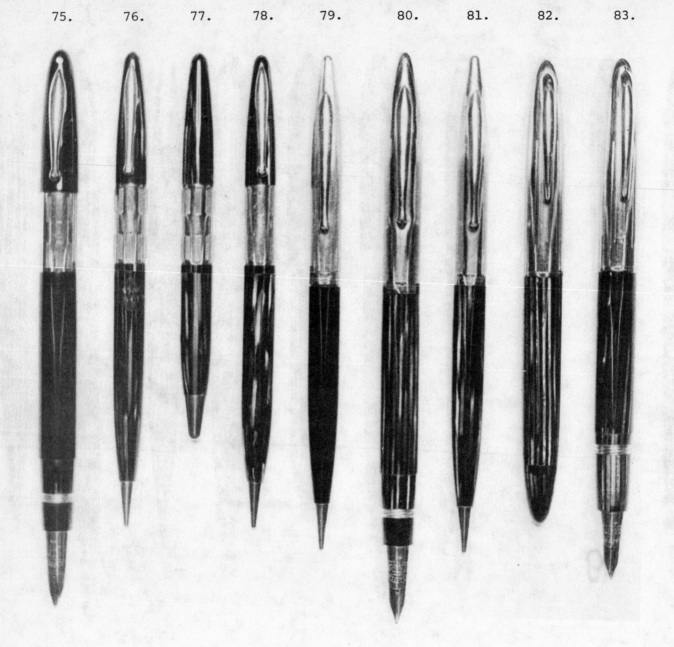

Plate No. 9

Sheaffer

75. 1942   Sheaffer Triumph Lifetime White Dot, Black, Gold Filled Trim, Vacuum Filler, Triumph Nib, Short Rigid Radius Clip, $30
76. 1942   Sheaffer Triumph Pencil, Caramine, Gold Filled Trim, Short Rigid Radius Clip, $25
77. 1942   Sheaffer Tuckaway Pencil, Caramine, Gold Filled Trim, $20
78. 1942   Sheaffer Triumph Pencil, Marine Green, Gold Filled Trim, Short Rigid Radius Clip, $25
79. 1943   Sheaffer Crest Pencil, Black Gold Filled Cap, Gold Filled Trim, Long Rigid Radius Clip, $35
80. 1943   Sheaffer Lifetime White Dot Crest, Gold Filled Cap, Golden Brown, Vacuum Filler, Long Rigid Radius Clip, $50
81. 1943   Sheaffer Triumph Crest Pencil #600, Gold Filled Cap, Golden Brown, Gold Filled Trim, Long Rigid Radius Clip, $35
82. 1945   Sheaffer Triumph Crest #1500, Lifetime White Dot, Golden Brown, Vacuum Filler, Gold Filled Cap (Closed), $50
83. 1945   Sheaffer Triumph Crest #1500, Lifetime White Dot, Golden Brown, Vacuum Filler, Gold Filled Cap, $50

84.   85.   86.   87.   88.   89.   90.   91.   92.   93.

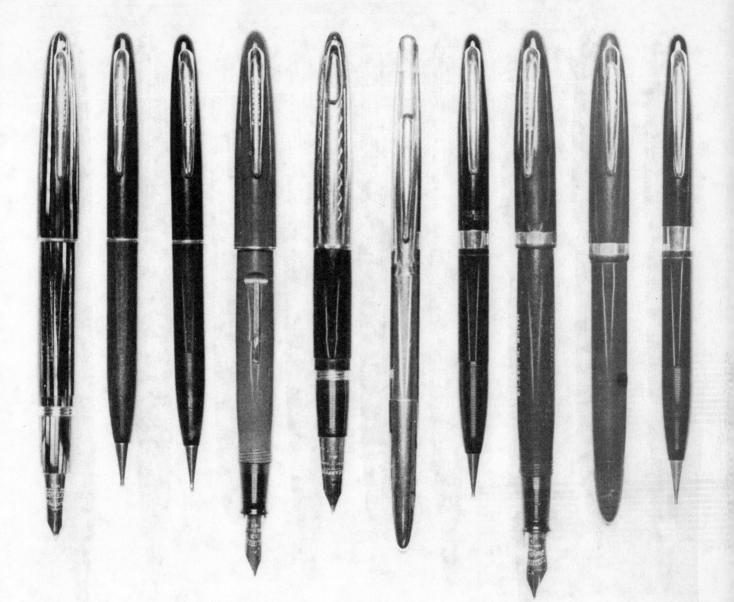

Plate No. 10

Sheaffer

84. 1945 Sheaffer Craftsman #875, Lifetime White Dot, Grey Pearl, Chromium Trim, Plunger Filler, Triumph Nib, $35
85. 1945 Sheaffer Craftsman Pencil, Burgundy, Gold Filled Trim, $15
86. 1945 Sheaffer Craftsman Pencil, Black, Gold Filled Trim, $15
87. 1946 Sheaffer Craftsman #350, Blue, Gold Filled Trim, Lever Filled, $25
88. 1947 Sheaffer Crest De Luxe Tuckaway, White Dot, Gold Filled Cap, Black Barrel, Vacuum Filler, Tuckaway Clip, Triumph Nib, $25
89. 1947 Sheaffer RAI Stratowriter Ballpoint, Gold Filled Barrel and Trim, Protective Cap $20
90. 1949 Sheaffer Admiral Pencil #400, Black, Gold Filled Trim, $20
91. 1949 Sheaffer Statesman Feather Touch, Burgundy, Gold Filled Trim, Touchdown Filler, $25
92. 1949 Sheaffer Statesman Feather Touch, Burgundy, Gold Filled Trim, Touchdown Filler (Closed), $25
93. 1949 Sheaffer Ambassador Pencil, Black, Gold Filled Trim, $35

94.   95.   96.   97.   98.   99.   100.   101.   102.

Plate No. 11

Sheaffer

94.	1949	Sheaffer Valiant White Dot, Black, Gold Filled Trim, Touchdown Filler, Triumph Nib, $35
95.	1949	Sheaffer Valiant White Dot, Black, Gold Filled Trim, Touchdown Filler, Triumph Nib (Closed), $35
96.	1953	Sheaffer Valiant Snorkel White Dot, Transparent Barrel and Cap, Gold Filled Trim, Triumph Nib, $65
97.	1950	Sheaffer White Dot, Chromium Cap, Gold Filled Trim, Pastel Green, Touchdown Filler, $30
98.	1950	Sheaffer White Dot, Gold Filled Cap, Black Barrel, Touchdown Filler, $30
99.	1953	Sheaffer Sentinel White Dot, Chromium Cap, Black Barrel, Gold Filled Trim, Touchdown Filler, Triumph Nib, $35
100.	1953	Sheaffer Sentinel White Dot, Chromium Cap, Pastel Green, Gold Filled Trim, Touchdown Filler, Triumph Nib, (Closed), $35
101.	1953	Sheaffer Lifetime White Dot, Black, Gold Filled Trim, Touchdown Filler, Triumph Nib, $40
102.	1954	Sheaffer Valiant White Dot Snorkel, Burgundy, Gold Filled Trim, Touchdown Filler, Snorkel Nib, $35

103.   104.   105.   106.   107.   108.

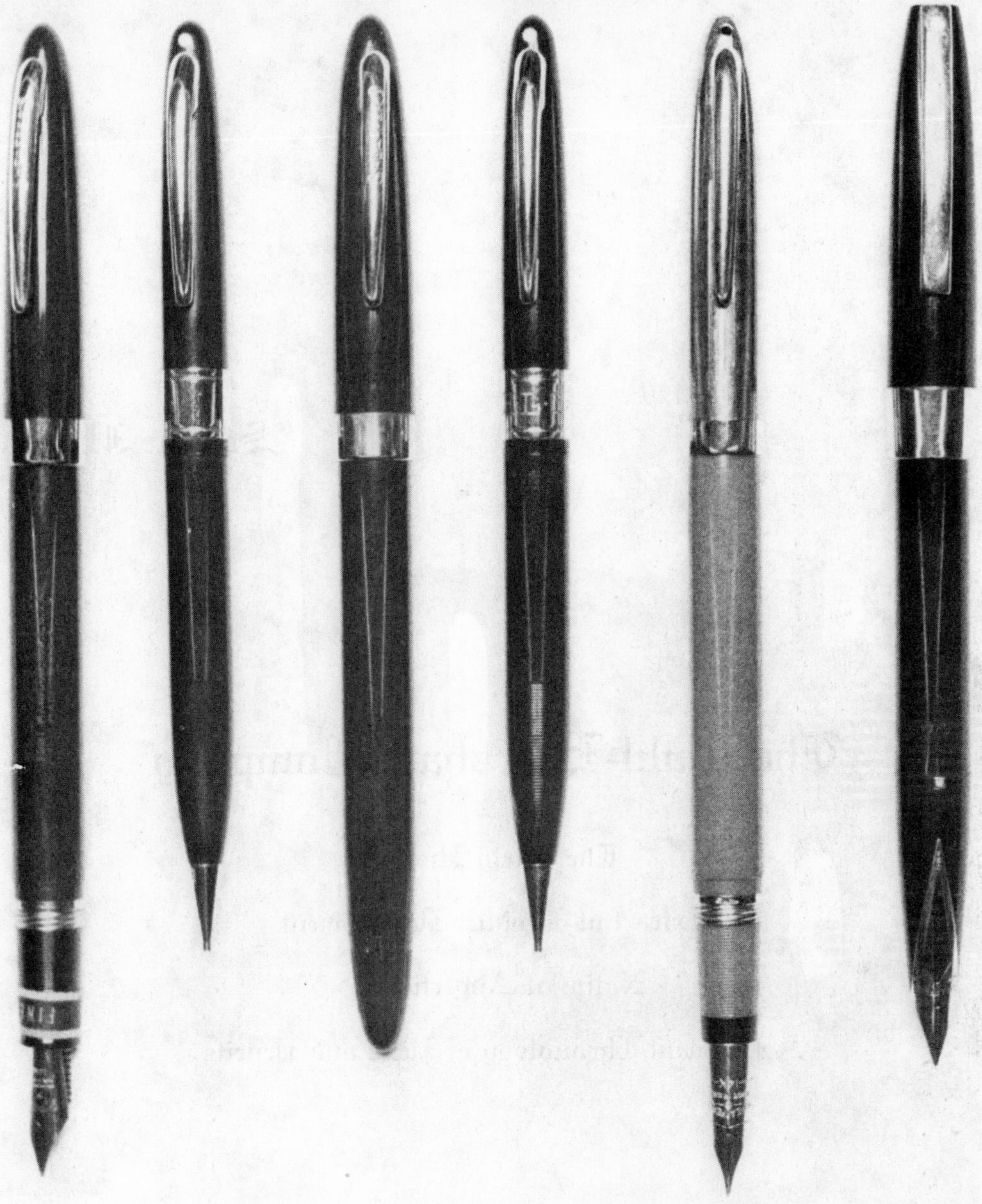

Plate No. 12

Sheaffer

103.	1954	Sheaffer Saratoga Snorkel, Burgundy, Gold Filled Trim, Touchdown Filler, $25
104.	1954	Sheaffer Statesman Pencil, White Dot, Burgundy, Gold Filled Trim, $25
105.	1954	Sheaffer Admiral Snorkel, Burgundy Cap and Barrel, Gold Filled Trim, Touchdown Filler (Closed), $25
106.	1954	Sheaffer Statesman Pencil, White Dot, Burgundy, Gold Filled Trim, $25
107.	1954	Sheaffer Sentinel Triumph Snorkel White Dot, Chromium Cap, Gold Filled Trim, Red Barrel, Touchdown Filler, Triumph Nib, $35
108.	1960	Sheaffer Imperial White Dot, Black, Gold Filled Trim, Touchdown Filler, $25

Section IV

The Wahl-Eversharp Company

The Early History

Extract of Product Development

National Advertising

A Pictorial Chronology of Pens and Pencils

Back of every Eversharp Pencil and every Tempoint Pen stands The Wahl Company, a two-and-a-half-million dollar concern of splendid international reputation and integrity.

Above is illustrated the great Wahl factory. Here are made the famous Wahl Adding Machine, the Tempoint Pen and the Eversharp Pencil, each representative of highest efficiency in its realm.

The Wahl Eversharp Company

The Early History

The Wahl Adding Machine Company was incorporated on September 7, 1905, in Illinois. Named for its founder, John C. Wahl, the company originally manufactured adding machines and metal products.

Meanwhile, a Japanese businessman by the name of Tokuji Hayakawa invented a fine mechanical pencil in 1912 that would soon change the direction of the Wahl Adding Machine Company. Named Ever-Sharp, the pencil was an all metal propel-type mechanical pencil. Hayakawa founded the Ever-Sharp Pencil Company to manufacture and market his new product.

In 1914 the Ever-Sharp pencil was exported to the United States where it gained wide popularity and sales. A year later, the Wahl Adding Machine Company purchased controlling interest in the Japanese firm and began manufacturing pencils in Chicago at 1800 West Roscoe Street. The Ever-Sharp pencil became so popular that its production and sales far outdistanced any other products manufactured by Wahl. The management soon was convinced that the road to further success was through an expanded writing instruments business.

Wahl leaped into the fountain pen field in 1917 when it purchased the Boston Fountain Pen Company and moved its operation to Chicago. The Boston pen was a proven quality product which helped assure Wahl a leadership position in the fountain pen arena. That same year the firm changed its name to the Wahl Company and two years later sold the adding machine portion of the business to the Remington Typewriter Company.

By late 1918, Wahl was producing a complete line of Tempoint fountain pens of hard rubber in addition to its metal pencils. Immediate acceptance of the Tempoint pens helped Wahl's net sales climb from $1.4 million in 1918 to nearly $7.4 million in 1920. By late 1920, Wahl had sold

1.5 million Tempoint pens and in excess of 12 million Eversharp pencils. This fantastic sales record shot the Wahl Company into first place in the quality writing instruments field.

It was fortunate that Wahl had leased space in a huge building since its two acquisitions had proven overwhelmingly successful. More than 1200 employees labored in three work shifts, day and night, to keep pace with Wahl's burgeoning sales.

Success had its drawbacks, however. According to C. A. Frary, vice president and general manager, production of the new pens became such a mess the Wahl Company seriously considered giving up pen manufacturing entirely (*Printer's Ink*, Nov. 30, 1922). The company had hired two of the best technical experts in the fountain pen field to oversee the manufacture of its Tempoints. Although they were excellent mechanics, they were "indifferent executives," said Frary. Rather than give up the pens, the company hired a top-notch executive who soon straightened out the production muddle.

Innovators in Mass Pen Production

The Tempoint with its rubber barrel and small ink capacity was replaced in 1921 with the Wahl Pen, a "distinctive" new pen designed with a metal barrel. The company placed great emphasis on developing the most efficient and modern manufacturing methods. Frary explained: "We developed automatic machinery and straight-line processing and introduced, even at very heavy expense, the equipment necessary for the most economical production under conditions of large quantity sales. That helped us to make the prices right — a consideration of fundamental importance."

As innovators in mass pen production, Frary said the

Wahl Company practically eliminated its competition. An all-out marketing and advertising program helped to ensure this success.

Less fortunate was Wahl's lack of mechanical innovation during its early years. It got into the writing instrument business by acquiring established pen and pencil companies and was slow in gaining expertise in research and development.

The Eversharp pencil, for example, soon became obsolete because of its simple propel mechanism. The pencil had a propensity to clog due to friction created by the lead with the inside of the point. The friction was designed to prevent the lead from falling out of the pencil. Meanwhile, Parker and Sheaffer developed propel-repel-expel mechanisms for their pencils which were far superior to the Eversharp pencil mechanism.

Wahl began losing a percentage of field to Parker and Sheaffer as the all-metal pencils began to lose popularity. After two years of falling sales, Wahl in July 1922 acquired yet another company, the Washington Rubber Company, to manufacture hard rubber for its pens and pencils. As it turned out, this acquisition did not enhance Wahl's competitive edge. DuPont had introduced a new plastic material that was lighter than rubber or metal and was break-resistant. Moreover, the new plastic could be produced in a variety of new vibrant colors not available in hard rubber. Sheaffer was the first to introduce the new plastic in its pens, and Parker soon followed. Meanwhile, Wahl had increased its production of rubber pens.

Wahl Introduces Plastic Pens

In 1928 Wahl finally introduced a dramatic new line of beautifully colored and Art Deco designed pens and pencils in break-resistant plastic. Initially, they were made in five colors — Coral, Jade Green, Lapis Lazuli Blue, Black and Pearl, and Rosewood. Wahl introduced the Gold Seal for its new pen line which was equivalent to Sheaffer's White Dot and lifetime quarantee.

The new pens were designed with the traditional yet unique roller ball clip developed by The Boston Pen Company. The pens and pencils designed in an Art Deco style were so popular that the company's sales jumped up fifty percent in 1929.

A Jet color was added in 1929 to the pen line and in 1930 the last and most spectacular color was added — Green and Bronze. Today, Green and Bronze is the most sought after and highly prized of the Art Deco pens.

A line of medium priced pens were introduced during 1930 and were called Equipoised. The pens were streamlined with tapered ends and slender barrels. The unique roller clip, trim and mechanics of the top of the line pens were designed into this line. The Equipoised pens and pencils were available in all the colors of the higher priced line.

By late 1931, Wahl introduced a new pen — the Doric. The new Dorics, as they were called, had twelve-sided shapes and were tapered at the ends. The Gold Seal Dorics were guaranteed for life and came in five beautiful oriental shades — Kashmir Green, Burma, Morocco, Cathay and Jet.

An inexpensive line of pens called the Wahl-Oxford pens also were introduced in 1931. They had 14K gold nibs and gold plated trim. The Wahl-oxfords were priced at $2 and $3 each, which for the times were a fairly good value.

In 1932 an adjustable point was introduced for the Dorics that could be adjusted to nine different positions. This was accomplished by moving a small slide button up or down the length of the exposed nib. This popular and heavily advertised device remained a Wahl-Eversharp feature until 1939.

The Dorics were slightly modified in 1935 by redesigning the pocket clip and dropping the unique roller ball. The cap girdle also was dropped in favor of a heavier cap band that strengthened the cap lip area.

A major new advancement in pencil mechanics was introduced in 1936 with the new Repeater Pencil. The leads were automatically fed into the magazine from the holding area inside the pencil as the leads were used up. More important, the pencil lead could be advanced with just one hand by pressing a crown button with the thumb. It was nicknamed the "clicker" because it made a click sound with each press of the button. One disadvantage was the lead had to be repelled manually. This technique eventually caused the clutch to loosen, and the lead would push back inside the point while writing.

The Safety Ink Shut-Off tab was another interesting mechanical feature introduced in 1936. The metal tab was designed to prevent ink leakage when the pen was not in use. The tab closed a valve between the ink reservoir and the nib when the cap was screwed on the barrel. Wahl brought out a beautifully designed all-metal gold filled pen and pencil set featuring the Safety Ink Shut-Off device. The pen was priced at $10 but never gained popularity in the prestige pen market. This may have been related to lack of public confidence in the Safety Ink Shut-Off feature. In fact, the Federal Trade Commission did not agree that the device did what was claimed and forced Wahl to drop the safety tab in late 1938.

Once again following Sheaffer's lead, the Dorics featured plunger fillers and transparent barrels in 1937. The oversized Dorics were dropped. Despite fairly strong sales, Wahl continued to lose its share of the pen market.

Straus Heads Up
New Management Team

On May 7, 1940, the Wahl Company was merged with its subsidiary, Eversharp, Inc. and Martin Straus took the helm along with a new management team. Straus introduced a new line of Eversharp pens and pencils called Skyline in the spring of 1941. The newly designed pens were guaranteed forever and the pen and pencil set sold for a very reasonable $8.75. The Skyline became the company's most successful selling pen of all time. It featured a high capacity ink filling system, an excellent lever filler mechanism and breather tube to prevent ink leakage during airplane flight.

Despite Skyline's success, Eversharp, Inc. reported a net loss of $346,000 for the fiscal year ended February 28, 1941. The profit loss was due in part to extraordinary expenses of more than $238,000 for developing the new Skyline designs.

Eversharp, Inc. bounded back in 1942 when sales were more than 100 percent ahead of the preceding year. This was due to the excellent new Skyline pen, an effective advertising and promotional campaign and Straus' management.

Eversharp sponsored a spectacularly successful radio quiz show called *Take It or Leave It* to promote the Skyline pens. The show became best known for its "Sixty-four Dollar Question," a special feature created by Straus himself. Magazine and radio promotion helped reinforce this popular show and the Eversharp name. The Fifth Avenue, another line of pens and pencils introduced in 1944, also was promoted on the show. The complimentary sets given to the show contestants had "6?4" engraved on their solid gold caps to symbolize the "Sixty-four Dollar Question," which was the earmark of the show.

Eversharp's future could not have appeared brighter. In 1945 it became the industry leader in sales. Straus introduced a solid gold Skyline set in 1944 called the "Gift of a Lifetime" which retailed for $125. The same pen set was reintroduced in 1945 and 1946 as the "Command Performance" and sold quite well.

To compete with Parker's "51," Eversharp introduced the Fifth Avenue line in 1944. The nib was hooded like the "51" and featured a gold filled slip-on cap. Unfortunately, it proved to be a poor competitor for the "51" despite being priced slightly lower at $10. The Fifth Avenue line was dropped in late 1946. However, strong sales continued for the Skyline pens helping to offset the failure of the Fifth Avenue line.

The Ballpoint Pen Makes Its Debut

In the early post war era, the ballpoint pen hit the U.S. market with all the hoopla characteristic of today's video/computer craze. Americans instantly fell in love with this convenient new writing instrument. Manufacturers and retailers scrambled to sell this marvelous new gadget which did not leak and held up to a year's supply of quick-drying, non-blotting ink in easy to replace cartridges.

Fascination with the ballpoint was evident in this description of Eversharp's new ball pen in the May 23, 1945, issue of the *Chicago Sun*: "The pen, which operates on the principle of capillary attraction, using a miniature ball bearing as its writing contact, will write on cloth or paper submerged in water or in an airplane at the ceiling of stratospheric air travel without leaking. In addition, it can be used on gloss, soft and blotting paper or cloth without spreading....The ink cartridge will be made in several sizes, the largest of which contains at least a year's supply, or enough for 257 continuous writing hours. The cartridge can be replaced in 20 seconds without staining the fingers."

Eversharp assumed it would become the undisputed king of the ballpoint. Eversharp, in cooperation with the Eberhard Faber Corp., acquired exclusive rights to manufacture and sell the Biro ball pen from the Eterpen Co. of Argentina in May 1945. Eversharp spent the next several months refining the Biro pen and developing its marketing strategy. The result was the "Capillary Action" (CA) ballpoint.

Right before Eversharp got its ballpoint on the retail market, it was shocked to discover it had been upstaged by a brand new company, the Reynold's International Pen Co. Reynold's was credited with making Americans ballpoint pen conscious when it introduced its $12.50 pen at Gimbel's Department Store in New York in October 1945. Gimbel's sold $100,000 worth of the pens the first day. Reynold's and Gimbel's launched an all-out advertising campaign — spurred by what they claimed were threats from Eversharp.

Reynold's and Eversharp sued each other — the first claiming restraint of trade and the latter alleging unfair trade practices. Eversharp found it fruitless to sue for patent infringement, since the pen with a rotatable ball originally had been patented in 1888 by John Loud, and the rights had long since expired.

Undaunted by this minor set-back, Eversharp forged ahead with an all-out marketing program. In 1946 the company enjoyed a spectacular rise in sales, thanks to its CA ball pointer. The *Chicago Daily News* on August 8, 1946, reported:

"Volume of business in the first four months of Eversharp's fiscal year, which began March 1, was approximately $4.5 million greater than the corresponding period last year. Estimated total sales for the present fiscal year are placed at $50 million, compared with $30 million last year and $20 million two years ago.

Looking back you find Eversharp's volume was only $2 million in 1939, when the present management took the helm.

A year ago the total number of employees was 2,300. Today it is 3,500, and a year from now, Bard says, there will be a need for 4,500 employees."

Unfortunately, the success was short-lived. By the end of fiscal 1947 (ended Feb. 29, 1948), the company experienced a net loss of more than $3.4 million. Three major problems contributed to the deficit: 1) the costly problem of overcoming the defects in the ball pen; 2) fierce price wars with other competitors, most notably the Reynold's Co.; and 3) spending heavily on new manufacturing plants to meet the demand of the ballooning ballpoint fad.

When the ballpoint pen first came out, many functioned

erratically; and the Eversharp pen was no exception. After the initial burst of sales, CA defects started cropping up. *Newsweek* on May 21, 1948, reported: "under its guarantee policy Eversharp called thousands of pens back; it lost $2,888,000 on 1947 inventory, another $385,000 on 'disposal of equipment,' $237,000 more to recondition dealers' stocks and $239,000 to replace defective cartridges for irate customers."

Then came the price wars. "Reynolds and other quick merchandisers cleaned up," continued the *Newsweek* article. "But to get out of the swift-moving razzle dazzle ballpoint pen business still wearing a shirt was a trick few could turn."

Eversharp kept its shirt on - but barely. Its deficit would have been even steeper had it not been for the profits from the company's burgeoning Schick Injector razor business which it had acquired in 1946 from the Magazine Repeating Razor Co. In 1948 Eversharp as a whole showed a profit of $1.2 million. The writing instruments division went in the red $2.3 million, but the company was saved by a $4 million profit before taxes in the razor division.

Overexpansion was the third problem plaguing Eversharp's financial health. "Dealers are killing us, screaming and tearing us apart for more ballpoint pens," complained an Eversharp honcho in mid-1947. The company invested heavily in new plants to meet the demand and continued to spend millions improving the ballpoint.

In late 1948 chairman Straus confessed that Eversharp had learned its lesson. It had "expended so great a portion of its time and attention in solving the problems of the ballpoint pen that certain developments in its conventional pen and mechanical business, were perhaps under emphasized," said Straus. He announced plans to shift emphasis back to the conventional pen and pencil business. Furthermore, Straus said he felt the price wars had ended as many smaller producers had come and gone, unable to withstand the intense competition.

Nonetheless, sales continued to drop in Eversharp's writing instruments division, and a bitter management battle ensued. The directors tightened the reins on Straus' duties and powers in January 1949, and in April accepted the resignation of Arthur J. Rogow as president. By mid-1949 there were cuts in payrolls and in selling and manufacturing expenses. The pen and pencil plant in Chicago was up for sale.

The showdown came in July 1949 when Straus was ousted as a director. Company officials charged that Straus had rushed into the ball pen market with a product which had not been adequately tested; compounding the problem had been ruinous price slashing.

The biggest blow to Straus reportedly was being deprived of the credit for inventing the "Sixty-four Dollar Question" on Eversharp's *Take It or Leave It* radio quiz show. The program had been his brainchild and contributed greatly to the success of the Skyline pen. The slap in the face came in a news release sent out two days before Straus' ouster as director in which the company stated, "The dramatization of the "Sixty-four Dollar Question" was the actual work of the Biow Co., our advertising agency."

Straus resigned as chairman in October 1949.

In an effort to turn around a serious sales decline, Eversharp in 1949 commissioned Raymond Leowy to design a new fountain pen. Introduced in 1950, the Leowy pens featured metal caps that were either chromeplated or gold filled and trimmed in the contrasting metal. Some models were designed with solid gold caps, while others were offered in sterling. Mechanically the pens were similar to the Skyline. The Leowy pens were not a big sales success, nor were any other pens introduced during the writing division's remaining days.

In 1952 Eversharp, Inc. brought a ballpoint infringement suit against the L. E. Waterman Co. A judgment resulting from a settlement between the two parties involved the payment by Waterman of substantial damages for past infringements and the issuance of a license to Waterman to permit it to continue with the sale of its ball pens.

Parker Purchases Eversharp Division

The Parker Pen Co. purchased the writing instruments division of Eversharp, Inc. in December 1957. Daniel Parker, executive vice president, announced the two businesses would operate separately. The Eversharp Pen Co. subsidiary would market lower priced ballpoint pens from a manufacturing plant in Arlington Heights, Illinois. Production of Eversharp writing instruments also continued from a Culver City, California, plant which also was purchased as a separate subsidiary.

In September 1958 the Eversharp Pen Co. introduced its first new pen — a low-priced triangular shaped ball pen. The triangular design was conceived by Desighn Dynamics of Chicago "for the natural triangle between the three writing fingers." The new "Fountain-Ball" pen retailed for 98 cents. The pen combined a new high density ink with a "honey comb metal" ballpoint, creating darker, more legible handwriting similar to that of a fountain pen.

The Civil War Centennial in 1961 prompted the Eversharp Pen Co. to offer two new ballpoint pens. One was Confederate gray and stamped with the Confederate flag. It was labeled "Johnny Reb." The second pen, labeled "Billy Yank," was a Northern blue stamped with the Stars and Stripes on a shield. Each had a clip designed like a saber.

Although the new ballpoints sold well for awhile, Parker was unable to turn the Eversharp Pen Co. into a profitable subsidiary, and the remaining assets were sold off and the division dismantled.

Wahl-Eversharp: Extract of Product Development

1905   The Wahl Adding Machine Co. was incorporated Sept 7.

1912   Tokuji Hayakawa invented the Ever-Sharp all-metal mechanical repel pencil.

1914   Wahl purchased controlling interest in the Ever-Sharp Pencil Co.

1917   • Wahl purchased The Boston Fountain Pen Co. and moved it to Chicago.
           • Wahl Adding Machine Co. changed its name to The Wahl Company.

1918   Introduction of an extensive line of hard rubber Tempoint pens. The gold nibs were hand
           hammered.

1920   The roller ball clip was introduced to the Tempoint pens.

1922   Wahl purchased the Washington Rubber Co. to produce hard rubber caps and barrels for its
           pens.

1924   Desk pens with base and taper were introduced.

1926   • Pens were introduced with interchangeable point-feed assembly sections
           • Nibs were available in 14 different pen point styles.
           • Colors were Black, Red, Rosewood.
1927   • Ladies brocaded enameled finish pen and pencil sets were available.
           • Manicure compacts called Eversmart were also available in chased gold filled metal, Blue
           Lizard over gold filled metal and Cloisonne of gold filled metal.
1928   • Beautifully colored break-resistant pens and pencils were introduced in Art Deco designs.
           They were made in five colors — Coral, Rosewood, Jade Green, Lapis Lazuli Blue and
           Black & Pearl.
           • The Gold Seal insignia was introduced and signified "Guaranteed for Life".
           • Wahl pens continued to be offered in all metal and in hard rubber models.
1929   Black was added to the plastic Art Deco line of pens and pencils.

Wahl-Eversharp Product Development Continued...

1930
- The most spectacular color of all was added to the line — Green and Bronze.
- An additional line of newly streamlined pens and pencils were introduced and called Equipoised. These were available in Black & Pearl, Jade Green, Coral, Rosewood, the new Green & Bronze and Jet.
- All pens and pencils (except the all metal models) up to and including this period were designed with the traditional, but unique roller ball pocket clip.

1931
- The Dorics, completely redesigned pens and pencils were introduced with 12 sided barrels, tapered ends, a modified roller clip and a new delicate cap band. The Dorics came in five new colors; Kashmir Green, Burma — a rich smoke/grey pearl color, Morocco — a medium burgundy and pearl color, Cathay Green and Jet.
- The economy line of Wahl-Oxford pens and pencils were introduced with 14K nibs and retailed for $2-$3.

1932 An adjustable point with nine different settings was introduced and with minor changes continued as an optional feature until 1939.

1935 The Dorics were slightly redesigned. The modified roller clip was discontinued as was the delicate cap band. A wide and heavier cap band was designed to fit around the cap lip for more durability
The Oversized Dorics were discontinued.

1937 Plunger fillers and tansparent barrels were added to the Doric line

1938 The Safety Ink Shut Off was discontinued as was the beautiful all metal pens of the same name.

1940 The company's name was changed from The Wahl Company to Eversharp, Inc.

1941 The dramatic Skyline pens and pencils were introduced. They represented a completely new design mechanically and in style. The pens featured a breather tube that prevented ink flow when not in use at high altitudes.

1944
- The Fifth Avenue pens and pencils were introduced with gold-filled slip-on caps and hooded nibs to compete with Parker's "51". The Fifth Avenue was discontinued after two years of production.
- A solid 14K gold set was introduced in the Skyline design. It was called "Gift of a Lifetime" and sold for $150 including federal tax.
- The "6?4" solid gold cap Fifth Avenue set was introduced and used as gifts for contestants on the famous radio quiz show "Take It or Leave It."

1945 The solid gold Skyline set was reintroduced in 1945 and 1946 and was called "Command Performance."

1946
- The Fifth Avenue sets were dropped from production.
- The revolutionary new non-leak ballpoint pen was introduced. This pen eventually cost the company millions in lost profits.

1950 Leowy pens were introduced with metal caps of chromeplate or gold-filled. Some models were available in solid gold or Sterling caps.

1957 The Parker Pen Co. purchased the writing instruments division of Eversharp, Inc.

1958 A triangular ballpoint with a honeycomb metal ball point was introduced.

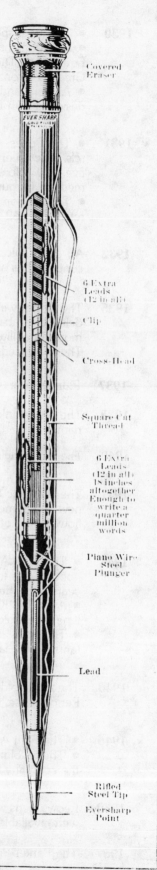

EVERSHARP PENCILS

The skeleton cut to the right shows the ingenious construction of the Eversharp Pencil.

The point is always sharp, never sharpened, for the Eversharp sharpens itself. No whittling, no lost motion, no lost lead, no interrupted thought.

And every stroke sharp and clean-cut. Easy writing, easy reading.

There's enough lead for a quarter million words, 18 inches of lead in all. Twenty-five cents at long intervals replenishes the supply—ten thousand words one cent.

There's a handy eraser, under cover until needed. Ready instantly.

The built-in Wahl pocket clip prevents Pencil from working out of the pocket.

The rifled steel tip insures a sharp, steady, ready point for every word and every dot. It tapers down to the lead itself, insuring that graceful writing quality and scholarly touch of pencil to paper so much appreciated by all good writers.

The Eversharp is constructed with jeweler precision throughout. It is as good to the eye as it is in the hand. If anything ever brought pride of ownership it is an Eversharp Pencil. Eversharp owners are discriminating people.

Eversharp Leads come in various degrees of hardness. From lead to cap the Eversharp is truly King of the Pencils— a striking advance in pencil construction and utility.

Reprinted From Wahl's 1919 Catalog.

THE PATENTED WAHL COMB FEED

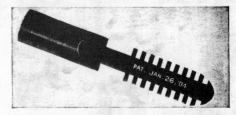

Built upon the principle of the comb. When the ink channel contains more ink than the pen point requires for writing, it flows back into the cavities formed by the teeth and the gold pen, and is held there until needed. The capillary attraction thus formed prevents the ink from dropping on the paper.

THE PATENTED AIR-TIGHT CHAMBER
The Safety Feature
(Enlarged View)

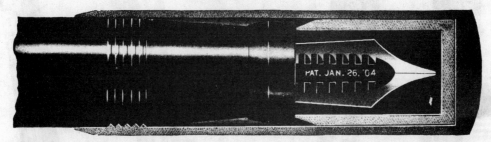

The air-tight chamber is simply a cap within a cap, and bevelled at its open end. When the outside cap is screwed on to the barrel tightly, there is a perfect contact on all sides between the open end or the inner-cap and the bevelled flange of the point section, making it air-tight and preventing any ink from escaping.

The pen point, so concealed within the inner-cap, remains moist and in condition to write the instant it touches the paper.

THE SEPARATE PARTS

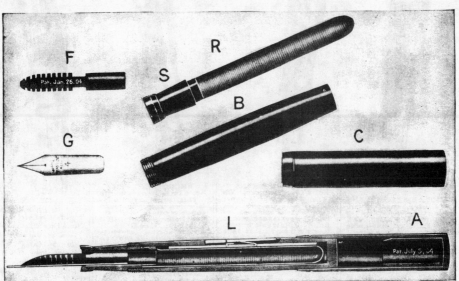

F—The Feed; S—The Point Section; B—The Barrel; C—The Cap; G—The Gold Pen.
The longitudinal view of the separate parts assembled.
Simplicity in construction and quality of workmanship and materials are the standards upon which the separate parts are made, and the complete pen assembled. Each pen is thoroughly inspected and tested before leaving the factory.

Reprinted From Wahl's 1919 Catalog.

WAHL - EVERSHARP
Personal-Point
FOUNTAIN PENS

These Nationally Advertised Pens, with a selection of fourteen nibs and numerous colors and styles of holders, afford every opportunity for purchaser to make an intelligent and very satisfactory selection.

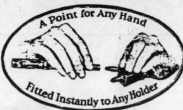

A Point for Any Hand

Fitted Instantly to Any Holder

"WAHL" EVERSHARP FOUNTAIN PENS are built with the precision of fine jewelry. The highly polished barrels have inner barrels of aluminum, insuring lightness and strength. Mounted with 14k Gold Filled Roller Clips, filler levers and bands. Unconditionally guaranteed defect-free. Fitted with exclusive "WAHL-EVERSHARP" feature—the interchangeable nib—any point may be transferred instantly by the dealer to any holder.

The House of Co-operation
Inc.
1889
1930

Reprinted from a wholesale catalog dated 1930

OVERSIZE CLIP PENS
No. 6 Interchangeable Nib
In such magnificent rich colors, as Black and Pearl, as illustrated, New Bronze and Green, or Jade Green, Lapis Blue or Rosewood. Pencils can be purchased to match, as described.

BLACK AND PEARL
No. 2673. Each.....$10.00
Eversharp to match is No. 2648.

BRONZE AND GREEN
No. 2674. Each.....$10.00
Eversharp to match is No. 2649.

JADE GREEN
No. 2675. Each..... $8.75
Eversharp to match is No. 2653.

LAPIS BLUE
No. 2676. Each..... $8.75
Eversharp to match is No. 2651.

ROSEWOOD
No. 2677. Each..... $8.75
Eversharp to match is No. 2652.

REGULAR SIZE CLIP PENS
No. 4 Interchangeable Nib
Like the OVERSIZE Clip Pens, the REGULAR SIZE CLIP PENS are obtainable in a beautiful Jade Green, as illustrated, Lapis Blue or Rosewood Colors, also such attractive color combinations, as Bronze and Green or Black and Pearl.

JADE GREEN
No. 2678. Each.....$6.25
Eversharp to match is No. 2655.

LAPIS BLUE
No. 2679. Each.....$6.25
Eversharp to match is No. 2654.

ROSEWOOD
No. 2680. Each.....$6.25
Eversharp to match is No. 2655.

BRONZE AND GREEN
No. 2681. Each.....$7.50
Eversharp to match is No. 2656.

BLACK AND PEARL
No. 2682. Each.....$7.50
Eversharp to match is No. 2657.

SHORT CLIP PENS
No. 4 Interchangeable Nib
Some folk like a short holder fountain pen. This style is nicely balanced, of finest workmanship and finish. Obtainable in such lovely colors, as Jade Green, Lapis Blue, Rosewood, or such exquisite color combinations, as Bronze and Green or Black and Pearl.

BRONZE AND GREEN
No. 2683. Each.....$7.50
Eversharp to match is No. 2661.

LAPIS BLUE
No. 2684. Each.....$6.25
Eversharp to match is No. 2659.

ROSEWOOD
No. 2685. Each.....$6.25
Eversharp to match is No. 2660.

JADE GREEN
No. 2686. Each.....$6.25
Eversharp to match is No. 2658.

BLACK AND PEARL
No. 2687. Each.....$7.50
Eversharp to match is No. 2662.

SHORT RING PEN
No. 4 Interchangeable Nib
This ladies' style fountain pen comes in such exquisite colors, as attractive Lapis Blue, Jade Green, or such beautiful combination of colors, as the New Bronze and Green or the popular Black and Pearl.

ROSEWOOD
No. 2688. Each......$6.25
Eversharp to match is No. 2665.

LAPIS BLUE
No. 2689. Each.....$6.25
Eversharp to match is No. 2664.

JADE GREEN
No. 2690. Each......$6.25
Eversharp to match is No. 2663.

BRONZE AND GREEN
No. 2691. Each......$7.50
Eversharp to match is No. 2666.

BLACK AND PEARL
No. 2692. Each......$7.50
Eversharp to match is No. 2667.

GOLD FILLED FOUNTAIN PEN
No. 4 Interchangeable Nib
Grecian Border Design
In the GOLD FILLED Fountain Pens, this is about the most exquisite creation on the market. A 14k Gold Filled Fountain Pen, richly engine turned and embellished with an exquisite Grecian Border design, fitted with a 14k Solid Gold No. 4 Nib. It is built with the precision of fine jewelry and as a writing instrument it compares with the very finest on the market.
No. 2693. Each......$10.00
Eversharp to match is No. 2668.

LONG CLIP PEN
No. 2 Nib, Not Interchangeable
This long clip is a wonderful value in a "WAHL"-"Personal-Point" Fountain Pen at a moderate price. Manufactured to a very high standard of excellence and finish. Like its companion Eversharp, it is furnished in a rich Rosewood color and fitted with a No. 2 14k Solid Gold nib. It makes a splendid inexpensive gift article, in which excellent service and satisfaction is assured.

No. 2694. Each......$3.75
Eversharp to match is No. 2669.

Note that plastic, rubber and metal pens and pencils were sold side by side. Also note that plastic pens and pencils were offered in three different cap band designs, Greek key, split ring and rhomboid.

WAHL - EVERSHARP
Pencils in Attractive New Colors Which Make Pleasing Gift Articles

EVERSHARP Pencils are standard for mechanical pencil values. Also Nationally regarded as standard among users everywhere. Built over inner barrels of aluminum, these pencils combine the utmost in balanced strength. All mountings are 14K Gold Filled. Pencils use standard thin lead; extra leads in magazine barrel. Renewable erasers under caps.

Beautiful in Design

As practical Christmas, Birthday, Graduation or Confirmation Gifts, Eversharp Pencils are Supreme.
Illustrations Actual Size

Dependable in Operation

GIFTS of UTILITY

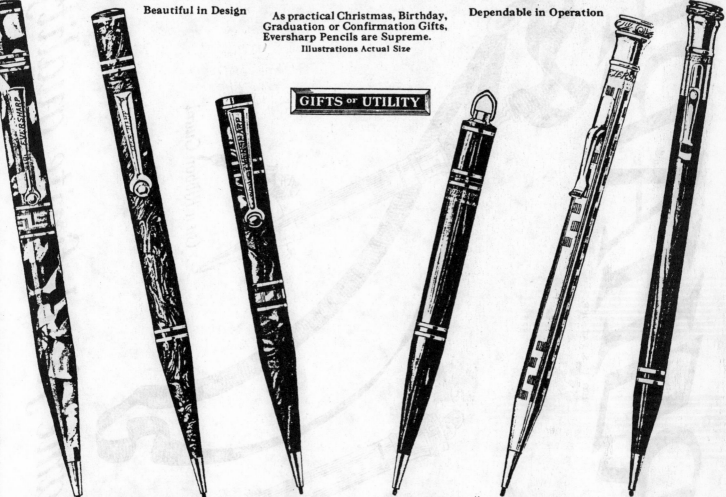

OVERSIZE CLIP PENCILS

In such beautiful colors Black and Pearl (as own), Bronze and Green, Jade Green, Lapis Blue Rosewood.

BLACK AND PEARL
. 2648 Each......$5.63
Fountain Pen to match No. 2673.

BRONZE AND GREEN
. 2649 Each......$5.63
Fountain Pen to match . 2674.

JADE GREEN
. 2650 Each......$5.00
Fountain Pen to match . 2675.

LAPIS BLUE
. 2651 Each......$5.00
Fountain Pen to match . 2676.

ROSEWOOD
. 2652 Each......$5.00
Fountain Pen to match . 2677.

REGULAR SIZE CLIP PENCILS

Like the OVERSIZE Clip Pencils, the REGULAR SIZE CLIP PENCILS are obtainable in Jade Green, Lapis Blue or Rosewood colors, also such attractive colors as Bronze and Green or Black and Pearl.

JADE GREEN
No. 2653 Each......$4.38
Fountain Pen to match is No. 2678.

LAPIS BLUE
No. 2654 Each......$4.38
Fountain Pen to match is No. 2679.

ROSEWOOD
No. 2655 Each......$4.38
Fountain Pen to match is No. 2680.

BRONZE AND GREEN
No. 2656 Each......$5.00
Fountain Pen to match is No. 2681.

BLACK AND PEARL
No. 2657 Each......$5.00
Fountain Pen to match is No. 2682.

SHORT CLIP PENCILS

A popular short EVERSHARP WITH CLIP in Jade Green, Lapis Blue or Rosewood, and color combinations, such as Bronze and Green, and Black and Pearl.

JADE GREEN
No. 2658 Each......$4.38
Fountain Pen to match is No. 2683.

LAPIS BLUE
No. 2659 Each......$4.38
Fountain Pen to match is No. 2684.

ROSEWOOD
No. 2660 Each......$4.38
Fountain Pen to match is No. 2685.

BRONZE AND GREEN
No. 2661 Each......$5.00
Fountain Pen to match is No. 2686.

BLACK AND PEARL
No. 2662 Each......$5.00
Fountain Pen to match is No. 2687.

SHORT RING PENCILS

Ladies who prefer the EVERSHARP with the SHORT RING, can obtain this pencil in their favorite color: Jade Green, Lapis Blue, Rosewood, or Bronze and Green or Black and Pearl.

JADE GREEN
No. 2663 Each......$4.38
Fountain Pen to match is No. 2688.

LAPIS BLUE
No. 2664 Each......$4.38
Fountain Pen to match is No. 2689.

ROSEWOOD
No. 2665 Each......$4.38
Fountain Pen to match is No. 2690.

BRONZE AND GREEN
No. 2666 Each......$5.00
Fountain Pen to match is No. 2691.

BLACK AND PEARL
No. 2667 Each......$5.00
Fountain Pen to match is No. 2692.

GOLD FILLED EVERSHARP

Long Pencil with Clip. Grecian Border

We feature this EVERSHARP—(Long style with Clip) in GOLD FILLED in the popular and beautiful GRECIAN Border design. It is built with the precision of fine jewelry and incomparable as a writing instrument. It has been for years one of the EVERSHARP'S best selling pencils. It is priced very low in this selling and makes a splendid gift article.

No. 2668 Each......$6.25

Fountain Pen to match is No. 2693.

LONG CLIP PENCIL

This long clip model pencil is of highly polished Pyroxalin in an exquisite ROSEWOOD COLOR. The cap pocket clip and band is of yellow gold filled. Like all companion pencils it is also fitted with eraser and 12 leads.

No. 2669 Each......$2.50

Fountain Pen to match is No. 2694.

SAME AS ABOVE IN OVERSIZED JADE GREEN

Silver Cap and Pocket Clip, Eraser and 12 Leads.

No. 2670 Each......$1.50

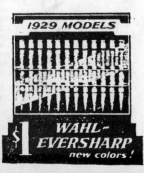

1929 MODELS

$1 WAHL-EVERSHARP new colors!

DOLLAR DECAGON PENCIL ASSORTMENT
Pictured at Left

Attractive counter display card mounted with ONE DOZEN "OVERSIZE" WAHL-EVERSHARP Decagonal Pyralin Pencils, three (3) Each Black, Blue, Coral and Yellow. This is the first time that genuine WAHL-EVERSHARP pencils in Pyralin could be obtained at this price. Uses standard thin lead; extra leads in magazine barrel. Nickel clip and eraser cap.
No. 2671 Pencil Assortment......$15.00
You make $4.95 on every assortment you sell.

New Oversize WAHL-EVERSHARP

60¢

SIXTY CENT "JUMBO" PENCIL ASSORTMENT
Pictured at Left

One of these assortments should be in your store on display. Here is another fast selling assortment, wherein you invest just a couple of dollars and make a nice profit.

Counter display card mounted with one dozen assorted "JUMBO EVERSHARPS" the utility pencils that were originally made to retail at $1.00. Uses standard thin lead; extra leads in magazine barrel. Nickel clips. Exposed eraser.
No. 2672 Pencil Assortment......$9.00
You make $2.97 on every assortment you sell.

Reprinted from a wholesale catalog dated 1930.

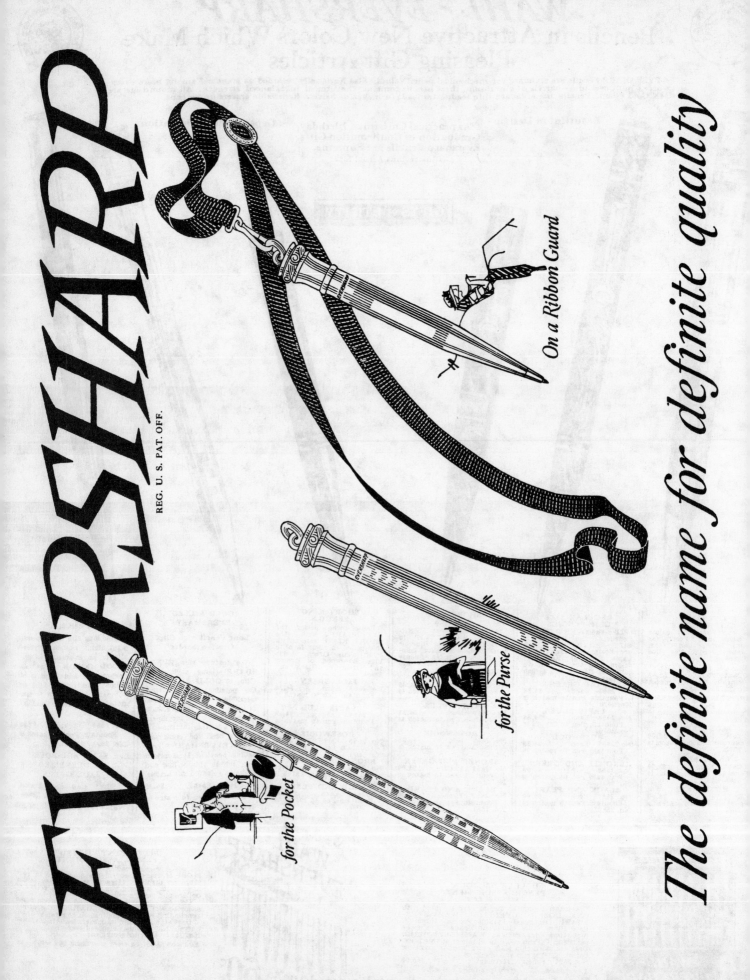

EVERSHARP

REG. U. S. PAT. OFF.

On a Ribbon Guard

for the Purse

for the Pocket

The definite name for definite quality

National Advertising

The Wahl-Eversharp Company

This is the symbol of perfect writing—the mark of the world's two greatest writing aids, the Eversharp Pencil and its perfect ink-writing mate, the Tempoint Pen. It is a guarantee of unusual worth, back of which stands a two-and-a-half-million-dollar concern.

Two Right-Hand Friends for Life

This perfect pointed pencil, and this perfect pointed pen bring a new efficiency to the realm of writing, and a new comfort, economy and pride of ownership to millions who write

In the Eversharp Pencil and the Tempoint Pen a striking advance has been made in pen and pencil construction.

Not a mere advance in but one or two respects, but a revolutionary advance in *every* respect.

The Eversharp Pencil is always sharp—never sharpened. Carries enough lead for a quarter million words—18 inches in all—and a real point for every word.

It is a thing of beauty and a joy forever. Constructed with jeweler precision and finish throughout. As much a mechanical wonder as a writing marvel.

Has a handy eraser—under cover until needed—and a built-in pocket clip. A quarter replenishes the lead supply, enough for another quarter million words—ten thousand words one cent!

* * *

The Tempoint Pen has a point of superb writing quality and wondrous durability. The gold is fused about the ample iridium tip—not annealed.

A further hammering process endows the pen with steel-like hardness and flexibility. The point cannot become "sprung" under severest writing nor weakened by harmful ink acids.

An exact flow of ink is maintained by the famous Wahl Comb Feed, automatically controlled by touch of pen to paper. No blots. No hesitant flow. You never have to coax the point with your thumbnail.

No sweating when carried in the pocket—the air-tight chamber about the pen prevents that. And it also keeps the nib moist for instant writing.

You never knew such pen-writing comfort.

* * *

Both Pencil and Pen are made for pocket, chain or milady's handbag. Pen is made in both Self Filling and Screw Joint styles.

Pencil prices, $1 and up; Pen prices, $2.50 and up. Sold by the better dealers everywhere. If yours is not supplied, write direct for descriptive literature to aid in selection.

THE WAHL COMPANY, 1800 Roscoe Street, Chicago, Illinois; Astor Trust Bldg., 5th Ave. and 42nd Street, New York

WAHL EVERSHARP
The Perfect Pointed Pencil
Always Sharp—Never Sharpened

Eversharp Leads made for Eversharp Pencils have a firmness, fineness and smoothness all their own. Many months' supply for 25c—1c for ten thousand words. Look for the Eversharp label on box

WAHL TEMPOINT
The Perfect Pointed Pen
(Heretofore known as the Boston Safety Pen)

Wahl-Eversharp Advertisement April 6, 1918

Everybody! Shop Early for Eversharps

Perfect pencil writing is embodied in Eversharp — always sharp — never sharpened.

Perfect pen writing is found in Tempoint — the pen with the tempered point.

Singly, or together, they constitute the gift of gifts — the gift that will make eyes pop open on Christmas morning, the gift that wins hearts and hands — and for all time.

EVERSHARP carries enough lead for a quarter million words, and provides a clean point for every word. Always sharp — never sharpened. No whittling.

A quarter replenishes the lead supply at long intervals — ten thousand words one cent.

TEMPOINT has a hand-hammered gold nib, impervious to the harmful effects of caustic ink acids. Unaffected by hard continuous writing. Never becomes "sprung." Always writes just like the owner.

There are nine other distinctive features that make Tempoint a writing friend for life — a lasting compliment to giver and user alike.

Eversharp and Tempoint are sold separately, or may be had together in a handsome jewel case. Pencil prices start at $1, and up. Pen prices at $2.50, and up. Both pens and pencils are made for pocket, chain, or lady's bag.

Note: Bear in mind that women, as well as men, appreciate the gift of perfect writing, as exemplified by Eversharp and Tempoint.

THE WAHL COMPANY
1800 Roscoe Street, Chicago, Ill., U. S. A.

EASTERN OFFICE: Astor Trust Building, 501 Fifth Avenue, New York
BERT M. MORRIS COMPANY, 444 Market Street, San Francisco, Cal.
Western Representatives for Eversharp Pencils and
Tempoint Fountain Pens
Canadian Representatives: Rowland & Campbell, Ltd.
Winnipeg, Manitoba

DEALERS: Write today for catalog and interesting proposition
on Eversharp and Tempoint

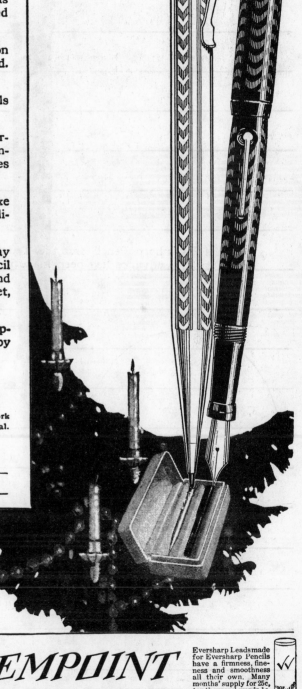

The symbol of perfect writing — the mark of Eversharp Pencil and Tempoint Pen.

EVERSHARP TEMPOINT

ALWAYS SHARP — NEVER SHARPENED   **THE PEN WITH THE TEMPERED POINT**

Right-Hand Mate to the famous Tempoint Pen   *Right-Hand Mate to the famous Eversharp Pencil*

Eversharp Leads made for Eversharp Pencils have a firmness, fineness and smoothness all their own. Many months' supply for 25c, ten thousand words 1c. Look for the Eversharp label on box. At all Eversharp dealers'.

Wahl-Eversharp Advertisement November 8, 1919

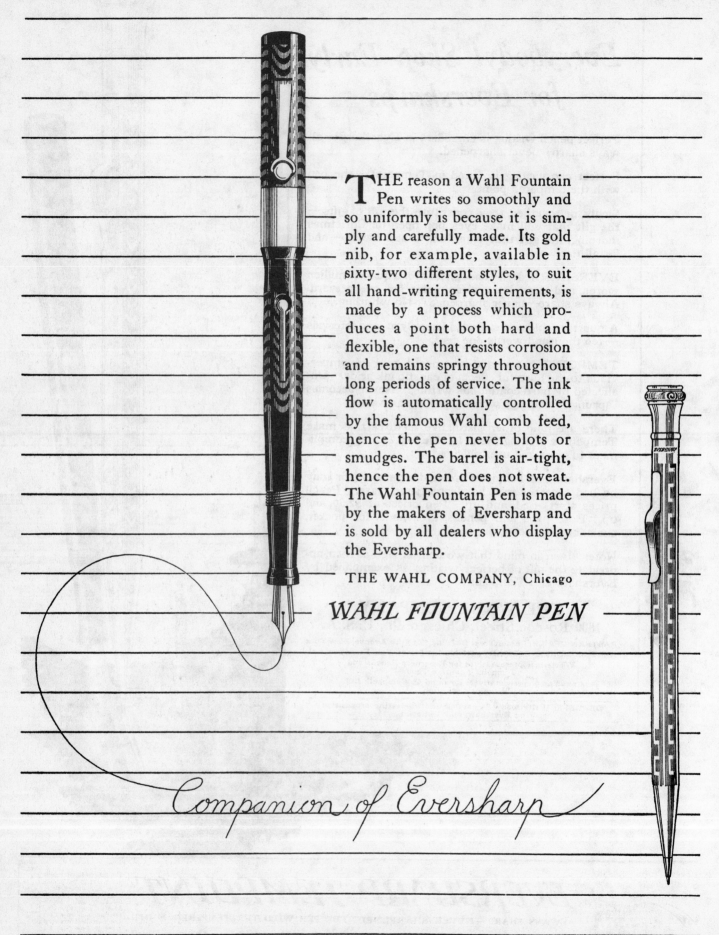

THE reason a Wahl Fountain Pen writes so smoothly and so uniformly is because it is simply and carefully made. Its gold nib, for example, available in sixty-two different styles, to suit all hand-writing requirements, is made by a process which produces a point both hard and flexible, one that resists corrosion and remains springy throughout long periods of service. The ink flow is automatically controlled by the famous Wahl comb feed, hence the pen never blots or smudges. The barrel is air-tight, hence the pen does not sweat. The Wahl Fountain Pen is made by the makers of Eversharp and is sold by all dealers who display the Eversharp.

THE WAHL COMPANY, Chicago

WAHL FOUNTAIN PEN

Companion of Eversharp

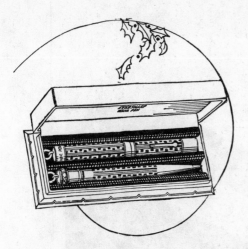

Gifts
$1 to $50

The gifts of *perfect writing* are here; at your price—in one perfect quality—in many forms of beauty—and with a name that is known wherever people write.

Give EVERSHARP—and your gift is supreme in quality; no other pencil has the exclusive rifled tip that keeps the lead from wobbling. Even if he has an EVERSHARP, give him another for his watch chain or for desk use. Ladies, from fourteen up, wear EVERSHARP on a ribbon, chain, or cord, for convenience and style.

Give WAHL PEN to match EVERSHARP. The indestructible all-metal barrel of WAHL PEN holds more ink, positively prevents leaking and will last forever. The iridium-tipped point writes as smoothly as a 2B lead. Priced as low as $4.

WAHL PEN and EVERSHARP make superb presents, singly, or matched in engraved designs, in velvet-lined Gift Boxes. Finished in gold or silver. See them at your dealer's.

Made in U. S. A. by THE WAHL COMPANY, Chicago
Canadian Factory, THE WAHL COMPANY, LTD., Toronto

EVERSHARP
matched by
WAHL PEN

"What's wrong with this man's pocket?"

Can it be possible that he still uses one of the ordinary whittle-and-sharpen lead pencils? He should know that Eversharp is the high-sign of efficient writing. For time-saving, convenience and sheer beauty, Eversharp has no equal. Have you one in your pocket?

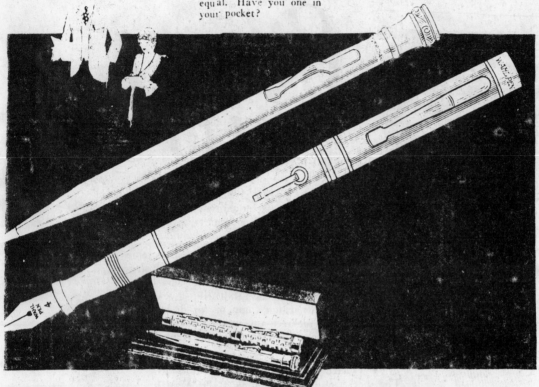

Your money buys excep—tional service in Eversharp
—and Eversharp can't be copied

When you pay $1 to $10 for Eversharp, you buy an extraordinary pencil. It has beauty, of course; its perfect balance doesn't tire your hand; and it writes without wiggle or wobble of its tale-smooth lead. Push it to the limit; it will keep on writing.

How long will Eversharp write? Twenty million Eversharps in use fail to complete the answer. From everywhere come service records so amazing, so convincing of Eversharp durability that you can count on an Eversharp serving you a lifetime.

Never a toy, always the leader, Eversharp, in beauty and writeability, is to-day the outstanding purchase. Buy it to-day—and for the years to come. Styles in gold and silver, for men and women, for pocket or purse, chain or ribbon.

The Wahl Pen is Eversharp's mate—matches in beauty and practical superiority. The all-metal barrel holds more ink, won't crack or split, lasts a lifetime. Prices $4 to $10. Eversharp and Wahl Pen in solid gold at higher prices. Wahl Pens in rubber, from $2.50 up. Look for the name on the pencil and the pen.

Made in U. S. A. by THE WAHL CO., Chicago
Canadian Factory, THE WAHL CO., LTD., Toronto

IMPORTANT. A pencil is no better than its lead. Don't use a poor quality lead in your Eversharp. Use Eversharp leads, which are recognized as the finest that can be made—a fact proved by over 200,000,000 which are sold every year. They are made to fit the pencil. Get them. Seven grades, from very soft to very hard. Ask for the new small-diameter colored leads, too! In the red top box.

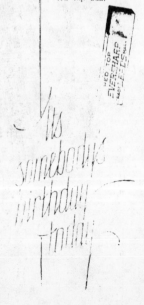

Wahl-Eversharp Advertisement — 1923

Its somebody's birthday today

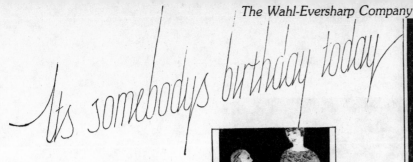

A write-hand combination with features that can't be copied

It's a happy birthday that brings to the owner of an Eversharp a Wahl Pen to match it. It's a doubly happy birthday that brings both these improved writing instruments to the person who still uses the old-fashioned kind.

Eversharp is the greatest pencil improvement ever made. It is beautiful. It does away with whittling and sharpening. It doesn't get lost. It is perfectly balanced for perfect writing ease. It is made to last a lifetime. And Eversharp's patented features can't be copied by other mechanical pencils.

The Wahl Pen, with its all-metal barrel, is indestructible—there's no limit to its length of life. It holds more ink. All parts fit as perfectly as the parts of a watch. No leakage in the pocket. No twisting of threads or cracking as with rubber.

Eversharp and Wahl Pen are made in gold and silver, in designs that match, and in various sizes, for pockets, purse, ribbon or chain. Eversharp, $1 to $10. Wahl Pen, $4 to $10. Solid gold at higher prices. Look for the name on the pencil and the pen.

Made in U. S. A. by THE WAHL CO., Chicago
Canadian Factory, THE WAHL CO., LTD., Toronto

EVERSHARP
matched by
WAHL PEN

Remember!
You can't have a good pencil unless you have good lead. Don't refill your Eversharp with "any old kind." Also—Eversharp Pencils and Eversharp Leads are made to *fit* each other. You can't be sure of the same results with any other combination. Two hundred million Eversharp Leads are sold per year. 15c in the red top box. Seven grades, from very soft to very hard.

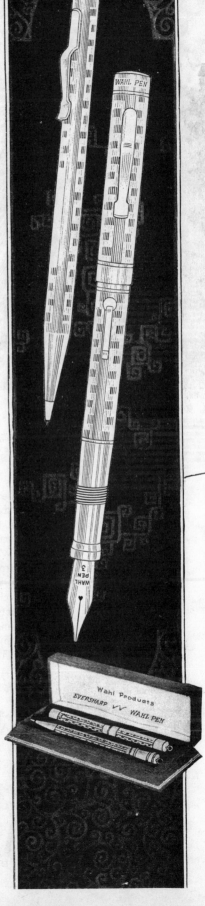

This Eversharp patent prevents a wobbly lead.

The Eversharp rifled tip is made like the inside of a rifle barrel. It cuts tiny grooves in the sides of the lead and holds the point like a vise until you are ready to move it. No slipping, no wobbling. Eversharp loads at the breech, like a rifle, and carries enough lead at one time to write 240,000 words.

Wahl-Eversharp Advertisement — April 1923

Copyright 1923
THE WAHL CO.

See the Wahl Pen at all dealers.
Gold-filled or Silver $4 to $10.

New Beauty—
and new practical usefulness

HOME-MADE
Gold point, iridium-tipped—the vital part. We make our own, carefully, painstakingly. Perfect points guaranteed.

FOR every hand that writes, for every man or woman who uses a fountain pen, there is a new idea—a beautiful, all-metal Wahl Pen of gold or silver.

Wooden pencils gave way to Eversharp metal pencils. The metal pen is just as modern and just as logical a development. For the Wahl Pen is practically indestructible. Drop it, lean against it, screw the cap too hard—nothing will break.

The all-metal barrel, thin yet strong, gives greatly increased ink capacity. Its better balance—the feel of the pen in your fingers—makes writing easier, smoother. The beautiful finish carries the Wahl Metal Pen into the hands of

men and women who appreciate the best in life, who know that fine, efficient instruments are definite factors in producing good work.

What made the Wahl Metal Pen possible

The self-filling fountain pen brought into use the rubber sac which actually holds the supply of ink.

Formerly the ink was contained in the barrel of the pen itself. And so it was necessary to use a material that the acid in the ink would not eat away.

The use of the rubber sac made possible the modern Wahl Metal Pen. The Wahl metal construction gives greater strength, greater ink capacity, and the beauty which is found only in engraved gold or silver.

Made in U. S. A. by THE WAHL COMPANY, CHICAGO
Canadian Factory, THE WAHL COMPANY, LTD., TORONTO

Manufacturers of the Wahl Eversharp and the Wahl All-Metal Fountain Pen

WAHL PEN

Wahl-Eversharp Advertisement — 1924

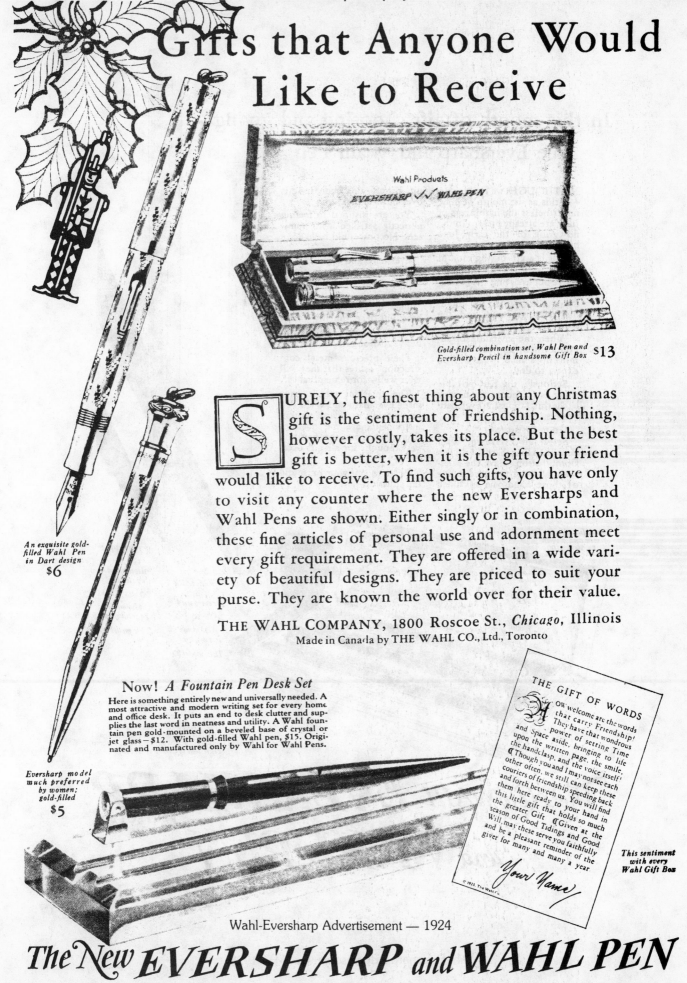

Gifts that Anyone Would Like to Receive

Gold-filled combination set, Wahl Pen and Eversharp Pencil in handsome Gift Box $13

An exquisite gold-filled Wahl Pen in Dart design $6

SURELY, the finest thing about any Christmas gift is the sentiment of Friendship. Nothing, however costly, takes its place. But the best gift is better, when it is the gift your friend would like to receive. To find such gifts, you have only to visit any counter where the new Eversharps and Wahl Pens are shown. Either singly or in combination, these fine articles of personal use and adornment meet every gift requirement. They are offered in a wide variety of beautiful designs. They are priced to suit your purse. They are known the world over for their value.

THE WAHL COMPANY, 1800 Roscoe St., *Chicago*, Illinois

Made in Canada by THE WAHL CO., Ltd., Toronto

Eversharp model much preferred by women; gold-filled $5

Now! *A Fountain Pen Desk Set*

Here is something entirely new and universally needed. A most attractive and modern writing set for every home and office desk. It puts an end to desk clutter and supplies the last word in neatness and utility. A Wahl fountain pen gold-mounted on a beveled base of crystal or jet glass — $12. With gold-filled Wahl pen, $15. Originated and manufactured only by Wahl for Wahl Pens.

THE GIFT OF WORDS

How welcome are the words that carry Friendship! They have that wondrous power of setting Time and Space aside, bringing to life upon the written page, the smile, the handclasp, and the voice itself. Though you and I may not see each other often, we still can keep these couriers of friendship speeding back and forth between us. You will find them here ready to your hand in this little gift that holds so much the greater Gift. Given at the season of Good Tidings and Good Will, may these serve you faithfully and be a pleasant reminder of the giver for many and many a year.

Your Name

This sentiment with every Wahl Gift Box

Wahl-Eversharp Advertisement — 1924

The New EVERSHARP and WAHL PEN

In this month of gift choosing and giving—
See Eversharp and Wahl Pen

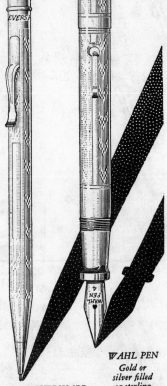

ALTHOUGH we look upon this as the month of May, nevertheless the harbingers of June are already present in the flowering of the early June brides.

This is a gift buying month!

Not only are the ministers active but even now the institutions of learning are loosing upon the world, the bold, masterful graduates and the sweet girl graduates.

When the invitation or announcement appears in your morning's mail, what do you expect to do?

Seriously, the best possible thing is to choose the nearest of the thirty thousand Eversharp dealers.

Go to his store.

Select an Eversharp, Wahl Pen, or an Eversharp, Wahl Pen Combination. Have the salesman put your purchase in one of those handsome silk-lined gift boxes—and everything is over but the pleasure.

You are justified in feeling perfectly satisfied with yourself. No one could have done better.

Eversharp and Wahl Pen are the products of the foremost manufacturer of fine writing equipment.

They have beauty to carry a heart full of sentiment.

They are useful, which signifies your thoughtfulness.

Their precious metal construction insures that they will wear well—for remembrance.

The qualities which have made Eversharp and Wahl Pen the world's standard writing instruments are the qualities that make them the first and best thought for all gift occasions.

Prices to suit your purse and the situation.

Beautiful gift sets for men and women $4.50 to $100

WAHL PEN
Gold or silver filled or sterling
$3 to $10
Also made in solid gold
This model $8

EVERSHARP
Models for every need
50¢ to $6
Also made in solid gold
This model $5

Wahl Eversharp and Wahl Pen
Made in U. S. A. by The Wahl Co., Chicago
Made in Canada by The Wahl Co., Ltd., Toronto
Prices same in Canada as U. S.

The New WAHL EVERSHARP PERFECTED and WAHL PEN

The big pencil with *the* easy grip *and the* big smooth-writing lead ~ ~

EVERSHARP "75"

PERFECTED

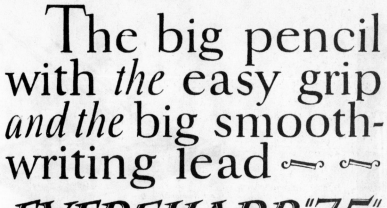

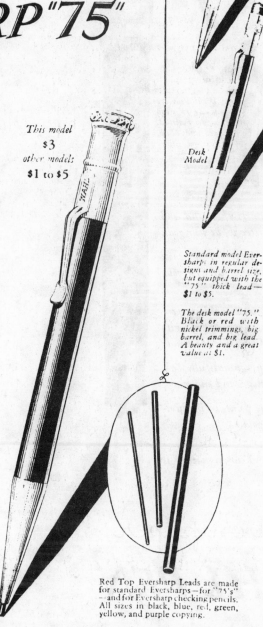

Standard Model

Desk Model

This model
$3
other models
$1 to $5

EVERSHARP "75" is the name of a new series of Eversharps using leads almost twice the thickness of those carried by the standard Eversharp.

You will like this big, smooth-writing lead. And Eversharp "75" is made in large barrel models—a big pencil as well as a big lead.

The big pencils have all the Eversharp features, including the famous, patented, rifled tip which holds the lead firmly *at the point,* so it cannot wobble or turn. They are obtainable in black, red, or mottled, with gold trim, at $3—in black or red, nickel trim, at $1. And all are handsome.

Regular model Eversharps with the new thicker lead complete the "75" family. Try the Eversharp "75" at your dealer's.

Wahl Eversharp and Wahl Pen
Made in U. S. A. by THE WAHL CO., Chicago
Made in Canada by THE WAHL CO., Ltd., Toronto
Prices same in Canada as U. S.

Standard model Eversharp in regular design and barrel size, but equipped with the "75" thick lead—$1 to $5.

The desk model "75." Black or red with nickel trimmings, big barrel, and big lead. A beauty and a great value at $1.

Red Top Eversharp Leads are made for standard Eversharps—for "75's" —and for Eversharp checking pencils. All sizes in black, blue, red, green, yellow, and purple copying.

Wahl Pens are made in new shades of mottled, red and black. This one sells at $7

A great team is the hand and brain, no matter what your goal.

Train them together, in school and in the game of life, for your victory.

One of the greatest aids to perfect play of the mind is a writing tool perfected for the hand:

A Wahl Pen—beautifully balanced, capacious, and enduring:

Your favorite point, in iridium-tipped solid gold.

√   √

Remember, "Your signature is you."

Put it on paper
WAHL PEN

Made by the makers of Eversharp

Wahl Fountain Pen Desk Sets from $7.50 to $30. Set illustrated, marble or glass base, two pens, $30.00

The Gifts that Santa Claus Himself would Choose

Here are gifts that echo Merry Christmas all the year around √ Wahl Fountain Pen Desk Sets and Wahl-Eversharp Writing Sets √ √ The desk sets are something entirely new √ √ A single gracefully tapered Wahl Fountain Pen, or a pair of them, perfectly balanced to the hand and set on a base of imported Italian Portoro Marble, Emeraline Glass, or Pearl Amerith √ √ Ball and socket joints that permit turning the pens to any angle or elevation √ √ Wahl-Eversharp Writing Sets—a Wahl Pen nested in an attractive gift box with its companion Eversharp—are *write* gifts for everybody √ √ At Wahl-Eversharp counters everywhere.

Wahl-Eversharp Writing Sets from $5.00 to $35.00. Set illustrated, gold-filled, $13.00

EVERSHARP
and
WAHL PEN

Marble base desk set,   *black rubber pen, $10*

Onyx base home desk set; rosewood pen $7.50

Ladies' brocaded combination set; pen, $7 pencil, $6

For Every *June* Occasion

Gifts — *gifts* — GIFTS!
For the best man and the ushers. For the matron of honor and the bridesmaids. For the happy pair themselves.

For the graduate.

For the lucky traveler who's going abroad the first time and of course will keep a diary.

Surpassingly lovely gifts. Surprisingly handy and superbly useful. From Wahl-Eversharp counters everywhere.

Such delightful aids to fashion as Eversmart Manicure Compacts. Such personal writing equipment as Eversharp Pencils and Wahl Pens,

in plain gold for gentlemen, perhaps in colorful brocade enameled finishes for ladies. Wahl Fountain Pen Desk Sets for office and home.

A treasure-house of these beautiful gifts, is every Wahl-Eversharp counter. And every article you choose from it is of Wahl-Eversharp manufacture, which means the guaranteed standard of materials, workmanship, jeweler design.

All with exclusive, original features. Eversmarts—nothing else like them. Eversharps—the famous rifled tip. Wahl Pens—14-karat, osmiridium-tipped points of solid gold—built to write, and to write well, always.

EVERSHARP
the name is on the pencil

WAHL PEN
Eversharp's write-hand companion

Eversmart, gold-filled, ripple design, $5   *Gold-filled Eversmart, blue lizard, $5*   *Cloisonné Eversmart, gold-filled, $10*

Men's gold-filled pen; matches Standard Eversharp $8

Standard Eversharp; gold-filled; rifled tip $5

© 1927, The Wahl Company, Chicago—The Wahl Company, Ltd., Toronto

Wahl-Eversharp Advertisement — June 4, 1927

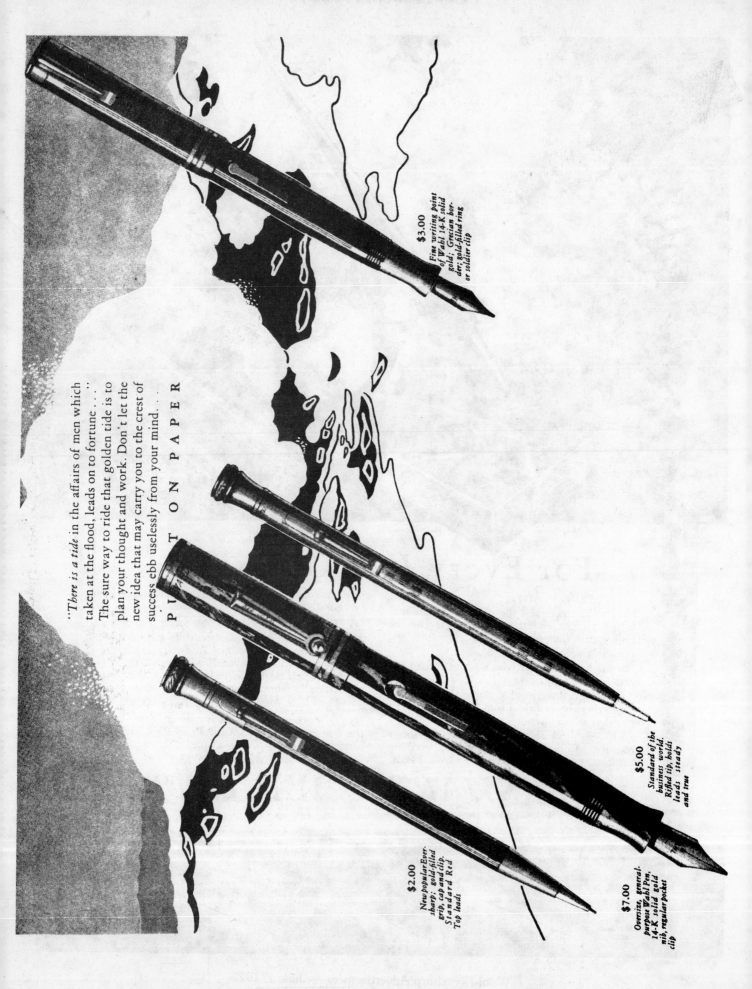

PI T ON PAPER

"There is a tide in the affairs of men which taken at the flood, leads on to fortune . . ." The sure way to ride that golden tide is to plan your thought and work. Don't let the new idea that may carry you to the crest of success ebb uselessly from your mind . . .

$3.00
Fine writing point of Wahl 14-K solid gold; Grecian border; gold-filled ring or soldier clip

$5.00
Standard of the business world. Rifled tip, holds leads steady and true

$2.00
New popular Eversharp; gold-filled grip, cap and clip. Standard Red Top leads

$7.00
Oversize, general-purpose Wahl Pen, 14-K solid gold nib, regular pocket clip

Keeping to the Point

Wahl workmen make good fountain pens in as many as 1500 different designs, sizes, colors and styles.

But Wahl workmen focus their skill chiefly on the working-end of the pen—the writing nib.

By thus keeping to the point they produce a pen that writes supremely well.

They tip everlasting solid gold with that hardest metal, osmiridium, and point and smooth and grind and polish it to writing perfection.

If you want a fountain pen that writes smoothly and tirelessly well, just try the Wahl pen.

And try it by the only test of a pen that means anything:

PUT IT ON PAPER

At any Wahl-Eversharp counter you'll find your choice of color, size or price in the pen that's "right as write can be"

WAHL PEN

write-hand companion of the famous

EVERSHARP

the name is on the pencil

$5.00
Easy writing nib of Wahl 14-K solid gold; osmiridium tipped; regular size

Wahl-Eversharp Advertisement — 1927

Money Can Not Buy a Better Writing Pen

From these 14 Wahl graduated, easy-writing points, pick the one that fits your writing stroke.

See your dealer today. He will gladly assist you in selecting the *one pen that was made for you.*

For real writing satisfaction pick your pen by its point. That means Wahl, a matchless value at this sensible price, five dollars.

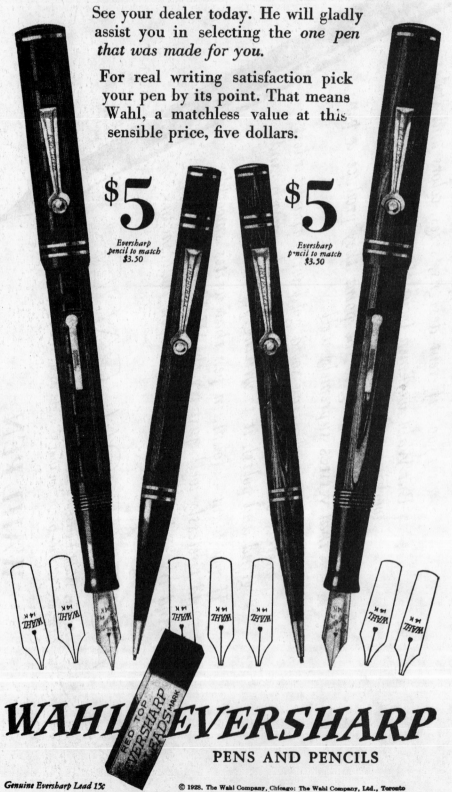

$5

Eversharp pencil to match $3.50

$5

Eversharp pencil to match $3.50

WAHL EVERSHARP
PENS AND PENCILS

Genuine Eversharp Lead 15c   © 1928. The Wahl Company, Chicago: The Wahl Company, Ltd., Toronto

Wahl-Eversharp Advertisement — 1928

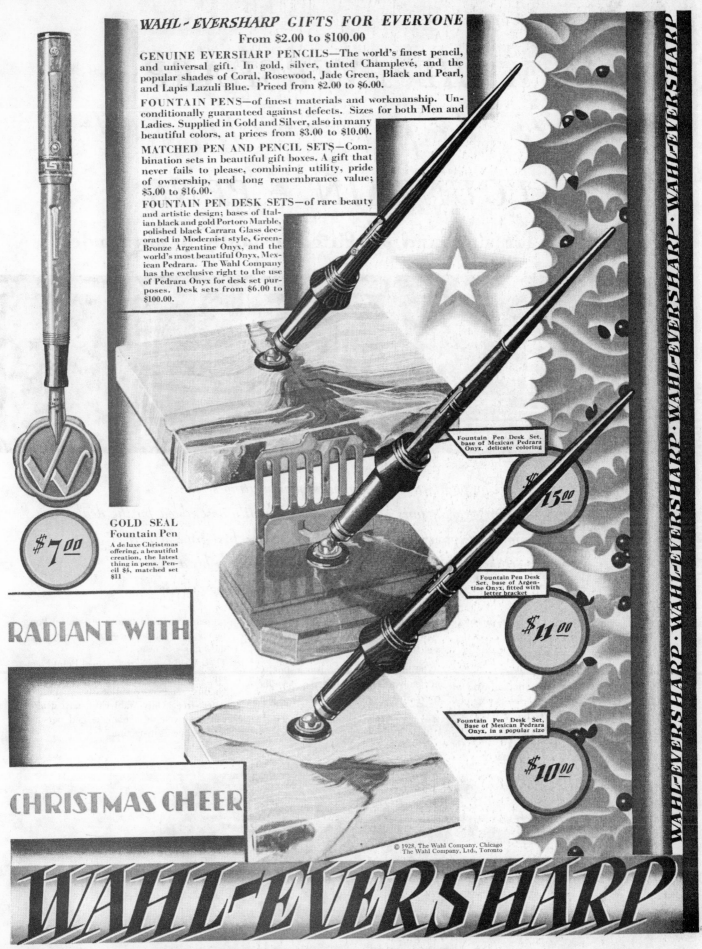

WAHL - EVERSHARP GIFTS FOR EVERYONE
From $2.00 to $100.00

GENUINE EVERSHARP PENCILS—The world's finest pencil, and universal gift. In gold, silver, tinted Champlevé, and the popular shades of Coral, Rosewood, Jade Green, Black and Pearl, and Lapis Lazuli Blue. Priced from $2.00 to $6.00.

FOUNTAIN PENS—of finest materials and workmanship. Unconditionally guaranteed against defects. Sizes for both Men and Ladies. Supplied in Gold and Silver, also in many beautiful colors, at prices from $3.00 to $10.00.

MATCHED PEN AND PENCIL SETS—Combination sets in beautiful gift boxes. A gift that never fails to please, combining utility, pride of ownership, and long remembrance value; $5.00 to $16.00.

FOUNTAIN PEN DESK SETS—of rare beauty and artistic design; bases of Italian black and gold Portoro Marble, polished black Carrara Glass decorated in Modernist style, Green-Bronze Argentine Onyx, and the world's most beautiful Onyx, Mexican Pedrara. The Wahl Company has the exclusive right to the use of Pedrara Onyx for desk set purposes. Desk sets from $6.00 to $100.00.

$7.00

GOLD SEAL
Fountain Pen
A de luxe Christmas offering, a beautiful creation, the latest thing in pens. Pencil $4, matched set $11

Fountain Pen Desk Set, base of Mexican Pedrara Onyx, delicate coloring

$15.00

Fountain Pen Desk Set, base of Argentine Onyx, fitted with letter bracket

$11.00

Fountain Pen Desk Set, Base of Mexican Pedrara Onyx, in a popular size

$10.00

RADIANT WITH

CHRISTMAS CHEER

© 1928, The Wahl Company, Chicago
The Wahl Company, Ltd., Toronto

WAHL-EVERSHARP

Wahl-Eversharp Advertisement — December 15, 1928

WAHL-EVERSHARP
Personal-Point
FOUNTAIN PENS

A point for any hand ··· Fitted instantly to any holder

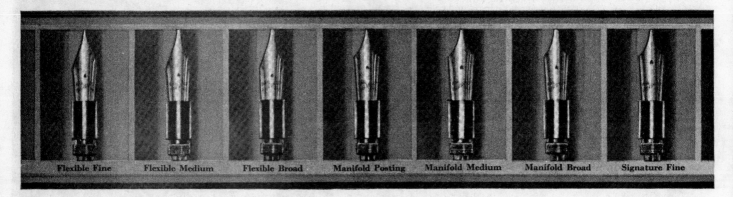

Flexible Fine   Flexible Medium   Flexible Broad   Manifold Posting   Manifold Medium   Manifold Broad   Signature Fine

*The point that exactly suits your writing stroke
and the holder that exactly suits your taste··permanently assembled by the dealer
in an instant···* YOUR PERSONAL PEN. *Now, for the first time, a perfected,
personalized writing instrument made possible by a new
Wahl-Eversharp invention···the* INTERCHANGEABLE NIB

Surely here is the easier, simpler, surer way to select a fountain pen.

When you try the points, never mind what type of holder contains them.

When you look over the alluring array of holder colors, sizes and styles—never mind what kind of points they happen to have.

But after you find *the point which writes like* you—after you choose the holder which suits your exact ideas of color, balance, price, size and style—

—let the dealer put the two instantly, permanently together! Then you have the entirely satisfying, strictly personal fountain pen.

It writes with gliding smoothness at just your natural angle—it responds to exactly the pressure you instinctively use—the ink flows precisely as you like it—from the pen you most enjoy to own.

These Wahl-Eversharp Personal-Point Fountain Pens are identified by the Gold Seal of Quality, and unconditionally guaranteed defect-free. Only Wahl-Eversharp dealers can offer you this complete and personal fountain pen satisfaction.

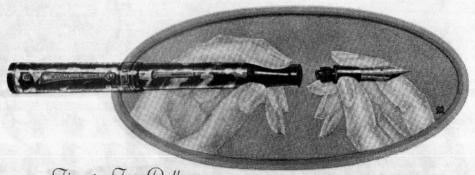

Five to Ten Dollars

Wahl-Eversharp Advertisement — June 1, 1929

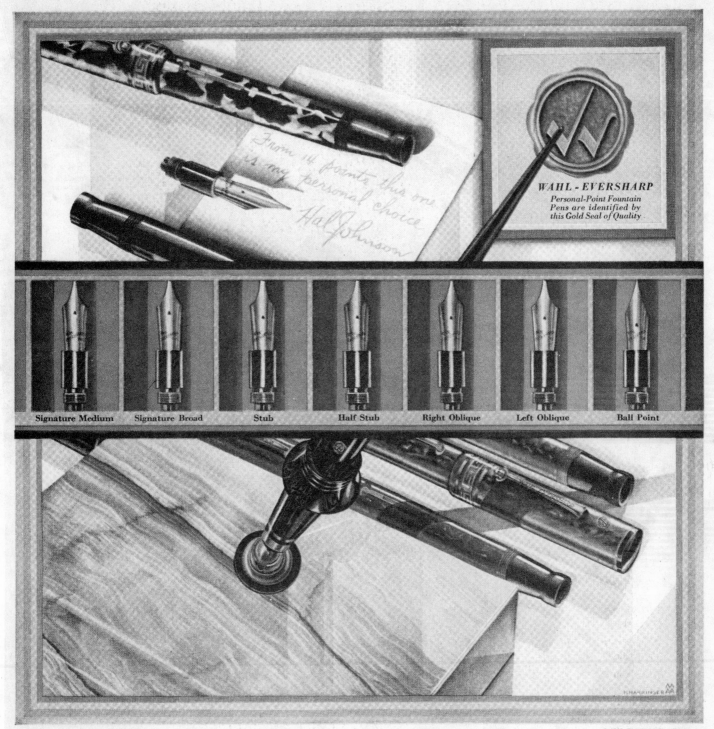

Signature Medium Signature Broad Stub Half Stub Right Oblique Left Oblique Ball Point

WAHL-EVERSHARP
Personal-Point
FOUNTAIN PENS

Wahl-Eversharp Advertisement — June 1, 1929

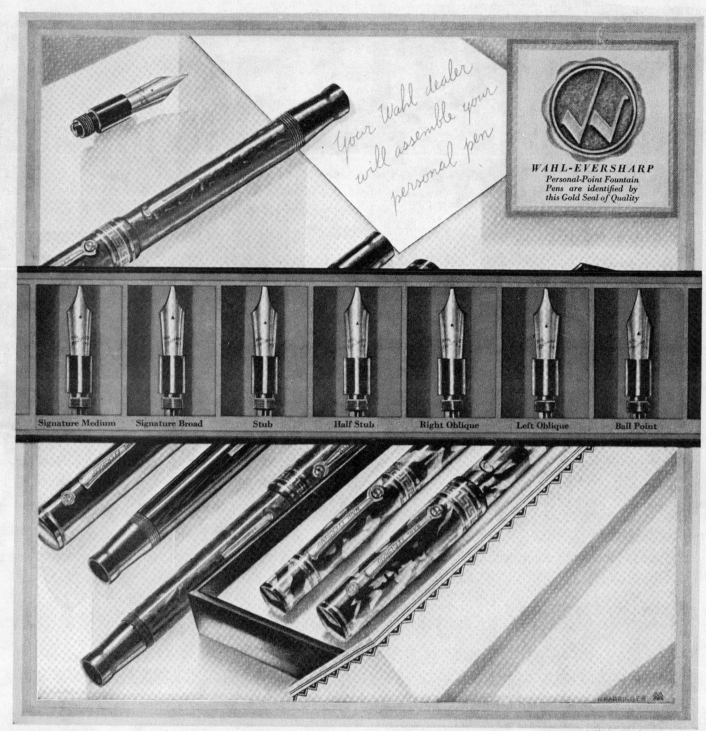

Your Wahl dealer will assemble your personal pen

WAHL-EVERSHARP
Personal-Point Fountain Pens are identified by this Gold Seal of Quality

| Signature Medium | Signature Broad | Stub | Half Stub | Right Oblique | Left Oblique | Ball Point |

© 1929, The Wahl Co., Chicago
The Wahl Co., *Ltd.*, Toronto

WAHL-EVERSHARP
Personal-Point
FOUNTAIN PENS

Wahl-Eversharp Advertisement — September 7, 1929

He writes like this

John J. Robinson

—so from among the 14 Eversharp *Interchangeable* Points, he selected the

MEDIUM SIGNATURE

Which point should YOU select? Obviously, that depends on your individual style of handwriting. Executives, who use fountain pens principally for signatures on letters or checks, require a sturdy, free-flowing, semi-flexible point—like the Wahl-Eversharp "Signature" —a point especially made for this purpose. There is an Eversharp Personal-Point built to fit your hand and need *exactly*, and you can secure it in a fountain pen that reflects your taste in color, size, and style.

The Eversharp Personal-Point is a separate unit of nib and feed, constructed and adjusted at the factory, which any dealer can fit into any pen holder at the time of purchase— while you wait. No other make of fountain pen has this revolutionary feature.

Buy your fountain pen this new and better way

Select by test your personal point

In a few minutes at any Eversharp counter you can choose the point that writes exactly the way you like to write

Then—choose the holder you like best

There are all kinds: the popular colors in all styles, shapes, and sizes—for men and women—for pocket or desk

The two are instantly assembled— by the dealer

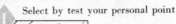

In a moment your point and holder are permanently united— a truly personal pen. Surely $5 to $10 is little to pay for such a personalized writing instrument

FINE SIGNATURE
Preferred by women for social correspondence

FULL STUB
Writes very wide lines, heavily shaded

HALF STUB
Lighter than stub, with same characteristics

FINE MANIFOLD
For bookkeeping, posting and Gregg shorthand

BALL POINT
Extra smooth, favored by older people

BROAD FLEXIBLE
For those who like a broad down stroke

MEDIUM FLEXIBLE
Best for the average hand and general usage

MEDIUM MANIFOLD
Makes carbon copies. Excellent for salesmen and accountants

RIGHT OBLIQUE
For stub pen writers who like an unshaded line

BROAD MANIFOLD
Same as medium—for "large" flowing hands

LEFT OBLIQUE
Specially made by Eversharp for left-handed writers

MEDIUM SIGNATURE
The executive's point for general desk work

FINE FLEXIBLE
For stenographers and Spencerian writers

BROAD SIGNATURE
Same as medium, writing a heavier, broader line

EVERSHARP
World's Standard Pencil in companion styles to match your Personal Point Pen—$4.50. Other styles 50c to $50

A POINT FOR ANY HAND—
FITTED INSTANTLY BY DEALER TO ANY HOLDER

WAHL EVERSHARP
Personal-Point
FOUNTAIN PENS

The Seal of Unconditional Guarantee

What Does Your Handwriting Reveal?
Tune in on the Eversharp Penman—8:30 P. M. Eastern Standard Time, Every Friday, on Columbia basic network stations

© 1930, The Wahl Company, Chicago
The Wahl Company, Ltd., Toronto

ONLY   EVERSHARP   PERSONAL-POINT   FOUNTAIN   PENS   HAVE   THE   INTERCHANGEABLE   POINT

Wahl-Eversharp Advertisement — March 1, 1930

She writes like this

Edythe Carpenter '34

—So She Chose Eversharp's
MEDIUM FLEXIBLE POINT
to Pen Her College Themes

If you want a fountain pen that *writes* as
well as it looks for your "write-hand" companion through college, mark this fact:
only the new Eversharp Personal-Point Pen
offers you the point that exactly *fits* your
individual handwriting—in an ultra-smart
holder any color, size and shape you most
desire! There is an Eversharp Personal-
Point for every writing style from the dainti-
est hand on Sorority Row to the mighty fist
of the varsity fullback. Every point is instantly *interchangeable* in any of the many
distinctive Eversharp holders—a revolutionary feature which enables you to secure
without delay any combination of point
and holder you personally select. If your
Eversharp is a gift, your dealer will gladly
exchange the point to suit.

*Buy your fountain pen
this new and better way*

**Select by test your
Personal-Point**

Each is a complete factory-
perfected unit, consisting of
hand ground 14K Personal-
Point and patented even-flowing Wahl Comb Feed

**Then—choose the
holder you like best**

A lavish assortment: the popular colors in all styles, sizes
and shapes—for men and
women, for pocket and desk

*The Two are Perma-
nently Assembled—
by the Dealer—Before
your eyes, your point and
your holder are instantly
united into your personal
pen for everlasting service*

EVERSHARP
World's Standard
Pencil to match your
Personal-Point Pen
—$4.00. Other styles
50c to $50

Use non-clogging Red
Top Leads for complete
writing satisfaction

RED TOP
EVERSHARP TRADE LEADS MARK

A point for any hand—fitted instantly by the dealer to any holder

WAHL
EVERSHARP
Personal-Point
FOUNTAIN PENS

$5 to $10

The Seal of Unconditional Guarantee

© 1930, The Wahl Co., Chicago
The Wahl Co., Ltd., Toronto

BROAD FLEXIBLE	FINE FLEXIBLE	RIGHT OBLIQUE	LEFT OBLIQUE	MEDIUM FLEXIBLE	FINE SIGNATURE	MEDIUM SIGNATURE	BROAD SIGNATURE	FINE MANIFOLD	MEDIUM MANIFOLD	BROAD MANIFOLD	BALL POINT	FULL STUB	HALF STUB
For those who like a broad down stroke	For stenographers and Spencerian writers	For right-hand back-handed writing	For left-hand back-handed writers	Best for the average hand and general usage; writes smoothly on any paper	Preferred by women for social correspondence	The executive's point for general desk work	For bold forceful hands; writes a heavy line	For bookkeeping and Gregg Shorthand	A stiff point; excellent for accountants	Makes carbon copies; ideal for salesmen	Extra smooth, favored by older people	Writes very wide lines heavily shaded	Finer than stub, with same characteristics

ONLY EVERSHARP PERSONAL-POINT FOUNTAIN PENS HAVE THE INTERCHANGEABLE POINT

Wahl-Eversharp Advertisement — September 13, 1930

A lovely Argentine Onyx Desk Set with *matched* Eversharp Personal-Point Pen for the home—$11. Extra with statuette.

Rich Black and Pearl, this Eversharp *matched* Personal-Point Pen and Pencil Set will please any man. Beautifully boxed—$10

Jet Black Eversharp *matched* Personal-Point Pen and Pencil Set with special clips, for ladies. Also in other colors—$8.50

Handsome desk set of Argentine Onyx, mounting two Personal-Point Pens and beautiful antique bronze lamp—$85. Pacific Coast—$95

Jade Green Eversharp Personal-Point Pen and Pencil *matched* set, specially designed for students. Attractively priced, in gift box—$6

Merry Christmas

No Other Gifts Like These

Points may be exchanged

AFTER CHRISTMAS

to suit any writing style

Individual pen-point preferences need not worry you when you give these ultra-smart new Eversharp *Personal-Point* Fountain Pens, Desk Sets and Combination Sets. They are the most personal of all writing gifts because those who receive them can exchange the points to *fit* their individual handwriting—at any Eversharp counter anywhere, without delay, after Christmas. Only Eversharp offers this *interchangeable-point* feature—a revolutionary new improvement which makes any lovely Eversharp gift as sure to give everlasting satisfaction as though it were personally selected by the one who will use it always. A lavish assortment in all colors, sizes, styles and prices, beautifully boxed, await your selection at better stores.

Milady's desk set—Black Carrara Glass base, with letter bracket and Personal-Point Pen. Also in marble or onyx—$10

A very attractive *matched* Personal-Point Pen and Pencil Set in the popular new Rosewood finish—for feminine purse—$5

Monarch of all writing equipment. Rich Black and Pearl Equi-Poised Personal-Point Pen and Pencil *matched* set—boxed—$15

Black and Gold Portoro Marble Desk Set, mounted with two Coral Personal-Point Pens and antique bronze golfer statuette—$27.50

Exquisite Bronze and Green—Eversharp's exclusive new color creation—makes this *matched* Personal-Point Pen and Pencil Set unique—$10

WAHL
EVERSHARP
Personal-Point
FOUNTAIN PENS

$5 to $10

The Seal of Unconditional Guarantee

14 POINTS
One for Every Hand—

There are 14 different Eversharp Interchangeable Personal-Points— one for every writing need. Each is a separate unit consisting of hand-ground 14-k gold point and even-flowing comb feed.

Ladies' Equi-Poised Eversharp Personal-Point Pen in exquisite new Jade Green. Equi-Poised insures tireless writing. $5

Men's Equi-Poised Eversharp Personal-Point Fountain Pen in the favorite new Bronze and Green. Gracefully tapered. $10

—INSTANTLY
Fitted to Any Holder

Any Eversharp Personal-Point can be instantly and permanently combined, by the dealer, with any handsome Eversharp holder you select—*while* you wait. Eversharp offers the widest variety of holders.

© 1930, The Wahl Co., Chicago
The Wahl Co., Ltd., Toronto

ONE OF THESE EVERSHARP *PERSONAL-POINTS* EXACTLY FITS YOUR HAND

Wahl-Eversharp Advertisement — December 6, 1930

CATHAY

MOROCCO

BURMA

The new

EVERSHARP

THE WORLD'S MOST

UTTERLY DIFFERENT IN DESIGN, these new Doric creations by Eversharp have a beauty beyond all other writing instruments—a smartness no picture can reveal. . . . Inspired by the fluted Doric columns of classic Greece, they are not round, but many-sided—shimmering like precious jewels from a dozen sparkling faces. **AND WHAT COLORS!** Elusive oriental treasure hues, never before duplicated. *Cathay*, the silvery-green of a mandarin's priceless porcelain. *Morocco*, from a historic Moorish mosaic. *Burma*, a rich smoke-grey pearl. *Kashmir Green*, from Persia. And *Jet*, gleaming with ebon beauty. . . . Finest of writing tools, tapering, slender, feather-weight —an end to bulging pockets, and infinitely more comfortable in the hand. A memorable commencement gift.

A POINT FOR EVERY HAND Fourteen Different Interchangeable Points — One for Every Style of Handwriting — **FITTED INSTANTLY** to the Holder of Your Choice

© 1931, The Wahl Company, Chicago
The Wahl Company, Ltd., Toronto

Wahl-Eversharp Advertisement — 1931

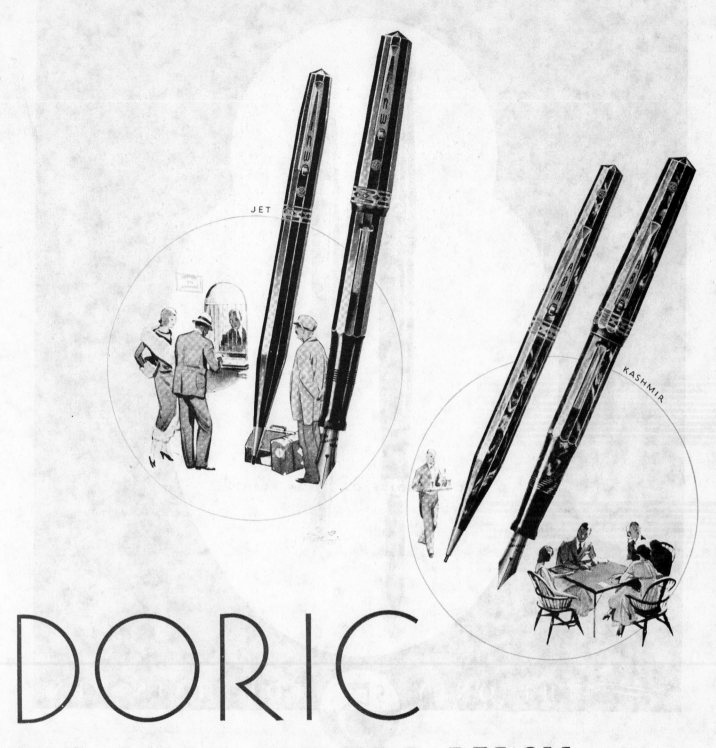

JET

KASHMIR

DORIC

BEAUTIFUL PEN AND PENCIL

WITH CHOICE OF 14 PERSONAL-POINTS. Regardless of how you hold your pen, Eversharp's exclusive interchangeable-point feature permits you to secure the point that exactly *fits* your hand—*instantly*—in any Doric pen...Dealers will gladly exchange points in gift pens to suit recipients. **YOUR INITIALS ENGRAVED—IN** DORIC

To identify your *hand-fitted* Doric pen as your very own, forever, Eversharp dealers will engrave your initials on the clip in lovely Doric letters—making it a doubly personalized possession.

EVERSHARP

Personal-Point

PENS AND PENCILS

EVERSHARP GOLD SEAL PENS AND PENCILS UNCONDITIONALLY GUARANTEED FOR LIFE

DORIC MODELS, PENS, $7.50 TO $10.00; PENCILS, $4.50 TO $5.00

Round Models, Pens, $5.00 to $8.00; Pencils, $3.50 and $4.00.   Other Eversharp Pens, $3.00 to $4.50.   Eversharp Pencils, $1.00 to $50.00

YOUR CHOICE OF 14 POINTS

THE ONLY **$5** FOUNTAIN PEN

individually fitted to your hand

Regardless of price, no other *round* fountain pen offers so much as this new $5 Eversharp Personal-Point Pen. It is modern, better balanced, slenderly tapered—an end to bulging pockets. It is unconditionally guaranteed for life! And in addition, Eversharp is the only pen that gives you a choice of 14 *interchangeable* points—one for every type of handwriting—backhand, shorthand, *any hand*. The dealer instantly assembles the point you like with the holder you prefer—creating a smoother-writing, *hand-fitted* fountain pen that is really worth treasuring forever.

Models for both men and women in Jade Green, Jet Black and Tunis, the rich new ruby and black offered only by Eversharp.

EVERSHARP

Personal-Point

PENS AND ⓦ PENCILS

ROUND MODELS—Gold Seal Pens, $5 to $8. Other Eversharp Pens $3 and $4.50. Eversharp Pencils $1 to $50.

© 1931, The Wahl Co., Chicago
The Wahl Co., Ltd., Toronto

Wahl-Eversharp Advertisement 1931

DORIC MODELS—Twelve-sided—in five oriental treasure colors—*the world's most beautiful pen and pencil.* Pens $7.50 to $10. Pencils $4.50 and $5. Solid-gold-mounted (14k) Pen and Pencil Sets—men's $25; ladies' $23.50.

UNCONDITIONALLY GUARANTEED FOR LIFE

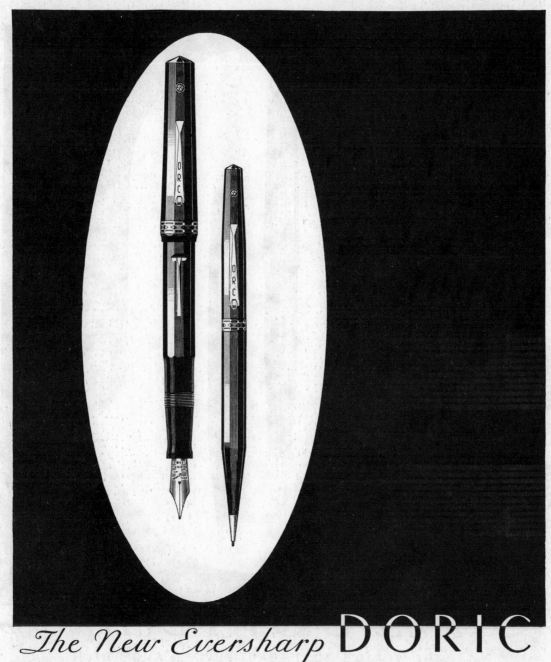

The New Eversharp DORIC

Twelve-sided • Utterly different • Slender, tapering sides cut like jewels • Gleaming, sparkling, featherweight • In five exotic oriental colors. De luxe writing instruments • Personalized with your initials engraved on the clips • And *hand fitted*, by the dealer, with your choice of 14 interchangeable points. ⓦ UNCONDITIONALLY GUARANTEED FOR LIFE

EVERSHARP
Personal-Point
PENS AND PENCILS
© 1931, The Wahl Co., Chicago; The Wahl Co., Ltd., Toronto

DORIC MODELS
Pens . . . . . . $7.50 to $10.00
Pencils . . . . . $4.00 and $5.00
ROUND MODELS
Pens . . . . . . $3.00 to $8.00
Pencils . . . . . $1.00 to $50.00

THE WORLD'S MOST BEAUTIFUL PEN AND PENCIL

Wahl-Eversharp Advertisement — October 1931

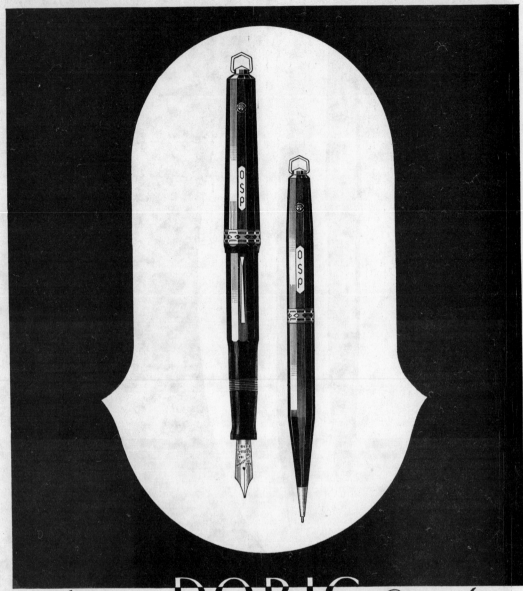

The New DORIC Eversharp

THE WORLD'S MOST BEAUTIFUL PEN AND PENCIL

A black diamond cut into a slender prism could be no more scintillating than these *twelve-sided* Doric pens and pencils in Jet— one of Eversharp's five new treasure colors. ...They are classic, jewel-bright, feather-weight—infinitely more comfortable in the hand.... The pens are individually *fitted* to your writing with your choice of Eversharp's 14 interchangeable points, instantly assembled in any holder.... Pens and pencils individualized with your initials engraved in Doric letters.

EVERSHARP
Personal-Point
PENS AND PENCILS

DORIC MODELS
Pens . . . . $7.50 to $10.00
Pencils . . . . $4.50 and $5.00
Solid-Gold-Mounted (14 K) Pen and
Pencil Sets—Men's $25; Ladies' $23.50

ROUND MODELS
Pens . . . . $3.00 to $8.00
Pencils . . . . $1.00 to $50.00
© 1931, The Wahl Co., Chicago
The Wahl Co., Ltd., Toronto

UNCONDITIONALLY GUARANTEED FOR LIFE

TO THOSE WHO RECEIVE
THE NEW **DORIC** EVERSHARP

Consider yourself doubly lucky this Christmas if you receive a new Eversharp Doric Pen and Pencil. Lucky first, because their modern twelve-sided shape, flashing jewel-brilliance, and radiant color tell you that you have the world's most beautiful writing instruments. Twice

lucky, because if the pen-point doesn't suit, you can exchange it—at any Eversharp counter—for whichever of Eversharp's 14 interchangeable points exactly fits your handwriting. . . . The set illustrated is the new Doric JET—personalized by the engraved initials on the clips.

EVERSHARP
Personal-Point
PENS AND *(W)* **PENCILS**

DORIC MODELS
Pens . . . . . . $7.50 to $10.00
Pencils . . . . . $4.50 and $5.00
Solid-Gold-Mounted (14 K) Pen and
Pencil Sets—Men's $25; Ladies' $23.50

ROUND MODELS
Pens . . . . $3.00 to $8.00
Pencils . . . . . . $1.00 to $50.00
© 1931, The Wahl Co., Chicago
The Wahl Co., Ltd., Toronto

UNCONDITIONALLY GUARANTEED FOR LIFE

Wahl-Eversharp Advertisement — December 1931

DORIC Pen and Pencil set. Pens, $7.50 to $10.
Pencils, $4.50 and $5

Noir marble desk set with green Argentine
and translucent onyx inlays, $15

Ladies' DORIC clasp set. Pens, $7.50 and
$8.50. Pencils, $4.50 and $5

© 1931, The Wahl Co., Chicago; The Wahl Co., Ltd., Toronto

receive an Eversharp writing gift

Remember, too, in choosing writing gifts for others, that Eversharps are by far the finest
made. There are the new DORIC Eversharps—*twelve-sided*, modern, jewel-bright, in five
new oriental treasure colors—the world's most beautiful pen and pencil. There are graceful
round models, too, slim and tapering for writing ease. And desk sets, mounted with single
pen, twin pens, or pen and pencil—at almost any price you care to pay. All models bearing
Eversharp's Gold Seal of Unconditional Guarantee for Life have the exclusive interchangeable
Personal-Point feature that insures your gift's being treasured always by the one who receives it.

ROUND MODELS—*Gold Seal pens with interchangeable points, $5 to $8. Other Eversharp pens $3 to $4.50. Pencils $1 to $50*

EVERSHARP
Personal-Point
PENS AND PENCILS

UNCONDITIONALLY GUARANTEED...
FOR LIFE

Wahl-Eversharp Advertisement — 1927

Claudette Colbert discovers the pen that writes 9 different way

New, Eversharp Adjustable Point delights famous screen star

WE ASKED Claudette Colbert to take a demonstration of one of the most ingenious fountain pens ever made—a pen that writes 9 different ways with *one point!* The Eversharp Adjustable Point Fountain Pen!

"Look at the top of this pen point," we said. "See this slider. It moves only one-quarter of an inch—to 9 different notches.

"Yet somewhere in that quarter-inch is the adjustment that will give you every kind of writing you'll ever be called on to do. . . . Here . . . try it . . . at Notch No. 1."

"Oh, that line is too fine," said Miss Colbert writing her name. "I like a broader writing line."

So we adjusted the slider to Notch No. 2—then No. 3 and No. 4. Finally at the sixth notch Miss Colbert exclaimed . . . *"That's it! . . . that's the kind of writing that suits me to a T!"* . . .

"And that's not all, Miss Colbert. The Eversharp Adjustable can do any kind of work you want. Simply regulate the slider—get as thin or thick a line you want—and write your check, your letters, sign your autographs, address your packages with the writing point best suited."

Writes perfectly . . . ALWAYS

With the Eversharp Adjustable Point Pen you get a flexible, medium or hard pen point, as quickly as snapping your fingers. You get exactly the kind of line you want —for your writing. You get a pen that fits you—that's as individual as your fingerprint.

Due to a little "breathing" device that regulates the flow of ink—the Adjustable Point

Wahl-Eversharp Advertisement — October, 1934

CLAUDETTE COLBERT, popular Paramount star, now appearing in "Torch Singer" using the Eversharp Adjustable Point in several different ways. (1) A fine, hairline stroke for writing small fill-in spaces of checks. (2) The same pen adjusted to the "medium" line for personal correspondence. (3) The same pen adjusted to "extra bold" line for addressing packages.

writes with a silky smoothness—is totally free from splattering, scratching or leaking.

Here, at last, is a pen that won't lose its "store manners." A pen that writes as easily and smoothly in 20 years as it writes today.

Go to your Eversharp Dealer today. Try the 9 different writing ranges. See if it doesn't excel by far any pen you've ever owned or used. The Wahl Co., Chicago, New York, San Francisco, Toronto. Makers of Eversharp Fountain Pens and Pencils.

The only pen you dare give as a gift

Does the "givee" write with a fine line? Or a broad line? A medium line? Or one that's extra bold? Forget your worries. Send an Eversharp Adjustable Point and let him adjust the point to write the way he likes best.

The secret?—*Using the cap of the pen, slide this control up or down over the tiny notches for any of 9 different widths of line you want! . . . The Eversharp Adjustable Point Pen is sold at stationery, jewelry, department and drug stores. Three prices . . . Eversharp Adjustable Point at $5 guaranteed for perfect writing. At $7.50 and $10 guaranteed for life . . . Eversharp Pencils to match $3.50 and $4.*

The Eversharp Adjustable Point is available only in the beautiful Doric and comes in smart modern colors.

EVERSHAR ADJUSTABLE POIN
FOUNTAIN PENS

For Distinguished Service—

THE EVERSHARP
$64 SET

WITH CAPS AND BARREL END OF FOURTEEN KARAT GOLD

Reproduced by permission of the United States Navy: the Navy Distinguished Service Medal . . . awarded for "exceptionally meritorious service."

THERE is no finer gift than the superb EVERSHARP $64 Set. Fourteen karat gold throughout . . . used generously in combination with modern plastics. EVERSHARP *self-blotting point* requires no blotter with quick-dry ink . . . writes perfectly with *any* ink! See this set—displayed at distinguished EVERSHARP dealers.

GUARANTEED FOREVER—Service on both pen and repeater pencil is guaranteed forever, subject only to a 35¢ charge for postage, insurance and handling—provided all parts are returned.

TUNE IN Phil Baker in "TAKE IT OR LEAVE IT"—CBS—Sunday Nights
Tune in Milton Berle in "LET YOURSELF GO"—Blue Network—Tuesday Nights

Give EVERSHARP—and you give the finest!

© 1944, Eversharp, Inc.

"Command Performance"

FOURTEEN KARAT GOLD THROUGHOUT

A NEW
EVERSHARP
CREATION

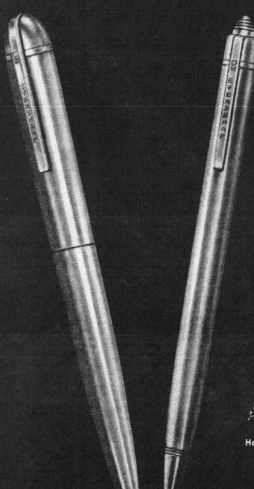

$125.00

Handsomely packaged
in a distinctive
presentation case.

EVERSHARP presents . . . for the one occasion that demands a truly beautiful and distinguished gift . . . a gift to be treasured throughout the years . . . the new Eversharp "Command Performance" pen and repeater pencil set . . . in fourteen karat gold. May be beautifully engraved with name, date, occasion, or military rank.

Service on both pen and
repeater pencil

**GUARANTEED
FOREVER**

subject to 35c charge for
postage, insurance and
handling provided all
parts are returned.

Tune in "TAKE IT OR LEAVE IT" with PHIL BAKER, CBS, SUN. NIGHTS.
Also Hear "LET YOURSELF GO" with MILTON BERLE, Blue Network, TUES. NIGHTS

Give EVERSHARP—and you give the finest!

© 1944, Eversharp, Inc.

Wahl-Eversharp Advertisement 1944

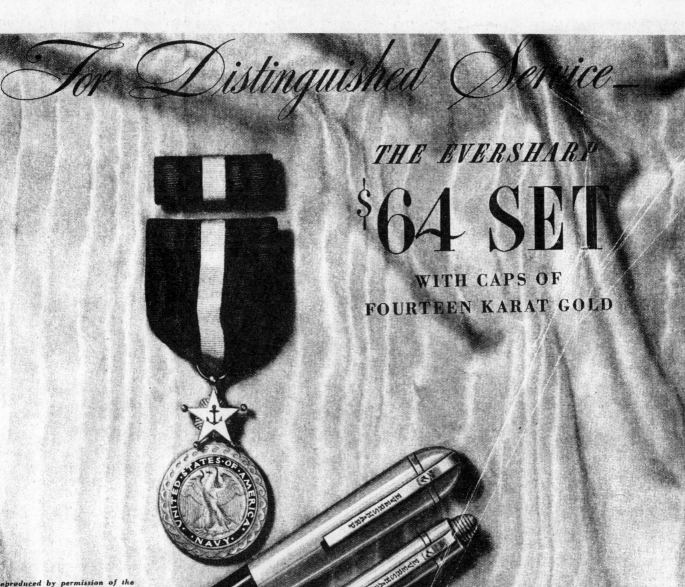

For Distinguished Service—

THE EVERSHARP

$64 SET

WITH CAPS OF
FOURTEEN KARAT GOLD

Reproduced by permission of the
United States Navy: the Navy
Distinguished Service Medal . . .
awarded to Naval personnel for
"exceptionally meritorious service"

THERE is no finer gift than this superb EVERSHARP
set . . . wrought of 14 karat gold throughout in generous combination with modern plastics. Magic Feed
prevents ink flooding or leaking high in a plane . . . so
at ground level too. The new Magic Point is so smooth,
you can't even *hear* it write. Now on display. Price:
$64 plus Federal tax.

Service Guaranteed Forever
If Your EVERSHARP Ever Needs Service . . . We Will Put It In Good
Order For 35¢. This Service Is Guaranteed—Not For Years—Not For
Life—But Guaranteed Forever!

Give **EVERSHARP** *and you give the finest!*

© 1945, Eversharp, Inc.

Wahl-Eversharp Advertisement 1945

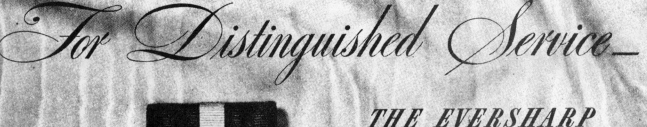

For Distinguished Service—

THE EVERSHARP

$64 SET

WITH CAPS AND BARREL END OF FOURTEEN KARAT GOLD

Reproduced by permission of the United States Navy: the Navy Distinguished Service Medal . . . awarded to Naval personnel for "exceptionally meritorious service"

THERE is no finer gift than this superb EVERSHARP set . . . wrought of 14 karat gold throughout in generous combination with modern plastics. The new EVERSHARP Magic Point is so smooth, you can't even *hear* it write. And the handsomely engraved *"64"* emblem on the caps identifies this as America's most famous set. Now on display at distinguished EVERSHARP dealers. Price: $64 plus Fed. tax.

GUARANTEED FOREVER — Service on pen and pencil is guaranteed forever, subject only to 35¢ charge for postage, insurance and handling — if all parts are returned to EVERSHARP. Slightly higher if handled by dealer.

TUNE IN Phil Baker in "TAKE IT OR LEAVE IT" — CBS — Sunday Nights and Milton Berle in "LET YOURSELF GO!" — CBS — Wednesday Nights

Give EVERSHARP— and you give the finest!

© 1945, Eversharp, Inc.

Chronology Of Pens And Pencils

The Wahl-Eversharp Company

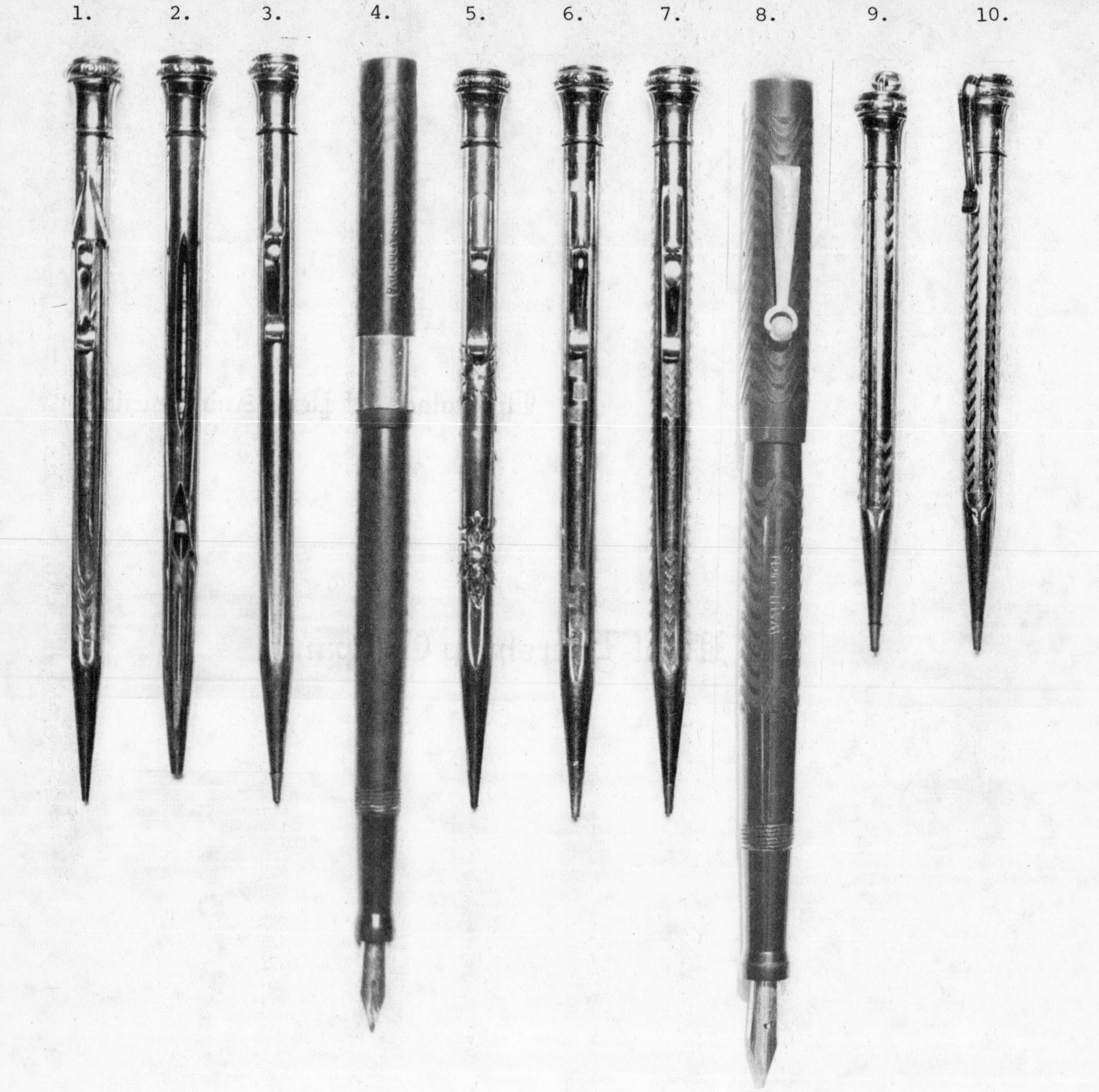

1.   2.   3.   4.   5.   6.   7.   8.   9.   10.

Plate No. 1

Wahl-Eversharp

1.	1915	Eversharp Pencil, Sterling, Chased Check Design, $50
2.	1917	Wahl-Eversharp Pencil, Silver Plated Plain Design, Cut-Away Demonstrator, $30
3.	1917	Wahl-Eversharp Pencil, Gold Filled Plain Design, $20
4.	1918	Wahl Pen No. 12, Black Chased Hard Rubber, Wide Gold Filled Band, Lever Filler, $20
5.	1919	Wahl-Eversharp Pencil, Sterling, Floral Design, $40
6.	1919	Wahl-Eversharp Pencil, Gold Filled Grecian Border Design, $20
7.	1919	Wahl-Eversharp Pencil, Gold Filled Checked Design, $20
8.	1920	Wahl Pen, Black Chased Hard Rubber, Roller Clip, $45
9.	1920	Wahl-Eversharp Pencil, Gold Filled Checked Design, Ribbon Ring, $15
10.	1920	Wahl-Eversharp Pencil, Gold Filled Checked Design, Crown Clip, $15

11. 12. 13. 14. 15. 16. 17. 18. 19. 20.

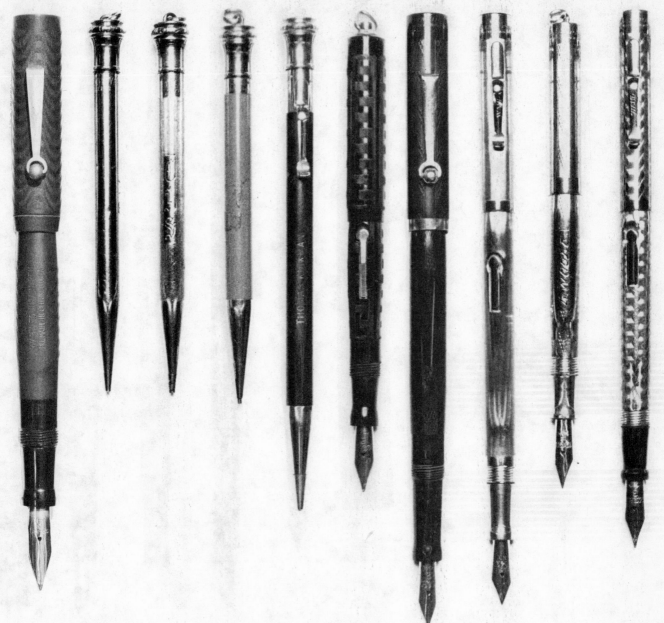

Plate No. 2

Wahl-Eversharp

11.	1921	Wahl Pen, Black Chased Hard Rubber, Roller Clip, $45
12.	1921	Wahl-Eversharp Pencil, Silver Plated Plain Design, Ribbon Ring, $15
13.	1922	Wahl-Eversharp Pencil, Sterling Lined Design, Ribbon Ring, $15
14.	1922	Wahl-Eversharp Pencil, Red Hard Rubber, Silver Plated Trim, Ribbon Ring, $25
15.	1922	Wahl-Eversharp Pencil, Black Hard Rubber, Gold Filled Trim, $25
16.	1922	Wahl Pen, Black Grecian Border Design, Lever Filler, Ribbon Ring, $25
17.	1923	Wahl Pen, Black Checked Design, Lever Filler, Roller Clip, $45
18.	1923	Wahl Pen, Gold Filled Metal, Lined Chasing, Lever Filler, $75
19.	1924	Wahl Pen, Gold Filled Metal, Wheat Design, Lever Filler, Ribbon Ring, $40
20.	1925	Wahl Pen, Gold Filled Metal, Wave Design, Lever Filler, $45

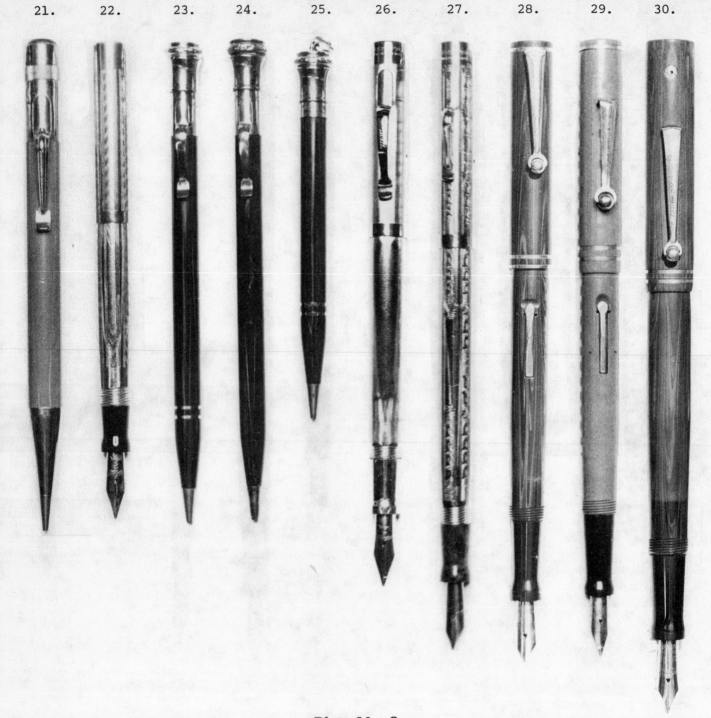

Plate No. 3

Wahl-Eversharp

21.   1925   Wahl-Eversharp No. 75 Desk Model Pencil, Red Hard Rubber, Nickel Trim, $20
22.   1925   Wahl Pen, Silver Filled Checked Design, Lever Filler, Ribbon Ring, $25
23.   1926   Wahl-Eversharp Pencil, Rosewood Design, Gold Filled Trim, $25
24.   1926   Wahl-Eversharp Pencil, Rosewood Design, Gold Filled Trim, $25
25.   1926   Wahl-Eversharp Pencil, Rosewood Design, Gold Filled Trim, Ribbon Ring, $25
26.   1926   Wahl Pen, Gold Filled Lined Design, Lever Filler, $65
27.   1926   Wahl Pen, Gold Filled Console Design, Lever Filler, $100
28.   1927   Wahl-Eversharp Pen, Rosewood Hard Rubber, Lever Filler, Military Roller Clip, $40
29.   1927   Wahl-Eversharp Pen, Red Hard Rubber, Grecian Border Design, Lever Filler, Roller Clip, $40
30.   1928   Wahl-Eversharp Gold Seal Pen, Rosewood Hard Rubber, Lever Filler, Roller Clip, $65

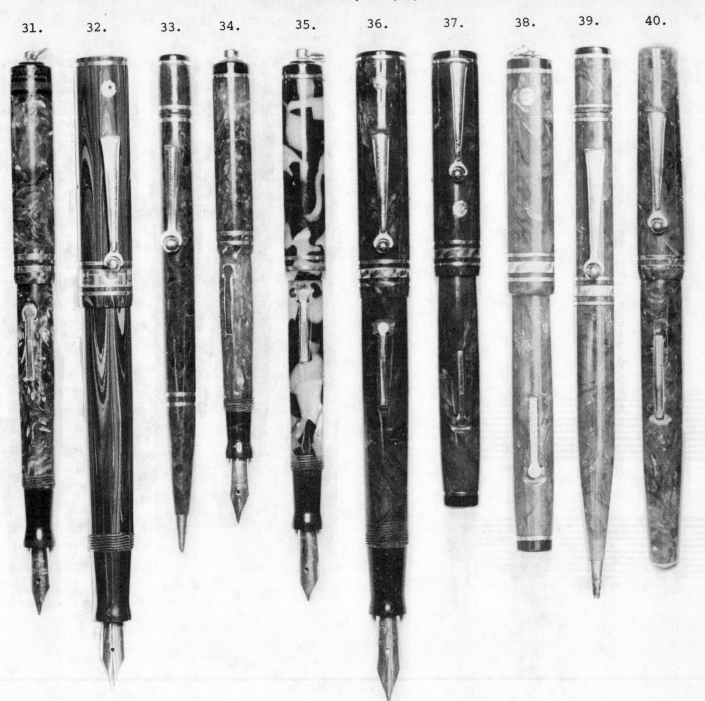

Wahl-Eversharp

Plate No. 4

31. 1928 Wahl-Eversharp Pen, Jade Green Pyralin, Black Ends, Lever Filler, Ribbon Ring, $25
32. 1928 Wahl-Eversharp Gold Seal Pen, Rosewood Pyralin, Greek Key Band, Lever Filler, Roller Clip, $100
33. 1928 Wahl-Eversharp Pencil, Royal Blue Pyralin, Gold Filled Trim, Roller Clip, $35
34. 1929 Wahl-Eversharp Pen, Green Jade Pyralin, Lever Filler, Ribbon Ring, $35
35. 1929 Wahl-Eversharp Pen, Black & Pearl Pyralin, Lever Filler, Ribbon Ring, $45
36. 1930 Wahl-Eversharp Gold Seal Pen, Bronze & Green Pyralin, Rhomboid Band, Lever Filler, Roller Clip, $150
37. 1930 Wahl-Eversharp Gold Seal Pen, Bronze & Green Pyralin, Rhomboid Band, Lever Filler, Military Roller Clip, $100
38. 1930 Wahl-Eversharp Gold Seal Pen, Bronze & Green Copyralin, Rhomboid Band, Lever Filler, Ribbon Ring, $125
39. 1930 Wahl-Eversharp Pencil, Bronze & Green Pyralin, Rhomboid Band, Roller Clip, $100
40. 1930 Wahl-Eversharp Equipoised Pen, Jade Green, Lever Filler, Roller Clip, $50

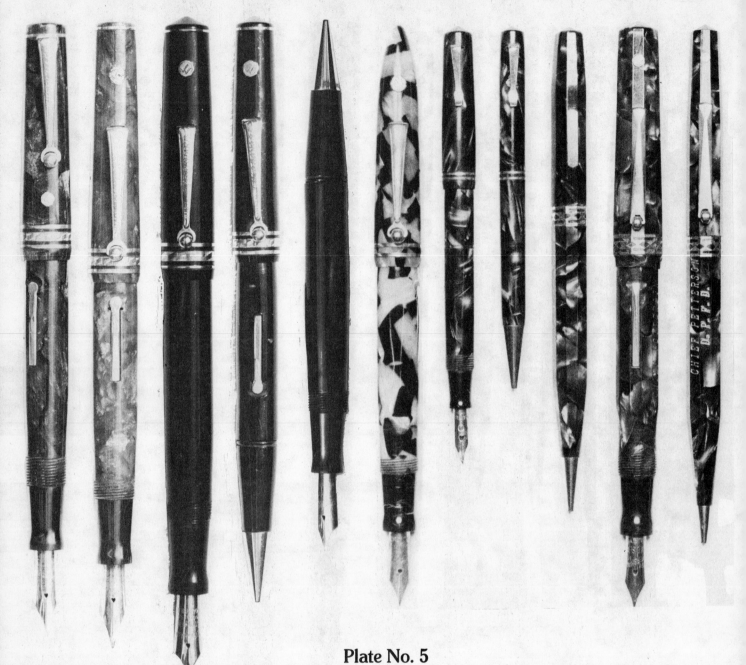

Plate No. 5

Wahl-Eversharp

41. 1930 Wahl-Eversharp Gold Seal Equipoised Pen, Bronze & Green, Rhomboid Band, Lever Filler, Military Roller Slip, $125

42. 1930 Wahl-Eversharp Gold Seal Equipoised Pen, Bronze & Green, Rhomboid Band, Lever Filler, Roller Clip, $140

43. 1930 Wahl-Eversharp Gold Seal Equipoised Pen, Black, Rhomboid Band, Lever Filler, Roller Clip, $150

44. 1930 Wahl-Eversharp Gold Seal Equipoised Pen & Pencil Combination, Black, Rhomboid Band, Lever Filler, Roller Clip, $175

45. 1930 Same As Above Without Cap

46. 1931 Wahl-Eversharp Gold Seal Equipoised Pen, Black & Pearl, Lever Filler, Roller Clip, $150

47. 1931 Wahl-Eversharp Miniature Equipoised Pen, Blue Pearl, Gold Filled Trim, $20

48. 1931 Wahl-Eversharp Miniature Equipoised Pencil, Blue Pearl, Gold Filled Trim, $15

49. 1931 Eversharp Doric Pencil, Morocco (Burgundy Pearl), Roller Clip (missing), $25

50. 1931 Eversharp Doric Gold Seal Pen, Kashmir Green, Lever Filler, Roller Clip, $75

51. 1931 Eversharp Doric Pencil, Kashmir Green, Roller Clip, $50

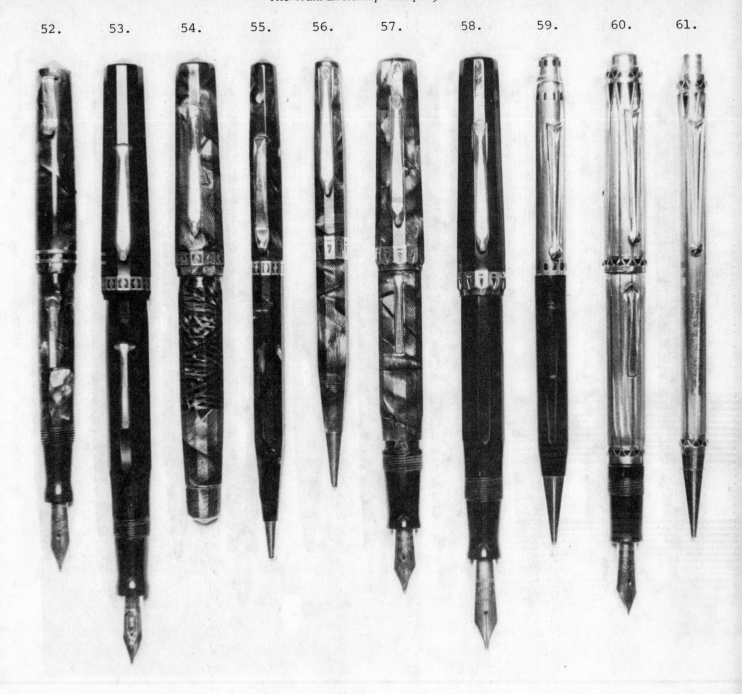

Plate No. 6

Wahl-Eversharp

52.	1932	Wahl-Eversharp Ladies Doric, Kashmir Green, Gold Filled Trim, Lever Filler, Short Clip, $30
53.	1933	Eversharp Pen, Doric, Black, Gold Filled Trim, Lever Filler, Adjustable Nib, $50
54.	1933	Eversharp Pen, Doric, Cathay (Green Lined), Gold Filled Trim, Twist Filler, $35
55.	1933	Eversharp Pencil, Doric, Morocco, Gold Filled Trim, $30
56.	1935	Eversharp Pencil, Doric, Morocco, Gold Filled Trim, $25
57.	1935	Eversharp Pen, Doric, Cathay, Gold Filled Trim, Lever Filler, $35
58.	1935	Eversharp Pen, Gold Seal Doric, Black, Gold Filled Trim, Twist Filler, $75
59.	1936	Eversharp Pencil, Repeater, Black Barrel, Gold Filled Cap, $25
60.	1937	Eversharp Pen, Safety Ink Shut-Off, Gold Filled Cap and Barrel, Pyralin Inlay, Lever Filler, $75
61.	1937	Eversharp Pencil, Repeater, Gold Filled Cap and Barrel, Pyralin Inlay, $50

62.   63.   64.   65.   66.   67.   68.   69.   70.   71.

Plate No. 7

Wahl-Eversharp

62. 1940   Eversharp Pen, Skyline, Maroon, Gold Filled Trim, Lever Filler (Closed), $20
63. 1940   Eversharp Pen, Skyline, Maroon Barrel, Red-Green-Gold Striped Cap, Gold Filled Trim,
            Lever Filler, $30
64. 1940   Eversharp Pen, Skyline, Black Barrel, Green-Gold-Black Striped Cap, Gold Filled Trim, Lever Filler, $30
65. 1941   Eversharp Pen, Skyline, Royal Blue, Gold Filled Trim, Lever Filler, $40
66. 1942   Eversharp Pen, Skyline, Maroon Barrel, Gold Filled Cap and Trim, Lever Filler, $20
67. 1942   Eversharp Pencil, Skyline Repeater, Maroon Barrel, Gold Filled Cap and Trim, $15
68. 1943   Eversharp Pen, Skyline "Gift Of A Lifetime" Solid 14K Gold Cap, Barrel, and Trim, Lever Filler, $250
69. 1943   Eversharp Pencil, Skyline Repeater "Gift Of A Lifetime" Solid 14K Gold Cap, Barrel and Trim, $200
70. 1943   Eversharp Pen, Fifth Avenue, "$64," Maroon Barrel, Solid 14K Gold Cap and Trim, Lever Filler, $75
71. 1943   Eversharp Pencil, Fifth Avenue, "$64" Repeater, Maroon Barrel, Solid 14K Gold Cap and Trim, $50

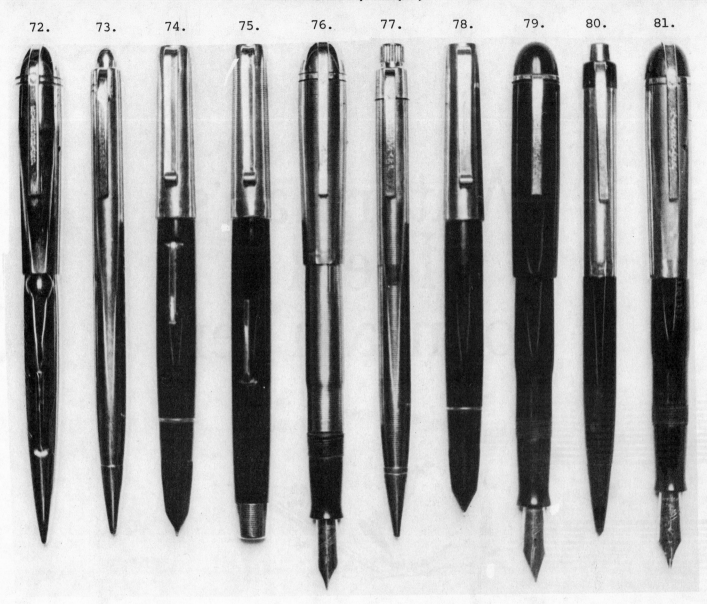

Plate No. 8

Wahl-Eversharp

72. 1944   Eversharp Pen, Skyline "Command Performance", Solid 14K Gold Cap, Barrel and Trim, Lever Filler (Closed), $250

73. 1944   Eversharp Pencil, Skyline Repeater "Command Performance", Solid 14K Gold Cap, Barrel, and Trim, $200

74. 1944   Eversharp Pen, Fifth Avenue, Royal Blue Barrel, Gold Filled Cap, Gold Filled Trim, Lever Filler, $30

75. 1944   Eversharp Pen, Fifth Avenue, Maroon Barrel, Gold Filled Cap, Gold Filled Trim, Lever Filler (Closed), $30

79. 1945   Eversharp Pen, Skyline, 14K Gold Filled Cap, Barrel and Trim, Lever Filler, $50

77. 1945   Eversharp Pencil, Skyline Repeater, 14K Gold Filled Cap, Barrel and Trim, $30

78. 1945   Eversharp Pen, Fifth Avenue, Brown Barrel, Chrome Cap, Gold Filled Trim, Lever Filler, $30

79. 1945   Eversharp Pen, Skyline, Black, Gold Plated Trim, Lever Filler, $20

80. 1945   Eversharp Pencil, Skyline Repeater, Maroon Barrel, Gold Filled Cap, Gold Plated Trim, $15

81. 1945   Eversharp Pen, Skyline, Royal Blue Barrel, Gold Filled Cap, Lever Filler, $20

Waterman's Ideal Fountain Pen

L.E.Waterman Company, 191 *Broadway*
NEW YORK CITY

Newark, 140 Thomas St. ~ Chicago, 129 South State St.
Boston, 40 School St. ~ San Francisco, 17 Stockton St.
Montreal, 179 St. James St. ~ Paris
London, 41 Kingsway, W.C.2.

Waterman No. 20 and Parker Black Giant — Actual Size
From Don Lavin's Collection

Waterman's Ideal Fountain Pen

Christmas

A gift that yields satisfaction by the handful. Christmas giving should be genuine, so pass the imitation and choose Waterman's Ideal,—ideal indeed in every respect. If it isn't an "Ideal" it isn't a Waterman. Best dealers have full stocks. Exchangeable always. Send for illustrated catalogue of our gift pens, and ink filler.

L. E. Waterman Co.
173 Broadway, New York.

8 School St., Boston.   160 State St., Chicago.   138 Montgomery St., San Francisco.
          12 Golden Lane, London.   107 St. James Street, Montreal.

L.E. Waterman Company

The Early History

Extract of Product Development

National Advertising

A Pictorial Chronology of Pens and Pencils

1837 - Lewis Edson Waterman - 1901

LEWIS EDSON WATERMAN was born on November 20, 1837, at Decatur, Otsego County, New York. He received limited schooling at Decatur and at the age of sixteen moved with his family to Illinois. Here he carpentered during the summer months and, as a result of self-instruction, taught school during the winter months. Later on he was, in turn, a publisher's agent, a teacher of shorthand and then an insurance agent. It was in 1884, while he was selling insurance, that Mr. Waterman saw the necessity for a dependable fountain pen and proceeded to invent the pen that is now known by his name around the world. From that time on, he was actively engaged in the fountain pen business until his death in 1901.

L.E. Waterman Company: The Early History

The Waterman history began in New York at the end of the last century. Mr. Lewis E. Waterman, a respected life insurance salesman, would methodically prospect the city, door to door, from neighborhood to neighborhood. The competition was very tough and Mr. Waterman spared no effort. He knew that insurance contracts had to be signed on the spot — if not he would surely lose the prospect. So, he never moved without his forms, his "nib and holder" and ink pot. The contracts had to be signed in ink.

One morning when Mr. Waterman was in his forty-fifth year, he was invited to call at a New York office to sign up for what in those days was a pretty big policy. Waterman found his prospect had been summoned to the site of a new building uptown and had left word for him to follow

Up to that time Waterman had used a little non-spillable ink bottle about the size of his thumb and carried it tied to a button on his waistcoat. But fountain pens had just come into the market. Waterman thought it would look good to have one of these new pens. On his way to the stagecoach to go uptown he bought one in order to try it out.

The insurance agent met his prospect, on whom he had been working for months. He presented the application blank and then the new fountain pen. The prospect put his foot on a rock and laid the blank on his knee. As he touched the paper with the pen — blot! He tried again — blot! He tried a third time — the pen was empty!

It was in vain that Mr. Waterman offered another application and an ordinary pen dipped in the old non-spillable ink bottle. The prospect was superstitious. He believed signing up for life insurance was like making your will. He regarded the failure of the pen as a bad omen.

Waterman was a mild-tempered, easy-going man. As a rule, hardly anything angered him. But that pen made him mad. It had worked all right for him. He had tried it, so as to be quite sure. The pen worked fine when full, but Mr. Waterman had tried it so much he nearly emptied it. That was why it blotted.

Had Mr. Waterman been a scientist he probably would have done what other scientific inventors of fountain pens did. Already there were dozens of them, and all were filling up the little insides of their pens with scientific mechanisms designed to overcome the difficulty of getting just enough air into the holder to let just enough ink out.

Evidently, the ink flow was the main problem to be resolved. He dissected the existing pens and concluded that none was satisfactory, because no one had thought to apply the well-known principle of capillarity. The best devised canal, even a dual canal, between the nib and ink tank, could not control the ink flood. It was necessary to find a way to create an inward draft of air to circulate with the ink but in opposite directions.

Burdened with poor health, Mr. Waterman went on a visit to his brother Elijah, a wagon builder at Kankakee. There he went at the pen problem with practical common sense unhampered by too much scientific knowledge. By a stroke of genius he solved the problem — and with a simplicity that no one else had ever thought of.

Mr. Waterman regarded the holder as a bottle to hold the ink. He saw no reason why the "feed" and the rear end of the pen point should not simply be the cork of that bottle. Along the side of the "feed" beneath the center of the pen he made a slot to let the ink down, and in the bottom of that groove he cut two or three fine slits to let the air up.

His sole tools were a pocket-knife, a saw and a file. His pen was made of hickory wood. His brother Elijah carved the holder out of a spoke of a broken old buggy-wheel that had been lying around in the shop for years.

Waterman's new pen attracted attention among his friends. Many of them tried to induce him to sell it. One day one of his life insurance prospects asked to be buy the pen, and Mr. Waterman felt it would be poor business to refuse. That was the first Waterman sale.

"Will it really work? asked the purchaser. "I guarantee it will work all right," replied its maker. "But won't it be going wrong all the time?" continued the buyer of the first Waterman. "If anything should go wrong with it at any time," replied Mr. Waterman simply and naturally, "let me know and I will put it right or make you another." And that was the start of the Waterman guarantee and service.

What eventually became of that first Waterman fountain pen is as much a mystery as the make of the pen that made the blot. Nobody had any notion then that the first Waterman pen would someday be worth many times its weight in gold as a historic relic.

Mr. Waterman gradually found he was making fountain pens instead of a living. It was more with the hope of combining pen-making with soliciting life insurance than of setting up in business that he took a little vacant space beside the cigar stand in the entrance of the office building at 136 Fulton Street in New York. He posted his first sign: "Waterman's Ideal Fountain Pen — Guaranteed for five years."

He made and sold his fountain pens for two years when in 1883 he applied for his patent, which was granted in 1884. In the first year he made and sold 200 pens; in the second, 500. All were made by hand, although by that time he was using hard rubber. The third year brought the next great step in his romance — the beginning of his advertising.

Mr. Waterman was a dreamer. Had he not been so, his straits in his first two years of pen-making would have disheartened him out of his enthusiasm as a pen-maker. In those two years he did not make enough money for food. His family recalled thinking he was able to keep going only because the landlady at the boarding house in Brooklyn where he and his wife lived was good enough to take the risk of not presenting her bill.

Though a dreamer, and a gentle, lovable man, likeed and trusted by all who met him, Mr. Waterman was not a visionary. He never had the remotest vision of the future. His great business came rolling along to him, riding on his guarantee and service.

As a matter of fact, he never wanted a larger business than he could manage personally. Every new customer meant a new friend. For years he kept the names and addresses of all his customers and would have regarded it as an unfriendly act if a purchaser had ceased to drop in when his pen needed attention. It was a blow to Mr. Waterman when he could no longer know every customer.

The visionary turned out to be a stranger who bought a pen and saw its future. He was E.T. Howard, the veteran advertising agent. Mr. Howard urged the pen-maker to advertise, and suggested a quarter-page ad in a well-known magazine, which had just begun to take general advertising and had jumped to a circulation of 300,000. Mr. Waterman hesitated.

Discovering the real reason was the cost, Mr. Howard offered to stake the required $62.50 and was not to be paid if the advertisement proved a failure. That was how Waterman advertising began. Mr. Waterman accepted the proposition, and together he and Mr. Howard wrote the first advertisement.

The advertisement paid all right. Orders poured in from every section of the country. To meet the demand, the first Waterman fatory was established with $5,000 loaned by a wholesale stationer. After the patent had been granted, on Mr. Howard's advice, the L.E. Waterman Company was formed with a capital of $25,000. The stock was purchased by a few friends.

Ever since the first piece of Waterman copy appeared in the *Review of Reviews* in 1883, it had been a Waterman tradition to advertise in each issue. The sale of the pen jumped to 2,000 the first year of the advertising to 5,000 the following year. By 1901, the year in which Mr. Waterman died, his pens were selling at the rate of 1,000 a day. Annual pen sales passed the half-million mark by 1903.

In his will Mr. Waterman left instructions that E.T. Howard, "the man with a vision," should be made a director for life of the company and that Waterman advertising should be handled by his agency as long as it desired to do so. Mr. Howard survived his friend more than long enough to see the annual sale of Waterman pens exceed five million.

A great New York pen house which subsequently became a maker of gold fountain pens in the early eighties was selling only gold nibs and stylographic fountain pens. It provided Waterman with his first gold nibs. The company had so much confidence in his fountain pen that it trusted Mr. Waterman with credit to the extent of as many as a dozen nibs at a time. Mr. Waterman and these gold pen people came to an arrangement when Waterman started making large purchases of gold nibs. So long as Waterman bought his points from them, they would not compete with him in the United States nor he with them in Europe. That house was Waterman's principal competitor outside this country — while in the U.s. it was comparatively unknown.

America was in full expansion during Mr. Waterman's time — every field was literaly in dynamic explosion. Mechanization accomplished marvels. A better understanding of work and productivity and an emerging awareness of the advantages of advertising made this truly a golden age for all who had a little bit of inventive spirit or business sense.

Mr. Waterman, unlike many inventors, had his feet firmly on the ground and a good sense of commerce. He knew from the beginning how to surround himself with efficient colleagues, such as William I. Ferris, a young man who began as a simple messenger. A few years later Ferris invented several ultra-perfected machines that were able to increase productivity and decrease hand labor.

The development of the firm was spectacular. It had a large sign on Broadway, a factory in Newark, New Jersey, a rubber company in Seymour, Connecticut, and selling outlets throughout the United States. Waterman's success in the U. S. led him to expand his business to other countries.

The highly valued and loyal Mr. Ferris established a factory in Montreal, Canada. Once more, the Waterman pen was a complete success and was sold from Quebec to Alaska by a team of traveling salesmen.

The company learned quickly the value of "feed-back" from the sales force and developed a series of reports strangely named *The Pen Prophet*. The reports were designed to communicate ideas and information to sales representatives throughout the world. The reports contained selling advice, duplicated posters and celebrities' pictures using a Waterman. *The Prophet* reflected in a picturesque way, the fashion, style and habits of the time. For example, it prophesied the future for the "Stylograph," an extravagant machine of five fountain pens designed to sign five bank notes at the same time.

During this time, Mr. Waterman's fame continued to grow. After the U.S. and Canada, Waterman expanded to Europe. What could be a better way to introduce the Waterman fountain pen to Europe than an exhibit at the World Exposition in Paris in 1900? Success, once more, found expression in a greatly prized medal for excellence bestowed upon Waterman.

Frank D. Waterman, Lewis E. Waterman's nephew, took his pilgrimage and became the ambassador of the company. He entrusted the sales representation of Europe to an Englishman, Laurence G. Sloan, a stationer in London, who some years later sold the territories of France, Switzerland and Belgium to a Frenchman, Jules Fagard. The result of this agreement was a veritable "armada" of salespersons, English and French, to travel all over Europe and the world to make the Waterman pen known. From Copenhagen to Singapore, from Hong-Kong to India, by sleigh, on a camel's back, or rickshaw they could be seen, as courageous pioneers, proudly posing for a picture which would immortalize their travels. Few firms at this time, were able to pride themselves on such worldwide success.

The fountain pen was no longer reserved for the businessman or writer. It became a part of daily life. The Waterman Company was still the undisputed leader in the field. It was a great age for fountain pens. Black pens were beautifully styled with gold and silver overlays, colors and designs increased and mechanical improvements made writing wth pens more convenient.

During World War I, many soldiers enjoyed writing from the trenches with a good fountain pen. Lloyd George even signed the Versailles Treaty with a Waterman on June 28,

1919. It was a wonderful golden fountain pen, on which was engraved a mysterious and short Welsh sentence.

The brand was so prestigious that Waterman became the purveyor by appointment to celebrities, royalty and politicians all over the world — from the king of Belgium to the emperor of China, from the queen of Romania to the president of the United States. A Waterman replica of the Lloyd George "Peace Fountain Pen" was given to Princess Mary.

Suzanne Lenglen, the tennis champion, autographed tennis balls with a Waterman. Fred Astaire was a regular customer — and Charles Lindbergh, the hero of the day, during his well-known Atlantic crossing in "The Spirit of St. Louis", took as his only personal possession, his Waterman. The list could go on a l'infini!

Years went by and Waterman remained in the avantgarde. The time had long since passed when pens were filled with an eye-dropper. Automatic filling systems had been perfected. The style of pens followed the fashion models. Between the two world wars, a rainbow of colors were created for fountain pens with mottled, striped, veined, rippled, and finely worked ring designs. Some Watermans had retractible nibs; others were equipped with a small light for reporters, stenographers, mining engineers, or anyone who needed to take notes in darkness. They could have even been used by secret agents! One client even ordered a clock fountain pen fabricated for his personal use.

After successfully representing Waterman for 12 years, Jules Fagaro in 1926 decided to establish a factory and start producing Waterman pens. Mr. Fagaro named his factory and organization "JiF"-Waterman. The new name represented Jules Fagaro's initials.

After Mr. Fagaro's death, his wife continued the business and led the way for a real dynasty of women. Mrs. Fagaro, a model wife, peaceful and middle-class, surprised everyone. JiF-Waterman did not lose ground as had been expected. In fact, the company flourished under Mrs. Fagaro's management.

One year later, Mr. Ferraud of JiF-Waterman invented the ink cartridge. It was so practical that it eventually became the most accepted ink filling method. Waterman France built a large modern ink factory in Issy-les-Moulineaux the same year.

Unhappily, the Second World War snapped everyone's momentum and weakened the business in the United States. Unfortunately, L. E. Waterman's heirs were not able to sustain the business and it collapsed under unsuccessful management. Consequently, Waterman-England fell into a state of lethargy. Only JiF-Waterman, under the leadership of Mrs. Fagaro, was able to continue.

Nevertheless, in this period, the public rapturously discovered the new writing gadgets, which were everywhere on the market. Since the ballpoint pen had been a huge success, JiF-Waterman introduced a fine ballpoint, the

"Pentabill," with five colors. The pen was an immediate success.

Some years later, in 1954, JiF-Waterman created a new pen named the "C/F," a marvelous fountain pen designed slightly like a rocket. It became a best seller and made the company the undisputed leader in the field in all of Europe, except perhaps, England.

When Mrs. Fagaro died, her chairmanship was given to her daughter, Elsa Le Foyer. The company's business slowed down; the management was old and top heavy. In 1969, the balance sheet was in deficit and the business was dangerously decaying.

Waterman-USA was bought by the Baron Bich, who was not in a hurry to boost the company. Waterman-England became a memory. Waterman-France was out of breath. The brand had never been so close to disappearance.

Just in time the third generation of JiF-Waterman women made her debut — Francine Gomez, Le Foyer's daughter. A woman of rashness and courage, she enjoyed taking risks and had the enthusiasm of a beginner. Mrs. Gomez worked hard and in less than four years succeeded in straightening out the firm and bought up the remaining Waterman holdings from Bich.

* Based on the article in *Printers' Ink Monthly,* "How Waterman Pen Business Grew from an Ink Blot," by Edward T. Tandy in 1921 and on an English translation of "Histoire d'un Stylo," by Pat C. Desmars, in a 1974 issue of the French periodical *Historama.*

The Pen Corner
New York

The Pen Corner
London

Main Factory

Newark
N.J.

The Pen Corner
Boston

Waterman Building
Chicago

L.E. Waterman — 1925

Rubber Factory, Seymour, Conn.

San Francisco Store

Waterman Building Montreal

Canadian Factory, St. Lambert, Quebec

L.E. Waterman — 1925

L.E. Waterman Company: Extract of Product Development

1884   The first patent of the first practical fountain pen was issued to L.E. Waterman. The significant development, the three fissure feed, allowed ink to flow smoothly and evenly from the pen.

1886   Waterman introduced a holder (barrel) that was machine chased.

1888   The L.E. Waterman Company was founded.

1890   Waterman introduced the first desk fountain pen with a tapered barrel end.

1892   A tapered cap was brought out for the fountain pen.

1898   Waterman introduced a hexagon shaped holder.

1898   Twist and cable styled holders were introduced.

1899   Waterman introduced a very large 14K nib, the #10.

1899   The spoon feed was developed by enlarging the original feed and adding overflow pockets.

1903   A pump type self-filling pen using the piston principle with a transparent barrel was manufactured but soon discontinued.

1904   Silver and gold overlays became part of the barrel and cap designs of some models.

1905   Waterman introduced a pocket clip riveted on the cap named the "Clip-Cap".

Waterman's Product Development Continued...

1907   The first safety type pen was made. It worked by withdrawing the pen point inside the barrel with the cap screwing on the barrel.

1908   A sleeve type self-filler was introduced.

1912   Under a special license, Waterman introduced a coin-filler from Conklin, but was discontinued after the first year.

1913   The lever self-filling pen was introduced.

1923   Waterman's Ripple rubber pens were first introduced; an exclusive pattern.

1929   The Patrician line was first offered. They came in Onyx, Turquoise, Jet (black), Emerald and Nacre (pearl and black) colors.

1932   Moss Agate added to Patrician line.

1933   The Tip-Fill ink feed was introduced on the No. 7 in Jet that allowed filling by submerging just the tip of the feed into an ink bottle.

1934   The Patrician line was reduced to three colors: Onyx, Moss Agate and Jet.

1935   Emerald Ray color was introduced on the No. 7 line.

1936   The Patrician pen line was phased out.

1936   Ink-Vue models were introduced in silver, copper and emerald transparent colors.

1936   Cartridge fillers were developed for Waterman pens.

1939   The No. 94 and No. 3 models that had been offered in Moss Agate and Steel Quartz were discontinued.

1939   Waterman introduced one of the most revolutionary styles ever in the Hundred Year Pen. The pens were ribbed and had gold barrel bands and transparent solid colors in a streamlined shape. Colors were Jet Black, Burgundy Red, Forest Green and Navy Blue.

1943   A sleek version of the Hundred Year Pen was introduced with a smooth barrel and a slip-on gold filled cap.

1943   Waterman offered a solid 14K gold Hundred Year Pen.

1943   The Taperite was introduced in response to competition from the Parker "51" and Eversharp's Fifth Avenue pens.

1946   Waterman introduced the "1003" pen that was similar in styling to the Patrician pen.

(No Model.)

L. E. WATERMAN.

FOUNTAIN PEN.

No. 293,545. Patented Feb. 12, 1884.

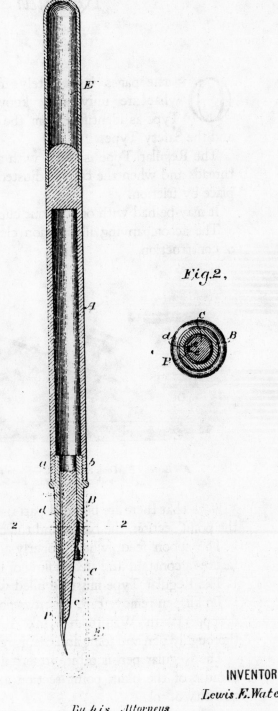

Fig.1.

Fig.2.

WITNESSES

Wm A. Skink?

Jas. S. Latimer

INVENTOR

Lewis E. Waterman

By his Attorneys

Pope Edgcomb & Butler.

L.E. Waterman's original fountain pen patent issued in 1884.

Regular Type

ON THE pages immediately following are illustrations of what are universally known as Waterman's Regular Type as identified from the Self-filling, the Pocket Type and the Safety Type.

The Regular Type is made with a plain point section without threads and when the cap is adjusted over the point it is held in place by friction.

It may be had with or without clip.

The accompanying illustration clearly indicates the simplicity of construction.

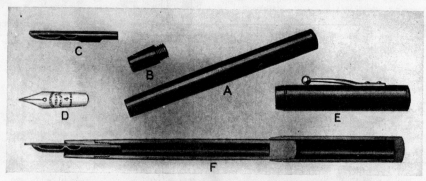

A—Barrel.   B—Point Section.   C—Spoon Feed.   D—Gold Pen.   E—Cap with clip attached.   F—Sectional View.

Note that there are but five parts: the pen point, the spoon feed, the point section, the barrel and the cap.

The spoon feed, when properly adjusted under the pen point, insures a constant and steady flow of ink when the pen is in use.

The Regular Type must be filled with a dropper.

To fill pen remove cap, unscrew point section, fill barrel (using dropper) with Waterman's Ink, readjust point section; wipe thoroughly pen and joint and pen is ready for use.

The Regular pen is often preferred for office or home desk use because of the plain point section and because it holds a large quantity of ink.

L.E. Waterman — 1925

REGULAR TYPE [Dropper Filling]   COMPARATIVE SIZES

Illustrations Are Actual Size

Chased with Clip No. 12½ $2.75	Chased with Clip No. 12 $2.75	Chased with Clip No. 14 $4.25	Chased with Clip No. 15 $5.25	Chased with Clip No. 16 $6.25	Chased with Clip No. 18 $8.25

L.E. Waterman — 1925

The Safety Type

For Women and Others

THE SAFETY TYPE differs from all other types of fountain pens. When the top is properly placed on a Safety Pen it is impossible for any ink to leak from it, no matter what position the pen assumes. This fact has made the Safety Pen popular among travelers, those who desire to carry a pen in the lower vest pocket, and among women who wish to carry a pen in their trunks, traveling bags or hand bags.

The Safety Type is positive insurance against inadvertent ink stains.

As the reward in service and security from the Safety Type is great, there is a compensating reason for the proper handling of the Safety Type.

Every one who sells and every man and woman who uses a Safety Type should clearly understand how to use it.

The accompanying illustration gives a clear idea of how it is made.

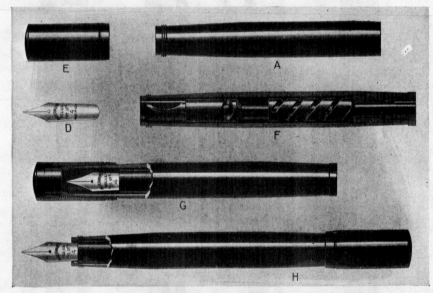

A—Barrel. D—Gold Pen. E—Cap. F—Sectional View.
G—Pen Closed. H—Pen Open.

The pen automatically disappears into the barrel when the friction end of the holder is turned and acts as a cork which seals the ink in the barrel and when the cap is adjusted the pen is hermetically sealed.

This is a perfect device for the prevention of ink leakage.

Every Safety Pen buyer should be carefully and accurately informed as to how to fill and to use the Safety Pen.

Lacking this knowledge, the buyer of a Safety may have trouble.

The directions are simple.

To fill, hold the pen in an upright position and screw off the cap. You will notice that the pen is sunk in the barrel. With a dropper fill the barrel to the top. Keeping the open end up, place the cap on the lower end of barrel and turn to the right. This will cause the pen point to rise from the barrel and lock the pen section securely in place. Now wipe all ink from the end and the pen is ready to write.

To close the pen, hold it in an upright position; turn the cap to the left and the pen point will recede into the barrel; keep on turning until the cap comes off the barrel; then place the cap over the pen end and screw securely into place. It is very simple.

Women particularly will buy the Safety Type if their attention is called to its efficiency and simplicity.

To open, fill or close this pen, hold in an upright position

L.E. Waterman — 1925

SAFETY TYPE 〔 Dropper Filling 〕   *Illustrations Are Actual Size*   **GOLD AND SILVER MOUNTED**

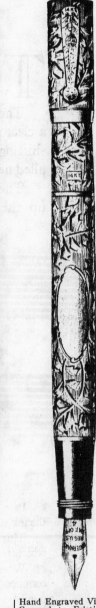

14 Kt. Solid Gold Plain Narrow Middle Band with 14 Kt. Solid Gold Clip	14 Kt. Solid Gold Plain or Scroll Wide Middle Band with 14 Kt. Solid Gold Clip	*Filigree Sterling Silver with Sterling Silver Clip	Plain Covered to Friction End, Gold Filled with Gold Filled Clip	Etched Covered to Friction End, Gold Filled with Gold Filled Clip	Hand Engraved Vine Covered to Friction End, 14 Kt. Solid Gold with 14 Kt. Solid Gold Hand Engraved Clip
No. 742½ $9.00	No. 742½ . . . $12.00	No. 442½ $6.00	No. 0542½ . . . $9.00	No. 0542½ . $11.00	No. 542½ . . . $35.50
No. 742 . . . . . . 9.00	No. 742 . . . . . 12.00	No. 442 . . . . . . 6.00	No. 0542 . . . . 10.00		No. 542 . . . . . 37.50
No. 744 . . . . . 10.00	No. 744 . . . . . 14.00	No. 444 . . . . . . 7.50	No. 0544 . . . . 11.00		No. 544 . . . . . 42.50
No. 745 . . . . . 12.00	No. 745 . . . . . 16.00	No. 445 . . . . . . 9.00	No. 0545 . . . . 13.50		
No. 746 . . . . . 14.00	No. 746 . . . . . 17.00	No. 446 . . . . . 10.00	No. 0546 . . . . 16.00		

*Filigree 14 Kt. Solid Gold with 14 Kt. Solid Gold Clip	Gold Filled with Gold Filled Clip	14 Kt. Solid Gold with 14 Kt. Solid Gold Clip			
No. 542½ . . . $25.50	No. 0542½ . . . $11.00	No. 542½ . . . $32.00			
No. 542 . . . . . 25.50	No. 0542 . . . . 11.00	No. 542 . . . . . 34.00			
No. 544 . . . . . 27.00	No. 0544 . . . . 13.50	No. 544 . . . . . 37.00			
No. 545 . . . . . 32.00	No. 0545 . . . . 16.00	No. 545 . . . . . 42.00			
No. 546 . . . . . 42.00	No. 0546 . . . . 19.00	No. 546 . . . . . 52.00			

L.E. Waterman — 1925

The Self-Filling Type

THE Waterman's Self-filling Type is today by far the most universally used fountain pen.

The ease with which it may be filled is the strong appealing feature.

The operations of the Self-filling Type should be clearly understood. Just as a clear mental picture of the gear shifts in an automobile assists the chauffeur in shifting gears, a clear vision of what happens when a Self-filling fountain pen is filled helps the person who fills the pen.

The accompanying illustration shows the six major parts which make up the Self-filling Type.

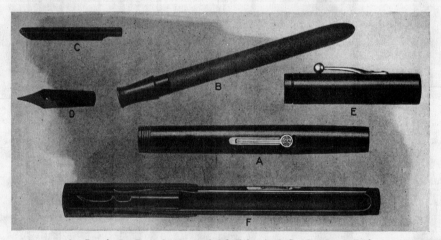

A—Barrel. B—Point Section (with Ink Tube attached). C—Spoon Feed.
D—Gold Pen. E—Cap with clip attached. F—Sectional View.

Part B shows the point section to which is cemented a flexible rubber reservoir which holds the ink supply.

This flexible reservoir when introduced into the barrel A rests against the filling device which is made part of the barrel.

When the lever, which you will notice on the barrel, is raised the air which the reservoir contains is immediately exhausted. When the lever is reset the rubber ink tube expands, drawing ink into the tube.

The process is very simple but very effective.

To fill the Self-filling Type all that is necessary is to pull out the lever, completely immerse the point section in a bottle of Waterman's Ink, replace the lever and after two seconds remove the pen and it is filled.

After filling, the pen and point section should be carefully dried.

The Self-filling Type is made with and without pocket clip because it is used for all purposes. It is made in all sizes and styles as shown in this Catalog and in black, mottled and cardinal, plain and ornamented, also with ring on the short lengths especially for women's use.

L.E. Waterman — 1925

SELF-FILLING TYPE   *Illustrations Are Actual Size*   GOLD MOUNTED

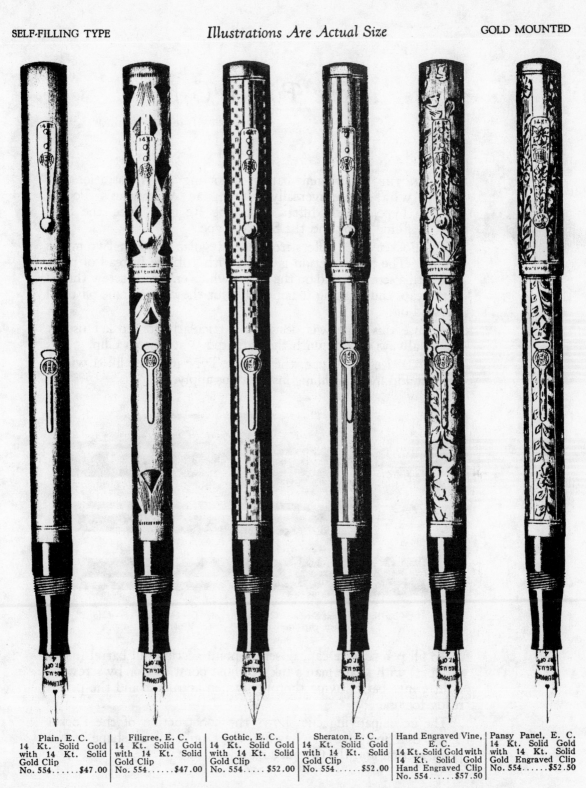

| Plain, E. C.
14 Kt. Solid Gold
with 14 Kt. Solid
Gold Clip
No. 554......$47.00 | Filigree, E. C.
14 Kt. Solid Gold
with 14 Kt. Solid
Gold Clip
No. 554......$47.00 | Gothic, E. C.
14 Kt. Solid Gold
with 14 Kt. Solid
Gold Clip
No. 554.....$52.00 | Sheraton, E. C.
14 Kt. Solid Gold
with 14 Kt. Solid
Gold Clip
No. 554......$52.00 | Hand Engraved Vine,
E. C.
14 Kt. Solid Gold with
14 Kt. Solid Gold
Hand Engraved Clip
No. 554......$57.50 | Pansy Panel, E. C.
14 Kt. Solid Gold
with 14 Kt. Solid
Gold Engraved Clip
No. 554......$52.50 |

Above pens are made in yellow and green gold

Any of the above pens may be had fitted with points as illustrated on page 59

L.E. Waterman — 1925

The Pocket Type

❦

O N THE pages immediately following are illustrations of
what is universally known as Waterman's Pocket
Type, which differs from the Regular Type, the Self-
filling Type and the Safety Type.

The Pocket Type differs from the Regular Type in two minor
details. The point section is made with a flange instead of plain
and with a screw thread on the barrel which engages a screw thread
in the cap, thus making it impossible for the cap to come off until
screwed off.

Because this type was designed particularly for pocket use, it
should always be sold with the patented Waterman's Clip.

Like the Regular Type, the Pocket Type must be filled with a
dropper and the same filling instructions apply.

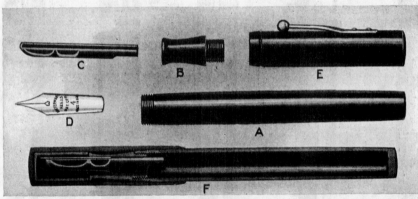

A—Barrel. B—Point Section. C—Spoon Feed. D—Gold Pen. E—Cap
with clip attached. F—Sectional View.

To fill pen remove cap, unscrew point section, fill barrel (using
dropper) with Waterman's Ink, readjust point section by screwing
tightly into barrel; wipe thoroughly pen and joint and the pen is
ready for use.

The accompanying cut shows the construction of the Pocket
Type, differing from the Regular Type only in the shape of the
point section and the threaded barrel and cap.

L.E. Waterman — 1925

POCKET TYPE [Dropper Filling]   *Illustrations Are Actual Size*   SILVER AND GOLD MOUNTED

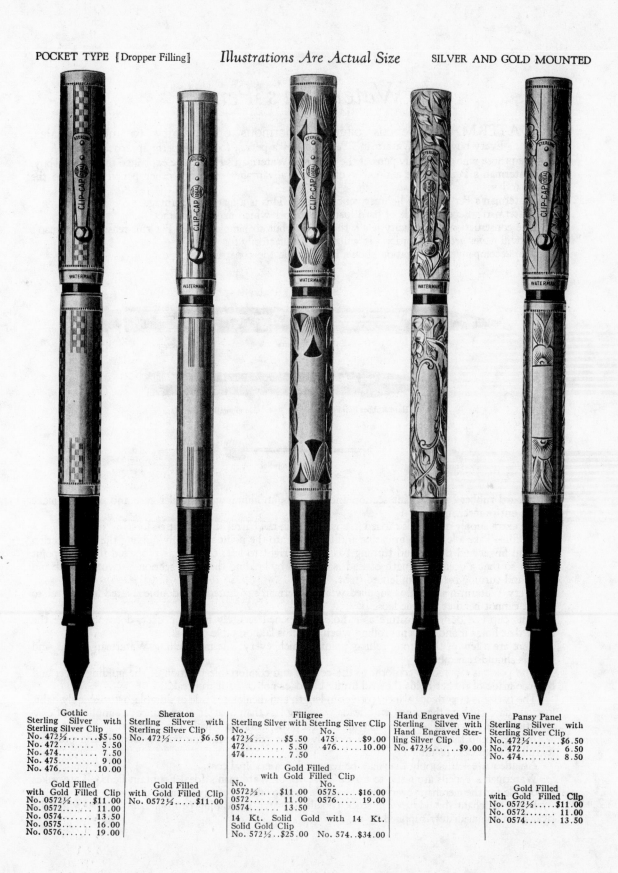

Gothic	Sheraton	Filigree	Hand Engraved Vine	Pansy Panel
Sterling Silver with Sterling Silver Clip	Sterling Silver with Sterling Silver Clip	Sterling Silver with Sterling Silver Clip	Sterling Silver with Hand Engraved Sterling Silver Clip	Sterling Silver with Sterling Silver Clip
No. 472½......$5.50	No. 472½.......$6.50	No. No.	No. 472½......$9.00	No. 472½......$6.50
No. 472........ 5.50		472½......$5.50 475.....$9.00		No. 472......... 6.50
No. 474........ 7.50		472........ 5.50 476....10.00		No. 474......... 8.50
No. 475........ 9.00		474........ 7.50		
No. 476........10.00				

Gothic — Gold Filled with Gold Filled Clip
No. 0572½....$11.00
No. 0572...... 11.00
No. 0574...... 13.50
No. 0575...... 16.00
No. 0576...... 19.00

Sheraton — Gold Filled with Gold Filled Clip
No. 0572½.....$11.00

Filigree — Gold Filled with Gold Filled Clip
No.   No.
0572½....$11.00   0575....$16.00
0572...... 11.00   0576..... 19.00
0574...... 13.50

14 Kt. Solid Gold with 14 Kt. Solid Gold Clip
No. 572½..$25.00   No. 574..$34.00

Pansy Panel — Gold Filled with Gold Filled Clip
No. 0572½....$11.00
No. 0572...... 11.00
No. 0574....... 13.50

L.E. Waterman — 1925

Waterman's Pencils

WATERMAN'S Pencils offer an enormous opportunity to increase sales. Every buyer of a Waterman's Pen will buy a pencil, too, if properly approached.

Even those who do not buy pens, if the merits of Waterman's Pencils are explained to them will buy.

Waterman's Pencils have a number of marked advantages over any other pencil offered to the public today.

Waterman's Pencil is the lightest pencil made. This is a marked advantage.

Waterman's Pencil is made of hard lustrous rubber which makes it attractive.

The construction is simplicity itself, there being but six simple parts. For this reason Waterman's Pencil will never get out of order. It will work satisfactorily for years.

The accompanying illustration shows how simple the construction is.

SECTIONAL VIEW

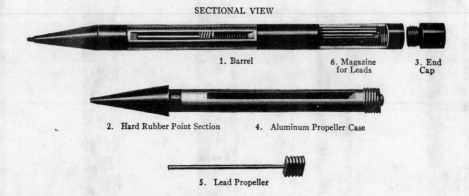

1. Barrel   6. Magazine for Leads   3. End Cap

2. Hard Rubber Point Section   4. Aluminum Propeller Case

5. Lead Propeller

A hard rubber barrel, point section and end cap, an aluminum propeller case and propeller make up the entire mechanism.

An extra supply of leads is carried in a magazine in the barrel at the butt end.

To fill—Take a lead from magazine and insert it into the point section by holding the point section between finger and thumb and turning barrel from right to left; the lead is propelled from the point section so that a desirable length of lead is exposed by holding the point section between thumb and finger and turning barrel from left to right.

Every Waterman's Pencil is supplied with Waterman's patented clip, double riveted into barrel, so that it cannot bend or become loose.

This clip is a desirable feature as it holds the pencil securely in the pocket, does not injure the fabric that holds it and prevents rolling when pencil is laid on table or desk.

Here are a few of the strong selling points which every salesman selling Waterman's Pens and Pencils should remember.

The point is tapered to conform to the correct and comfortable position of the guiding finger and because made of rubber holds the lead firmly but does not cause it to break.

The barrel is in perfect balance, correct in length and diameter; made of durable, astonishingly light, lustrous hard rubber; the pencil with leads weighing less than quarter of an ounce; a simplicity of construction that accomplishes with unerring accuracy the work for which it is intended.

A safety clip that holds the pencil securely in the pocket until the writer needs it and prevents its rolling from desk or table.

An adequate lead supply that may be renewed at a nominal cost.

Waterman's Pencils are made to match all styles of Waterman's Ideal Fountain Pens. This makes it possible for the merchant every time he sells a pen to offer a pencil of similar design.

Every merchant should carry in stock pencils to match his leading pen numbers. Styles which he lacks can be immediately supplied by us.

WATERMAN'S PENCIL   GOLD MOUNTED

Illustrations Are Actual Size

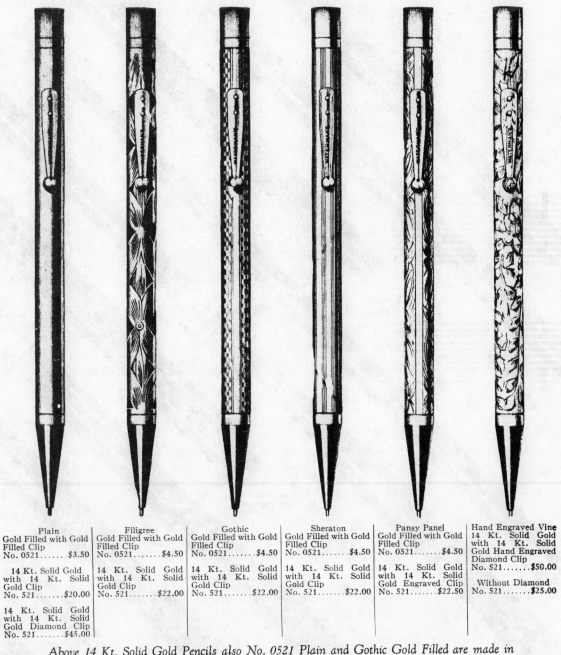

| Plain
Gold Filled with Gold Filled Clip
No. 0521......$3.50

14 Kt. Solid Gold with 14 Kt. Solid Gold Clip
No. 521......$20.00

14 Kt. Solid Gold with 14 Kt. Solid Gold Diamond Clip
No. 521......$45.00 | Filigree
Gold Filled with Gold Filled Clip
No. 0521......$4.50

14 Kt. Solid Gold with 14 Kt. Solid Gold Clip
No. 521......$22.00 | Gothic
Gold Filled with Gold Filled Clip
No. 0521......$4.50

14 Kt. Solid Gold with 14 Kt. Solid Gold Clip
No. 521......$22.00 | Sheraton
Gold Filled with Gold Filled Clip
No. 0521......$4.50

14 Kt. Solid Gold with 14 Kt. Solid Gold Clip
No. 521......$22.00 | Pansy Panel
Gold Filled with Gold Filled Clip
No. 0521......$4.50

14 Kt. Solid Gold with 14 Kt. Solid Gold Engraved Clip
No. 521......$22.50 | Hand Engraved Vine
14 Kt. Solid Gold with 14 Kt. Solid Gold Hand Engraved Diamond Clip
No. 521......$50.00

Without Diamond
No. 521......$25.00 |

Above 14 Kt. Solid Gold Pencils also No. 0521 Plain and Gothic Gold Filled are made in yellow and green gold.

Any of the above pencils may be had with leads of varying degrees as listed on page 67

L.E. Waterman — 1925

Fifty Years of Style Changes in
1884

No. 1
The world's
first practical
fountain pen,
1884.

No. 2
Waterman's
second model.

No. 4
An early type
of desk pen,
1890.

Waterman's
original
"three-fissure"
ink feed.

No. 3
The "chased"
holder intro-
duced in
1886.

Nos. 5 and 6
Two types of
tapered pens,
1892.

Two types of
twist holders.

No. 7
The hexagon
holder, 1898.

Waterman's
Spoon-Feed
patented in
1899.

No. 8
Cable twist,
1898.

No. 10
Cone cap, 1899.
With clip, 1905.

No. 13
Sleeve pulled
down to permit
operation of
filling device.

Waterman's Ideal Fountain Pens

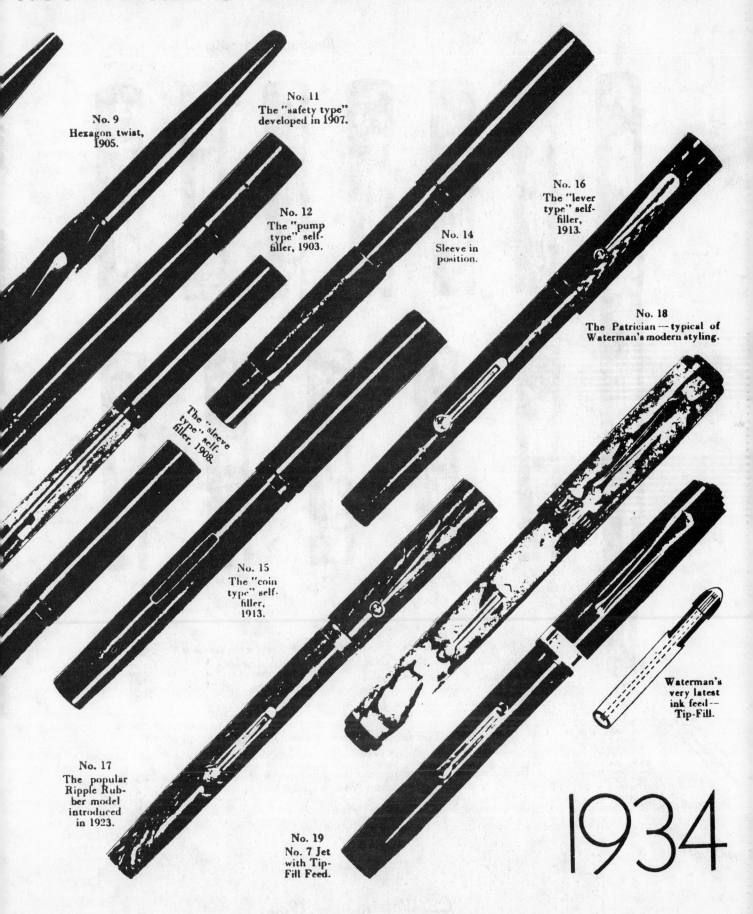

No. 9
Hexagon twist, 1905.

No. 11
The "safety type" developed in 1907.

No. 12
The "pump type" self-filler, 1903.

No. 14
Sleeve in position.

No. 16
The "lever type" self-filler, 1913.

No. 18
The Patrician — typical of Waterman's modern styling.

The "sleeve type" self-filler, 1908.

No. 15
The "coin type" self-filler, 1913.

No. 17
The popular Ripple Rubber model introduced in 1923.

No. 19
No. 7 Jet with Tip-Fill Feed.

Waterman's very latest ink feed — Tip-Fill.

1934

EMBLEM MOUNTINGS   *Illustrations Are Actual Size*

Knight
Templar

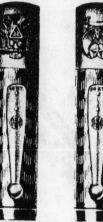

Scottish
Rite

Mystic
Shrine

Blue
Lodge

Odd
Fellows

Knights
of
Pythias

Knights
of
Columbus

Royal
Arcanum

Rotary

B. P. O. Elks

Eagles

No. 554
Plain
14 Kt. Solid
Gold with
14 Kt. Solid
Gold Clip and
Blue Lodge
Emblem
$44.00

No. 854 Self-Filling Pen, with 14 Kt. Solid Gold Lever, Clip, Mounting and Emblem at Top of Cap.

Knight Templar	$19.00	Knights of Columbus	$17.00
Scottish Rite	19.00	Royal Arcanum	17.00
Mystic Shrine	17.00	Rotary	17.00
Blue Lodge	17.00	B. P. O. Elks	21.00
Odd Fellows	17.00	Eagles	17.00
Knights of Pythias	17.00		

Emblem Pens furnished only in Yellow Gold, Roman Finish.

*These Emblems may be mounted on any other style of Waterman's Ideal
Fountain Pen at a special price.*

L.E. Waterman — 1925

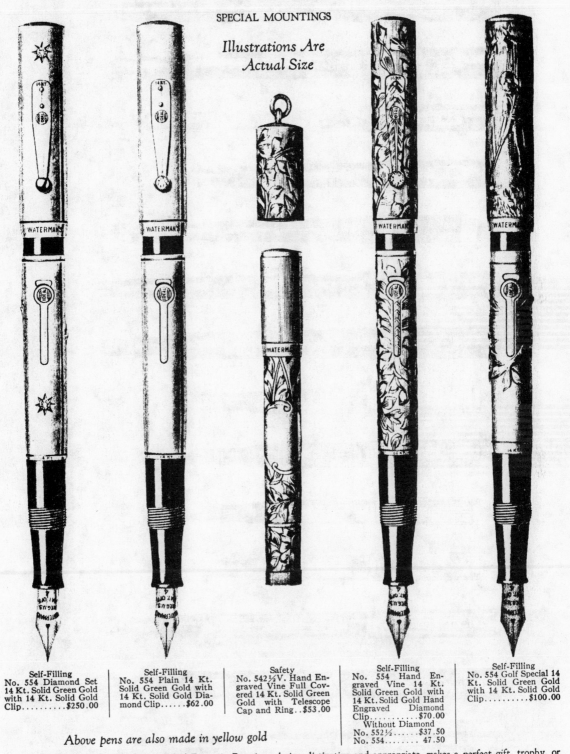

SPECIAL MOUNTINGS

*Illustrations Are
Actual Size*

Self-Filling
No. 554 Diamond Set
14 Kt. Solid Green Gold
with 14 Kt. Solid Gold
Clip..........$250.00

Self-Filling
No. 554 Plain 14 Kt.
Solid Green Gold with
14 Kt. Solid Gold Dia-
mond Clip......$62.00

Safety
No. 542½V. Hand En-
graved Vine Full Cov-
ered 14 Kt. Solid Green
Gold with Telescope
Cap and Ring..$53.00

Self-Filling
No. 554 Hand En-
graved Vine 14 Kt.
Solid Green Gold with
14 Kt. Solid Gold Hand
Engraved Diamond
Clip..........$70.00
Without Diamond
No. 552½......$37.50
No. 554....... 47.50

Self-Filling
No. 554 Golf Special 14
Kt. Solid Green Gold
with 14 Kt. Solid Gold
Clip..........$100.00

Above pens are also made in yellow gold

\ handsomely mounted Waterman's Ideal Fountain Pen, in a design distinctive and appropriate, makes a perfect gift, trophy, or souvenir. We are prepared to furnish special mountings for any purpose or occasion, and upon request will submit suggestions and prices.

L.E. Waterman — 1925

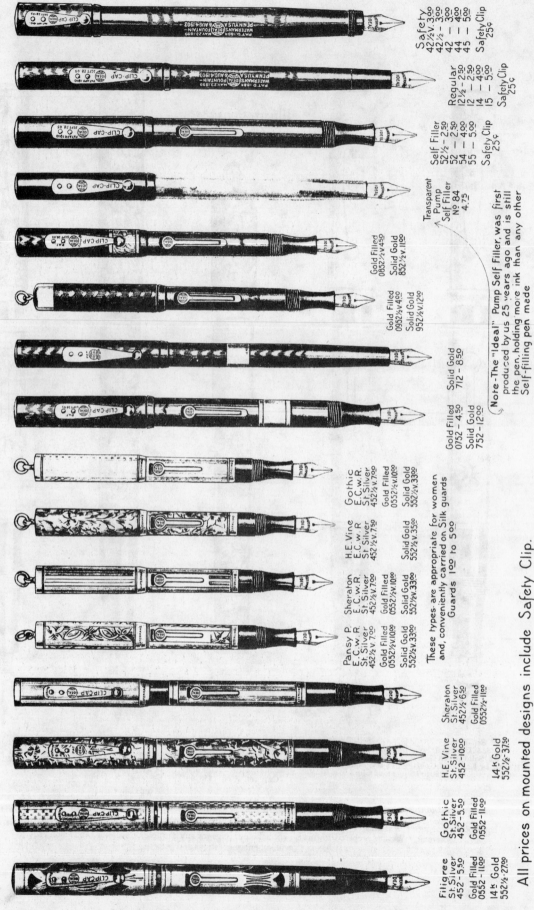

Safety
42½ v. 3.00
42½ — 3.00
44 — 4.00
45 — 5.00
Safety Clip
25¢

Regular
12½ — 2.50
12 — 2.50
14 — 4.00
15 — 5.00
Safety Clip
25¢

Self Filler
52½ — 2.50
52 — 2.50
54 — 4.00
55 — 5.00
Safety Clip
25¢

Transparent
Pump
Self Filler
No. 84
4.75

Gold Filled
0852½ v 4.50
Solid Gold
852½ v. 11.00

Gold Filled
0952½ v 4.00
Solid Gold
952½ v. 12.00

Note—The "Ideal" Pump Self Filler, was first produced by us 25 years ago and is still the pen, holding more ink than any other Self-filling pen made

Gold Filled
0752 - 4.50
Solid Gold
752 - 12.00

Solid Gold
712 - 8.50

Gothic
E. C. w. R.
St. Silver
452½ v. 7.90
Gold Filled
0552½ v 10.00
Solid Gold
552½ v. 33.00

H. E. Vine
E. C. w. R.
St. Silver
452½ v. 7.90
Solid Gold
552½ v. 35.00

Sheraton
E. C. w. R.
St. Silver
452½ v. 7.90
Gold Filled
0552½ v. 10.00
Solid Gold
552½ v. 33.00

Pansy P.
E. C. w. R.
St. Silver
452½ v. 7.00
Gold Filled
0552½ v 10.00
Solid Gold
552½ v. 33.00

These types are appropriate for women and, conveniently carried on Silk guards
Guards 1.00 to 5.00

Sheraton
St. Silver
452½ v 6.50
Gold Filled
0552½ - 11.00

H. E. Vine
St. Silver
452 - 10.00

14 K Gold
552½ - 37.50

Gothic
St. Silver
452 - 5.50
Gold Filled
0552 - 11.00

Filigree
St. Silver
452 - 5.50
Gold Filled
0552 - 11.00
14 K Gold
552½ - 27.00

All prices on mounted designs include Safety Clip.

Key to Standard Numbering System

THE following table will fully explain the system which is used in the numbering of all Waterman's Ideal Fountain Pens. We believe that this table, with the accompanying explanation of the meaning of each figure in every number, will greatly facilitate the re-ordering, checking and billing of all fountain pens of our make.

SIZE OF GOLD PEN is indicated by number in unit column, i.e., 2–4–5–6–8–10

TYPE OF HOLDER is indicated by number in tens column, i.e., 0–1–2–4–5–7.

Thus:

- Regular Type (Straight Cap)....... =0 in tens column
- Regular Type (Cone Cap).......... =1 in tens column
- Regular Type (Taper Cap)......... =2 in tens column
- Safety Type...................... =4 in tens column
- Self-Filling Type................ =5 in tens column
- Pocket Type...................... =7 in tens column

MOUNTINGS are indicated by figures in hundreds and thousands columns, i.e., 2–3–4–5–6–7–8–9.

Thus:

- Sterling Silver Barrel covered .... =2 in hundreds column
- 14 Kt. Solid Gold Barrel covered .... =3 in hundreds column
- Sterling Silver Barrel and Cap covered ... =4 in hundreds column
- 14 Kt. Solid Gold Barrel and Cap covered . =5 in hundreds column
- Two 14 Kt. Solid Gold Bands on Barrel... =6 in hundreds column
- One 14 Kt. Solid Gold Middle Band on Barrel =7 in hundreds column
- One 14 Kt. Solid Gold Band on Cap...... =8 in hundreds column
- 14 Kt. Solid Gold Band Top of Cap...... =9 in hundreds column
- One 14 Kt. Solid Gold Band at Lip of Cap =1 in thousands column
- Two 14 Kt. Solid Gold Bands on Pen, one at upper end of Cap, the other at end of Holder.............................. =2 in thousands column

Gold filled mounting indicated by prefix 0. Slender holder is indicated by suffix ½. Short (V) length indicated by suffix V. Ring on end of Cap indicated by suffix w.r. For example: 01852½V.w.r. would indicate Slender, Short (V) length, Self-Filling, with narrow gold filled band at lip of cap with gold filled ring and with gold pen, size 2, i.e.

- Prefix ....0—Gold Filled
- Thousands Column ....1—One Narrow Lip Band
- Hundreds Column...................8—Gold Band on Cap
- Tens Column.......................5—Self-Filling Type
- Unit Column.......................2—Gold Pen size No. 2
- Suffix............................½—Slender
- Suffix............................V—Short (V) length
- Suffix............................w.r.—With ring

Mountings are Sterling Silver, Gold Filled 18 Kt.—1/10 gold and Solid Gold 14 Kt.
Mounting extending over the closed end of the barrel indicated by the suffix E.C.

This KEY TABLE is made by using No. 2 in the unit column in all instances, i. e., fitted with No. 2 size gold pens—see below.

Types of Holders	Full Length	Short (V) Length	Slender Size	Two Gold Filled Bands on Barrel	Gold Filled Middle Band on Barrel	Gold Filled Band on Cap	Gold Filled Band Top of Cap	Sterling Silver Barrel and Cap covered	Gold Filled Barrel covered	Gold Filled Barrel and Cap covered	14 Kt. Solid Gold Barrel covered	14 Kt. Solid Gold Barrel and Cap covered	Narrow Gold Filled Band at Lip of Cap	Narrow Gold Filled Band at end of Cap and at end of Holder
Regular Type (Straight Cap)..	02	......	......	0602	......	......	......	402	......	......	......	502	......	......
Regular Type (Cone Cap)....	12	......	12½	0612	0712	......	......	412	0312	0512	312	512	......	......
Regular Type (Taper Cap)...	22	......	......	0622	0722	......	......	422	0322	0522	322	522	......	......
Safety Type............	42	42½V	42½	0642	0742	......	0942½V	442	......	0542	......	542	......	......
Self-Filling Type........	52	52V	52½	0652	0752	0852V	0952½V	452	0352	0552	352	552	01852	02852
Pocket Type..........	72	72V	72½	0672	0772	0872V	0972½V	472	0372	0572	372	572	......	......

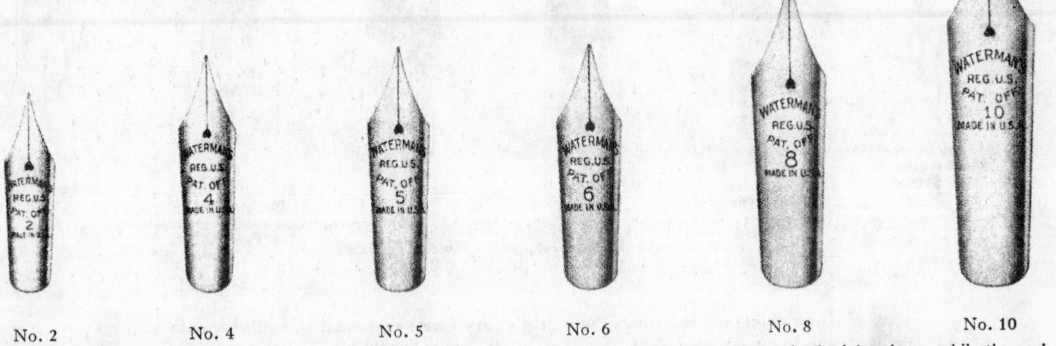

No. 2 No. 4 No. 5 No. 6 No. 8 No. 10

In the above table all types of holders in which Waterman's Ideal Fountain Pens are made are shown in the left column while the various styles in which each holder is made are shown across the top of the table.

The finish of the holder or the *design* of the mounting, however, is always indicated by the addition of a descriptive word after the number, for instance:

"Plain" or "Chased," "Cardinal" or "Mottled" on the unmounted pens. "Plain" or "Sheraton" on gold banded pens. "Gothic" or "Filigree" etc., on gold or silver mounted pens.

Size of Gold Pens is indicated by the figure in the unit column of all numbers, *i. e., Safety pen, plain, fitted with No. 6 gold pen is No. 46.*

Above illustrations are full size. *For comparative sizes of Gold Pens see page 59.*

The PATRICIAN

Patrician
Moss-Agate
Pen $10

Patrician
Onyx
Pen $10

Patrician Jet
Pen $10

Patrician Emerald
Pen $10

Patrician Nacre
(Chromium mountings)
Pen $10

Patrician
Turquoise
Pen $10

The Patrician is known as the world's very finest and most beautiful fountain
pen for men—a triumph of nearly a half century of Waterman's achievement.
It is a large size pen in a distinctive, modern design and with all the built-in
excellencies that have ever characterized a Waterman's. Perfect balance.
Extra generous ink capacity. Always dependable ink feed. And with an
over-size point especially hand-crafted for this very finest of Waterman's.
The Patrician can be had in a wide range of points—as outlined on page 9.

The LADY PATRICIA

Lady Patricia
Onyx
Gold-filled mountings
Pen $5

Lady Patricia
Jet
Chromium mountings
Pen $5

Lady Patricia
Nacre
Chromium mountings
Pen $5

Lady Patricia
Turquoise
Gold-filled mountings
Pen $5

Lady Patricia
Persian
Chromium mountings
Pen $5

 Lady Patricia is designed expressly for the woman who demands not only a perfect writing instrument but one attractive enough to be used as an accessory for her handbag. It embodies many features dear to the feminine heart—dainty, jewel-like design—slender grip—and a chic, modern clasp that secures Lady Patricia conveniently upright in even a crowded bag. The polished disc on top of cap offers an ideal place for engraving. Lady Patricia can be had with any of the points described on page 9.

The NUMBER FIVE

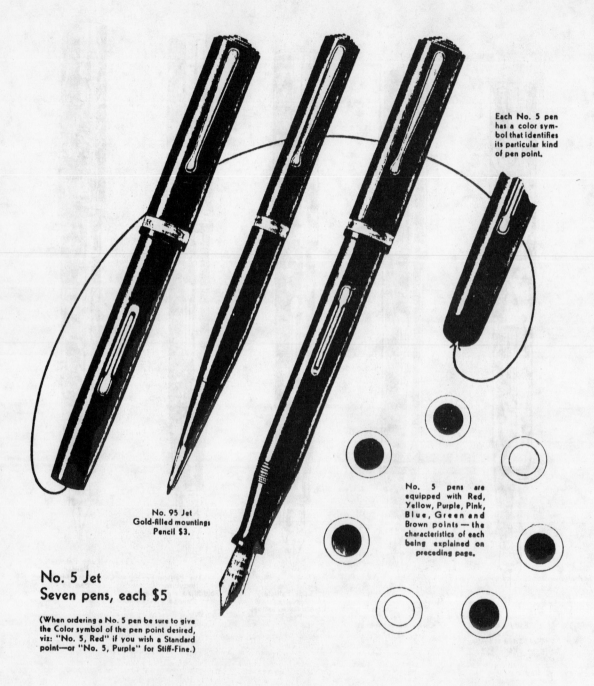

Each No. 5 pen has a color symbol that identifies its particular kind of pen point.

No. 5 pens are equipped with Red, Yellow, Purple, Pink, Blue, Green and Brown points — the characteristics of each being explained on preceding page.

No. 95 Jet
Gold-filled mountings
Pencil $3.

No. 5 Jet
Seven pens, each $5

(When ordering a No. 5 pen be sure to give the Color symbol of the pen point desired, viz: "No. 5, Red" if you wish a Standard point—or "No. 5, Purple" for Stiff-Fine.)

Although smaller than No. 7, the seven No. 5 pens have the same range of points and employ the same method of point identification as used by the No. 7 group. See preceding page. No. 5 is the choice of those who prefer a moderate size, conservative pen. Perfectly balanced and with every Waterman's excellence, including a liberal ink capacity. Gold-filled mountings—the clip being placed high to allow pen to set low in pocket. Pencil of same design and equipped with eraser and an extra supply of leads.

The NUMBER SEVEN

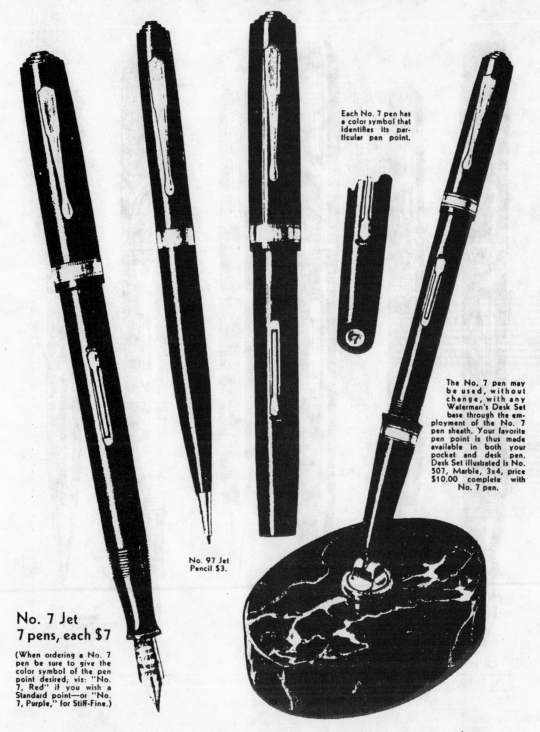

Each No. 7 pen has a color symbol that identifies its particular pen point.

No. 97 Jet Pencil $3.

The No. 7 pen may be used, without change, with any Waterman's Desk Set base through the employment of the No. 7 pen sheath. Your favorite pen point is thus made available in both your pocket and desk pen. Desk Set illustrated is No. 507, Marble, 3x4, price $10.00 complete with No. 7 pen.

No. 7 Jet
7 pens, each $7

(When ordering a No. 7 pen be sure to give the color symbol of the pen point desired; viz: "No. 7, Red" if you wish a Standard point—or "No. 7, Purple," for Stiff-Fine.)

The world's most practical pen! Each No. 7 has a specific kind of point identified by a color symbol—as explained on opposite page. Because of No. 7's exclusive, patented "Tip-Fill" feed the nib need be inserted in ink just deep enough to cover keyhole vent for complete filling. Holder does not touch the ink—therefore, cleaning after each filling is eliminated. Ornamental band is amply wide for engraving. Perfectly matching, latest propel-repel-expel type pencil—with an eraser and an extra supply of leads.

The NINETY-TWO

No. 91
Red and Gold
Pencil $1.50

No. 91
Jet
Pencil $1.50

No. 91
Green and Gold
Pencil $1.50

No. 92
Red and Gold
Pen $3.50

No. 92
Jet
Pen $3.50

No. 92
Green and Gold
Pen $3.50

The No. 92 pen and matching No. 91 pencil are made of unbreakable material in snappy—yet simple—lines. Clips are mounted high to allow them to set low in pocket. The holder in size and weight is suitable for smaller hands, yet the pen has an unusually liberal ink capacity and a sturdy nib. No. 92 can be had with any of the points listed on page 9. The pencil is strongly constructed for long writing service. It both propels and repels the lead and contains a convenient eraser fountain supply of leads.

The NINETY-FOUR

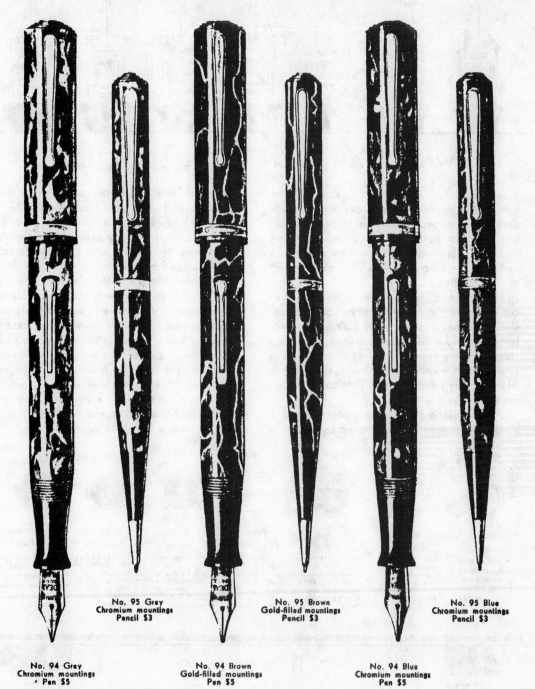

No. 95 Grey
Chromium mountings
Pencil $3

No. 95 Brown
Gold-filled mountings
Pencil $3

No. 95 Blue
Chromium mountings
Pencil $3

No. 94 Grey
Chromium mountings
Pen $5

No. 94 Brown
Gold-filled mountings
Pen $5

No. 94 Blue
Chromium mountings
Pen $5

The No. 94 pen is a moderate size, unbreakable pen in colors that the average man prefers. An ideal pen for those looking for an attractive, thoroughly dependable writing instrument at a moderate cost. Liberal ink capacity. Sets low in pocket. Can be had with any of the various points described on page 9. The matching No. 95 pencil is of the latest propel-repel-expel type. Gauged for standard, small size leads. And each pencil has a conveniently placed eraser and a supply of leads.

WATERMAN'S PEN POINT SELECTION

Waterman's has always recognized the importance of providing the proper pen point for each writer to secure permanent pen satisfaction. But we have found—through our long service to fountain pen users—that from a certain seven different points 95% of all writers can be satisfied.

These seven different points form the basis of our exclusive No. 7 method of pen point selection. Each one of these seven points is shaped, tempered and ground to a certain never-varying standard for a specific kind of writing, and is identified by a color. The characteristics of each of these points and its identifying color symbol are shown below.

A pen point preference once determined can always be matched or duplicated by means of our Color Chart. This is particularly easily done in our seven No. 7 pens (and also the No. 5 pens) each of which has a different type of pen point identified by its individual color symbol on butt of pen holder and also by its color name stamped on the nib.

While the No. 7 and the No. 5 pens are the only Waterman's showing color symbols and color names, *any* Waterman's pen in this catalogue may be had with a point to duplicate the action of any of the points shown in the Chart. To secure a particular point for the desired Waterman's *order the point by its color,* viz: "Patrician Moss-Agate with a Red point" (if you desire this pen with a Standard point)—or "Patrician Moss-Agate with a Purple point" (if you want a Stiff-Fine point).

RED	**YELLOW**	**PURPLE**	**PINK**	**BLUE**	**GREEN**	**BROWN**
Standard	*Rounded*	*Stiff-fine*	*Flexible-fine*	*Blunt*	*Rigid*	*Fine*
A splendid correspondence point of medium flexibility. Suits most writers.	The tip is ball shape. Writes smoothly on any paper in any direction. Fine for left-handed writers.	Makes thin, clear lines and small figures. Ideal for accountants and Gregg shorthand.	A smooth-writing, fine point. So flexible it will shade at any angle. For Pitman shorthand.	An improved stub, slightly oblique. Makes thick or thin characteristic stub strokes as desired.	A durable stiff point of medium width. Best for carbon copy work. Won't shade under pressure.	A finely tapered point for general use. Writes smoothly, does not scratch.

OTHER POINTS

In addition to the points described above, we stock other points for various writing preferences—such as Extra Broad, Extra Fine, and Oblique —and for special uses like the Music Point and the Artist Point illustrated, and the Duo Point with its two nib actions—fine and medium in one point, etc. In fact, we will be glad to suggest a pen point for any special writing requirement as we can duplicate, on special order, the action of any steel pen in a long-lasting 14-kt. solid gold point.

The music point and a specimen of its work.

The artist point and a specimen of its work.

National Advertising

L.E. Waterman Company

Waterman's (Ideal) Fountain Pen

for convenience in your summer writing

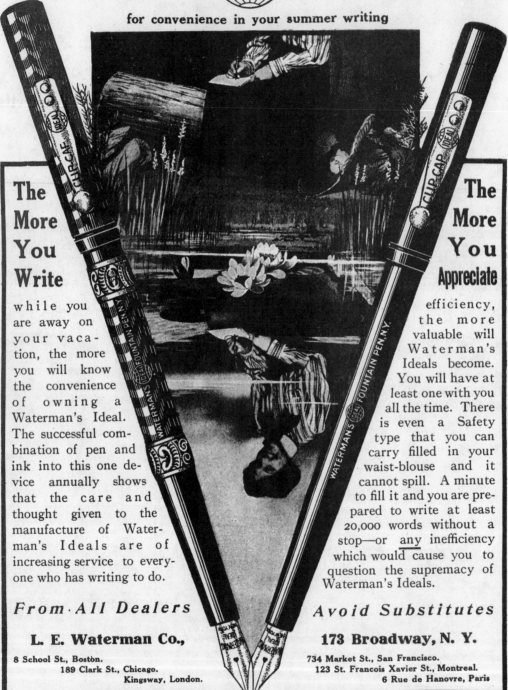

The More You Write

while you are away on your vaca- tion, the more you will know the convenience of owning a Waterman's Ideal. The successful com- bination of pen and ink into this one de- vice annually shows that the care and thought given to the manufacture of Water- man's Ideals are of increasing service to every- one who has writing to do.

From · All Dealers

L. E. Waterman Co.,

8 School St., Boston.
189 Clark St., Chicago.
Kingsway, London.

The More You Appreciate

efficiency, the more valuable will Waterman's Ideals become. You will have at least one with you all the time. There is even a Safety type that you can carry filled in your waist-blouse and it cannot spill. A minute to fill it and you are pre- pared to write at least 20,000 words without a stop—or any inefficiency which would cause you to question the supremacy of Waterman's Ideals.

Avoid Substitutes

173 Broadway, N. Y.

734 Market St., San Francisco.
123 St. Francois Xavier St., Montreal.
6 Rue de Hanovre, Paris

Waterman Advertisement — 1910

Waterman's Ideal Fountain Pen

The Most Important Part Of Your Vacation Outfit

THERE is nothing more necessary to the convenience of those who travel than a reliable fountain pen. Remember that it is the superior writing qualities of Waterman's Ideals that will serve you best. Wherever you go take your Waterman's Ideal, and you will at once appreciate that your letters home and friendly post cards can be written with the ease and comfort for which present day pen making has proficiently provided.

Booklet on Request

Our Safety Pen

is made to carry in any position you want to. It can roll around in your grip or trunk and cannot spill. The barrel is sealed by the cap (as illustrated). The gold pen screws out into place for writing by a simple little twist, when the cap is off.

All Dealers

Avoid Imitations and Substitutes

L. E. Waterman Co., 173 BROADWAY, NEW YORK

8 School St., Boston - 189 Clark St., Chicago - 734 Market St., San Francisco - 123 St. Francois Xavier St., Montreal - 12 Golden Lane, London

Waterman Advertisement — September 1913

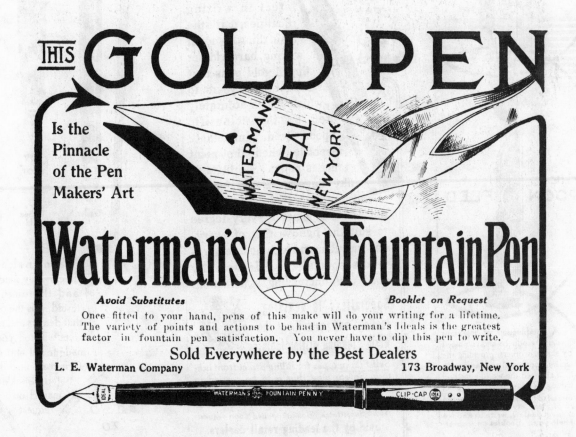

Waterman Advertisement — June 1914

3 Famous Features of Waterman's Ideal Fountain Pen

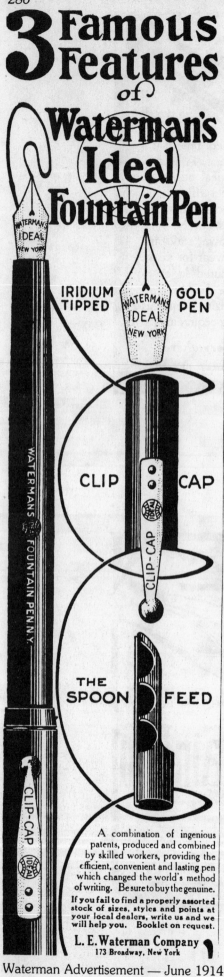

IRIDIUM TIPPED — GOLD PEN

CLIP — CAP

THE SPOON FEED

A combination of ingenious patents, produced and combined by skilled workers, providing the efficient, convenient and lasting pen which changed the world's method of writing. Be sure to buy the genuine. If you fail to find a properly assorted stock of sizes, styles and points at your local dealers, write us and we will help you. Booklet on request.

L. E. Waterman Company
173 Broadway, New York

Waterman Advertisement — June 1914

Ink where ink is wanted, and in no other place: Ink when ink is wanted, your swiftest thoughts to trace

Waterman's Ideal Fountain Pen

Self-Filling Regular & Safety Types

$2.50 TO $50.00

Principally perfect in writing qualities, that's the main thing. Smooth writing, hard iridium tipped gold pens that last for many years, to which ink is accurately fed by the scientific Spoon Feed. Immediate response when the point touches paper. No blots or inky fingers. Every feature accurately tested as to fit and finish. Gold points of every degree to suit the handwriting of everyone; peculiar and technical requirements specialized. Universally used with increasing satisfaction.

Specialists in devising, testing and exploiting the world's leading writing tools.

Self-Filling types for filling direct from inkwell, Safety type that may be carried in any position, and the standard Regular type. Prices $2.50, 3., 4., 5., to $50.00. Avoid Substitutes. Booklet mailed upon request.

Sold by the leading retail dealers.

L. E. Waterman Company, 173 Broadway, New York.
Boston, Chicago, San Francisco,

Advertisement — May 1914

For School and Collegiate Use —

Waterman's Ideal Fountain Pen

The Standard Pen

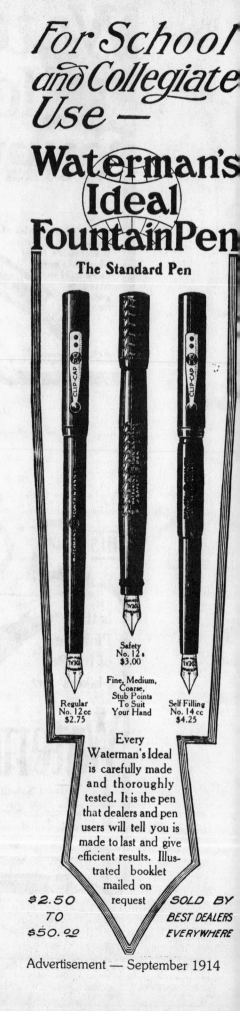

Regular No. 12 cc $2.75

Safety No. 12 s $3.00

Fine, Medium, Coarse, Stub Points To Suit Your Hand

Self Filling No. 14 cc $4.25

Every Waterman's Ideal is carefully made and thoroughly tested. It is the pen that dealers and pen users will tell you is made to last and give efficient results. Illustrated booklet mailed on request

$2.50 TO $50.00

SOLD BY BEST DEALERS EVERYWHERE

Advertisement — September 1914

Waterman Advertisement — June 1915

Advertisement — September 1915

Advertisement — December 1915

This Year
Give

Waterman's Ideal Fountain Pen

This is the particular year for · practical presents. Waterman's Ideals are a certain fulfillment of the happy Christmas gift sentiment. They are suitable on every gift list. Waterman's Ideals are universally known as the standard pens. There are two generations of pen-making in back of them. They are handsome in finish and design, and made to last and do good work for years. According to the purse or the person, you can select perfectly plain pens or those handsomely mounted in gold or silver. Some mounting is generally preferred for gift pens. Gold points can be had to suit every hand and character of writing and may be exchanged until suited. Waterman's Ideal pen service can be had throughout the world. From the Regular, Safety or Self-Filling Types of Waterman's Ideals can be selected appropriate pens for business, social or student life for men, women or the young folks.

IDEAL

Self-Filling	Safety		Pocket	Regular
12 S. F	12½ S		412 Poc.	14 G M M
$2.50	gold		Filigree	$5.00
also gold	banded		Sterling	also
banded	$4.00		Silver	Plain
$3.50	without		$5.00	$4.00
Clip-on-Cap	band		Clip-on-Cap	Clip-on-Cap
25c extra	$3.00		50c extra	25c extra

Illustrated Waterman's Ideal gift folder mailed upon request. Prices $2.50 to $50.00.

Insist upon the genuine Waterman's Ideal. In attractively designed boxes for Christmas.

Sold Everywhere at the Best Retail Stores.

L. E. Waterman Company, 173 Broadway, New York

24 School St., Boston   115 S. Clark St., Chicago   17 Stockton St., San Francisco
107 Notre Dame St., W., Montreal   Kingsway, London   408 Calle Lima, Buenos Aires

Waterman Advertisement — January 1915

Self Regulating!

The Patent & Inimitable Spoon Feed

on every

Waterman's Ideal Fountain Pen

Regulates the Ink Flow to the very last drop in the Pen

There are other flat feeds, but not Spoon Feeds

Just as the impulse to walk faster or slower automatically increases or reduces one's speed, so the desire to write heavily or lightly reflects itself unconsciously in increased or decreased pressure upon the nib.

Such pressure upon a Waterman's Ideal regulates the ink flow. In this way: The patented Spoon Feed—a system of fissures and reservoirs—holds in check and readiness the ink stored in the barrel. The slightest pressure on the pen releases a certain quantity of ink, which travels to the pen point just as quickly as it can be utilized. Under heavy pressure a more ample supply of ink is fed to the nib, but without blotting. Just sufficient ink for the need of the moment. No more, no less. Here lies an important part of the great success of Waterman's Ideals. *The service cannot be estimated on the surface.*

L. E. WATERMAN CO.
Cortlandt St. and Broadway
New York

Boston, Chicago
San Francisco
Montreal
London

ASK YOUR DEALER

Gold Pen Points to suit the characteristics of every hand

Waterman Advertisement — April 1916

Waterman's Ideal Fountain Pen

*14 Kt. Gold
Set with Diamonds*
$150.00

From making a diamond-set pen for a Persian Prince to a special pen for a court stenographer, the extent to which individuality may be expressed in Waterman's Ideal is limitless.

Every Waterman's Ideal is a finished and tested example of the pen maker's Art.

From the plain mountings, to meet popular demand, to those richly trimmed in silver, gold and precious stones, the craftsmanship of our jewellers played its part in embellishing this, the world's universal writing instrument.

Every Waterman's Ideal, down to $5.00, $4.00 and $2.50, has two generations of pen making back of it, and bears the manufacturer's stamp and guarantee — the name Waterman's Ideal.

At the Best Stores

L. E. Waterman Co.
New York

For Presentation—

Pens with Lodge Emblems, College Colors, many patterns in gold and silver, chatelaines, etc. More useful than a loving cup or medal.

Waterman Advertisement — August 1916

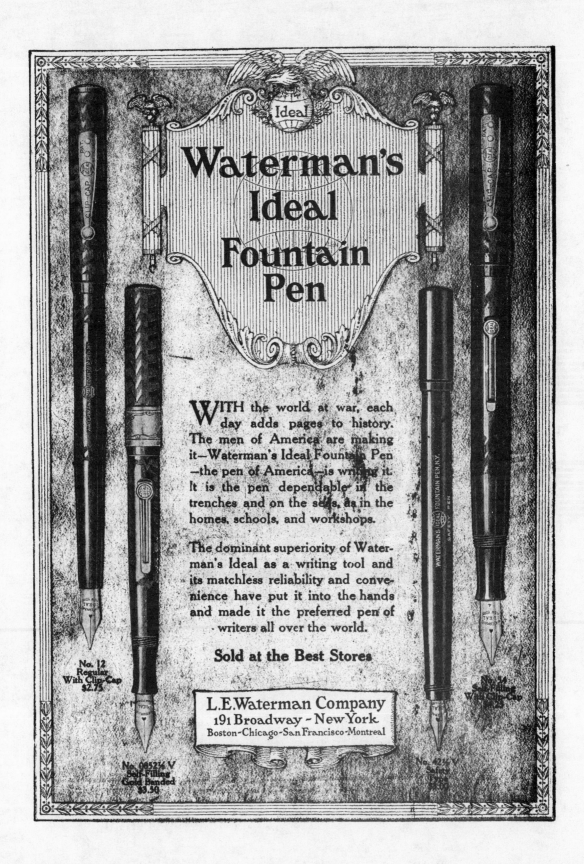

Waterman Advertisement — December 1917

From "Somewhere"—To Home

Waterman's Ideal Fountain Pen

is the pen that brings home the real personality of our boys. With it they can write freely anywhere, without pen annoyances. Waterman's Ideal is keeping the home ties alive. We long for their letters; they need ours. Keep the letters going. Make them long and cheerful. You cannot work a Waterman's Ideal Fountain Pen too hard or too fast. It lasts for years.

Sold at the Best Stores

In Self-Filling, Safety, and Regular Types, $2.50, $4.00, $5.00, and Up

L. E. Waterman Co., 191 Broadway   **New York**

Give him
Ink
in Pellet Form
Ask for our
ARMY AND NAVY
Ink Pellets

Make Ink
by adding water

Waterman's Ideal Fountain Pen

The Appreciated Present

Waterman's Ideal Fountain Pen

THE world-wide reputation of Waterman's Ideal Fountain Pen suggests it as the perfect present for every member of the family.

In addition to pride of possession, it brings with it years of faithful service that endear it more and more each year.

THREE TYPES:

Regular   Safety   Self-filling

with a choice of natural iridium pointed gold nibs to fit any individual pen preference.

$2.50 *to* $250

Selection and Service at Best Dealers the World Over

The quality standard in all Waterman's Ideal Fountain Pens is the same. The difference in prices is determined by size or ornamentation.

L. E. Waterman Company
191 Broadway, New York

129 So. State Street, Chicago
24 School Street, Boston
17 Stockton St. San Francisco

Waterman Advertisement — December 1921

The Appreciated Gift

Waterman's Ideal Fountain Pen

"The Daddy of Them All"

THE whole world knows and accepts Waterman's Ideal as the fountain pen standard for quality, beauty, reliability and long service.

Made in Plain Black, Chased, Cardinal, Mottled, Gold and Silver Mounted, and Jeweled.

Over 44,000 dealers in the United States sell it.

Easy to buy — Easy to send.

Waterman dealers everywhere will assist you in making a fitting selection for man, woman or child.

$2⁵⁰ *to* $50⁰⁰

L. E. Waterman Company
191 Broadway, New York
Boston   Chicago   San Francisco
London   Paris   Montreal

No. 454
Gothic
Sterling
Silver
$7⁵⁰

No.
0952½V
$4⁰⁰

No. 55
Mottled
Gold Filled
Lever&Clip
$6⁵⁰

Waterman Advertisement — December 1923

© 1924 by
L. E. W. Co.

Because it Breathes

Waterman's Spoon Feed
(Patented)

Follows the principle of human breathing—inhales air and exhales ink in exact proportion to the speed and pressure of the writer—never too much, never too little.

Waterman's Spoon Feed is the most soundly scientific fountain pen feed made—the one that holds in perfect control the flow of ink from the barrel to the point of the pen without skipping or blotting.

Size for size, Waterman's Ideal Fountain Pen is the most beautifully proportioned and finely balanced of all writing implements.

The exact length, depth and position of channel ways and pockets was scientifically determined in the Waterman Research Laboratory.

Waterman's Ideal Fountain Pen

"The Daddy of Them All"

The most Popular of all Vacation Companions and Commencement Gifts

$2.50 to $50.00

Sold at Resorts, on Ocean Liners and by Best Dealers the World Over

No. 52
with
Clip Cap
$2.75

No. 55
with
Clip Cap
$5.25

L. E. Waterman Company, 191 Broadway, New York

Chicago   Boston   San Francisco   Montreal

Waterman Advertisement — June 1924

The Pen of Accomplishment

Waterman's Ideal Fountain Pen

"The Daddy of Them All"

SPECIAL MOTTLED
Red & Black Rubber
$7.50

Uniquely beautiful in appearance. The blending of the red and black produces designs that do not duplicate. Ask your dealer to show it to you.

Other Waterman's from $2.50 to $50.00 in barrel sizes and point tempers to fit the hand and preference of individual owners.

Pen illustrated ⅞ actual size.

Every age in pen-ownership has its appropriate

Waterman's Ideal Fountain Pen

The sturdy pen of school day utility, dependable aid to neatness and accuracy

The appreciated companion of office and campus hours—a pen selected to keep pace with growing hands and more exacting employment.

Finally, the insignia of success—the handsome gold mounted pen of the man of affairs, dignified as his treasured time piece and as efficiently ready for instant call.

Pride of possession goes with every Waterman's Pen that's sold.

Selection and Service at Best Dealers Everywhere

L.E.Waterman Company

191 Broadway New York

Chicago   Boston   San Francisco   Montreal

Waterman's Ideal Ink—Best for fountain pens and general use Writes blue, dries black.

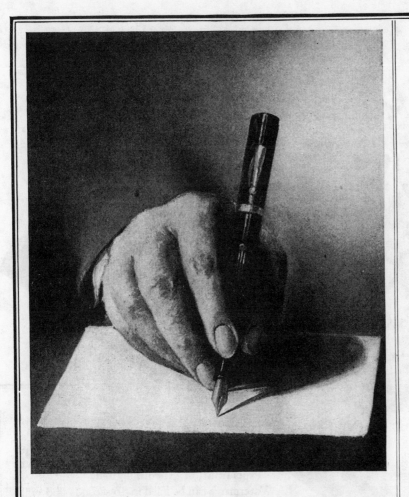

Your hand and your pen

are partners in the expression of your thought

Waterman's Ideal Fountain Pen is the choice of millions because it makes thinking and writing easier. There are no annoying hindrances when a Waterman's is used— just a steady flow of perfectly written words.

Made with different sized holders and different pen points to suit all hands and styles of writing.

50,000 merchants have selected Waterman's as the best pen to sell because they know it satisfies all who buy.

Ask a nearby merchant to show you Waterman's lip-guard models (see illustration) with mottled, black and cardinal holders, then select a pen you like, at a price you will be glad to pay.

Waterman's Ideal Fountain Pen

L. E. Waterman Company, 191 Broadway, New York

Boston : Chicago : San Francisco : London : Paris : Montreal

Mottled
with Gold Filled Lever, Clip and Narrow Band at Lip of Cap. Holder exact size.
No. 01855 - - - $6.50

Waterman Advertisement — June 1925

With a few strokes of a pen LINCOLN freed the slaves —

WITH one filling a Waterman's pen would have written many times the entire Emancipation Proclamation Lincoln signed.

A Waterman's can be filled in 10 seconds and will write ten thousand words. Easy to fill; it holds an abundance of ink.

Waterman's Ideal Fountain Pen

satisfies every pen need perfectly

Different sized holders to fit different sized hands; with pen points to suit every style of writing.

The LIP-GUARD, the CLIP-CAP, the SPECIAL FILLING DEVICE and the SPOON-FEED are four outstanding features.

Ask any one of 50,000 merchants to show you style illustrated; with cardinal, black or mottled holders. Make your selection at $4.00, or in larger sizes at $5.50 or $6.50

L.E.Waterman Company

191 Broadway, New York

Chicago   Boston   San Francisco   Montreal

Illustration is exact size of $4.00 model. Made with cardinal, black or mottled holders.

*With a few strokes
of a pen*
RICHELIEU
*demonstrated that "the
pen is mightier
than the sword"*

SINCE Richelieu's day, Waterman's has added even more to the power of the pen, and men as great as he have selected it because of the exceptional service it always renders.

Waterman's Ideal Fountain Pen

satisfies every pen-need perfectly

Made with different sized holders to fit different sized hands, pen points that suit every style of writing, and an ink capacity that is unequaled in pens of the same size.

... The LIP-GUARD, the CLIP-CAP, the SPECIAL FILLING DEVICE and the SPOON-FEED are four outstanding features.

Ask any one of 50,000 merchants to show you the style illustrated; with cardinal, black or mottled holder. Make your selection at $4.00 or in larger sizes at $5.50 or $6.50.

L. E. Waterman Company

191 Broadway, New York
Chicago, San Francisco, Boston
Montreal

Illustration is exact size of the $4.00 model. Made with cardinal, black or mottled holder.

One of These Two Pens Will Suit You Perfectly

Both Are Waterman's

Each is as perfect as a pen can be made. They differ only in size and price.

For more than forty years the pre-eminence of Waterman's pen has been recognized. Each feature of excellence is outstanding. Every pen point is iridium-tipped and hand ground. Every holder is pure Brazilian rubber. Every filling device is a perfected mechanism.

$4.00

$7.50

Both pens shown are 018 models. They are made in red, mottled and black holders, with flexible lip-guard to protect cap and pocket clip to prevent loss. May be had with different pen points to suit different styles of writing.

Waterman's are guaranteed to give perfect service without time limit. Ask any one of 50,000 merchants to explain their merit.

Waterman's Ideal Fountain Pen

L. E. Waterman Company, 191 Broadway, New York

Chicago   Boston   San Francisco   Montreal

Waterman Advertisement — June 1926

He Chooses the Treasure Chest

AT Christmas time no happier selection can be made than a Waterman's fountain pen and pencil — a gift that causes immediate delight and acts as a reminder of your generous thoughtfulness for years to come.

Ripple-Rubber pen and pencil shown, in Treasure Chest, $8.50. Other gold- and silver-mounted models $10 to $50.

Sold by 50,000 reliable merchants.

Waterman's Ideal Fountain Pen

L. E. Waterman Company
191 Broadway, New York
Chicago   Boston   San Francisco   Montreal

Waterman Advertisement — December 1926

PICK YOUR PEN POINT *by* COLOR

The color band on the holder tells the story. It enables you to quickly choose a pen-point that exactly suits your writing.

Ask to See
Waterman's Number Seven

The following colors indicate the different pen-points:

Red—STANDARD—Suits most writers. A splendid correspondence point. Medium flexibility. For home and general use.

Green—RIGID—Tempered to armor-plate hardness. Will not shade even under heavy pressure. Unequaled for manifolding. The salesman's friend.

Purple—STIFF; FINE—Writes without pressure. Makes a thin, clear line and small figures with unerring accuracy. Popular with accountants.

Pink—FLEXIBLE; FINE—As resilient as a watch-spring. Fine, tapered point; ground fine to shade at any angle. Loved by stenographers.

Blue—BLUNT—An improved stub point. This point makes a broad line. May be held in any position. Liked by rapid writers.

Yellow—ROUNDED—A different pen point. The tip is ball shape. Makes a heavy, characteristic line without pressure. Suits left-handed writers.

Merchants who sell Waterman's will be glad to let you try all six points. Do this and select the one that suits you best.

When you buy a Waterman's you buy perpetual pen service.

Guaranteed since 1883 and until 1983—100 years of pen service

L. E. Waterman Company
191 Broadway, New York

Chicago   Boston   San Francisco   Montreal

$7.00

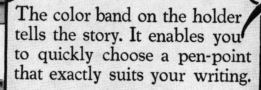

Number Seven
Beautiful, resilient *Ripple* stainless rubber holder. Made with protective lip-guard and an unequaled patented filling device.

Waterman's

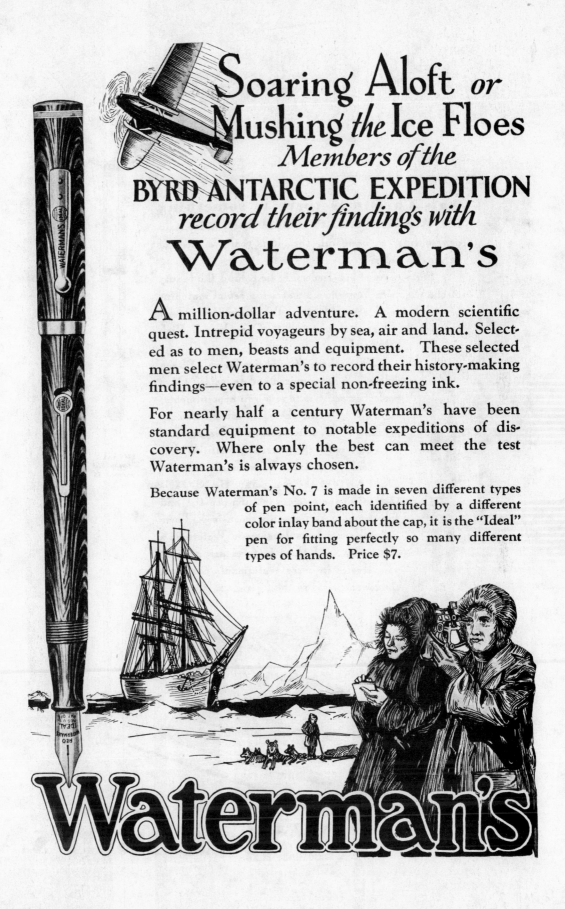

Soaring Aloft *or* Mushing *the* Ice Floes
Members of the
BYRD ANTARCTIC EXPEDITION
record their findings with
Waterman's

A million-dollar adventure. A modern scientific quest. Intrepid voyageurs by sea, air and land. Selected as to men, beasts and equipment. These selected men select Waterman's to record their history-making findings—even to a special non-freezing ink.

For nearly half a century Waterman's have been standard equipment to notable expeditions of discovery. Where only the best can meet the test Waterman's is always chosen.

Because Waterman's No. 7 is made in seven different types of pen point, each identified by a different color inlay band about the cap, it is the "Ideal" pen for fitting perfectly so many different types of hands. Price $7.

Waterman's

This Christmas there is something NEW—Waterman's Patrician, a fountain pen so fine, so beautiful, that it is really a piece of personal jewelry.

Forty years of pen-leadership lie behind the beauty of the exquisite Waterman's Patrician set of matching pen and pencil shown below. Tawny streamers shoot through the creamy whiteness of its Onyx barrel. Rich gold bands it.

What other gift so choice for only fifteen dollars? What so prized and desirable? Or so perfect an addition to your own appointments?

Then there are these four other Patrician beauties: Turquoise, Emerald, Nacre, and Jet. All with those writing qualities that can come only from Waterman's HAND-CRAFTING of the pen point, HAND-FIN-ISHING of the precious iridium pen-tip, and the patented Waterman's spoon-feed. These improvements have long made Waterman's the leader, and these features are now at your service in every Waterman's pen from the lowest priced to the Patrician.

NACRE
The pen . . $10
The pencil . $5

JET
The pen . . $10
The pencil . $5

EMERALD
The pen . . $10
The pencil . $5

TURQUOISE
The pen . . $10
The pencil . $5

Waterman's
patrician

ONYX
The pen . . $10
The pencil . $5

Waterman's

Waterman Advertisement — December 1929

Why do many more millions of men and women all over the world use Waterman's fountain pens than use any other make? Ask some of them—their answers will mean more to you than anything we may say.

Perhaps they will first mention the unquestioned advantages of fountain pens in general—the convenience of having your personal pen-and-ink ready at hand the instant you want it. Then they will move on to those features that are peculiarly Waterman's—the ink capacity which, size for size, outranks other pens—Waterman's exceptionally wide selection of pen points—the smoother finish of the writing point—the flexibility which Waterman's alone has seemed able to work into a gold pen—the beautiful new colors and smart modern designs—the jeweler's finish of the trim—the Waterman's patented spoon-feed that flows the ink so evenly without skimping or blotting.

And they are likely to sum it all up by saying: "Waterman's pens write better—they last almost forever".

Waterman's pens may be had in a wide variety to fit every taste and every purse. Used with Waterman's inks they give even better service. Every Waterman's is guaranteed forever against defects. Service Stations are maintained at the addresses below for the purpose of making good our guarantee and for servicing our pens as required.

L. E. Waterman Company
191 B'way, New York • 129 So. State St., Chicago
609 Market St., San Francisco • 40 School St.,
Boston • 263 St. James St., Montreal, Canada

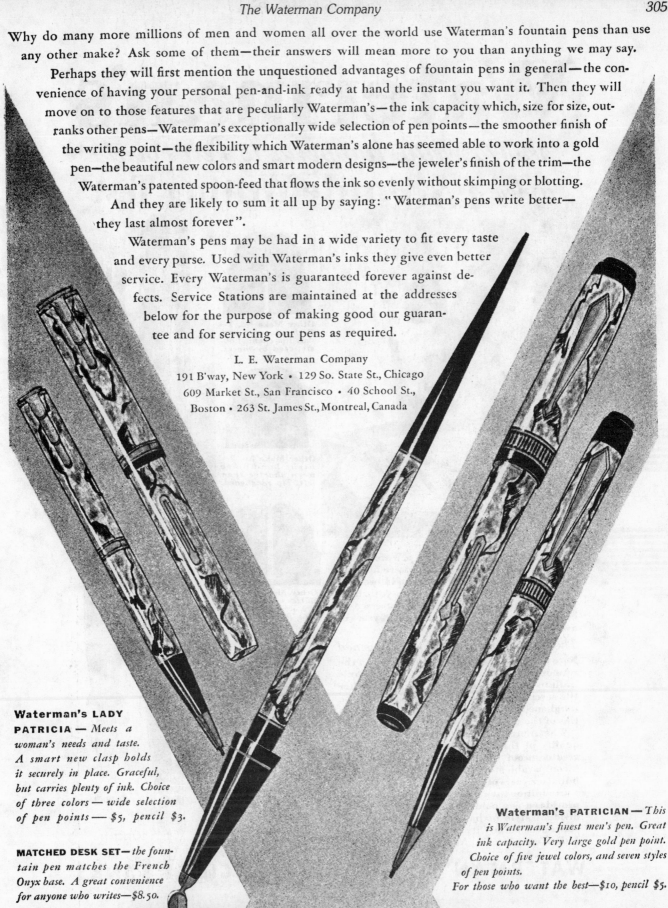

Waterman's LADY PATRICIA — *Meets a woman's needs and taste. A smart new clasp holds it securely in place. Graceful, but carries plenty of ink. Choice of three colors — wide selection of pen points — $5, pencil $3.*

MATCHED DESK SET — *the fountain pen matches the French Onyx base. A great convenience for anyone who writes—$8.50.*

Waterman's PATRICIAN — *This is Waterman's finest men's pen. Great ink capacity. Very large gold pen point. Choice of five jewel colors, and seven styles of pen points. For those who want the best—$10, pencil $5.*

Waterman's

Waterman's
shows what happens to Pen Points after a 38-mile Writing Test

Other Make No. 1— *Both point tips worn flat. Ink channel obstructed by metal.*

Other Make No. 2— *Right hand point worn shorter than left. Tip roughened.*

Other Make No. 3— *Ridges worn into entire writing surface. Tips flat and pitted.*

FOUR new pen points . . . a Waterman's and three other makes . . . were fitted to the holders in a writing machine in order to test their comparative ability to withstand wear. A distance of 38 miles was traversed by each pen point . . . the equivalent of years of average usage.

The Microscope Shows What Happened
Note the microscope-photos herewith . . . the roundness and smoothness of the Waterman's iridium point . . . its freedom from wear, after the severe 38-mile test, in contrast with the roughened writing surface and worn-down tips of the other pen points.

What more convincing evidence of the super-quality of the Waterman's point . . . what greater proof that Waterman's writes with incomparable smoothness not only when new, but after years of usage?

In addition to enduring quality, Waterman's provides a pen point to suit exactly every individual style of handwriting. Whether for yourself or as a gift, it pays to get a Waterman's. *L. E. Waterman Co., New York.*

Waterman's—Perfect roundness and smoothness unaffected by 38-mile test.

Do you know you can get a Waterman's . . . the world's finest writing instrument . . . for as little as $2.75 ?

LADY PATRICIA

PATRICIAN

WATERMAN'S · PENS · PENCILS · INKS

Waterman Advertisement — September 1932

Chronology Of Pens And Pencils

L.E. Waterman Company

Plate No. 1

WATERMAN

1. 1899   Waterman, Red and Black Cable Twist Hard Rubber, Slip Cap, Eye Dropper Filled, $75.
2. 1901   Waterman, Gold Barrel and Slip Cap, Eye Dropper Filled, (Closed), $100
3. 1902   Waterman, Gold Barrel and Slip Cap, Eye Dropper Filled, $100
4. 1906   Waterman, #12 Black Chased Hard Rubber, Slip Cap, Eye Dropper Filled, Nickel Plated Clip, $25.
5. 1906   Waterman, #12 Black Plain Hard Rubber, Slip Cap, Eye Dropper Filled, Nickel Plated Clip, $25
6. 1907   Waterman #18 Black Plain Hard Rubber, Slip Cap, Eye Dropper Filled, #8 Nib, Nickel Plated Clip, $300
7. 1907   Waterman, Ideal Safety, 18K Rolled Gold Cap and Barrel, Eye Dropper Filled, $250
8. 1908   Waterman, #0942½V Safety, Black Chased Hard Rubber, Gold Crown, Eye Dropper Filled, Ribbon Ring, $30
9. 1908   Waterman #12 SF Black Chased Hard Rubber, Slip Cap, Sleeve Filler, Nickel Plated Clip, $35

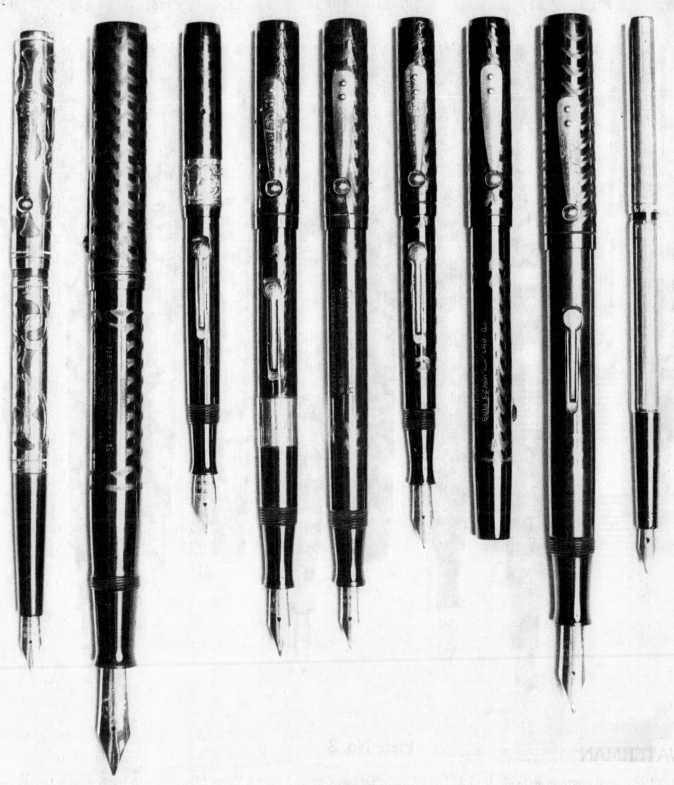

WATERMAN

Plate No. 2

10. 1912   Waterman, #0512 Gold Filled Filigree, Slip Cap, Manifold Nib, Eye Dropper Filled, $75.
11. 1913   Waterman #18 Black Chased Hard Rubber, Eye Dropper Filled, #8 Nib, Nickel Plated Clip, $300.
12. 1913   Waterman #52½V Black Chased Hard Rubber, Gold Filled Trim, Lever Filler, $25.
13. 1915   Waterman #54 Black Chased Hard Rubber, Gold Filled Trim, Lever Filler, $35.
14. 1915   Waterman #52, Black Chased Hard Rubber, Nickel Plated Trim, Lever Filler Double Waterman Mark, $25.
15. 1917   Waterman #52½V Black Chased Hard Rubber, Nickel Plated Trim, Lever Filler, $15.
16. 1917   Waterman #52 Black Chased Hard Rubber, Nickel Plated Trim, Lever Filler (Closed), $20.
17. 1918   Waterman #56 Black Chased Hard Rubber, Nickel Plated Trim, Lever Filler, $75.
18. 1919   Waterman #0512½ Gold Filled Plain Cap and Barrel, Slip Cap, Eye Dropper Filled, Ribbon Ring, $30.

19.   20.   21.   22.   23.   24.   25.   26.   27.   28.

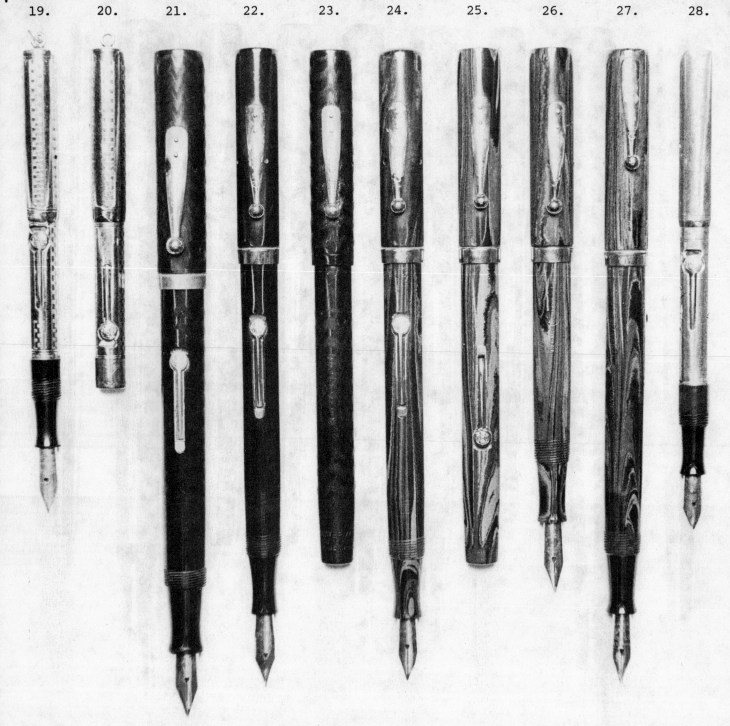

WATERMAN

Plate No. 3

19. 1920   Waterman #0552½V Gold Filled Gothic Design Cap and Barrel, Lever Filler, Ribbon Ring, $30.
20. 1920   Waterman #0552½V Gold Filled Gothic Design Cap and Barrel, Lever Filler, Ribbon Ring (Closed), $30.
21. 1921   Waterman #56 Black Chased Hard Rubber, Lever Filler, Nickel Plated Clip and Trim, $75.
22. 1922   Waterman #52 Black Plain Cap and Barrel, Gold Filled Trim, Lever Filler, Double Waterman Mark, $35.
23. 1922   Waterman #52 Black Chased Hard Rubber, Nickel Plated Trim, Lever Filler, Double Waterman Mark (Closed), $25.
24. 1923   Waterman #52 Red and Black Ripple, Gold Filled Trim, Lever Filler, Double Waterman Mark, $40.
25. 1923   Waterman #52 Red and Black Ripple, Gold Filled Trim, Lever Filler, Double Waterman Mark (Closed), $40.
26. 1923   Waterman #52V Red and Black Ripple, Gold Filled Trim, Lever Filler, Double Waterman Mark, $30.
27. 1923   Waterman #54 Red and Black Ripple, Gold Filled Trim, Lever Filler, Manifold Nib, $60.
28. 1923   Waterman #452½V Sterling Cap and Barrel, Lever Filler, Ribbon Ring, $40.

29. 30. 31. 32. 33. 34. 35. 36. 37 38.

Plate No. 4

WATERMAN

29. 1924   Waterman #52½V Red and Black Ripple, Gold Filled Trim, Lever Filler, Double Waterman Mark, $25.
30. 1924   #0552 Gold Filled Sheraton Cap and Barrel, Lever Filler, $150.
31. 1924   Waterman #0552½ Gold Filled Sheraton Cap and Barrel, Lever Filler (Closed), $50.
32. 1925   Waterman #52 Black Chased Hard Rubber, Gold Filled Trim, Lever Filler, Double Waterman Mark, $35.
33. 1925   Waterman #55 Red and Black Ripple, Gold Filled Trim, Lever Filler, Double Waterman Mark, $75.
34. 1925   Waterman #55 Pencil, Red and Black Ripple, Gold Filled Trim, $50.
35. 1926   Waterman #52½V, Black Plain Hard Rubber, Gold Filled Trim and Crown, Lever Filler, Double Waterman Mark, $25.
36. 1926   Waterman #52 Black Chased Hard Rubber, Nickel Filled Trim, Lever Filler, Double Waterman Mark, $25.
37. 1926   Waterman Pencil, Gold and Red Ripple, Gold Filled Trim, $50.
38. 1926   Waterman #52 Red and Black Ripple, Gold Filled Trim, Lever Filler, Double Waterman Mark, $40.

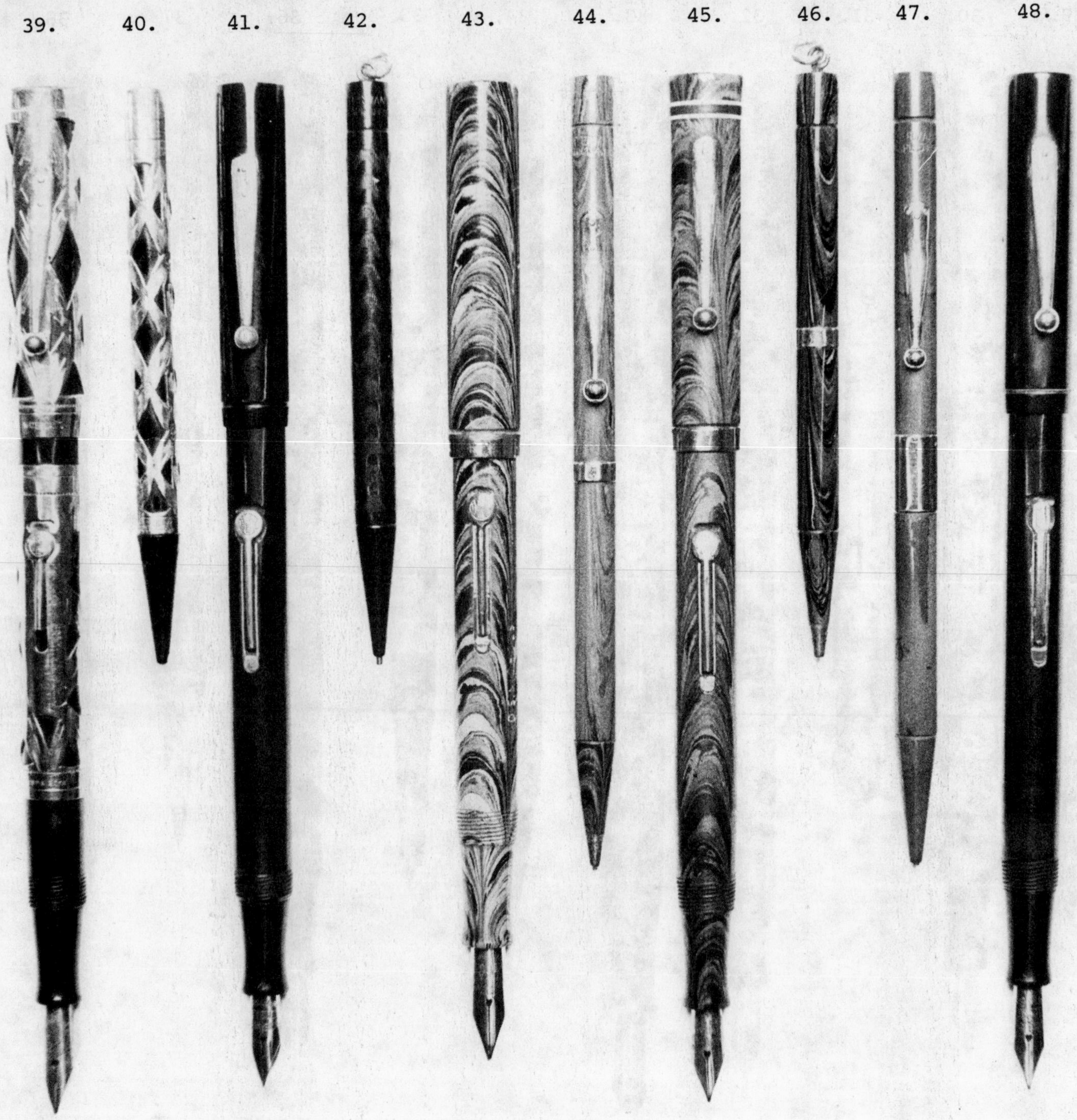

Plate No. 5

WATERMAN

39.	1927	Waterman #0552 Gold Filled Filigree Cap and Barrel, Lever Filler, $125.
40.	1927	Waterman Gold Filled Filigree Pencil, Ribbon Ring, $20.
41.	1927	Waterman #12 PSF Black Plain Cap and Barrel, Nickel Plated Trim, Lever Filler, $20.
42.	1928	Waterman Pencil, Black Chased Hard Rubber, Ribbon Ring, $20.
43.	1928	Waterman #94 Gold Ripple, Gold Filled Trim, Lever Filler, $100.
44.	1928	Waterman #52 Pencil, Red and Black Ripple, Gold Trim, $35.
45.	1928	Waterman #7 Red and Black Ripple, Gold Filled Trim, Lever Filler, Double Waterman Mark, $75.
46.	1928	Waterman #52½V Pencil, Red and Black, Gold Filled Trim, Ribbon Ring, $15.
47.	1928	Waterman #52 Pencil, Olive Hard Rubber, Gold Filled Trim, $35.
48.	1928	Waterman #52 Black Plain Hard Rubber, Nickel Plated Trim, Lever Filler, $15.

49.   50.   51.   52.   53.   54.   55.   56.   57.

Plate No. 6

WATERMAN

49.   1929   Waterman #3 Black Plain Hard Rubber, Nickel Plated Trim, Lever Filler, $20.
50.   1930   Waterman #32 Blue and Tan, Nickel Plated Trim, Lever Filler, $25.
51.   1930   Waterman Pencil, Blue and Tan, Nickel Plated Trim, $20.
52.   1933   Waterman Pencil, Lady Patricia, Pearl and Black, Chrome Plated Trim, $25.
53.   1935   Waterman #84-S Black Ray, Chrome Plated Trim, Ray Filler, Red Nib, $30.
54.   1935   Waterman #84-S Silver Ray, Chrome Plated Trim, Ray Filler, Brown Nib, $40.
55.   1936   Waterman #5116 Pencil, Black, Chrome Plated Trim, $15.
56.   1937   Waterman #3 Moss Green and Red Agate, Nickel Plated Trim, Lever Filler, $20.
57.   1937   Waterman #3 Silver and Brown Agate, Nickel Plated Trim, Lever Filler, $20.

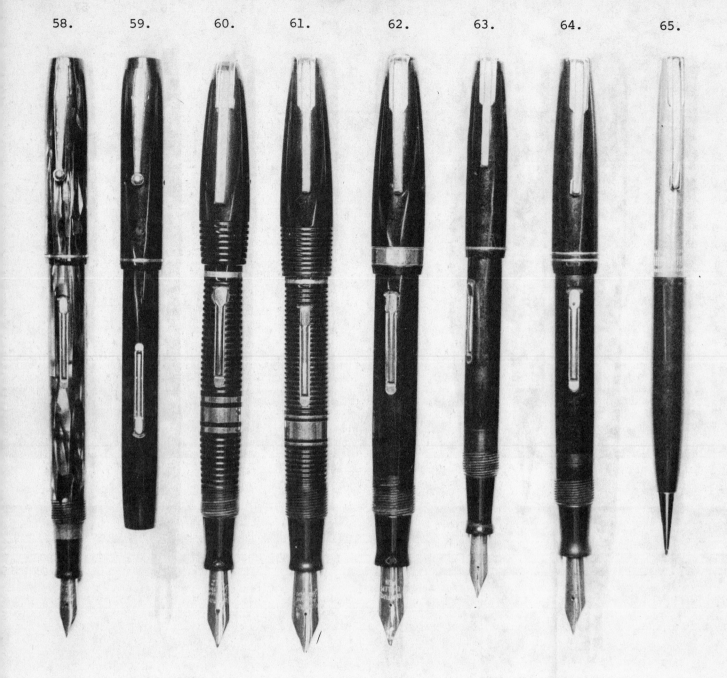

Plate No. 7

WATERMAN

58.	1938	Waterman #32A Red and Silver, Nickel Plated Trim, Lever Filler, $20.
59.	1938	Waterman Thorobred, Black, Nickel Plated Trim, Lever Filler, Account Nib, (Closed), $15.
60.	1939	Waterman Hundred Year Pen, Transparent Blue Ribbed, Gold Filled Trim, Lever Filler, Barrel Bands, $100.
61.	1940	Waterman Hundred Year Pen, Transparent Red Ribbed, Gold Filled Trim, Lever Filler, Barrel Bands, $150.
62.	1943	Waterman Emblem, Maroon, Transparent Amber Barrel End, Gold Filled Trim, Lever Filler, $100.
63.	1943	Waterman Black, Chrome Plated Trim, Lever Filler, $15.
64.	1943	Waterman Commando, Black, Gold Filled Trim, Lever Filler, $20.
65.	1944	Waterman Taperite Pencil, Grey Barrel, Aluminum Cap, Chrome Plated Trim, $20.